OUR MAN
ELSEWHERE

I0165817

IN SEARCH OF
ALAN MOOREHEAD

THORNTON M^cCAMISH

Published by Black Inc.,
an imprint of Schwartz Publishing Pty Ltd
Level 1, 221 Drummond Street
Carlton VIC 3053, Australia
enquiries@blackincbooks.com
www.blackincbooks.com

This work was developed with the assistance of the Merlyn Myer Biography Stipend.

SIDNEY MYER FUND

National Library of Australia Cataloguing-in-Publication entry:
McCamish, Thornton, author.
Our man elsewhere: in search of Alan Moorehead / Thornton McCamish.
9781863958271 (hardback)
9781863959339 (paperback)
9781925203110 (ebook)
Moorehead, Alan, 1910–1983.
War correspondents—Australia—Biography.
Journalists—Australia—Biography. Historians—Australia—Biography.
Authors—Australia—Biography.
070.92

Cover design by Peter Long
Text design and typesetting by Tristan Main
Photographs on pages 96, 261: National Library of Australia, Papers of Tom Pocock, MS8377.
Photograph on page 242: National Library of Australia, Alan Moorehead Papers, MS 5654.

CONTENTS

For Gracie, Jonah and Hughie

1

NOTES ON A DISAPPEARANCE

In the mid-1960s, Alan Moorehead dusted off the notes he had accumulated over the previous twenty years and, in a little stone-walled workroom he had built behind his house in Italy, knuckled down to serious work on an autobiography. He was then probably Australia's most internationally celebrated writer – the *Washington Post* would soon call him one of the best writers in the English language – and he was producing some of the most acclaimed and most enduring work of his career. But the autobiography was a struggle. He'd gotten as far as drafting some chapters a decade earlier, but had put them aside and now he wasn't finding it easy to get back into it. Though still only in his mid-fifties, he found writing wasn't as easy as it had once been. Producing his daily quota of words, Moorehead told a friend, was 'like straining shit through a sock'.

Moorehead scratched away at drafts and rewrites, a few weeks here, a few there. He'd put his notes away in the drawer for months at time. In one fragment he did manage to squeeze through the sock is a petulant sentence about the craft of which he was widely considered a master, a craft that had not only made him famous, but had also paid for his house and, to his enormous satisfaction, half a yacht: 'The choice and arrangement of the words is an excruciatingly difficult thing and I do not see how anyone could enjoy doing it.'

He later crossed it out.

The problem can't have been lack of material. It was probably the oppo-site, the cause of most writers' block: the problem of having too much to say and no idea where to start. At one point he jotted down a rough chronology of his life and its highlights, and also a sketchy plan for the chapters and themes. This dog-eared sheaf of foolscap still exists. It was when I first saw it, in the National Library of Australia, that I realised I wanted to write a book about Moorehead and his work.

This strangely bemused stocktaking of a man's life is an intriguing doc-ument: it's an odd mix of complacency and bitterness, and also something like wonder at just how much of it there is. There are some desultory notes on childhood; the themes of this section were to be boredom, the ordi-nariness of suburban Australia, the discovery of girls, and the desperate longing he always felt for the excitement he imagined was to be found elsewhere. At seventeen, he wrote, he was determined to become a writer whose books were 'all to be masterpieces, *acclaimed* masterpieces ... in my imagination I went off like a hound dog in pursuit of my quarry, which was fame and immortality'. As an adult, though, his fantasies became fixed on The Trip, the great journey that would take him from nowhere (Melbourne) to somewhere (Europe).

He was in his mid-twenties when he finally got away. In 1936, the Melbourne *Herald* reporter left with £500 in his pocket, an unconcealed relief at escaping Australia, and dreams of becoming a famous author. (*This break with Australia*, Moorehead jotted in his notes, *was the first of two great breaks of my life.*) His timing was fortuitous. He arrived in Europe in time to witness the scenes of a historic year at close range. The abdication of King Edward VIII, the outbreak of the Spanish Civil War, sybaritic Paris and the savage pomp of the Berlin Olympics – he took it all in his stride. There's an irresistible swagger to his letters home from this period. The gap-year cavalier gives a suave account of his trav-els, but you can almost hear his eyes popping out of his head: 'I've had a gun shoved into my ribs and seen a certain amount of sudden death in Spain, I've spent a night with 50 naked prostitutes in a Paris dive, I've seen brother Hitler heiling down the Unter den Linden, I've drunk gal-lons of the nectar they call beer in Germany, I've been in a car smash,

I've slept with an Austrian governess in Berlin, etc., etc., etc.'

When the money ran out there was no question of going home. He wouldn't go home for another ten years, and then only reluctantly (*In effect broken off with family, friends – the idea of Aus. Had deliberately put Aus out of mind*). In 1937 he found freelance work reporting for Lord Beaverbrook's *Daily Express* from Gibraltar, and the next year was appointed to the paper's Paris bureau. He was running the *Express*'s Rome office when Germany invaded Poland. From there, with what was fast becoming a signature knack for getting to the right place at the right time, he blagged his way to Egypt, where General Wavell's tiny Army of the Nile was facing off against Graziani's massed Italians in Libya. He arrived by flying boat in May 1940, just in time to organise a uniform and report the first clashes of the Desert War.

Moorehead knew nothing about war. In Cairo, he was issued with a revolver he had no idea how to use. But here, the only front where British forces faced their enemies on land, in the arid vastnesses that would become famous for the battles of Tobruk, Beda Fomm, Badia and El Alamein, Moorehead's talent underwent an alchemical expansion that startled everyone, himself included. This was his *annus mirabilis*. Enterprising, ruthlessly adaptable, he thrived in the emptiness and heat of the desert battlefields, and made himself at home among the top brass, intrigues and late-imperial languor of GHQ in Cairo. Within a year, the journeyman from Melbourne had become the *Daily Express*'s star reporter in the battle zone. He was well on his way to becoming Britain's best-known war correspondent. Between fighting seasons he dashed out the first instalment of what would become a classic work about the war in the Western Desert, the *African Trilogy*, whose battle scenes the *Observer* ranked beside those in *War and Peace*. In 1943 Moorehead followed Montgomery's Eighth Army to Italy; he accompanied the invasion fleet into France on D-Day and was with the Allied armies all the way into Germany. Bashing out his reports in a terrific, jerky rush, in jeeps, tents, on the kitchen tables of requisitioned farmhouses, he relayed all that he saw – including the horrors revealed by the Wehrmacht's retreat – with a fluency and vividness that made his reports essential breakfast reading for millions of Britons. When the Third Reich collapsed he was exhausted, and sick to death of war, but he nonetheless hied back to the Kent countryside to complete *Eclipse*, a fourth and final volume of eyewitness war history.

The war was over and Moorehead was a superstar. *Things gone well in war* – he notes – *4 books; not masterpieces hoped for but good criticism … From small fry to chief off for D Express and name in big type almost every day.* He was on a huge salary, and he had a growing literary reputation and a contact book fat with influential names. But he was finished with daily journalism. Moorehead wanted to write more books. He wanted to be a famous author, like Hemingway, his idol since his early days on the *Herald*. When his ties to the *Express* were acrimoniously cut in early 1946, he was free to try.

The break with daily journalism was the second *great break* of Moorehead's life, and not a great success. (*Now things began to go wrong…*) The postwar decade was one of frustration and malaise. He tried sitting still, with his wife and two children, at Portofino, near Genoa; then in Fiesole, near Florence. When that didn't work (*Florence too soporific …*) he went back to constant travelling, producing a stream of upmarket pieces for the *Observer*, and soon the *New Yorker*, from Kashmir, Lebanon, Berlin, Italy and Australia. (*But still not settled.*) There were more books. There was a biography of Montgomery, with whom Moorehead had established a warm rapport, largely based on the high opinion both men had of Montgomery. Then there were two novels, both of them duds, Moorehead thought, though one of them, *The Rage of the Vulture*, was nonetheless made into a movie starring Alan Ladd and Deborah Kerr. For all the *accidie* and false starts, Moorehead still had a high reputation. When Ernest Hemingway proposed a piece on postwar Venice to the *New Yorker*'s Harold Ross in the late 1940s, the legendary editor had to turn him down – he was hoping Alan Moorehead was going to do something on the city. (*Yet what sort of writer was I?*) While he pondered this question, his hardwon success seemed to be pouring through his fingers.

Then, in the mid-1950s, he found out what sort of writer he was. Forget novels. Moorehead had discovered a new kind of book to write: popular histories written with the urgency and immersive detail of eyewitness journalism. In the next ten years he would write half a dozen of these, including *Gallipoli, The White Nile, The Fatal Impact* and *Cooper's Creek*, travelling histories of war, exploration and discovery which made his worldwide reputation for a second time. His books sold in prodigious quantities across the English-speaking world, including in abridged and junior illustrated editions, and in translations into more than a dozen languages. *All successes*, he wrote in his notes next to these titles. It was the plain truth.

All this achievement was knotted into a few handwritten pages. But those pages of notes refused to expand into a coherent book of autobiography. It's not as though he couldn't rise to the necessary levels of candour. He was planning to incorporate a long piece he'd written earlier about the life-changing friendship he formed during the war with rival correspondent Alexander Clifford – the most intimate material he'd ever written – and his drafts included stories of adolescent humiliation and some frank stuff about sex. Whatever the precise nature of the block was, Moorehead kept putting his notes aside for other books, for other projects, preferably ones demanding long and rugged trips away. And so time ran out. An early working title for the autobiography, *It Is Later Than You Think*, proved to be horribly apt. Moorehead had been suffering persistent headaches for months when, towards the end of 1966, he went into hospital for an angiogram. The procedure triggered a stroke, and the emergency operation that followed miscarried disastrously, leaving him paralysed and barely able to speak. Moorehead lived for another seventeen years, slowly regaining the ability to walk, speak a few words and even paint. But he never wrote again.

Nonetheless, the elusive autobiography finally appeared, in 1970. It was his wife, Lucy, who put *A Late Education* together. Moorehead's great protector and helpmate was a gifted journalist and editor, and, as far as I've been able to tell, she assembled the book from parts of three separate manuscripts. Chapters on Moorehead's growing up she shuffled in with the story of his friendship with Alexander Clifford, and sections on late 1930s Europe. This fragmentary scheme puzzled some when the book came out – James Cameron, a wartime colleague, called it 'exasperatingly cavalier with continuity'. Others wondered why the story ended so abruptly at 1950. Where was the rest? Overall, though, the reviews, particularly in the British papers, amounted to a kind of *festschrift* for an honoured comrade, a man so many readers had first come to know during the Second World War, and who had been producing wonderful books ever since. There would be no more of those.

§

Every book-lover knows the thrilling experience of discovering a writer whose work changes the way they see the world. It can happen more than once; it had already happened to me several times before I picked up *A Late Education* in my late twenties, so I knew what was happening as I read – I'd found a writer who would forever be indispensable to my imaginative sense of the past. But it was still a shock. I hadn't expected to feel that way about a journalist and popular historian I'd never heard of before.

A Late Education was the first Moorehead book I read. It was the germ that led, slowly at first, then with a feverish rush, to something like an obsession. I read *The Africa Trilogy* next – that sprawling, headlong story of the war as it unfolded, which many admirers considered his masterpiece, and then *Eclipse*, the book about the end of the war in Europe. Then *The White Nile* and *The Blue Nile*. And then, within a year or so, and with the help of online secondhand booksellers, I'd tracked down the rest. All fourteen of them.

I couldn't get enough. Moorehead seemed to speak out of the past with a voice that felt astonishingly contemporary: alert, curious about everything, companionable. It was like getting letters from a rather brilliant friend who happened to be visiting Tunis in 1943 – or Kashmir in 1954, or Nigeria in 1963; or shadowing Burton and Speke as they sweated inland from Zanzibar in 1854. Long letters you didn't want to end, letters steaming with atmosphere, thick with vivid detail that raced from thought to thought with just one intention: to make you see how amazingly interesting it all is.

And almost all of it *was* amazingly interesting, partly because Moorehead lived in amazingly interesting times. In hindsight, he seems to have lived in an era perfectly shaped for the expression of his talent, energy and wanderlust. It didn't always seem that way to him, though, especially during that mid-career funk. In its gloomiest depths, in the late 1940s, Moorehead was living in Fiesole, outside Florence, trying to decide what to do next. There he met often with his illustrious neighbour, the American art critic, scholar and all-round fabled personage Bernard Berenson. A very old man then, Berenson allowed himself to be adopted as a mentor and literary confidant: perhaps he couldn't resist, Moorehead wrote later, 'the Johnsonian pleasure of instructing a young disciple'. Berenson gave Moorehead the run of his superb library at his villa, *I Tatti*; he listened to his protégé's confused ideas; he gave encouragement; sometimes he pointedly withheld it. One day Moorehead announced that he'd decided to write a biography of the Medici poet Poliziano, in whose Renaissance villa Moorehead was then living. Berenson wasn't sure. Poliziano was 'an interesting chap but with no real intellect', he explained. 'You might dip him into what I call the sauce of the epoch but then the little shrimp would disappear.'

That, obviously, would be a wasted effort. But ever since I'd read *A Late Education*, I'd been wondering what would happen if you dipped Moorehead again into the sauce of *his* extraordinary epoch. He'd already disappeared once; maybe, by some strange reverse alchemy, he could be made to reappear.

§

Moorehead was a literary giant in his time, but by the time I discovered him, he'd fallen into deep obscurity. His work was easy enough to find, but only if you knew it was worth looking for. Among those with long memories, the popular histories of the '50s and '60s are still cherished as classics of yesteryear. In the highbrow literary reviews, critics dust off the *Nile* books now and then and hold them up as benchmarks against which some unlucky new book of African travel writing or military history is – almost always – judged minor or dull. Moorehead's war books have been regularly reissued over the decades. As eyewitness accounts they enjoy a

lingering half-life in Second World War historiography. A biography cen-
tred on the war years was published in 1990, but couldn't arrest Moorehead's
slow fade-out;* nor could a fine monograph focusing on Moorehead's
achievements as a historian which appeared in 2005.†

In 2008 I knew plenty of keen readers in Melbourne, the city of his
birth, who had no idea who he was. This wasn't surprising, really. It would
be hard to imagine a writer more unfashionably dead, white and male.
His books are almost exclusively about men, and deal mostly with subjects – war, spying, exploration, wild animals, far-off adventures in far-off
times – that might have been chosen to appeal to an Edwardian schoolboy. It was possible to believe, as I fed my growing infatuation, hunting
down an obscure 1974 reissue of *The Traitors* (1952) through military
bookstores or delightedly swooping on a rare first edition of *Rum Jungle*
(1953) I spied propping up a potted cactus at a charity shop in Queenscliff,
that I had joined a memorial cult with only one member. This notion
wasn't without its perverse appeal. It felt almost transgressive to find myself
identifying so strongly with a writer whose themes seem so remote and
obsolete; as if the inner Edwardian schoolboy I didn't know dwelled within
was rummaging around in the dead-white-male dress-ups box, trying on
dented pith helmets and old flying goggles.

But a regressive yearning for adventure wasn't what made me read
Moorehead's entire published output. It was that voice I'd first heard in
A Late Education; it was the time-machine of the prose.

Here's his first glimpse of the waterfront of Toulon, in southern France,
as a 26-year-old, the first taste for this pilgrim from the New World of the
intoxications of the Old. The *Ormonde* steamed into Toulon harbour in
bright morning sunshine and anchored out in the roadstead. Passengers
were ferried towards the mirage of the waterfront ('some turreted town
from the East, floating on the edge of the water') in little boats that ran
right up to the stone coping of the docks. 'I date my life from this moment,'
Moorehead wrote:

---

* Tom Pocock, *Alan Moorehead*, The Bodley Head, 1990.
† Ann Moyal, *Alan Moorehead: A Rediscovery*, National Library of Australia, 2005.

You stepped from your boat straight on to the cobblestones, and all about you yelling women were selling oysters and mussels, lobsters and crabs, shrimps and limpets and sea urchins; they were all alive, reeking of the sea, and piled on top of one another in sagging wicker baskets. Beyond these stalls there was a short open space and then the cafés began, dozens of rickety little tables in the sunshine, with coloured sunshades, and sitting there, idly surveying the universe, sipping their vermouth-cassis, were the bottomlessly cynical French clientele. Wonderfully gay little men, chattering like monkeys. And girls. French girls, doing things or having things done to them, right there in the open in a way that would have caused a riot back in Park Villas, Melbourne. Before my eyes a man casually reached up his hand to the waitress, pulled down her head, and kissed her on the mouth. When, after a long time, she lifted up her head again and caught my eye she smiled pleasantly ... This was it. This was what I had come for. Here in this market and among these people was the missing thing. From now on there was no more time to be lost: I must learn the language, I must understand what they were saying and thinking; and I must see all the other markets, the buildings, the paintings, and the peoples of Europe.

Like many Australians before and since, I knew this sensation of arriving in Europe and recognising that 'missing thing' that was both foreign and deeply familiar. But I hadn't seen it described as hungrily as this, or in prose which took so much pleasure in observed details that you want to crawl into the page and roll around in it. He 'has a mind like one of those small and enormously expensive cameras,' the *Times Literary Supplement* declared in 1946, 'whatever he sees, up goes the camera, and you have, in any light, a beautifully defined picture.'

That descriptive gift went beyond word pictures. He had a casual brilliance for atmosphere, for conveying the distinctive air pressure of time and place. In that first decade of his European career, he was reporting from the rolling catastrophe of the Second World War, which meant that the atmosphere he described is the one that still haunts our culture through endless TV documentaries and movies and spy novels. All the dark ambience is there in Moorehead. If you were so inclined, you could read him now just to lose yourself in the texture of that dark dream: the desolation of cheap travellers' hotels with creaky iron-grille lifts, whisky breath at secret conferences, tramp steamers tied up alongside foggy docks, the blacked-out nightclubs, blackmarket nylons, the cryptic telegrams, and always the background static of emergency.

But in Moorehead it sounds brand-new, as if he were the first writer to cross the border into a new world – the Middle East and Europe in the throes of modern, technological war – and the first to send back news of how it felt to ordinary people and what it was doing to them. The Victorian essayist Walter Bagehot wrote that Dickens describes London 'like a special correspondent for posterity'; in the *African Trilogy*, Moorehead does something similar for Middle Eastern towns and deserts undergoing historic transformation, constantly tugging at your sleeve to show you another surreal detail, to make you stand in the right place so that you see what he sees. 'He wrote effortlessly,' a wartime colleague later recalled, 'the only man I knew who could type a story and hold a conversation at the same time.' And that's how his copy read: like a conversation on paper. Moorehead's biographer, Tom Pocock, called it his 'buttonholing intimacy': this is a writer who wants you to see and understand, and to do that, you have to be there, too, feeling the heat on your back, the dust in your tea mug, swatting flies at a briefing, smelling the smoldering charcoal in the brazier of an abandoned Bedouin village.

As early as 1941 you can also see the promiscuous curiosity of the travel-writer Moorehead was becoming, his knack of seeming to fit in wherever he is while maintaining the detachment of an outsider seeing everything for the first time. In May that year he flew to Iraq to report on what turned out to be a sideshow skirmish over the oil fields there, and tossed off a memorable sketch of one tiny disregarded corner of the embattled Empire:

> Before it is too late and all the English clubs of the tropics are gone, let me just record my memory of this one. It was almost a perfect specimen ... a ramshackle single-storied wooden building by the river, with a library, a billiard room and a bar. A wide verandah and a big reception

room for the dances and social evenings on Saturday night. Barefoot servants in white robes and turbans, a broad table on which lie six months' old copies of the *Tatler*, the *Bystander*, the *Sketch*, the *Sphere*, the *Illustrated London News*, *The Times* and the *Daily Telegraph*, the *New Statesman*, the *Forum*, *Truth*, *Punch* – a lot of *Punches*, bound copies too – the *Windsor* and *Strand Magazines* and a pile of engineering and trade papers and one or two local journals. The wicker chairs are just as they should be and always have been. So is the boy who presents a chit for you to sign for your drinks. So are the silver cups and the shield in the corner. Only the wireless set is out of place. When the day's work is done, launches slide down the river and drop off the white-trousered English residents and they call for drinks as they slump down in the wicker chairs among their friends.

Moorehead's prose grew leaner over time. As he himself became less easy and less eager to impress, so did his style. *Detachment* and *polish* were the qualities he was aiming for in his histories of the '50s and '60s. Moorehead was capable of *tour-de-force* passages that still make you want to leap out of your chair and find someone to read them out to, but there's no straining for effect in his mature prose and little conspicuous panache. In the late works some grandiloquence creeps in, as though the language is trying to rise to the august standing of its author. You start to notice an over-fondness for the word 'scene' ('now we must imagine the *scene* ...' 'into this *scene* burst', etc. etc.), and brolly-twirling phrases ('One even fancies that one can descry Mount Athos ...' he grandly reports in *Gallipoli*). In Moorehead there are sentences to which, given a moment, you fancy you could descry some potential improvements: maybe a fresher verb here, or a more pungent noun there. But this rarely feels true of a Moorehead *page*. In full flight his story-telling is so lucid and swift and sensible that it feels inevitable, and so nearly transparent the pages seem to be turning themselves. All you notice, and only after a while, is the sensation of being borne along by the story's eagerness to be told, an irresistible current that barely ruffles the surface.

§

So I read it all. The outdated histories, the obscure biographies, even the despised novels. At one level, it was pure escapist pleasure I was after, a chance to ride shotgun on a wonderful adventure and to experience a lost world with almost teleporter immediacy. But there was also a fantasy identification with Moorehead himself, who had, after all, set out from my own home town in search of fame and excitement, and been unimaginably successful in finding it.

Only months after reading *A Late Education* for the first time, in 1999, my wife and I moved to London, and on the way passed through Cairo, and stayed at what our guidebook described as a perfectly preserved colonial-era hotel. On the first night we came down to the lounge in an antique elevator that moved in an open ironwork shaft and had tricky folding doors that had to be precisely latched before the thing would budge. We sat up at the bar. The whole place had been styled – or deliberately neglected – to give a convincing impression of a scene from 1940s British Cairo. We admired the wainscoting and the clubby armchairs with their cracked leather and the brass frosted-glass lamps that gave the room its polleny glow. Then a TV crew arrived to film a scene for an Egyptian soap opera. Gaffers erected arc lights and ran flex under rugs. It was only then, sitting decoratively in the background of the shot, that it dawned on me that this was Moorehead's hotel: by complete coincidence, we'd chosen among hundreds of hotels the one where Moorehead lived in 1940 during the first months of the Desert War. I'd had a couple of drinks by then, which may have contributed to my excitement. It was like a hallucinated sensation of connection across time – maybe it had been three or four drinks – and this was somehow concentrated *in the elevator*, in its clattering quaintness. Down that very elevator had come a young man from my home town on the other side of the world. I could almost see him drawing back the accordion grill of the elevator car, releasing a gust of big-band mood music, and stepping out neat and alert, tie tightly knotted, folded cap tucked under the epaulette. I could see him dropping into a club chair *right there*, ready to set out on a brilliant career. Right *there*.

This sense of the atmosphere of a lost world was crucial to my interest in Moorehead. His account of the mid-twentieth century was somehow inseparable from the battered old books and magazines it came in. The cloth boards of the cheap old hardbacks I was collecting were often pie-bald from palm sweat, or had that slightly convex buckling that comes from being left in the sun. They had coffee cup half-moons and pot-plant rings. Some had spindly fountain-penned gift inscriptions from the '40s and '50s. They were tangible links to the actuality of a time before this, related to ours, but also fundamentally foreign. And this half-real, half-dreamed aroma of the past seemed strongest in the maps that so often came in Moorehead's books, showing the string of battlefields along the Libyan seaboard, or the half-guessed interiors of nineteenth-century Australia and Africa. Sometimes they were glued into the inside covers; sometimes, if you were lucky, they were gatefold inserts, like the one in my copy of *The Blue Nile*, printed on delicate, translucent paper that folded out from the spine like a rustling quarto miracle. But they all showed that the world looked and felt different to people once, before it was sat-mapped to the last pixel.

Moorehead's books and travel pieces are soberly anchored in their historical periods, but they seem to have acquired another dimension now: a pathos that comes with the simple passing of time. Reading them, I felt the same vague longing for vanished places that made vintage postcards from the '50s and '60s so appealing and also haunting – those panoramas of the Eiffel Tower or Naples or Hong Kong, with their saturated Kodachrome blues and glowing whites that seemed to represent the eternal summertime of the tourist's globe. Moorehead's writing produced the sensation of disquieting transport, to an era that can feel today like a lost world.

Of course, it may have just been me. I still hadn't met anyone else who'd read any of his books.

§

Joseph Brodsky wrote somewhere that once you've read a certain amount of a writer's work you find yourself wanting to know what she or he looks like. I already knew what Moorehead looked like, and from his books I'd been able to compose a partial identikit image of his character. Moorehead mostly wrote non-fiction, and he is visible in all of it to varying degrees.

Eclipse, for instance, the most personally revealing of his war books, is partly a journal in which Moorehead is the most vivid character, improvising feasts in Sicilian villas with his comrades between battles, objecting to shabby billets and raiding wine cellars for claret to fuel hours of talk of the future and grand metaphysical bollocks. He is companionably present in the travel pieces he filed for *Holiday* and the *New Yorker* in the '50s; we see him in a different way – both unconvincingly masked, and pitilessly naked – in the clunky postwar novels. But in the late histories he recedes from view, without ever quite disappearing. One of the most distinctive effects in Moorehead's mature prose is the way that he sets a scene and then, like a personable tour-guide, steps back to contemplate it with us, his fellow-inquirers into the sheer strangeness of things.* As you read the *Nile* books and *Cooper's Creek* and *The Fatal Impact* you're always conscious of the author nearby, organising his tale. You can hear him in the background, stomping along the old tracks, setting out the camp stools on a weedy old battlefield at dusk. You can hear him *thinking*.

But I knew what Brodsky meant. After I'd read all the books, what I wanted was to see the room Moorehead worked in.

A compulsive traveller, Moorehead wrote books all over the place. But one place stands out: for the last ten years of his writing life he was based in a house he and his wife, Lucy, built just above the little seaside village of Porto Ercole, on Italy's Monte Argentario. One day late in 2010 I drove down the west coast of Tuscany from where I was staying in Umbria to see if I could find it.

On the map it looked like a few hours each way at most – an easy day trip – and an adventure on the right scale for the whim that I told myself this was. I didn't know the precise address of the house, after all. I was just going to poke around, and take a look.

---

* A typical passage, from *The Blue Nile*: 'Nothing is more intriguing in African exploration in the nineteenth century than the casualness with which it was often undertaken. A group of friends meet and discuss a trip abroad. Shall it be Vienna, Naples, or the Canary Islands? Or possibly Africa? Yes, of course, Africa. They know nothing about Africa, no shipping lines exist, no one can tell them anything very definite about the climate, the kind of medicines required on the journey, the local languages, the food, the money or the inhabitants; maps are unobtainable. But presumably … All these things will be made clear as they proceed along their way. The gunsmith in the Strand supplies them with firearms, the banker gives them a draft on Cairo, the hatter furnishes sun-helmets with flaps at the back, and off they go as light-heartedly as if they were setting off for the south of France to avoid the English winter.'

For reasons I can't remember now, my wife and I decided it might be a nice idea to take along our small children. They would research gelati while I tried to find the house. After three long hours of 'I Spy' and 'Guess the Animal', we were still shooting south at the usual unnerving *autostrada* speed, through mountains thick with gothic pine forest. When the freeway finally swept us down from the hills, spat us out an exit ramp and onto the coastal plain, we soon became lost in a maze of little crooked roads with signs pointed puzzlingly into the hedges of overgrown corn on either side. Another hour passed while we found the causeway across to the peninsula and made our way around the coast to Porto Ercole.

We crawled stickily out of the car and took our bearings. Porto Ercole is one of those rustic fishing villages that has held its ancient shape while the decades have cluttered its edges with cheap flats. Between two high bluffs, each capped with the ruins of a medieval fortress, the town zigzags down a steep slope to a strip of waterfront cafés and shops facing the boardwalk, a pebble beach and a marina where hundreds of little white boats suckle at their piers. It was early autumn. It wasn't deserted, but it was quiet, in that appealingly neglected way that summer towns have when all the holiday-makers have gone home. In the boutiques expressionless shopgirls tapped at keyboards or rearranged trinkets in the windows. Now and then a moped blattered up a steep cobbled street to the main road, but in the following silence all you could hear was the clink of wires against aluminium masts and the slap-suck of water against rocking hulls.

I felt a surge of excited purpose – I was so close now! But I had no address for the Moorehead house, only vague descriptions of its approximate location. Distracted by the difficulty and unlikelihood of ever getting to this place from Melbourne, I'd overlooked this detail; I'd assumed that if I made it this far, finding the house would be the easy part. I hesitated, wondering whether coffee would help. Then I recalled that Moorehead had experienced a moment like this himself. In 1937, during the Spanish Civil War, he was based in Gibraltar, a junior stringer for the *Daily Express* in London, reporting on the shipping war raging in the Mediterranean. On the hunt for a scoop, he persuaded his paper to let him go to Istanbul to see what he could dig up there. But when he arrived in Istanbul, a city seething with rumour, spies, criminals and profiteers – or so everyone said – he realised he had come ashore 'without a single coherent idea of what I was to do next'.

> I wandered out into the streets and stood for a while gazing at the statue of Kemal Ataturk. He was carved boldly in stone and he was wearing a dinner jacket and turned-up cuffs on the bottom of his trousers. Camels and mules and street vendors with their handcarts passed by, covering the statue's elegant legs with dust. Somehow, I thought, I must discover the technique of the high-powered foreign correspondent. He would not stand here, in the midday heat, with his hands in his pockets staring at a statue of Kemal Ataturk. He would be dining at embassies, telephoning Cabinet ministers, sending off long political cables, perhaps interviewing Kemal Ataturk himself. But how did one begin? … How did you penetrate that magic world?

Well, quite. How did you?

I left the kids pinging stones into the water and made for the tourist office. On the way I noted, with disappointment, no sign of a 'White Nile Café' among the village's bars, no '*Trattoria* Moorehead'. The tourist office was in a modern, low-slung building that fronted a car park. The two women behind the desk inside looked pleased to have a customer. They listened encouragingly to the faltering Italian phrases I'd rehearsed for this moment, but when I finished they seemed nonplussed. Now I saw a quite specific look of feminine pity that I'd noticed a lot in Italy and which seems to be reserved for grown men who, for whatever reason, ought to know better. They'd never heard of Alan Moorehead. They were terribly sorry, one said, in perfect English.

That was that, then. My best shot at finding the house had come to nothing. Feeling foolish, I turned to go. But then one of the women gasped and flung out a palm. Wait. Yes, yes! A famous writer, you say? Yes! She nodded at her colleague in triumph. There was a rapid exchange in Italian. The other woman's eyes widened. Oh yes! *Si, si*. My heart leapt. They had him now. I realised how excited I was to be this close to the house. I beamed with gratitude. The women nodded at me proudly. He is American, yes?

American? No. I explained again, in English. He was Australian. Or British, if you like. An expat.

The first woman frowned happily at her municipal map, tracing thoughtful circles in the air with a pen. There *was* a famous American writer's house in the town, she said. She glanced up, a little impressed, I thought. You *know* him?

Not exactly, I admitted. Not really.

Do you have his telephone number?

Er, no. No telephone number. You see …

But you must have his telephone number if you're going to visit?

I didn't have the famous writer's telephone number.

Evidently this was a serious setback.

I tried again. Perhaps I should have mentioned earlier, I said, he's been dead for thirty years.

At the word 'dead' the women visibly tensed.

I tried for my most placid smile. No – I said – I just want to *see* the house. From the outside. The women were watching me carefully. Because I love his books, you see? I am a fan. I'm just a … *fan*. (I have always hated the word 'fan'.) I kept smiling, like a harmless fan. 'I just want to see where he lived.'

At that, the tension dissipated. Clearly I was telling the truth – why admit to such nonsense unless it was true? They had me print the name, ALAN MOOREHEAD, on a scrap of paper. Then they studied it from different angles, as though it were a cryptic clue, and cross-checked it against their map, looking from one to the other. Each woman pronounced the name experimentally. *Mourhid. Morr-hayde.* One picked up the phone – twice – as if to make a critical phone call, and then, hesitatingly, put it down. I recognised the kindly pantomime. I'd seen it the week before, in the tourist office at Fiesole, near Florence, another old home of the author, another place where Moorehead's name had returned a regretful blank, where no local memory survived of the writer whose work I had become so helplessly consumed by. Neither woman knew the name, or the books; neither could think of anyone who would. They were out of ideas and very sorry. Never mind, I said: it doesn't matter at all. Just a whim.

It mattered a lot, of course. Now I was desperate to find it.

§

The pilgrimage to the writer's house is a cliché, but it's still one of the oddest things readers do. What is in the reader's heart when she goes to see a famous writer's house? Prurience? Reverence? Hope? We know our memory of the books won't be there, yet we go anyway, to experience the strange, simple fact – the same old fact, but strange every time – that the intimate journey we took with the mind of someone else can be traced to a person sitting at a desk in a room somewhere, gnawing their nails and wondering if the mail's come yet. We want to pay our respects, I think, and to stake a claim. We demonstrate to ourselves, if to no one else, how important a writer's work has become to us.

My failure at the tourist office was a blow, but there was still hope. I had the description in Robert Hughes' memoir of walking drunkenly back to the Moorehead house from the village fifty years ago. It is a brief passage, and was never meant to be used as a map. But it might serve as one. The cemetery. Pine trees. Ten minutes' walk up the hill. But which hill? And how far does a half-schickered art critic walk in ten minutes?

We had lunch, then piled back into the car. Past the cemetery there was a road that did, indeed, wind up a hill. But it quickly narrowed to a track barely wide enough for our car, let alone any that might happen along from the other direction. Dusty foliage pressed on either side; it was impossible to see anything except the shaded track ahead, which kept forking. We chose at random. It was like a game where the goal is to become lost as fast and as comprehensively as possible. We kept climbing. You could tell from the driveways, most of them solemnly gated, their letterboxes unmarked, that plenty of properties were tucked away behind the trees and scrub. Now and then through gaps in the foliage you could glimpse ordered shadow where tiny vineyards and olive groves clung to the hillside. We could be close, and we'd never know. I thought again about how long ago 1965 was, when Moorehead was in full flight, writing *The Fatal Impact* in daily increments up here somewhere among the trees, working in the mornings, strolling down to the town for dinner.

It was hopeless. A four-hour return trip loomed. The sun was getting lower. At least, I told my stupefied children, we've seen the town. Everyone was quiet while I tried to find a driveway I could use to squeeze the car around and begin the drive back. I found one. At the entrance was a plain wooden sign. *Casa Moorehead.*

I marched up the driveway alone. I had no idea what I was going to say, and tried not to think about it. I just followed my feet. The track made a sharp hairpin bend, then continued steeply uphill before it opened out to a broad gravelled area. There was the house – the back of the house, I guessed, from what I'd seen of photographs – a simple, two-storey building with creepers hugging the windowsills like delicate bunting, and a shuttered garage and no sign of anyone at all.

I was about to knock on the door when I glanced to my left and saw what I'd come to see, and then I forgot all about knocking on the door. About fifty yards or so up the hill from the house was a small cabin of rough honey-coloured stone wedged into the sloping ground. Moorehead's writing studio – 'His little shithouse, with no view,' Robert Hughes called it. 'Do you want your little studio – how pathetic that sounds – run up right away?' Lucy Moorehead wrote to her husband in early 1960. As so often, Moorehead was away on a trip, and Lucy was attending to business, in this case, the business of seeing their dream home built. He *did* want it straightaway. And here it was, so small. I walked over and gazed at it, checking with all my senses that it was real, feeling that strange old sensation of seeing, right in front of you, a thing you have imagined so often that you can't quite believe it exists outside the imagination.

Everything was very still. All I could hear was birds, and the scrape of my shoes on the gravel. A lawyer friend once told me that, technically, you're only trespassing after someone has asked you to leave the property. But biography, or reader's obsession, is itself a kind of trespass. Nothing you can do about it. And no one had asked me to leave yet.

§

I'd been trespassing for a while now in any case. A few years before, when I finished reading everything Moorehead wrote himself, as well as everything I could find that was written about him, I realised I hadn't finished. So I flew up to the National Library in Canberra to inspect the collection of personal papers he gifted to the nation in 1971.

The National Library is where Australia keeps the documentary remains of its glorious dead, and the Manuscripts Reading Room, where anyone with a card and the inclination may inspect those remains, felt like an annex to a well-run mausoleum. When I arrived one winter morning, and unpacked my laptop, I had a crisis of nerve. Coming here felt like a fateful escalation of my interest in Moorehead. In that sensible room, with its rows of sensible-looking readers absorbed in ledgers and passenger manifests, the glamour drained out of my quest. While I waited for my first order slip to be processed, I wandered over to the windows and looked out into the windy day, the oystery sky. Beyond the car park below I could see a few monumental concrete buildings spaced out among gum trees and fields of asphalt, some flagpoles and, at the edge of Lake Burley Griffin, an ornamental row of trees long-sufferingly heeled over in the winter wind. It was a sharply unromantic view that asked questions I didn't want to think about.

But then a trolley appeared bearing the first box of Moorehead's papers and my anxieties were forgotten. I sat at my canted reading table and, with tingling fingertips, began to pick through the fragrant debris of a mid-century literary life. Here were the very cables Moorehead had received on board a freighter running illicit fuel supplies into Republican Spain in 1937; scalloped-edge photographs of mysterious beaming bathers; a girl's name scrawled on the back of a Tangier nightclub flyer from 1937; the notebooks in which Moorehead had jotted one-line impressions as he rode behind the tanks through Normandy in 1944. Rejection letters from publishers. Letters from readers, from agents, other writers. Royalty statements. Fan-mail. Sketches for abandoned projects. The poignant letters from Father, as Moorehead always called him, full of achingly muffled pride at each new book his startling son produced.

For hours, I was euphoric. I'd begun to identify with Moorehead, I realised – no, more than that, I'd started to feel as though I owned him. And here was my man, swimming off the rocks near St Jean in 1938; here are his pictures of the port at Istanbul in 1937. The letters of introduction for a promising young fellow from 1936; the in-house bulletins from the *Express*'s editor praising another Moorehead dispatch to the skies in 1945.

Over the next couple of years I came back several times, whenever I could scrape together a few days. Haunting the cheapest motels on the capital's fringes, I lived on library coffee and half-thawed sandwiches from petrol stations, and made daily forays into the Reading Room in a series of rental cars. Each day felt like another deep-dive into piles of old paper, from which I would emerge with a fresh haul of disorganised notes. In the evening I would trudge away from the glowing temple of the library towards the dark, stumbling over fist-sized sods in the empty paddock that had been full of cars when I'd parked there in the morning. It never felt like work. It felt like losing myself in a time-current. I was feeling my way back into the everyday texture of Moorehead's life, trying to place the factiveness of these fragments in the popular-memory glamour of Moorehead's milieux – pre-war Paris, expat Italy in the '40s, the early jet age.

It was the speed and scale of his success that stood out first. From one neat little archival box to the next you could trace Moorehead's rapid progress, and his excitement at seeing so much so soon, and doing so well. But over time, as old mysteries deepened and new ones appeared, I began to see some encouraging answers to the oldest mystery: why such a celebrated writer had become so hard to place so soon. This was crucial, since the alternative – that Moorehead had faded from sight because he and his work simply hadn't been interesting enough to last – was too dispiriting to contemplate. But here, happily, was evidence suggesting that Moorehead had *always* been hard to place. For all his professional achievements, he had never loomed large in the public imagination. Moorehead wasn't famously irascible, or vicious, or brilliant in company. He lacked the popular artists' vices of the time. He became quietly notorious for his womanising in some circles, including, painfully, his wife's; but that was a private matter. To the reading public, he wasn't a fabled boozer, or a tremendous hater, communist or talk-show raconteur. He was highly ambitious for his writing, but never too fastidious to grind out mediocre copy for newspaper deadlines (he was always pragmatic about the relationship between writing and paying bills), and he wasn't a natural self-promoter. One of his few recorded maxims for the writing life was: 'Avoid publicity as much as you can, above all television.' That reads like a misprint now, but Moorehead could afford to let the work speak for itself. He was, he once wrote to Lucy, 'prim at heart and too serious. I'm only good and strong when I'm working, really working.'

It might all be too mild, perhaps, if he hadn't been consumed by his work. He was a ferociously hard worker. Work, and the travel it involved, was the governing compulsion of his life. *Comes over one an absolute necessity to move*, wrote DH Lawrence, an author he admired. Moorehead would suffer the long stretches of internment necessary to write his books, but the only time he concentrated on staying still, writing novels in Italy after the war, he sickened like a captive animal. Restlessness fuelled his work. It shaped his life. It links the brash colonial who strode down the gangway onto the wharf at Plymouth in 1936 – the dasher-off of suave, flirty letters, the curious but easily bored young player who can still be glimpsed in the weary celebrity of 1945 – and the unillusioned materialist, the master artisan who replaced him in the '50s and '60s. It was the restlessness – and the recklessness that went with it – that intrigued me. Moorehead hated getting stuck, and would escape whenever possible, without any apparent fear about where he might end up, or at what cost to his conscience. This appealed to me enormously, in the way that reckless adventure has always appealed to the couch-bound. His propulsive ambition called out to half-buried frustrations and desires of my own, my own baulked attempts to escape Australia and fear of getting stuck in my beloved Melbourne, my queasy fascination with the Second World War, a naïve faith in the glory of travel.

One afternoon at the National Library I settled into a cubicle to listen to an oral history interview Moorehead recorded in 1964. I donned the plush headphones. This would be the first time I'd encountered his spoken voice, though I had an idea of what to expect. When he first arrived in London in 1936, Moorehead had been appalled when a girl he was sleeping with told him he had a 'cockney' accent. He didn't – but he got rid of it anyway, and old friends he met during the war and after often remarked on the change. It was still a shock. This imposter was an English aristocrat with blocked sinuses and a drawling tenor voice. Moorehead had shed his Australian accent, but he'd replaced it with something one might acquire at a gentlemen's outfitters. 'You sounded just as I had hoped you would,' one Mrs Barker of Birkenhead, Cheshire, wrote after she heard a BBC radio talk he gave in 1944, 'and not what my son calls a chromium plated accent.' But anything more chromium-plated was hard to imagine.

I was thrown by this for a while. It felt like a rebuke for my presumption, for getting overfamiliar with the past.

§

To most people I spoke to, Moorehead was a vague figure who fell vaguely into the category of remaindered Australiana. Up close, however, he didn't seem to fit into any category at all. Not even Australian. He discarded his provincial origins as soon as he could; within a decade of leaving he was well on his way to becoming a multilingual cosmopolitan, capable of blending in anywhere.

And so now he seemed to belong nowhere. John Hetherington, a former wartime colleague, wrote that Moorehead's 'dominating purpose for many years now has been to appear an Englishman, a European'. The expatriate option is the oldest sore in Australian cultural life: to stay or to leave? and if to leave, to return? The sheer scale of Moorehead's overseas success sent many Hetheringtons back to pick at the scab, even as it inspired the next generation to test its talent abroad. Clive James, Philip Knightley and Robert Hughes, who would enjoy international success from the early 1970s, are just three who publicly acknowledged the importance of Moorehead's example.

It didn't help that Moorehead's prodigal return to Australia twenty-five years later coincided with a historic moment of cultural reassessment and self-contemplation in which the views of fly-in expatriates were hardly more welcome than they are today. At the 1964 Adelaide Arts Festival the speech Moorehead gave at an exhibition of paintings by his friend Sidney Nolan received mixed reviews. 'Alan Moorehead opened it,' wrote the novelist Xavier Herbert in a letter the next day. 'What a pompous bore. As I said to Judah [Waten]: "He's not one of our mob," to which J said: "Definitely not." He lives in Spain, has a castle there ...'*

---

* Moorehead's European home wasn't a castle, and it wasn't in Spain, but the fact that it existed at all was probably enough for Herbert.

If Moorehead himself haunts Australian passport control like an ambivalent shade, sometimes hoping to be let in, sometimes not, but in any case mostly disqualified on the grounds of old grudges or visa irregularities, then his books are equally hard to classify. '[*Gallipoli*] placed Moorehead in a unique literary category,' the *Sunday Times*'s obituarist noted in 1983. You can try to place him among that generation of travel writers set moving by the war – Eric Newby, Jan Morris, Norman Lewis, Peter Fleming, Freya Stark – or perhaps with other generalist historians working in the '50s and '60s – William L Shirer or Barbara Tuchmann – but when you do, what you see most clearly is how he doesn't quite fit. Even at the time, no one was sure what he was up to, or precisely why it read so well. 'He really can see through the eyes of others,' wrote Australian critic Max Harris, taking a stab at the elusive Moorehead quality in 1965. 'As a result he is the living master of a modern literary genre which lies between history on the one hand and journalism on the other.' The English novelist CP Snow tried to isolate the literary *genus* this way:

> There is a kind of writing at which our age ... has been out of comparison better than any previous one. It is a kind or category for which no one has yet found a suitable name, but one can indicate it by a few examples – Vincent Sheehan's personal history, Barbara Tuchman's *Guns of August* ... much of Arthur Koestler's non-fiction, Cyril Connolly's *Enemies of Promise*, some of Aldous Huxley.
>
> Somehow this writing seems to have been squeezed out by the pressures of our artistic climate: as novels have become more esoteric, and history more doggedly professional, gifted and independent persons have tried to find an interstice between the two ... Let us call it high journalism. Of all its practitioners, Mr Alan Moorehead is one of the most masterly.

For most professional historians, Moorehead was a mere populariser. But there was a sly art to these narratives, and a distinctive aesthetic to which ordinary readers responded in huge numbers.

But those readers have gone. Decades ago they began to dwindle away, along with the middle-class subscribers to *Horizon* and the *Saturday*

Evening Post, and the Book-of-the-Month Club, and avid readers of *Time* or *Life* magazine features. The virtues of Moorehead's work haven't faded, but perhaps they're harder to see out of context. And the context was an era in which his reports from distant places were a magic carpet ride of escape and adventure most people couldn't get anywhere else but in books and *National Geographic* and the glossy magazines. This was the Western world on the cusp of ubiquitous television and mass travel.

Moorehead's generation of writer-travellers was the last to see so many cultures existing in anything like an 'unspoilt' state, whether it was the Dinka people of Sudan ('almost as naked, as primitive and as unresponsive to the healthy dreariness of modern civilization, as they ever were'), or even – perhaps especially – the last authentic fag-ends of the British Empire. In East Africa and Asia Moorehead didn't stay in the kind of hotels top-end travellers do today, where colonial ease and elegance is expensively simulated in repro teak and tiffin lunches. He stayed in hotels that were authentic remainders of the colonial period, whose fraying wickerwork and decades-old copies of *Punch* were the actual, tattered decor of the Imperial sunset.

$$\S$$

It's enough to make him seem like a citizen of a different world. Of course it *was* a different world. From my earliest days in the archives I'd been struck by the realisation – a truism to historians, but new to me – that people's lives were so very different to ours only a few decades ago. Whenever I read through his *New Yorker* pieces I found my eyes drifting from Moorehead's copy to the strip adverts running alongside. How the ads have aged around him, I thought, these ads for defunct airlines and gizmos that were obsolete before I was born, from Braniff Airways to Magnavox radio-TVs.

Yet there is something else, particular to Moorehead, that roots the work of the '50s and '60s so firmly in its period: his imagination seemed to face backwards. Increasingly, he looked for stories from other times, stories of exploring, destroying and suffering, in which the great subject of his career finally reveals itself: the spread of European civilisation 'like a proliferating plague' over distant lands, its 'aggressive curiosity', its self-destructiveness, and its often bloody retreat.

Moorehead was a product of the British Empire, and at some level remained one, even as a fellow-travelling young socialist, and then later as a roaming witness to the Empire's abrupt dissolution. The young dreamer who'd started out all agog at Hemingway's trailblazing prose style had, by the late 1940s, lost interest in literary innovation. But he didn't need new forms to tell fresh stories. The carefully cultivated qualities in his prose – the shrewdness, and independence, the rhythmic clarity, the immunity to fads and cult personalities – were what gave his books their unassuming authority. Of pop culture and the social revolution that transformed Western life in the late 1960s there is hardly a trace in his work. Current affairs rarely intrude on his 'Reporter at Large' dispatches from across the world. But he never lost his ability to spot the big picture behind small details. His later books are quietly prescient about the rise of environmentalism and the fate of the postcolonial world.

Most of all, he never lost faith in the revelatory pleasure of the story. From the mid-'50s on, the story was everything. To read Moorehead's work now is to be reminded of how we once told stories about the world to ourselves. It's inevitable that the flaws and dated tics of his work should stand out in retrospect, particularly the paternalistic assumptions, and the unreconstructed terms in which he describes 'native' peoples. But there are also qualities that we have perhaps forgotten how to value: the open-hearted view of adventure as a worthwhile thing in itself; and a kind of intelligent, unironic wonder at the world and how much of it there is to see.

§

In *A Late Education*, Moorehead described the various rooms he'd worked in over the past thirty years as 'self-inflicted prisons where the writer sits incarcerated for so many hours each day'. He probably wrote those words while he was sitting in *this* stone cell at Porto Ercole, I thought. A cell he'd designed himself. For straining shit through a sock.

I tried to put the question of trespassing out of my mind long enough to survey the *scene*, as Moorehead might say. I noted the window with its dust-streaked glass, a window which had been deliberately oriented so that the inmate couldn't be distracted by the pretty view of the sea and the hills and the harbour. I am not a prowler, I told myself, I am a *fan*. I edged closer to the window: no sign of the author. No angle poise lamp. No trace of the desk, a copy of Dr Livingstone's that Moorehead had had specially made up. The place was a storeroom, crammed with holiday lumber, with inflatable pool toys and old fishing rods. Some gardening tools.

I stepped back. In his forties and fifties, Moorehead himself made many trips like this to significant sites. He did all the usual desk-bound research, finding his way into the minds of his long-dead characters through their diaries and journals. But then he liked to track his stories back to their settings to feel the landscape under his boots. He always 'walked the course', as one friend put it. Sometimes there was a residual tremor of drama. But mostly he was surveying, fossicking for remains, adjusting his bearings and perspective.

For Moorehead, the crucial dimension wasn't space, but time. In his books explorers and scientists and soldiers act out their fates in alien, often vast landscapes, but also in the unpitying wastes of eternity. The quiet and neglected air of places abandoned by the onrush of history fascinated him. It made its way into his books in a distinctive way, in what one writer called 'sudden pools of contemplative and passive quiet – a sort of cool stagnancy, into which the narrative … sinuously slides forward'. Behind all the action and wonder of *The White Nile* and *Cooper's Creek* and *The Fatal Impact* is always this feeling of the universe's indifference: to the pageant of history itself, its striving and pathos and absurdity. It's there in his journalism, too, as in this stage-setting passage from a 1962 *New Yorker* piece beginning at the town of Bonny, at the mouth of the Niger Delta:

> The old town of Bonny is a labyrinth of mud walls and rusting galvanized-iron roofs – the mud of Africa, the iron of Europe – and is full of tumble-down buildings and derelict little workshops that are declining away to nothing … A ragged parrot, too old or too lazy to fly away, pecked at a pile of rubbish in the roadway, and an ancient man in a daze of

inertia offered for sale a handful of kola nuts and half a bottle of Pepsi-Cola . . . Beyond the town, one had a glimpse through the mango trees of a modern school and the great, gleaming aluminium forms of the new oil-storage dumps, with tankers from Norway and Japan lying off the shore. It was terribly hot, and I tried to bathe among the mangrove roots but got covered with mud and slime.

We recognise the mood. It's the fed-up gloom of the traveller who wishes they'd taken an earlier bus. But in Moorehead, traveller's ennui can be a sweet melancholy that feels existential; there's a kind of Sunday after-noon listlessness to it, an unfocused yearning for other ages and places. I could feel it right here, in Porto Ercole. This was in every sense a Moorehead scene. Thirty years after his death, this little building radiated an air of gentle abandonment. The glorious indifference of time was all around, in the late afternoon sunshine catching wisps of spiderweb in the mortared stones, the hushing sound of a wind moving through the cypresses on its way to somewhere else.

But it was the sturdy actuality of the shed that struck me most. It was a solid link to a real life that, till now, existed in a past-haze of black-and-white footage and mid-twentieth-century atmospherics. Seeing it had made the four-hour drive worthwhile. But I knew I wouldn't learn anything here about Moorehead's struggle to become the writer he was, or the world in which that struggle took place. This humble building belonged to the com-fortably established end of Moorehead's working life, when success had largely soothed the itch of constant striving and doubt. I needed to start with an earlier version, the younger man who'd caught my imagination in the first place: the charming, pushy chancer who arrived in pre-war Europe full of wild dreams, and afraid that he was running out of time.

2

CUMDEAD ETWOUNDED

Moorehead arrived in Gibraltar by third-class steamer in March 1937 and checked into the Rock Hotel, a magnificent white palace halfway up the steepling mountain-side. 'There was a brightly striped Moorish counterpane on the bed,' he recalled, 'and from my balcony, which was entwined with flowering creepers, I looked across the blue water of the straits to the coast of Africa, fourteen miles away.' It's hard to imagine a more delicious vista for a young colonial who'd dreamed of the great world since he was a boy. 'I used to go down to the docks at Port Melbourne and read on the sterns of the vessels the names of the wonderful places from which they had sailed. Valparaiso. Liverpool. San Francisco. Le Havre. Tokyo. One day, I said to myself . . .' Now, from the terrace, he could gaze down onto British warships racked into Gibraltar's South Mole like tokens in a game of Battleship; further around were crowds of merchant vessels whose home ports were every bit as evocative as the ones he'd pined for back in Port Melbourne.

He was twenty-six. He'd reached London eight months earlier and immediately set out on a summer spree in Europe, thrilled to be 'at the centre of things' and exulting in his freedom. When he ran out of money he returned to London and took a job with an Australian press agency. London was only a short-term answer to wanderlust, though. By the end of the summer colleagues were packing their bags for Spain, where a

military coup was fast descending into a brutal civil war between rebel
Nationalist troops under General Franco, among others, and Republican
forces loyal to the government. Moorehead didn't want to miss out. He
asked for help from Noel Monks, an old friend and colleague from the
Melbourne *Herald*, who was flourishing on the *London Daily Express*,
whose proprietor, Lord Beaverbrook, a Canadian, was an Empire-first
conservative who made a point of employing journalists from the dominions. There were no staff jobs going, but the *Express* was looking to hire
someone in Gibraltar to cover that end of the Spanish Civil War, and if
Moorehead was going there anyway – he wasn't, but Monks had implied
that he was – then they'd be happy to have him as a string-man. So here
he was: a foreign correspondent, sort-of, with the world's highest-
circulation newspaper, in a vital port, with a panoramic view of the kind
of story that could make a newspaperman's career.

Across the top of every cable Moorehead collected from the telegraph
office, and there were eventually hundreds of them, was printed the motto
'*Gibraltar: Travel Key of the Mediterranean*'. Gibraltar was also a strategic
strongpoint. The Rock had long been home to the British Mediterranean
Fleet; it was now becoming a bazaar for deals and information, and a
turnstile for traffic in and out of Spain. The border area had been under
Franco's control since the first days of the war, though in recent months
there had been sporadic shooting in nearby La Línea and Algeciras. It
had been quieter since February, when Franco's forces had pushed east
from their southern stronghold, capturing Málaga, and triggering a tragic
exodus of tens of thousands of refugees. The British, 'in the isolation of
neutrality, had watched the pleasant spectacle across the bay of the fires
and the tracer bullets.'

By the time Moorehead was plumping his pillows at the Rock Hotel,
the British weren't so sanguine. In La Línea, in plain view of Gibraltar's
terraces, hundreds of Spaniards toiled under the hot sun and the direction
of German engineers, building concrete gun emplacements for batteries
that would directly menace the Rock. Five miles around the bay, also in
plain view, was a naval base Franco had established at Algeciras. 'The warships in and out of the harbour, the air raids on the neighbouring Spanish

coasts, the warplanes roaring over the Rock, the barrage of heavy guns at practice, searchlights sweeping the sky at night, the nightly war talks on the radio, the gloomy groups of refugees lounging about the town – all these things have given Gibraltar an attack of nerves.'

Technically, Moorehead was a 'lineage stringer'. The *Daily Express* had agreed to pay him a fairly meagre weekly retainer of £5, topped up with another £4 in expenses. Anything more would depend on how many lines of news he managed to produce for the paper. For a while, there would be very few. Despite all the tension and intrigue, there was precious little to file from this hot company town, and Moorehead was forbidden to cross into Spain. More senior reporters were constantly coming and going from the war, and often snaffling the best stories on the way in. On 9 April Noel Monks popped across the border to dash off a signed story about Republican planes bombing ammo dumps behind Algeciras. When Italian engineers began cementing several large howitzers into place a few miles away at Tarifa, Monks was the one who told the British public about that, too. On Gibraltar itself, naval authorities had most of the newsworthy information and Moorehead found them genially disinclined to share it. In his first week, Moorehead received a formal invitation to dine with the governor, but if any insights came of the meeting they didn't make it into the paper. When he then called upon the chief secretary, 'quite a pleasant fellow', Moorehead was informed that while there certainly wasn't anything as rum as censorship going on – goodness, no! – he could expect to find himself marched off the Rock quick smart if he published anything 'subversive'.

Publishing *anything* was the challenge. Moorehead went to work, searching for some news behind the Admiralty's bluff communiqués. He eavesdropped on the dull garrison talk. He trudged from shipping agency to harbour, to pub, where he read the papers, and then back again. He arranged a permit to enter the North Mole so that he could get closer to the freighters that docked there, but there were no buses or trams, so whenever he wanted to check out a newly arrived ship he had to take a cab down to the dockyards (1/6 each time, his pocketbook balefully notes). He noted ship numbers and registrations, he studied the defences of the Rock, recorded details of foreign shipping and the armaments of visiting warships. His notes show how he was putting together an informal payroll of sources: hotel porters, 'men at the look-out stations', and dock workers who would telephone whenever they had a scrap of information to toss his way. ('These also might cost 10/.') On the backs of cables and invitations he jotted down the few snippets his efforts yielded: brief descriptive phrases, rumours, dates.* One of the best sources of information unfiltered by the Gibraltar authorities was the freighters arriving from Spanish ports, but many of these anchored in the bay. To reach them Moorehead had to shell out for a motorboat ride ('at the cost of anything between 10/ and £1'). It was a lonely life, brightened only by occasional visits from Monks. When he was in town, the old pals would spend the evening in a beerhouse, drinking and playing the fruit machines.

A few short and unsigned news briefs finally made it into the paper. Ever since he began at the Melbourne *Herald* in 1933, Moorehead had experienced an acute and undiminished pleasure from seeing his work in print. But if there was a special thrill to seeing his first paragraphs in the world's highest-circulation newspaper, there's no sign of it. In mid-May, Moorehead wrote to the foreign editor.

> Dear Mr Sutton,
>
> Now that I have been six weeks at Gibraltar for *The Express* there are one or two aspects of the job on which I would like to ask for advice . . . Chiefly I am anxious to know if you are getting the sort of stuff from me that you want; whether it is too much or too little and whether the treatment of it is satisfactory. Up to now I have thought it wiser to give the news as simply and directly as possible. A good deal of my time and money goes in chasing agency rumours . . .

---

* Notes like this:
  Rock Defences
  New anti-aircraft guns & guns to fire on ships . . . [illegible] built on Mole
  On Rock new directional beam wireless for Admiralty & other equipment being introduced
  Dutch ship covers guns whenever anyone attempts to look.
  Gunpowder nest on rock.

Chas Sutton's reply is lost. But he can't have been too dissatisfied with his man in Gibraltar. The *Express* kept Moorehead on the Rock for another seven months.

§

In most summaries of Moorehead's career, the time he spent in Gibraltar, and Paris and Rome afterwards, is mentioned, if at all, as a minor phase obscured by the professional glory he achieved in the Second World War. But Moorehead was deeply affected by these years. 'Six years of fighting made a massive insulation,' he wrote, when the war was over: 'they muffled the memory almost entirely and hardly an echo got through.' But memories of Gibraltar and Spain and pre-war Paris got through: sharp, visceral, sometimes overwhelming. At war's end, the first thing Moorehead did after squaring away his final campaign books – *Eclipse* (1945) and *Montgomery* (1946) – was write an autobiographical novel or memoir (no one, Moorehead least of all, was quite sure which) about his three years in Europe on the eve of its catastrophe.

That novel was never published. 'I read the proofs,' Moorehead told an interviewer in 1962, 'and just couldn't bear it.' Yet dispersed among the pages of clunking dialogue and anguished introspection are some passages of classic Moorehead description, as lucid and infelt as anything he ever wrote. And they were going to help me track him down in modern Gibraltar.

§

The Rock Hotel was new in 1937 – erected by the 4th Marquess of Bute only five years before – and it still gleams bone-white in the sunshine on its perch halfway up the Peak. I went up there one afternoon and ordered a drink on the terrace, and peered down through the bougainvillea to the bay and all that dramatic space falling away below. There were yachts heeling out into the white-blue horizon of the sea, tankers plonked about on the deep cerulean of the bay waiting their turn at the docks. At a nearby table an English family was talking about some tiresome people they wished they hadn't had to invite to the wedding.

I took out a passport photograph I'd copied and was carrying around in my shirt pocket as a kind of charm. Moorehead was, it was generally agreed, a good-looking young man. A slightly frog-like appearance one friend remembered from university days had matured into a 'generous mouth', as Alexander Clifford once described it, and a profile 'which, in certain photographs, has evoked references to Gary Cooper'. He had neatly waxed, parted hair and an intense brow. His much-remarked upon blue eyes are not apparent in the black and white, and his neck seems awkwardly stuffed into his collar, but he certainly photographed well, and the ironic look he was giving the camera suggests he knew it. The passport makes him 5'8", which was a bit of a stretch. In built-up shoes, maybe. *Il piccolo col basco*, the locals called him in Italy during the war – the little one with the beret. His shortness was what people tended to notice, especially when they found him pushy.

But he was well endowed with what Henry James called 'that supreme quality without which a man can never be interesting to men – the capacity to be tempted', and I found it easy to wish him well. He'd made such a demon-stration of leaving Australia; he'd gambled his pride on his lunge for a life in more exciting places. I liked the thought of the hungry colonial at large, revelling in his freedom, and chasing as much experience as he could fit in before Europe fell apart.

It seemed strange that he didn't relish this first professional posting in Europe more. It all looked pretty good to me, especially from up here. When I was growing up in a rural district north of Melbourne there was a battered tin advertising sign that used to stand outside the general store. It was an ad for cigarettes that showed an open packet against a radiant sky, with fags fanned out of the box at staggered lengths, a staircase of nic-otine climbing towards the sky. And above it, in that endless blue, soaring heavenward at the tip of its brilliant contrail, was a Concorde. You could just tell that the Concorde was pointed to Europe, towards ABBA and James Bond movies, which were the twin poles of my elsewhere at the time. I thought of it now because from the Rock Hotel, Gibraltar seemed a very Concorde kind of destination: a fantasy sky-blue place very far from home.

Among the nodding flowers and the rustle of intercontinental breezes, it didn't take much work to imagine Moorehead's Gibraltar, especially with the English family nearby still idly denouncing people whom I took to be old and dear friends. 'People ate shrimps in the Almeda gardens,' Moorehead remembered:

> the officers went to dinner dances on Saturday nights at the Rock Hotel
> and the garrison wives debated endlessly over little teas the scandals of
> the service rates of pay and the habits of their servants. This was peace,
> secure and timeless. The long uneventful dreariness of garrison life had
> its own peculiar fascination; it atrophied the mind quite pleasantly and
> painlessly, and life went by in a tide of talk.

Every time I walked down a street, inhaling the smell of spilt beer and sea wind, shading my eyes against the low autumn sunlight, I must have been retracing his routes, as he ducked from telegraph office to café, from North Mole to pub and back to the hotel. It was easy to picture him shouldering through the glass-doored offices of shipping agents in the bright heat of late spring, lining up at the Thomas Cook office, sweating in his shirt-sleeves as he clambered up through the Almeda gardens to the Rock Hotel in order to avoid paying for a cab.

He felt close, but between his Gibraltar of seventy years ago and the one I could see lay a force field of kitsch. Gibraltar was a giant duty-free emporium. If someone built a fun park called British Empire Land it would look just like this. Every street bristled with John Bull heritage: the themed street-names; fortified walls so thick they seemed part of the Rock itself; the thundering cannonades at the top of the hour. Those shops that weren't selling tax-free Winstons and scotch to cruise-ship passengers – or stuffed monkeys, or commemorative tea towels – were selling naval memorabilia. An entire shop was devoted to old photos of warships. Inside, people flipped through the racks like collectors brows-ing vintage vinyl.

In Moorehead's time, of course, Gibraltar was still a serious fortress with more on its mind than Jubilee teaspoons and plush-toy apes. I won-dered what he would have made of the milling crowds and day-trippers' tat. He might have preferred it. 'Generations of army and naval occupa-tion had managed to create a town and dockyards of unexampled utility and ugliness,' he recalled. 'It was … a prime contender for the distinction of being the leading eyesore of the Mediterranean.'

What grated most was the 'smugness', by which he meant the born-to-rule complacency of the largely pro-Franco British officers who ran it, and the strict social hierarchy laid over the listlessness of garrison life: bridge with the 'assistant bank manager and the shipping accountant', ten-nis with the major and his wife, '(if you rated a major)'.

He was bored, which was always a volatile state for him. To leaven the tedium, he took weekend furloughs across the Strait to Morocco. Two hours on a crowded Bland Line steamer and he was in the fabled port city of Tangier. It was, he wrote in his unpublished autobiographical novel, a 'blowsy trollop' of a place:

> [a] roaring mixture of squalor and easy earthy glamour. Everything that
> was done in secret and meanly in Gibraltar was here performed shamelessly

in the open; prostitutes paraded the streets along with money lenders who looked and behaved like Barbary pirates, and on every hand one saw drunks and paralytics, touts and fortune-tellers, professional gamblers and procureurs, spies and thieves, agents-provocateurs and sellers of drugs and pornographic books.

You might think Tangier just the spot for a young man keen on getting 'a thrill out of living'. Here was a shady milieu right out of the Beau Geste thrillers Moorehead had devoured as a boy. He stayed at the El Minzah Hotel, another extravaganza recently authored by the Marquess of Bute, which offered the traveller sensational cabarets, tennis and delicious black Moroccan figs served by turbanned waiters. But the novel won't crack a smile. Its hero looks back sourly at a waste of time. All Tangier's pleasures 'were a little too near decadence. No matter how glamorous a dinner party you attended at the El Minzah Hotel, how rich the guests, how good the wine, the moment would come when you stepped outside into the street to be confronted at once with a diseased and whining beggar'.

This isn't Moorehead's best or most likeable prose. But we're close to a nerve. One of Moorehead's chief themes in these years is an exaggerated horror of being pinned down, of getting stuck, and the absolute necessity of avoiding it, either in a place, or with a woman, or – worse – with a wife and the prams and toddlers and suburban front yard he assumed came with one. He'd escaped Australia only to find himself caged on the Rock. 'I was nagged by the feeling that I should have arrived in Europe at least five years earlier, and that now there was not much time left, that war was bound to come or that revolutions would break out or some other catastrophe would intervene and shut me off from these strange and famous places before I had had a chance to know them.'

In 1937, as he well knew, Moorehead's future lay out there in the 'matchless blue' of the sea lanes. The escalating barbarity of the civil war had led, in April, to the establishment of an international Non-Intervention Committee. The idea was to restrict the flow of arms and matériel into the Spanish bloodbath. British, French, Italian and German navies all signed up to policing operations in the Med, but at sea, at least, non-intervention was a doomed charade. The Russians continued to funnel fuel, weapons and advisers into the Republic, while Germany and Italy did the same for Franco. By mid-year, the Italian navy had begun looking for merchant vessels sailing from the Black Sea into Republican-held ports, particularly tankers wallowing westward brimful of oil. None of this was openly known; it was just speculation, gossip and disinformation, part of the 'mysteries of the Mediterranean these days', as John Dos Passos put it when he visited Valencia in April – along with 'the unannounced blockades, the unreported sinkings, the freighters with their names painted out that run without lights slipping through the blockades … Europe is in such a tangle these days that nobody has yet unravelled.'

§

At the end of May, Moorehead's funk on Gibraltar abruptly ended, thanks to a stroke of luck. It was luck that took the form, as is so often the case in the career of a war correspondent, of someone else's disaster.

On 29 May, Republican warplanes at Ibiza attacked what they thought – or claimed they thought – was a Nationalist cruiser, but was actually a German ship, the heavy cruiser *Deutschland*. Thirty-one sailors were killed and many more wounded. Badly damaged, but still afloat, the ship made for Gibraltar, and entered the harbour the following evening. Moorehead scrambled down to the dock with his camera and little black tooled-leather notebook. He was a poor photographer, but in the failing light he managed to capture some underexposed shots of the *Deutschland* and snub-nosed ambulances full of wounded Germans. '[A]t seven p.m. the *Deutschland* appeared, moving dead slow,' read Moorehead's unsigned report:

> As she turned into the docks three ambulances raced into the yard from the military hospital, where wards had been cleared and doctors and nurses summoned from dinner …
>
> Standing stiffly at the stern of the German warship two white-clad sailors mounted guard over the flag-swathed dead.

Moorehead returns to this incident twice in later writings and both times with an intensity that suggests the sight affected him more deeply than you'd guess from his first report. In *A Late Education* he wrote that:

> there was an air of suppressed tension among the crew, something almost bordering on hysteria.
>
> The sailors who ran to lower the gang-plank fumbled with the ropes and finally dropped the unwieldy thing with a clatter on the wharf. Twice more they hauled it up and dropped it again before it was made secure at last. Other sailors who had gone off to carry the coffins to the shore stumbled about the deck in a confused and awkward way ... All this time in the gathering darkness groups of British officers and sailors who had been suddenly called from their evening meal were eyeing the strange scene from the wharf. [This] was the first time they had seen the famous ship which had been built with so much secrecy ... It was, moreover, their first real vision of war, of the power and the harm of high explosive. The Rock of Gibraltar reared up behind us like the wall of a chasm, dark at the top where the guns were hidden, sprinkled with the lights of the town at the base, and the sea was unusually calm all the way across the Straits to Africa.

In that deepening gloom, we can just make out the moment when these young men and women first apprehend the scale of the coming catastrophe, the one that will kill and maim some of them and forever alter the lives of the rest.

But for Moorehead it was thrilling. A moment of 'ghoulish release,' he wrote, 'and I enjoyed every minute of it.' It was also front-page news worldwide. Diplomatic phone lines ran hot. Gibraltar's naval radios crackled with a stream of messages to patrol ships and Spanish consular offices. Hitler was said to be incensed. The *Deutschland* had, after all, been patrolling, quite legally, under the aegis of the Non-Intervention Committee. What would he do? Eventually he would use the attack to justify withdrawal from the tedious strictures of Non-Intervention. More immediately, there was the street-brawler's craving for revenge. At 6 a.m. the next day, a German heavy cruiser, *Admiral Scheer*, moved into position offshore at the Republican-held port of Almería, 150 miles up the coast, and methodically shelled the unsuspecting town for half an hour, killing at least twenty people and wounding perhaps a hundred more. As Moorehead put it: 'the new Dark Ages had started in Europe.'

On Gibraltar, Moorehead was trailing a funerary procession of coffins draped with swastikas through Gibraltar's streets, still haplessly snapping away with his camera and capturing a lot of ankles. Telegrams from the *Express*'s foreign desk began flowing in. They're all on almost translucent Cable & Wireless Limited forms, headed with a world-map logo in fire-engine red, and seventy years on they still softly crackle in the fingers. There were congrats from Noel Monks: 'NICE WORK FELLA SUTTON PLEASED KEEP GOING'. But most of the telegrams were from Chas Sutton himself, lord of the foreign desk, and master of penny-pinching telegramese. At 12.56 p.m.:

> ADVISE WHAT CHANCES YOU GETTING ANYTHING EX ALMERIA SMORNING IS IT POSSIBLE ARRANGE SOME NEWS SERVICE EXTHERE PERBOAT ADVISE E EARLIEST WHAT YOU LIKELY GET TODAY STOP ... HAVE YOU ANY PICTURES DEUTSCHLANDS ARRIVAL YESTERDAY CUMDEAD ETWOUNDED

At 3.14:

> ADVISE WHAT CHANCES GOOD ALMERIA BOMBARDMENT STORY EXYOU TODAY STOP CAN YOU GET TO ALMERIA ETHOW LONG WILL IT TAKE PICTURES GREATEST IMPORTANCE

And at 5.52pm:

> GERMAN WARSHIPS POSTSHELLING ALMERIA GONE MELILLA CAN YOU CONTACT MELILLA OTHERWISE FIND SOMEBODY MELILLA GET GERMAN SAILORS STORY

And so they go on.

On the back of one cable Moorehead jotted the latest figures for the *Deutschland*'s wounded: *19 seriously 23 lightly*. That was yesterday's story. What the paper urgently wanted was eyewitness accounts and especially pictures from shelled Almería. Moorehead packed fast. By evening, he was down at the dock with his camera and bag; as the shadows of warehouses lengthened over the harbour, he leapt into a water taxi that ran him out to a passenger cargo-steamer, the *Nailsea Vail*. He was finally off the Rock. This was more like it – a serious mission, with maybe a front page at the end of it. He was, however, still being peppered by telegram. 'Great scoop if you can rush out pictures,' Sutton cabled, as the steamer turned east and began its run up the coast at a languorous 12 knots.*

The details become a bit vague now, but what's clear is that once Moorehead disappeared over the horizon in his dithering steamer things began to go badly wrong. His attempt to work his way north-east along the coast to Almería was plagued by mishaps, hold-ups and missed connections. The *Express* didn't get its pictures until Monday, 7 June, and they weren't Moorehead's: he hadn't yet arrived on the scene. Because of a muddle in his itinerary, he was actually further up the coast in Alicante, where, to his chagrin, he found 'the port was as peaceful as an English fishing village'.

'As it turned out I chose the worst way to get to Alicante,' he wrote to Sutton when it was over. 'I was held up at one place after another by the lack of transport, and petrol and the general disorganisation of things . . .' He eventually stumbled into Almería more than a week after the bombardment, with no choice but to put a brave face on a fiasco. 'The debris of the town was still an appalling thing to see and the incidents of that fatal morning were of course very fresh in the people's minds,' he reported lamely. Days before, the *Express* had run a front-page dispatch from 'Jean Ross, British woman journalist who travelled to Almeria from Valencia yesterday'. Moorehead hadn't yet got his name on a single story. The photos the *Express* printed show the elegant curved façade of a four-storey bank building gouged open, the walls sagging around its terrible wound. But someone else took them. The tiny scallop-edged photos Moorehead took resemble snaps from a terrible holiday. You can just make out the port in one airy photo with lots of sky; elsewhere there's some street-level rubble, dust gleaming in high sunlight; an ox, some peasants wheeling a

---

* By comparison, the warship that had attacked Almería, *Admiral Scheer*, could make almost 30 knots.

cart; another dingily lit and ill-focused pic of some people sitting in a café, one of them glaring at the camera, or maybe its owner.

Back in Gibraltar, Moorehead sent in his expenses claim for the trip ('I am sorry it is so much for so little result') and moved down into the Hotel Bristol, cheaper and closer to the waterfront. Things were starting to look up – which is to say, news from the sea lanes was growing more and more alarming. On 18 June he made the front page with a story about an Italian steamer that hobbled into Gibraltar after an attack from the air. The work he'd put into grooming his contacts at the port was paying off – by the time he'd assembled some quotes from the crew, it sounded as if he'd been on board himself. 'For forty minutes the ship tossed and shuddered while thirty high-power bombs fell to port and starboard, cascading great waves of spray across the decks.' He was learning how to apply a hand-coloured tint to secondhand facts, a skill highly prized at the *Express*. Mr Sutton was prepared to overlook the Almería debacle. 'I am well satisfied with your service,' he wrote, in a letter for once. 'I can imagine the amount of work you are putting into the job ... your stories are regarded as authentic. They are also written in the *Daily Express* manner.' There was another letter, this one from his old boss on the *Herald*. He was pleased to hear Moorehead was working in 'such an interesting city as Gibraltar. It is delightful to know that young *Herald* journalists push to the front ...' He reminded Moorehead that there was always a job for him back at the paper.

Nothing could have been further from Moorehead's mind. On 21 July 1937, after nearly four months on the Rock, he finally got his name, or something like it, on a story. 'Italy Puts Guns on Majorca. 20,000 Ready to Land in Spain', reported 'Alan Moorhead'. The next day he provided a colourful feature on Gibraltar life which took up most of page 10, and began with laconic élan: '*Gibraltar was front page news on two counts yesterday.* Franco's big guns are said to be trained on it. Playwright Noël Coward has deigned to set a foot on it.'*

His name was on that story, too – sort of: it was 'Allan Moorhead' this time. But these were red-letter days. 'NOW PERHAPS YOU'LL BELIEVE ME,' cabled Monks, 'THAT YOURE HEADING PROTHE BIG DOUGH STOP EYEM DELIGHTED FELLA REGARDS NOEL.'

He was right. The fact that the *Express* printed by-lines at all was another of Moorehead's lucky breaks. At more upmarket papers, such as the *Telegraph* or the *Times*, articles usually ran without them. The *Express*, on the other hand, shamelessly pumped up its star reporters. In the popular press, this was the era of the unconstrained and colourful use of the first person in news reporting. The reporters themselves called these pieces, when personal adventures were woven into the news, "'I' stories". Moorehead took to 'I' stories with aplomb. He seemed to have no trouble hitting the right tone, or finding what he called 'the right amount of sensationalism for the *Express*', and in the coming months he would have plenty of opportunity.

'Scarcely had the fires of Almeria died down,' Moorehead wrote in the postwar novel,

> than it was reported that an oil tanker, making its way from the Black Sea to the eastern coast of Spain, had been sunk by an unidentified submarine off the coast of Africa. There was another sinking and then another. A period of outright piracy had begun in the central Mediterranean.

On Moorehead's Mediterranean beat, this was *the* story of the year. At the height of summer, Mussolini decided to let loose his submarines against Soviet merchantmen shipping fuel and matériel into Republican ports. On 12 August the tanker *Campeador*, bound for Republican Valencia, was sunk by torpedoes. A handful of the crew were rescued by British ships in the area and brought to Gibraltar, where Moorehead was waiting to wring the details out of them.

His *Campeador* story led the paper. It earned from Sutton an uncharacteristically friendly cable of congratulation which was followed, more characteristically, with demands for more. Who was responsible? 'ENUMERATE FRANCOS SUBMARINE STRENGTH COMPARED COMBEGINNING WAR ETACTIVITIES ITALIAN SUBMARINES STOP ANXIOUS GET THIS PIECE SECRET WAR HISTORY'.

---

* Coward had arrived, Moorehead reported, 'in a white duck suit', and describing himself as 'a refugee from Cannes'.

Secret war history: a three-word antidote to boredom. Moorehead had a very busy August. In his little black notebook, there is a list of all the ships attacked during the month in the western Mediterranean. Moorehead reported every story, mostly from the Gibraltar waterfront, where he could quiz dockworkers, buy seamen pints in the bars or take water-taxis out to anchored freighters. There was no real doubt about what was happening. 'The blatant nature of these attacks,' remarked the *Naval Review* decades later, 'carried out when Italy was not at war and when nothing was done to disguise the nationality of the pirates, is astonishing, even after thirty-five years'. When an Italian sub accidentally attacked the British destroyer *Havock* at the end of August, it looked as though the jig was up. The fresh outrage sent Sutton into a frenzy of excitement: he immediately demanded to know where his stringer was ('IF YOURE NOT YET BACK RETURN IMMEDIATELY ETCOVER ALSO ADVISE WHAT DOING'). Moorehead was actually in Tangier – he had nipped over to follow up on a lead and enjoy some low-lit R&R in the cabarets – but he scurried back in time to throw together some quotes and file a story for the front page.

§

Emboldened by his run of signed stories, Moorehead now made an ambitious pitch. What would Mr Sutton think of him taking a cruise of the Mediterranean, from Algiers out to Istanbul, and then back again aboard a freighter bound for Republican Spain – on, that is, precisely the kind of ship Mussolini's subs were sending to the sea floor every other night? 'The scheme at first may seem a little ambitious,' he wrote, 'but I am convinced after talking with the navy people and merchant captains here that it would yield some good stories in an entirely new field.' After grumbling about the cost, and fretting about who was going to keep an eye on things in Gibraltar, Sutton approved the mission: 'OK GO AHEAD ... ETLOOK PROAS MUCH TROUBLE AS POSSIBLE STOP'.

The cage door was open. Within twenty-four hours Moorehead was in Algiers. He immediately began door-knocking the shipping agencies for a berth to Istanbul, and hoovered up all the gossip he could find. The haul of dockside rumour from the first day alone half-filled a sheet of

Aletti Hotel stationery: *Canaries being warned of Spain bound ships by Italian planes & destroyers … Only protection from planes is to zig zag … Italy getting more oil here than ever. They send ships across to Italy to pick up oil brought from Persia …*

The mission involved no danger as yet, just the risk Mr Sutton might change his mind. That risk was quite real. Sutton was an editor who lived in terror of his correspondents missing anything. He soon starts to sound as though he's regretting his decision: 'YOU MISSED GOOD STORY YESTERDAY … BATTLE ONGOING INTEREIGHT WARSHIPS STOP' – and is getting quite tetchy when Moorehead suggests that he *fly* to Istanbul ('UNWANT AIRTRIP OR STORYLL BE TOO EXPENSIVE'). By the next day, though, it was too late to call his stringer back. Moorehead had found a berth on a German ship. The caviling would continue (day 4: 'YOUR TRIP INPRODUCTIVE SO FAR MESSAGES TOO SHORT INSUFFICIENT DETAILS FOR USE – SUTTON') but Moorehead was away, watching the African coast pass by from the bridge of the *Achaea*, and chatting to the ship's captain, a fat and fatalistic old salt who didn't like where all this seemed to be heading. 'It is impossible to continue,' he told Moorehead. 'The English will not understand. It will be war.'

'Now at last,' we read in *A Late Education*, as Moorehead sails into Istanbul, 'I felt I was getting into the war. What actually happened was that I was catapulted into the world of Eric Ambler and Graham Greene.' Which is to say, into the world of the espionage thriller.*

It's true: there's a subtle but unmistakable genre-shift in Moorehead's adventures in Istanbul and the Mediterranean, a self-conscious drift into the sinister atmospherics and suspense of film noir. I'd always loved those bits of *A Late Education*, but it was only after a lucky find at the National Library that I guessed why they sounded that way. When he sketched out this part of the memoir in the mid-1960s, Moorehead had drawn heavily on his unpublished, overheated novel; in fact, pages-long chunks had simply been lifted out of it and dropped in, with barely a comma altered. The

---

* By astonishing coincidence, Moorehead arrived in Gibraltar just days after Ambler arrived in Tangier to recover from an appendectomy. Lolling feebly in the sunshine, Ambler spoke to several young sailors from the *Deutschland* just weeks before their ship would deliver its salutory preview of wartime to Moorehead.

novel's first draft of memory explained the magic-lantern glow mood of the memoir, its grace notes of detail, introspection and – more than anything – nostalgia for youth. And perhaps this willingness to marble fact with fiction points to something else: a sense that Moorehead saw himself as malleable, a self-invention still very much in progress.

Moorehead booked into Istanbul's Pera Palas Oteli (Agatha Christie's favourite) on 19 September. Then he headed out onto the street and, as we have seen, stood helplessly for a moment before that dusty statue of the Ataturk. 'How did one begin?' Well, in the world of Ambler, and, it seems, in this Istanbul of 1937, with its oil and gun-running, and spying, its milieu of semi-secret commercial dealings and war profiteering, you need only stand still for a paragraph or two, and trouble found you.

Moorehead takes a seat in a café. 'A plump little man in a crumpled linen suit' appears. He's a journalist called Andropolous, a stringer for Agence Havas press in Istanbul, 'neither French nor Turkish nor Greek, though possibly a mixture of all three' – and he has the good oil on the companies running matériel into Republican Spain. They buy up decrepit tramps so cheaply, he explains, they turn a profit after only a couple of runs into Valencia, so even if a few get sunk, everyone's still making money. Moorehead can barely contain himself. Could he get a berth on such a ship? Why naturally, it could be arranged, but it was a 'secret and difficult business'. Andropolous will put Moorehead in touch with a friend of his, a White Russian businessman. 'I should not bother very much with his name,' he says. 'You may call him Mr Brandt.'

A chauffeur-driven American saloon arrives that evening. Moorehead is whisked to an address on the southern side of the city, where he takes tea in a private garden with the mysterious Mr Brandt. Brandt is a physical grotesque – 'a large fleshy man with an enormous head which gave him a certain toad-like appearance' who 'wore a crumpled grey palm beach suit, and as we talked flapped a purple fly-whisk languidly in the air'. He even has a supervillain's horrible puss, a 'gross and hay-coloured Persian cat', which he tenderly strokes throughout the meeting. Moorehead and Brandt now enter a pas de deux of polite suspicion, discussing (through a translator) the quality of drinking water in Istanbul, the weather, the beauty of the Blue Mosque. Brandt cuts to the chase. Why Spain? What is Moorehead's interest there? Moorehead explains why the sinkings are such a big story for his newspaper. It will be very uncomfortable, Brandt muses; he can't understand why Moorehead would want to take the risk.

'It's my job,' I said, and then thinking over what he had just said I added: 'I'm not an agent or a spy if that's what you are thinking.'

'My dear sir!' He raised both flabby hands in the air and waved them deprecatingly. 'What a droll suggestion.' We both laughed merrily.

They both seem to have learnt their parts from the movies. But Brandt, or someone like him – with or without cat – can be made out in Moorehead's notes from 1937, under a different name: *Russian in Istanbul now worth 10 m. Further – owns several houses – made money out of Spain war. Has 5 ships (10) trading from Costanza to Spain. Mostly tankers . . .*

And 'Brandt' duly provided a ship for Moorehead to sail in. It was a decrepit old tub named the *T/S Beme*, renamed *Tinos* in *A Late Education*, and carrying 8000 tons of petrol from Romania.

As Moorehead approaches the ship, his account seems to take on an extra intensity of attentiveness and fearful pleasure that doesn't let up for the next twenty pages. Written ten years after the events it describes, every lucid detail in it gleams with a cherished quality, as though remembering is itself a kind of joy.

In the rowboat taking him out to his ship: 'the lights of the city had come up, making long quivering yellow snakes across the water, and in the distance the domes of the mosques had the appearance of floating on a mist between the city and the sky . . . Every now and then a gobbet of phosphorus came out of the black sea on the blade of an oar and shimmered briefly for a second before it was churned back into the wake of the boat.'

Once aboard, we enter a new universe, a new genre. With a few details Moorehead manages to evoke the grubby, bitter life of the ship. Someone years ago had made an attempt at elegance in the captain's saloon: the tasselled crimson velvet cloth on the table; the black leather chairs stuffed with horsehair; a pendant light hanging from a heavy brass bracket in the shape of flying angels. 'All this intensive décor must have been a stimulating sight some thirty or forty years before ... But now the mirror was discoloured, the horsehair had burst through to the surface of the cracked leather seats, two of the brass angels had lost their wings, and the crimson cloth was marked with a solar system of grease spots revolving around a particularly heavy blot at the captain's end of the table.'

For the next ten days, Moorehead wanders about the ship, attuning himself to the rhythms and customs of this enclosed world, and trying to avoid the captain, a big, bluff, taciturn bully who is trailed everywhere by a Chinese-Russian steward in baggy Turkish pantaloons. He counts off the meals and changes of watch, waiting for the moment when the ship will make the final run up to Valencia past the Balearics and the German fighter-bombers. A routine develops to fill the days of ennervating boredom. In the mornings he paces the ship, he chats with the mate on the bridge, lunches or reads on his cot, watching the 'play of green and yellow light reflected from the water onto the white paint' on the bulkhead above his bed. After a nap he paces the ship again, 'pausing at my favourite places, the chicken coop where four withered hens crouched listlessly on the hot iron deck, the wheelhouse, the portside lifeboat, the stern where the *Tinos* shuddered and wriggled like a dog shaking his tail and the wake came frothing up to the surface in streams of blue-white bubbles.' Apart from the mate, he has no one to talk to. So he watches the sea and sky. If bombers come, he has heard, they will come diving out of the sun. But nothing comes out of the sun. Even the painterly seascapes of these pages have an undertow of helpless waiting about them. The 8000 tons of petrol focus the mind. When the ship passes Malta, the mate asks Moorehead, as a British national, to send a message to the Admiralty requesting protection. (A sheepish-sounding draft of this telegraph is in Moorehead's papers.) No escort is forthcoming.

But then on the sixth day Moorehead awakes to see through the grimy porthole by his pillow an unforgettable thing. The great battle cruiser *Hood* is steaming along just a few miles off, attended by a small brood of freighters gratefully hurrying to keep up. For Moorehead, *Hood* is a stirring sight, a vision of Imperial sea power: prepotent, vast, magnificent. *Hood* was not only one of the largest warships afloat but 'by some accident of genius or design the most beautiful. She gives no impression of dead weight or immensity; she is shaped in the lines of a yacht and if she was strong then it was a graceful strength.' *Tinos* immediately joins the motley flotilla, but the comfort is temporary. That evening, *Hood* increases speed and slips away over the darkening horizon.

§

On the tenth day came the storm. By the time Moorehead reached the bridge, alarmed by the swaying of the saloon's pendant lamp, 'the whole ship was full of the noise of sighing and straining woodwork.' People were running along the catwalks. Some were even milling about the lifeboats. Only a precaution, the Greek mate explained: *We turn north. Plenty bombs ... Get boats ready.*

The storm immediately freshened the stale mood on board. A nice rough storm would protect them from submarines and bombers. The storm they got was much worse than that. When Moorehead awoke the next morning, it was building to its violent pitch, breaking bones, smashing gear, even sucking into the sky one of those wretched hens from the coop. Moorehead's storm is superb and terrible. What's remarkable is that it's all done so simply, with plain grainy sentences arranged in the natural rhythm of thought:

> I went directly on to the bridge. It was difficult to recognise either the *Tinos* or the sea. The accustomed world of yellow sunshine and blue water had vanished entirely; everything had turned to grey. A heavy grey rain flew almost horizontally across the ship, and it hit the waves with such force that they were pockmarked with a million little splashes; and the waves themselves had mounted up into furious grey mountains, forever collapsing and renewing themselves out to the jagged horizon, where there was no break in the forbidding sky, nothing but a torrent of racing grey-black clouds which almost touched the sea. There was a screeching, maniacal quality in the wind; it tore and tore at every obstacle as though it would pluck it out of existence, as though it would pluck out your eyes.

During all this even the captain is redeemed by his uncomplaining endurance. Moorehead finds him at the helm, staring out at the insensate rage of the storm 'with that set expression of men who have become fixed in the attitude of waiting, so that the mere act of waiting had become an end in itself, a test of endurance, a kind of rational defiance against the uncontrollable fury of the sea.'

Tinos survived the storm, of course. And the next day, in calm sea and sunshine, the ship passed through the critical danger point near Ibiza entirely without incident. The voyage had ended in blissful anti-climax. In the novel, this anti-climax wouldn't do, so Moorehead brings down some German fighter-bombers to plaster the docks with high explosive and blast *Tinos* into a towering fireball. Rewind history onto its spool, play it again, and things could easily end that way. But in *this* life, Moorehead went ashore in perfect safety. For the *Express*, Moorehead gave it the full treatment. His report was headed 'I Run Pirate Zone in Tanker' – an 'I' story par excellence. In Valencia he checked into the Victoria Hotel and carefully recorded the room and its simple furnishings, the plain iron bed, the washbasin, the chipped wardrobe. The anonymous hotel room, more or less shitty or luxurious: ground zero for the writer-traveller Moorehead was becoming, and his real address for much of the next thirty years. A place to work, sleep and dream uneasy dreams.

3

ARRIVAL

W hen he left Australia, Moorehead was twenty-five and had been a working journalist for six years. But he seems so young. In his luggage he carried letters of introduction from the premier of Victoria and the governor, from his editor at the Melbourne *Herald* and the headmaster of his old school: it's as if he's been carefully packed off on his adventure by his elders. His efforts to sound like a seasoned observer of life make him seem even younger. First landfall in Europe was at Naples. 'I was drunk when I got back,' he wrote to Beth Thwaites, a close (platonic) friend from university days.

> I went with a nice Australian girl on the boat deck and told her that the discovery of a frying-pan and pieces from a chess-board in the ashes of Pompeii had disproved the existence of God. We sailed along under the cliffs of lovely islands piled with palaces and churches and I told her that everything was all wrong with everything. That Naples had the beauty of an over-ripe melon. That its beauty was superstition … Then I went to bed.

But Moorehead's determination to make a life for himself in Europe, and to do it by becoming a serious writer, was already in place. It's impossible to miss. A friend from the time recalled that he 'struck us as being very ambitious – knew he wanted to be a great writer.' Well before the *Ormonde* reached England, Moorehead fished a novel out of his trunk and asked Frank Sullivan, a *Herald* colleague he was travelling with, to look at it. Frank had contracted double pneumonia during an on-board fancy dress party, and may not have been at his most critically receptive, but he thought the novel was dreadful, and more or less said so. If this is the typescript I think it is, a shapeless story of a locust plague in Victoria's wheat belt, I can only agree. Its forlorn pages have an unmistakable odour most writers would recognise from the bottom drawer. They show, more than anything, the dogged determination, in the face of all reason and good sense, to *just keep typing*. Moorehead wasn't unduly dismayed. When they off-loaded poor Frank in Tilbury, now in a coma, Moorehead went ashore with him and stayed by his hospital bedside for several days before setting out for London.

In *A Late Education*, Moorehead makes much of the shock of arrival, the can't-quite-believe-it sensation of finally seeing a place so exhaustively previewed in the imagination. A few days earlier there had been the delicious shock of Toulon and its market with the fish baskets spilling and the women kissing; now, a park in suburban Plymouth provides another epiphany: a tree. Never has a tree seemed so *tree-like*, 'the dampest and greenest tree in the whole world'. Yet he scuttles on: the homing beacon was drawing him to London. It was early summer when he arrived. It was raining constantly. It was wonderful. 'To be known by no one, watched by no one,' he wrote, 'to join in the ant-like anonymous procession – this was a new and exhilarating kind of privacy.' He stayed with a colleague from the *Herald*, Erl Gray, near Victoria Station; then Noel Monks found room for him in his bedsit in Bloomsbury. Moorehead and his friends sat in tea shops, swapping gossip about Fleet Street jobs and studying the newspapers in which they intended to make great careers, but the call of adventure was too strong to get bogged down in work right away. At a time when the hand-to-mouth literary heroes of Orwell's *Keep the Aspidistra Flying* or Patrick Hamilton's *Hangover Square* were subsisting in principled poverty on a few pounds a week, Moorehead had £500-worth of freedom burning a hole in his pocket.

He hatched plans to head to Spain with a South African journalist called Guy Young. If they could get to Burgos, they might be able to find work with an American journalist Young knew. From the London office of the *Herald*, Moorehead extracted a commission to write some articles about the riots in Spain. They were on the next boat train to Paris.

Moorehead didn't just enjoy travelling; he had an inborn talent for it that seems to have been unlocked by his arrival in Europe. From the moment he docked in Plymouth – and for the next thirty years – he embarked on the simplest trips with an openness to experience that seems undisappointable. 'Who will ever forget his first sight of a prewar French railway terminus at the rush hour? ... The porters in blue smocks and cloth caps careering by with agitated families in their wake, the loudspeakers booming "*En voiture s'il vous plaît*," the locomotive hissing steam like a great beast impatient to be off...' Money was too tight for a sleeper for the trip south to Hendaye, so he and Guy Young squeezed themselves into a crowded compartment and passed the night sleeping fitfully, pinned upright by the crush.

> I woke in the morning when the first warm shaft of sunshine travelled up my legs, growing wider and more yellow and warmer as it advanced, until it struck me full on the face. My skin felt like parchment and the faces of the other passengers were lined and dirty and tired. And yet, despite the foetid air, the chaotic mess and staleness of the compartment and the dryness of my throat, all my anxieties of the night before flew away. There was a rush of bright green foliage outside, and this, as I rubbed my eyes, resolved itself into fields of hop poles strung with necklaces of green leaves, and tall bamboos, and red and yellow roofs of Cordova tiles, and donkeys with spilling bags of carrots and onions on their backs, and beyond all this the clear racing blue of the Atlantic. It was a lovely day.

But that day in June 1936, the border was closed. Their attempt to gate-crash the excitements of Spain were casually rebuffed by guards with rifles. They slunk back to the spindly iron tables and persistent flies of Hendaye's Café Internationale to regroup. Edging east along the border they found a gap at Dancharia and crossed into Spain a couple of days later on a motorcycle. At Pamplona a Carlist official advised them to turn around, but they pushed on to Burgos anyway, until they gave up in the face of constant road blocks, curfews that curtailed night-time adventures, and dismal food.

So Spain was a bust. Why not celebrate his twenty-sixth birthday in style? They returned to Paris where they met Erl Gray and went to the Folies Bergère to see Josephine Baker dancing in her girdle of bananas. Berlin was next, where they spent a couple of weeks soaking up the sunshine, and the heady atmosphere of the Olympics. Moorehead wangled a press pass, and managed to get close to the athletes, and to the disquieting cult of body worship he detected in the Reich. He studied the pagan virility of Nazi statuary at the Olympic stadium: 'the great bull-like young men with truculent sexual parts and huge-bellied women carrying sheaves of wheat.' He glimpsed Hitler at a procession on the Unter den Linden, but it was the look on the face of a German girl in the crowd that stuck with him: 'the shining-eyed look of ecstasy that overcame her face ... the look of a girl meeting her lover.'

This could be any backpacker's Continental itinerary from the past thirty years – fall off a motorbike, drink yourself silly in places you don't remember – if not for the impending catastrophe that looms over the late

'30s, ready to engulf everything in its path. And also for the exultant tone of Moorehead's letters, as he registered the scarcely believable freedom. 'I didn't want to pause and understand what I was observing,' he wrote later, 'so much as I wanted to go on and on seeing new places and meeting new people'. All this freedom tore through his savings, and the summer spree lasted barely a month.

Moorehead wrote that leaving Australia was the first of 'two great breaks' of his life. But it's not the leaving itself that constitutes the critical break; it's the staying away. For the next two years Moorehead's adventures in Europe are a record of fierce, but shapeless hunger for experience, in which the satisfaction of getting what he wanted never seems quite as intense as being quit of what he didn't want. The speed and thoroughness with which he shed his Australian manners, friends and accent is striking, and over the years the disavowal rankled with many of his Australian peers. It still seems to require an explanation. 'Can you explain to me,' a friend asked when I first got interested in Moorehead, 'why this guy isn't just another ersatz Englishman?'

I took his point – not a good thing to be, an *ersatz Englishman*, least of all in a creative field. Any Australian artist who longs simply to *become* English is someone who has ducked the specific burden of being an artist in Australia and left it to others to sort out. But Moorehead thought the cost-benefit analysis was pretty straightforward. 'To stay at home,' he wrote much later, not defending himself, just explaining, 'was to condemn yourself to non-entity. Success depended on an imprimatur from London … to be really someone in Australian eyes you first had to make your mark or win your degree on the other side of the world.'

But in the late '30s he seems to be guarding his escape so fiercely – like a prized possession that could be snatched away at any time – that it's as though Australia had done something unforgivable to him. But what? No satisfying answer is provided by *A Late Education*. It's true that the boyhood he depicts there was, apart from thrilling holidays in the bush or at the windy camping grounds of Philip Island, a doleful tale of underachievement and quiet misery. Unhappy at school, dull in classes, uncoordinated on the muddy sports fields, and bored, bored, bored.

Moorehead's beloved older sister, Phyllis, didn't remember it this way, though; she remembered him as a sunny, lively little boy. The sparse evidence available suggests Moorehead enjoyed a safe and reasonably comfortable suburban childhood. His father, Richard Moorehead, was a journalist and editor; in 1904 he married Louise Edgerton, a painter who had trained at Melbourne Art College. The marriage produced three children: Phyllis (b.1905), Bernard (b.1907) and Alan (b.1910); and it seems to have been unusually contented. Louise was a popular and gregarious woman. She is lovingly recalled by subsequent generations for her independent spirit, her golf swing, her indifference to housework and her fits of eccentric home decoration. Richard would often come home to find the furniture reshuffled among rooms. Once he came home to find his wife painting every one of the thousands of tiny flowers on the living room's wallpaper. She became a keen traveller in later years; in a 1950 article Moorehead praised her exemplary approach to travel ('She took things how she found them') and the pragmatism of her kit, which consisted, among other things,

> of a green-lined umbrella, a bottle of smelling salts, a small blind for attaching to uncurtained windows, a flask of brandy (for accidents), a spirit lamp and ingredients for making her own tea, a red flannel cummerbund, and that invaluable Baedeker which assured her that the touts in Marseilles were apt to be insolent and that the water everywhere was undrinkable.

Richard has left fewer traces. His letters suggest a thoughtful, warm, slightly indecisive man who was almost as bewildered as delighted by his son's remarkable success. There was some wanderlust in his DNA too: he was editor for a while of the monthly trade journal *Transport by Land and Sea* and accompanied a 1934 trade delegation to Batavia (Jakarta). The Torajan death statues of South Sulawesi that he saw on this trip so fired his imagination he wrote a pulp adventure novel about them.* He made a respected, but slightly disappointing career, and despite his 'Micawberish

---

* Called the *Mists of Macassar*, Richard's novel was the usual sort of thing – rugged white adventurer finds love in the exotic tropics – and it wasn't published until ten years later, in 1946, when it was comprehensively outsold by his son's *Montgomery*.

and futile optimism' he was never quite as solvent as he would have liked. In the last decade of his life, when he was tending a lemon orchard at his home in Croydon, he gratefully accepted regular cheques from his son.

For most of Alan's childhood, Richard was a freelance journalist, which explains the obscure state of degentrification in which the Mooreheads existed by the early 1920s. They were 'genteel poor', Moorehead remembered; his parents maintained a façade of prosperity that crumbled a little more every time a tradesman called about an unpaid bill. Despite the 'humiliating struggle to keep up appearances', young Alan revelled in the mayhem of moving house, and fully approved of his parents' determination to keep up the charade – 'we were not working class and that was that'. But as an adult, he came to wonder whether there wasn't also 'a great distress behind this restlessness', each move a fresh attempt 'to escape from the squalid pettiness of counting every penny'.

Somehow though, funds were found to send both boys to Scotch College, one of the city's most exclusive schools. There young Alan wallowed unhappily at the bottom of the class. There are no signs of precocity except, perhaps, in ambition – Moorehead's plan to become a great and famous writer was fully formed by age fifteen. University fees were beyond the family's means, so when he matriculated at sixteen, without undue distinction, he went to work as a copy boy at an advertising agency. Then, showing an early glimmer of his almost eerie self-certainty, he fronted the editor of *Table Talk* magazine and proposed writing a weekly column of news from the university. The column paid £2.10s a week; combined with the money he made selling university exam results to the *Herald* newspaper (all he had to do was copy down results posted on campus noticeboards and type them up), he had enough to pay his way through three years of an arts degree at the University of Melbourne, then a further two of law. During these Depression years he lived at home, but often coming home very late after long days playing pool in the student clubhouse, trying, without much success, to seduce girls at social smokers, and writing for the university magazine. Moorehead's politics were mildly leftist at this time, and though he wasn't much of a joiner he was attracted to the contrarian glamour of the campus radicals – 'we were all for Karl Marx and the brotherhood of man'. Many of

the young men he befriended would reappear in his life on the other side
of the world as war correspondents, editors and authors, people like Sam
White, Cyril Pearl, Chester Wilmot and Alwyn Lee. In September 1933 he
sat down to his final law exam, only to realise there was no point – he'd never
wanted to be a lawyer. As a hall full of candidates bent over their papers,
Moorehead gathered up his pencils, caught a tram to the offices of the *Herald*
on Flinders Street and asked for a job. They gave him one on the spot.

Nothing went wrong here, either. He made close friends on the paper, he
progressed from the court round to more interesting assignments. He thrived.
Yet he was increasingly desperate to get away. The ship-spotting daydreams
hardened into something more concrete, especially after he watched Noel
Monks sail for Europe in 1935. Moorehead was becoming someone for whom
frustrated daydreams had a propulsive, ruthless force – enough, in 1936, to
make him tear up his lucky, happy start in life and begin all over again.

§

Back in London after his Continental tour, he got busy making himself
anew. He moved in a large circle of friends and colleagues, meeting for
drinks and tea and long talks about books and politics. He began an affair
with an English girl, 'the prettiest girl I had ever seen', who was about to
be married to an older man but meanwhile took great pleasure in introducing a wide-eyed colonial to the capital. 'She peels off her stockings,'
Moorehead dreamily recalled thirty years later, 'and unhooks her belt with
a quick decisive air and I feel that I am a very fine chap indeed'. Soon he
was out of Monks' Bloomsbury bedsitter and into 'rather grander quarters' in Gloucester Road. He got work with an Australian news agency
where colleagues remembered him staying behind late, bashing away on
a typewriter into the long winter evenings. In the background, behind the
lone driven writer and the late-night clacking of his Underwood, we can
see the great events of the times moving like shadows across the wall.
There was Spain, on which Moorehead was now indignantly anti-Franco.
There was the abdication. When Australian prime minister Joseph Lyons
visited London ahead of the coronation, it was Moorehead who handed
around the whiskies at the PM's afternoon press conferences.

Then his girlfriend got married. Alas, this happy event only seemed to intensify her interest in her Australian lover. Moorehead was suddenly out of his depth. He badly needed to get away. Thanks to Noel Monks, he was on the boat to Gibraltar within a week.

§

There are few traces of Moorehead in London in the pre-war years. There are suggestive glimpses of a young man on the make in the unpublished notes from interviews that Tom Pocock, Moorehead's biographer, conducted in 1989. Moorehead had 'drive', Erl Gray confirmed: 'But he could be great fun.' Frank Sullivan, who was battling old age and emphysema when Pocock found him in a retirement home in Lorne on the Victorian coast, recalled a 'a sense of destiny about Alan. He did nothing by design – inclined to be lazy. [But] when the war broke out he was all ready to go.'

The most tantalising relic from that period in London was a novelty voice recording that Alan and Erl made in a booth in Piccadilly Circus, and posted home to the Mooreheads. I could hardly contain myself when I found it in the archives and realised what it was: a message direct from 1936, a shot of pure oxygen in the biographical smog. This might the key to the self-transformation, I thought. My glee evaporated when I realised that I had no way of playing it, and never would. I slipped the glossy disc from its paper sleeve, and just stared for a while at the shellac filigree where the sound of Moorehead's young voice had lain undisturbed for seventy years, as if it might be possible to lift it out of the grooves by mind-power alone.

§

The late '30s were, if nothing else, a great time to embark on a newspaper career. The popular newspapers commanded a power and cultural influence that is hard to grasp today in this twilight of newsprint, and the *Daily Express* was the biggest of them all. Its editor was 32-year-old Arthur Christiansen. Known to his reporters as Chris, Lord Beaverbrook's brilliant boy had been taken on at just twenty-nine with orders to boost circulation by a million copies in ten years. He did it in five. Christensen liked a front page with impact. 'Give them stardust' was his motto. A stocky man, with dark curly hair, Christiansen was, an irreverent *Time* magazine profile said, 'personally kind but professionally exacting', and his newspaper 'at its best on stories about murders, sex, abandoned babies and the more maudlin doings of Soho underworldlings'. That wasn't entirely fair. The *Express* was never a yellow rag – salacious divorce stories, for instance, were forbidden. For Geoffrey Cox, a rather earnest figure who'd been lured from the sober *News Chronicle* to Christiansen's dazzling circus, the *Express* simply 'outshone its competitors', interweaving 'a strong element of sophistication with its quest for hard news and sensation'. Under Christiansen the paper also took a lively interest in the world beyond its readers' London suburbs.*

In 1936 Beaverbrook moved his empire into a new building, 'Black Lubyanka', they called it in Fleet Street: a modernist wonder of chrome and curved coal-black glass. The reporters' room inside, where Moorehead laboured anonymously in the winter of 1938 after his return from Gibraltar, was a scene to send any old-school hack into transports of nostalgia, with its clattering teletypes and the fug of cigarette smoke. In the evenings, shirt-sleeved subeditors huddled over their desks under brilliant strip lighting, reporters hurried in with late stories, office boys ran to and fro with proofs and pages of agency tape and lights flashed above booths indicating that a foreign correspondent was waiting to phone in some copy. The great printing presses thrummed in the basement. As the first edition hit the presses, Christiansen himself would return from the opera or the club, roll up his French cuffs and get to work on the front page, resizing headlines, culling unsightly stubs and demanding rewritten leads.

Christiansen was a vital figure in Moorehead's life: not just a boss, but a mentor, confidant and powerful supporter. But not yet. After Gibraltar Moorehead dashed off a rugged account of his Mediterranean exploits to the *Herald* back home, which was reported in the paper's in-house newsletter. But there are no mentions of Moorehead's name in the editor's daily bulletins at the *Express*, or even in the paper itself. In fact, sometime late in 1937,

---

* Evelyn Waugh's satirical novel *Scoop* was published while Moorehead was finding his way at the *Express*. The farcical adventures of its accidental hero, sent to cover an African war resembling the one in Abyssinia in 1936, clearly had some basis in truth: in the 1960s, the *Express* still had in its inventory a camel acquired in the 1930s to carry a correspondent to some long-forgotten desert dateline.

or early the year after, Moorehead was amicably fired. He hadn't done anything wrong; it was just time to give someone else a turn. This disastrous setback lasted barely ten minutes. Moorehead seems cloaked in an auspicious mist of destiny in these years, so it's not surprising that before he had even begun boxing up his desk ornaments, he looked up to see striding towards him Steve Foley, the new foreign desk editor. Foley needed a deputy bureau chief in Paris, and he was wondering whether Moorehead spoke French.

§

Just as Moorehead was shipping his trunks across to Paris, Beaverbrook set out his paper's philosophy in a front-page editorial. Our policy, he wrote, 'demands for each of us social equality and equal opportunity ... And the joy of living must not be restrained, limited or confined by any measures whatsoever. The *Express* is allied to the group of human beings who like to have a good time.'

In which case they had appointed the right man for the Paris job. The City of Light was in the grip of a last-dance euphoria and mass neurosis that seems to have burned itself into the collective memory of everyone who saw it. Paris was bursting at the seams. Along with exiled White Russians and the usual mix of hustlers and tourists dabbling in bohemian adventures and looking for 'one last hectic spending bender', thousands of refugees were fleeing Nazi persecution. But fears of a general European war were in abeyance, and Paris was a wonderful place to be young, well-paid and interested in trying everything.

Moorehead plunged into the sensory feast. *This* is what he had been promised in Toulon:

> every week a new night club opened in Montparnasse, and there was an
> another parade or an exhibition on the boulevards; every day there was
> a new song, a new scent, a new novel, a new race horse ... Paris was a vast
> bazaar full of music and movement and quick business; full of sex and
> easy living.

The *Express* group office comprised two large rooms in the seven-storey *Paris-Soir* building in the Rue de Louvre. There was a bar on the roof where

Moorehead and his colleagues could take a lunchtime drink and gaze out over their tremendous good fortune, at a city whose libertine spirit seemed so far from the dour Presbyterianism of Moorehead's boyhood.

The Paris bureau of the *Express* was not celebrated for fearless attacks on corruption or privilege. One of the paper's heavyweights, Sefton 'Tom' Delmer, had been disgusted to find himself 'required to report the parties of Woolworth heiress Barbara Hutton ... follow up the Paris end of British crime stories, and keep a watch on tourists and trippers'. Now the bureau chief was Geoffrey Cox, but the job was the same. 'Every day,' Cox remembered, 'there seemed to be yet another member of the aristocracy who had eloped to Paris with someone else's wife, about whom the news desk was frantic for a story ("The Beaver's especially interested, old boy: he knows them both well")'. Cox welcomed his new lieutenant by putting him on the trail of the Duke and Duchess of Windsor, who were scoping Paris for a suitable love nest.

Moorehead's daily routine from here is worth noting, if only for its otherworldly ease and the barely credible quantity of drink it involved. His supercharged pounds (ten per week, plus expenses) funded a cook and houseboy from French Indochina (1 pound 10s/week) who each morning prepped young monsieur for work, fetching his slippers, brewing fresh coffee and bringing him a stack of morning papers for perusal. After breakfast it was off to the Racing Club in the Bois, for an hour's sunbathing by the pool with those papers Moorehead hadn't gotten to yet. Back into the car – a zippy Matford – for the drive into the city. He got in at around midday. Barely time now to toss one's hat on the hook before it's 1 p.m., the appointed hour for a *coupe de champagne* at the bar on the roof before an enormous lunch where 'we tried to limit ourselves to a half carafe of white wine each and one small brandy afterwards'. Now, during a few hours' work, moderation supervened – 'a single glass of beer and perhaps a couple of glasses of champagne was the ration in the office before dinner' – until dinner itself, where there was more to drink at a little restaurant named for the plump white rabbit that shuffled around its sawdust-sprinkled floor. Then, until midnight, some actual work. When it was time to head home, Moorehead would stop at a favourite bar, the *Café des Sports*, for one last *pression* before climbing back into the Matford. When he confessed in a letter home to having packed on some pounds, his father was all admiration. 'Didn't I tell you long ago that fat means force?'

Elsewhere had again fulfilled its promise, as it had so sensuously in Toulon, and in wet shades of green in suburban Plymouth. How gratifying it must have been to be found in this worldly state by Chester Wilmot, his confrère from Melbourne Uni days. 'Taxi to office of *Daily Express* to see Alan Moorehead. He's been wonderfully successful. He came over here two years ago ... Sent to Gibraltar last year and then into Spain and now is in Paris – earning a very good salary indeed.'

It was a social posting, and it suited him. He didn't always make it to his French lessons, but he didn't miss a chance for a picnic in the woods on weekends, or a drive out along the Seine. The Paris bureau received a steady flow of visitors from London, too. Important businessmen, who came into the office with tightly rolled umbrellas and 'an air of taut and pallid restraint', had to be entertained. That meant a rich meal with firm talk about Hitler, then, invariably, a front table at the Bal Tabarin. 'Naked, six-foot girls come whirling from the roof and debouching from the walls. They rise in glittering tableaux on lifts beneath our feet and their breasts are not a yard away from the visitor's noses. Girls on horses, girls in cages, girls in mountains of flowers ...'

A late bloomer at university, Moorehead had thereafter impressed observers with his eagerness to make up for lost time. In November he wrote to Lucy Milner, fashion editor of the *Express*, about late-night sessions in Montmartre nightclubs. 'Result was I washed up in the backstreets of Paris at 7 a.m. without the faintest idea of where my new home was. And this definitely is the end of my debauchery – it just mustn't happen again, not until Friday night anyhow.' It's disconcerting to realise that the courtship between Alan and Lucy, which would culminate in their marriage in 1940, had already begun when she received this and other such letters. They would also meet in Paris a number of times over the next year. Lucy's job required her to make frequent trips to review the collections the French fashion houses were still pumping out with glorious insouciance. But Moorehead would continue to goad her even as he flirted, bragging about the 'gross sport' of his evenings, the variety of his pleasures, the inconstancy of his heart.

§

Moorehead's flat in Paris was on the seventh floor of a new building in outer-suburban Saint-Cloud. A few hundred feet below his floor-to-ceiling windows, he could watch as:

> the Seine made a wide sweep round the Renault factories at Billancourt, and all the foreground was filled with the green woods of the river, the racecourse at Longchamps, and the Bois de Boulogne. Paris itself floated in a grey mist at the further side of the green belt, and from this height it showed merely as a jagged line of buildings on the horizon. Here and there the great landmarks of the city jutted up into the sky, and they looked like tiny models of themselves – the Invalides and the Tour Eiffel on the left bank, the square block of Notre Dame in the centre of the river, the Arc de Triomphe on the right bank, and then, far to the north, higher and more beautiful than all the rest at this distance, the tiny gleaming Byzantine domes of the Sacre Coeur on the topmost crest of Montmartre.
>
> At dusk all this became blurred with a rose and purplish light like the paintings of the early impressionists, and at night … all the valley of the Seine where Paris lies became a black bowl strewn with glittering beads of light as though a part of a tropical sky had fallen on the earth.

In 2013 I went out to Saint-Cloud to see if the apartment was still there. There had been a confusing change in the street-numbering system since the late '30s, but there it was, with its fresh-looking cream stone, its vertical detail of 'portholes' designed to suggest an ocean liner. Geoffrey Cox had lived nearby with his family, which is probably why Moorehead chose the neighbourhood. But it was odd to find him here, in this pretty suburban street dappled with leaf-shade of lush European trees.

This bourgeois calm was badly ruffled early in 1939 when police discovered the bodies of three murder victims in the basement of a Saint-Cloud villa belonging to a German national, Eugene Weidmann. Weidmann was eventually convicted of killing six people in what became a sensational criminal case. This sort of thing was catnip for the *Express* and its happily horrified readers. Cox put his young deputy onto the story. Moorehead was there on the sparkling early summer afternoon to see Weidmann escorted to the scene of his last murder by a crowd of police, officials and reporters. At Fontainebleau, this solemn assembly followed the killer through the pretty woods, going 'up and up through glades of mossy rocks and last year's leaves were still lying on the ground in their autumn colours'.

In the cave where the murder took place, Moorehead got close enough to study Weidmann's face carefully. As the killer helpfully took the judge through the fine points of the killing, Moorehead 'could see his great dog-eyes gleaming faithfully in the match-light and his face was in a transport – quite placid and serene but utterly engrossed'. A charming, charismatic, apparently intelligent German mass-murderer: an intriguing figure in late '30s Paris. Moorehead came to remember him as a kind of portent of the coming age, in which millions of ordinary people would find themselves cast in the role of victim, or executioner. 'I believed that I had found in him a synthesis, a sort of catalyst, for all my restless won-derings about myself ... and the inevitable fate that appeared to be closing in upon us.'

§

That sense of inevitability, what Moorehead called 'a quality of impending disaster in the background of people's lives', was only growing stronger. The Munich crisis at the end of September 1938 produced a sudden spike in anxiety. Until Chamberlain and Daladier made their infamous peace bar-gain with Hitler, war seemed likely to break out at any time. Bombing was the immediate threat. In Paris, street lights were hooded; citizens had been given sand for putting out incendiaries and told to head for the coal cellars when the bombing began. Henry Miller was one resident who took no com-fort from these precautions. Having heard that German bombers would flatten the city on 30 September, he fled to Bordeaux. 'If this is cowardice,' he wrote, 'then I am the vilest coward of any man on earth.' On that day, thousands of Parisians stepped out onto the Boulevard Saint-Michel to get a look at the massive German air armada which was scheduled to devastate Paris, so rumours said, at midday. Moorehead was among them. 'I think we knew that we were condemned to war at that time,' he recalled, in a piece commissioned for the twentieth anniversary of the crisis. 'There was the most lively horror at the prospect of what would happen if cities were bombed from the air or if poison gas were used again ...'

Nothing happened at noon on the 30th. Thousands of upturned faces in the streets, but no sign of the Luftwaffe. All was quiet. When I was in Paris I went to the Boul'Mich and tried to recreate the moment in my mind. I suppose the Parisians of 1938 saw what I saw when I looked up – a dusty blue sky with a few clouds in it, smelt the same odour of roasting chestnuts and stale pee. It was the massed quiet that's hard to recapture; the sound of a huge crowd of people from the past standing in the street, waiting for the future to arrive.

§

A week after Wilmot's visit in March 1938, Moorehead was ordered to Saint-Jean-de-Luz, a resort and fishing village half an hour north of the French–Spanish border. The war in Spain appeared to be approaching a terrible climax. In the worst air raids of the war – the worst yet seen anywhere – German Heinkels bombed Barcelona on 16 and 17 March. Supported by fresh squadrons of warplanes from Italy and Germany, the Nationalists were rapidly gaining ground east towards Lerida and north to Huesca, driving thousands of refugees towards the French border high in the Pyrenees.

Till now, Saint-Jean had been a quiet holiday and fishing town; Moorehead the carefree tourist had seen it in 1936 soaked in southern sun and refreshed by breezes off the Bay of Biscay. Now it swarmed with spies, journalists, arms contractors, refugees; Francoists and Republicans co-existed in cordial hatred. 'In all Spain itself there is hardly a town that lives and breathes in the odour of war as St. Jean does,' Moorehead told *Express* readers in a colourful backgrounder Moorehead published towards the end of the Spanish war. 'Here Franco makes his business deals with the outside world; the spies and the counter-spies hang round the pavement cafés to listen.' The epicentre of all this sedition and war-profiteering was a place on the main street called the Bar Basque. The single telephone was in a booth tucked away near the men's toilet. Whenever a reporter approached the phone to shout a story down the line to London or New York, every Francoist flunky in the place discovered a pressing need to pee.

On this 1938 trip he was refused a visa to enter Nationalist Spain, so he spent the next few weeks ranging up and down the French side of the forbidden frontier, trying to follow Spanish radio reports on hotel wireless sets. Late one night a huge blue bus rattled into Perpignan and jerked to a standstill in front of the café where he was sitting. Five infants were among the eighty or so refugees aboard. 'Bus Runs Babies Through Warzone' ran on page two. The plight of refugees like these – exhausted, half-starved, harried by enemy planes all the way from Madrid – made a powerful impression on Moorehead. In early April, he drove himself up to Luchon, a remote, pretty mountain hamlet, where he witnessed the saddest thing he saw in Spain. With a small crowd of local onlookers and soldiers of the French *Gardes Mobiles*, he stood on the snow-bound precipice looking down into Spain itself, 'a vast and frightening chasm broken by many sheer precipices of solid ice and white ravines that fell down out of sight,' and watched in silence as some 5000 refugees – women, men, children and soldiers – toiled up the icy slope to the French border. When the refugees finally stumbled over into safety, they were disarmed, fed soup, deloused with powder. Then, in groups of fifty or so, they were herded down into the town. Among the exhausted remains of a Government division Moorehead spotted a 'gaunt-faced, six-foot Catalan officer, wearing blue fur boots'. He watched, as 'with rare tact, the black-helmeted mobile guards had stepped aside to give him the honour of leading his men into retreat'.

The colonel stuck in his memory. He reappears, more fully imagined, in *A Late Education*. Now the man's 'humiliation seemed more complete than for the others, and his pride had had so much further to fall'. Moorehead watches a pompous little French officer march up to the colonel, salute, and invite him, in Spanish, to lead his defeated troops down to the valley. In this tableau of suffering, it was an act almost of grace:

'I still did not understand what tug of conscience, what sudden delicacy of feeling could have prompted that sensitive and kindly gesture.' When the wounded colonel understood what he was being asked to do, he called his men to their feet. They 'stopped and quickly grabbed up their bundles from the snow as if they had suddenly woken from a trance'.

> The colonel did not look back to see if they were following. He marched ten paces ahead, swinging his one good arm, and it was not possible to watch that pathetic figure in the blue boots or see the pride in the tattered men behind him without breaking into tears.

Moorehead didn't see any fighting in Spain, but he got close enough to be infected by the romanticism so many writers associated with the lost cause of the Republic. The week he spent in Valencia at the end of the Tinos trip in late 1937 became, in his memory, a glimpse of a makeshift utopia, where 'wildly and irrationally generous' Spaniards fought a great struggle for freedom with 'insouciance' and indomitable optimism. The pathos of this scene at Luchon is strongly reminiscent of a line from Simone Weil, who also reported from Spain and described being moved by the 'love and fraternal spirit, and, above all, that concern for honour which is so beautiful in the humiliated'.

§

In March 1939 Moorehead received a letter from his old friend and London flat mate Erl Gray. Erl's European spree was over for now. He was back in Melbourne and feeling it as a come-down. He found himself surrounded by 'suburban hedge cutters' whose 'world is a jerry-built villa with the "good woman" waiting eternally for "her man" to come home and imprison himself behind his front fence, prop his feet in the air, and lie smugly before his built-in-Japan grate … The years ahead of the same thing after the same bloody thing never cause them mental anguish.'

It could be a letter from anywhere – anywhere remote from what Moorehead thought of as the *centre of things*. But the particular flavour of the suburban monotony is recognisable enough as my own home town to make my face prickle to read it seventy years later, in Canberra, which is an unlikely place to find yourself mortified by your home town.

I have no idea where Moorehead read this letter but I'll put him in the Café des Sports, perched up at the L-shaped bar after work. If he lifted his eyes from Erl's typed report he would see the familiar red leather banquettes, sporting scenes painted on the walls, clientele leaning over the pintables and shouting about politics in a language he never quite got the hang of. What did he feel, so far from home, being reminded of his childhood, an existence shrouded always in his memory, he wrote later, by 'the dead hand of suburbia'? Horror? Relief that he was here and not there, with Erl? When he read *Kangaroo* soon after this, he was fascinated by Lawrence's vision of Australia, but repelled by the memories it revived. He wrote to Lucy Milner: 'I know if I went back it would, octopus-like, close round me again bit by bit so that in the end I would say, "Well, it's a damn sight better than decayed Europe anyhow."'

It wasn't, of course: Europe's political crises were giving Moorehead Zelig-like entrée into some of the epoch's defining scenes. In early 1938, for instance, he crossed the Spanish border once more to supply correspondents installed at the Barcelona's legendary Hotel Majestic with pesetas, whisky, cigars and other necessaries.

> Hemingway came running down the stairs with Martha [Gellhorn] behind him, calling my name. He put his arms round my shoulders, and he was smiling with that famous bearded smile. 'Where is it?'
>
> I showed him the case of whisky. He ripped it open on the floor and took out a bottle. 'That's for you for a start.' You could not get whisky in Barcelona then, not at any price, and it soon went.
>
> And now [Herbert] Matthews [of the *New York Times*] arrived for his cigars and they wanted to hear everything I had to say, how I had come through the border, how the refugees had blocked the road.

Only a couple of years had passed since he'd sat around with some other would-be novelists in Melbourne pubs debating *Fiesta* and *The Green Hills of Africa*, and feeling a million miles from everything. Now here he was, in Europe's hottest warzone, with his idol's heavy arm draped over his shoulders.

Conscious that time was running out, Moorehead was desperate to keep moving. When Mussolini invaded Albania in April 1939, Moorehead disingenuously misread Sutton's instructions (Sutton had intended the more senior Cox to go) and caught the first train to Belgrade to report on the crisis. Then he swung south through the Aegean, visiting Istanbul and Rhodes, where he slept in a hotel bed recently occupied by Dr Goebbels.

Back in Paris, there was a different kind of spectacle he was determined to see. Moorehead had a press pass to Weidmann's public execution; he went along with a friend from the *Express* office, Jerome Willis. The event was scheduled for dawn, but at midnight a large and restive crowd of some 20,000 people had gathered. People made the most of all-night licence extensions at nearby cafés; jazz poured from hundreds of radios along the street. As official invitees, the journalists drank their *fin à l'eau* at café tables behind a barricaded VIP area close to the guillotine. Moorehead smoked the hours away. The worst thing about the long night was the same thing, he reflected later, that made watching the preparations for an attack during the war so ghoulish: the cold, methodical planning for slaughter.

> I kept perversely remembering [that night] when I had stood hour after hour on the cobblestones outside the prison in Versailles ... They had erected the guillotine, tested it, roped off the crowd, backed the hearse into the square and then with the utmost punctuality they had brought Weidmann out at dawn and cut off his head.

It's possible to watch the execution on YouTube, though I don't recommend it. The footage itself, not just the spectacle, looks pre-modern: there's no sound, officials hurry around at the odd accelerated tempo of old film. Even in a grainy little box on the screen the way Weidmann's lopped trunk slowly slides away from the blade is one of those things that's impossible to unsee. Moorehead found it remarkably quick. There were only two 'disgusting things', he told Lucy in a letter: the blood in the gutter and on the knife, and the 'sanctimonious' voice of the official in a blood-flecked shirt who afterwards described Weidmann's behaviour in his last moments to the press pack. 'I'm glad I saw it, and especially the bloody [sic] hungry crowd.'

There's no sign of Moorehead in the footage. I can't make him out in the dark blur of the crowd, which is only surprising because Willis from the office had hoisted his smaller colleague onto his shoulders to give him a better view.

§

24 August 1939: Moorehead is on a train, taking him from London via Paris to Rome, where he is to take up his appointment as bureau chief there. He has farewelled the Saint-Cloud flat and the houseboy; the Matford is sold. It's a promotion, but he has mixed feelings. He and Lucy have decided to get married, and as the train takes him further from her in London, he is missing her badly. But the spell of travel slowly works its magic on our forlorn hero. As he gazes out the window of his first-class sleeper at the snowy Alps and then at signs of cheerful life in the plains of northern Italy, his taste for adventure flows back. He makes his way to the dining car for breakfast, where he finds the Italian waiters packed around a breakfast table, smoking and arguing and jabbing fingers in chests. They've heard a rumour that Russia and Germany have signed a peace deal. Is it true, *signor*? Moorehead tells them it can't be true. With *Russia*? No. Meanwhile, he raises a spoon hopefully. Any chance of some breakfast?

But it was true. Moorehead got his breakfast – bacon and eggs, half a grapefruit and tea – but the Molotov-Ribbentrop Pact, which he read about in a paper when the train paused at Turin, meant the waiting was almost over. With the USSR out of the equation, Hitler was ready to unleash his panzers on Western Europe.

Moorehead checked into a hotel in Rome near the Spanish Steps, right in the middle of a large and welcoming British expatriate community. On the first day, Sydney Morrell, who had been covering Italy until Moorehead arrived, introduced his replacement to everyone who might prove helpful. 'What a collection,' he wrote to Lucy:

> The shrewd little German doctor in the news agency, who said he had it
> for certain that there would be war in the morning; the 15 dozen Italians,

who assured me there wouldn't be war at all; the Americans, who just didn't know and were twice as efficient as anybody else. Nobody seems to really care about it – the weather is too hot. Everyone who can goes down the beach at Ostia and swaps rumours.

At work, he kept his ear to the ground, trying to decipher the local tremors set off by geopolitical rumblings from Berlin, London and Poland. Perhaps his ear trumpet needed fine-tuning: his first report from Rome, his first as a senior foreign correspondent, assured readers that there were no warlike preparations underway in Italy. The Italian papers were urging a peaceful resolution over Poland, and all the signs pointed to a peace settlement.

Only ten days later, Europe was at war. Italy was still neutral, but on 1 September the *Express* sent Moorehead a sealed package containing 'war emergency funds' in American dollars in case communications broke down. This was a bit alarming, thrilling too; but Moorehead still believed Mussolini would remain neutral. He wrote to Lucy urging her to take leave and come to Rome so that they could be married. While he waited for her, he continued his bachelor existence in bars and nightclubs, chatting to friends from the embassy, sometimes talking to young fascist officers. These were grimmer places than those he'd left behind in Paris. 'Mussolini had banned dancing,' he noted.

> Even in the Ambassadors no one seemed to laugh any more, and the play-girls and the trollops sat around the night clubs like the Florina and the Ulpia talking moodily to their clients over bad champagne or listlessly trailing off with their lovers to dark bedrooms up above.

Somehow, despite all the turmoil, Lucy managed to get there in mid-October. And so, amid all the epochal tremblings of war came a brief season of love.

Lucy Milner was a doctor's daughter who had grown up in Bournemouth, in an atmosphere of stifling middle-class respectability. A very bright student, she got into Oxford, but couldn't afford the fees. She went into journalism instead. A friend of Moorehead's called Lucy 'a tall, witty, statuesque girl'. I like that *girl*, because as the years go on, Moorehead's boyishness can make her seem like the only grown-up in the room. She was popular at the *Express*, and highly regarded. She was slightly older than her fiancé, and taller; and in photographs her reserve and self-possessed air can seem severe as the years go on. But Moorehead adored her. Almost despite himself, as he never failed to remind Lucy in his letters.

§

Nothing about Moorehead's era seems more subtly foreign than the tenor of relations between young middle-class men and women, at least as manifested in Alan and Lucy's largely epistolary courtship. Moorehead had always been fiercely attached to his own freedom, of course; even in his postwar novel, his protagonist is nervous about surrendering any of his independence to a wife ('God knows we'll be trapped soon enough . . . It's all coming towards us like a hangman's noose . . .'). In one letter to Lucy from 1939, Moorehead wrote, with more honesty than gallantry: 'I had a fine barrage up against the world of suburban homes and respectable wives and there is momentarily a hole in the barrage now.'

Moorehead had all but proposed in March 1939, but Lucy remained, understandably, unpersuaded. Both wondered whether the costs of marriage, even a happy one, were too high. For Lucy, marriage and family could only be got at the expense of a career she relished. And perhaps there was also a mild terror of trading self-reliance for dependence on someone so proudly unreliable, and who seemed to be having so much sex elsewhere.

Most of Lucy's letters to Moorehead from this time are lost, so we usually have to deduce her side of the conversation from his; but it's clear that Lucy, and several close advisors, including her sister, had concerns about Moorehead's way of life. 'It is only the world and the devil which really keep us apart,' he wrote in March '39: 'only the fact that you want to go on with your job and I with mine. We already have so much separately that we are not struggling hard enough to be together.' There's plenty of passion in the tangled pas de deux of the letters, but also a striking hard-headedness. They were both nearly thirty, after all.

'What I dread so much is this,' Moorehead wrote,

that you will insist that anything short of the perfect dream is not enough. My dear, do you think I prefer half-baked affairs and living in and out of brothels, of never having a let-up in the complete knowing of one person in the world? ... I tell you again that I am not 'perfectly' in love – I never will be. And I tell you that more than any other woman in the world, I want you. Can't you see? There will always be a barrier. Cannot you accept that? ...

It seems that I am giving you everything except the one thing you really want – constant overwhelming proof that I am deeply and perfectly in love. And I am sure that this is the trouble between us, the thing that makes us altogether too heroic and serious ...

The letter ends, rather more in the style of an inter-office memo than a *billet-doux*, with a recapitulation:

1. I am not perfectly in love.
2. I want to marry you.
3. I want in the short time of peace ahead to travel, meet a lot of people, be a success in journalism, to eat and drink well.

And yet it is clear they adored each other, and that each was the other's considered choice of intellectual companion. Moorehead wrote to Lucy with an almost feverish frequency whenever they were separated through the war years. It's as though none of the world-historical events he witnesses are quite real until he's described them for her. She becomes his first reader and was, Caroline Moorehead told me, 'a huge, a total fan of my father. She really admired him as a writer.' She believed in him long before he did; her belief supplied something essential to Moorehead's work, to his growth, productivity, confidence and survival as a writer.

The wedding was in October. They drove up to the Palazzo Senatorio in Michelangelo's Piazza del Campidoglio on the Capitoline Hill, where they were wed by 'a stout gentleman with a colored sash round his torso'. The marriage document provided spaces for the names of thirteen children – the kind of patriotic output the regime encouraged. Mussolini's government blessed the nuptials with a free railway trip to a destination of their choosing, which meant they could honeymoon on Capri.

Lucy and Alan, c.1948

Lucy stayed in Rome for nearly two months. In the expat community around the Spanish Steps and Galleria Borghese, the newlyweds cut a romantic dash. They attended drinks parties at the embassy. They ate Tuscan steaks at Nino's. Lucy befriended Countess Yvonne Pallavicino, a useful connection given that Yvonne presently married Hamish 'Jamie' Hamilton, who would become Moorehead's lifelong publisher. They took walks among the tumbled columns and broken arches at the Foro Romano. 'And we wondered: would we ever see the Foro Romano again?'

Then, when Lucy returned to London, Moorehead was miserable, and so was Rome. 'Everything is grey and sombre and old with the indefinable smell of old age and decay … It seemed you could not escape this sense of doom and despair.'

The unreality of the Phoney War set in; in January 1940 Lucy was back in Paris to appraise the spring collections, as if an entire German army wasn't perched on the French border with engines running. Italy remained neutral. Moorehead filled the waiting with more travels, to Egypt, and to the Adriatic, where he spent ten days aboard the destroyer *Galatea* as it prowled the mouth of the Adriatic for illicit cargoes and Nazi agents. Before he left the ship, Admiral Cunningham invited him to address the ship's company on the life of the foreign correspondent. Moorehead hated public speaking. But he gamely climbed up onto a gun turret so that everyone could see him and hear his newly rounded vowels above the breeze whipping off Valletta harbour.

In March he returned to Lucy in London and stayed six weeks. He wanted to stay indefinitely, but when Germany invaded Denmark and Norway in April, Christiansen needed him back in Rome to cover Mussolini's next move.

'Within two hours of reaching Rome I saw everything had changed.' There was a new menace in the Blackshirts' swagger. Anti-British posters were being pasted up overnight on the big hotels. In Moorehead's Swiss pensione on the Piazza di Spagna, German and English residents shared a breakfast hour, but fought a phoney war of their own by asserting the primary rights of English or German newspapers to space on the table. 'Hating it all, a gentle old aristocrat said to me: "It isn't that we hate you in England. It's just that we're afraid you aren't going to win."' The fascist police kept a file on young Moorehead; his room was searched three times.

Yet he doesn't seem much alarmed. There was a shy German art student also living at the pensione; he took her out once or twice to a 'pseudo-German' beer hall. He made almost daily trips to the beach. He had got hold of a sports car somehow and bowled down the highway to Ostia for a bathe in the sea. Surrounded by paper, I kept forgetting this physicality in his nature, his animal spirit, his lightness of step – like a dancer's, someone said. When Lucy wrote in May to tell him she was pregnant, he replied with a whoop of delight. If it's a boy, he wrote, he will be 'a tiger, full of great appetites. Not one of those damn public school pansies with a squeaking voice.'

Moorehead was in the Piazza Venezia on 10 May, the day Hitler was finally ready to set his panzer army on France and Belgium. A few students were trying to whip up the crowd with chants of 'Down with England – We want Tunis'. But Mussolini restrained himself. 'I have watched many demonstrations in the Piazza Venezia,' Moorehead advised readers. 'Today's seemed to me surprisingly good-humoured and un-warlike.'

Time was running out. In theory, correspondents were, with diplomatic staff, guaranteed safe passage if war should be declared, but the *Express* decided not to chance it. On 22 May Moorehead flew to Athens and checked into the Hotel Grande Bretagne, joining a number of other correspondents awaiting instructions from their papers. Prevented from writing anything much by 'insurmountable' censorship, most were enjoying a holiday in the lovely sunshine, shopping and meeting up with old friends. It was a nice, if slightly fantastical spot to be in. You could swim in the sea. You could have a tailor run you up a nice white linen suit.

On his second afternoon there Moorehead went upstairs to visit a colleague who was laid up with the flu. He stepped into the hotel elevator with a tall, frowning figure who looked vaguely familiar and seemed to be grimly avoiding eye-contact. It was Alexander Clifford of the *Daily Mail*. The two had met briefly in Saint-Jean two years before when Moorehead, newly arrived in the border town, had approached a couple of reporters in a bar for advice about hotels. Clifford had been sullen and curt, Moorehead thought. Now the snooty bugger was here again. Worse, he was on his way to visit the same man. Neither spoke. In the sickroom, they addressed all their remarks to the patient. Then a doctor came and ordered them out.

Marching in ludicrous silence to the lift, Moorehead cracked, and suggested a drink. To Moorehead's surprise, and possibly Clifford's, the quiet Englishman agreed. They found a *taverna*, and took a table on the pavement. They stayed there for three hours. It was the beginning of the most intense and rewarding friendship of Moorehead's life. They talked and argued and drank ouzo, which Clifford could order in effortless Greek. He spoke six languages, and could fumble by in several more. Diffident, brilliant and solitary, Clifford was much that Moorehead wasn't, and conjuring him up it's hard to avoid a caricaturist's doodle: Moorehead's sociable eagerness v. Clifford's Brahmin aloofness; Moorehead's ambition v. Clifford's watchful self-sufficiency. Clifford had worked for Reuters, and now had a roving commission in the Balkans for the *Daily Mail*, the *Express*'s fiercest rival. As Clifford fluently unpacked the situation in Greece and Yugoslavia, Moorehead decided that the unfriendliness that had stung him in Saint-Jean was just an acute case of English reserve. 'I have not talked so well with anyone for so long,' he wrote to Lucy. On subsequent days Clifford proved himself to be a strong swimmer, too, only increasing Moorehead's admiration.

All the world was watching France, where the British and French armies were still reeling before the German assault. If Italy came into the war, the new friends reasoned, there would be action in Africa. All they needed was permission to go. So they cooked up a scheme: Moorehead reported to the *Express* that Clifford of the *Daily Mail* was heading to Cairo, information which was sure to send the foreign desk into conniptions of anxiety. Clifford was off; shouldn't he follow? Clifford did the same thing at his end. This transparent ruse worked beautifully. They were both promptly ordered to Egypt, each shadowing the other into god only knew what.

4

A DESERT WAR

I'd forgotten how hot it was in Egypt. When I went back in 2011 the worst of summer was over, but the dusty light persisted; my flinching pupils seemed to recognise it, like a sense memory of a migraine. What would be ideal, I thought, after about five minutes in the baking streets, would be to spend as much time as possible indoors.

By now I knew that my epiphany in that hotel bar a decade before – the semi-mystical imagining of Moorehead coming down in the antique iron elevator – had taken place in *the wrong hotel*. In my excitement, I'd confused the Windsor with the Carlton. This time I checked into the Carlton Hotel, which has also survived seventy years without any perceptible upgrades to the fittings or carpets. The foyer was small, dim and cool. There were brass lamps in understated Orientalist style; at the top of a short flight of marble stairs was a lacquered filigree screen with mother-of-pearl inlay. To the right of the entry vestibule was a waist-high wooden gate enclosing a sitting area. *That* was where Moorehead must have sat, seventy years earlier, reading his cables, nursing a drink, perhaps listening to the radio.

This was the first stop for him and Clifford when they arrived in mid-May 1940. They checked into the Carlton and reported to the Kasr-el-Nil barracks on the river to be fitted for uniforms. As accredited war correspondents attached to the brand-new Public Relations Unit, they would be entitled to the rank of captain, and to green shoulder tabs with the words

'British War Correspondent' stitched in gold thread. Their kit included knee-high khaki stockings, khaki drill shorts that buckled high on the waist, a pith helmet to guard against sunstroke, and a revolver to guard against restive locals. They also located the three separate censors who would have to rubber-stamp each dispatch sent back to London – making the rounds of all of them would take, Moorehead later estimated, four hours or more.

They started making calls to whatever numbers they could find, introducing themselves to potentially useful contacts at GHQ. The calls began in confusion since no one had yet heard of Public Relations ('What in the name of God is that?') and often moved into open hostility once it was explained to them.* But mostly they just took in the noise, filth, variety and hallucinogenic plenty of colonial Cairo. They bought silk in the bazaar, fended off touts selling stomach pumps and books on how to avoid income tax, and wandered streets where the sunlight lay in 'thick drowsy slabs between the tall buildings'. Rationing was in force in England, but here French wine could be had and hawkers' barrows groaned with fresh bananas and mangoes. In the evenings pungent camels wandered in from the country with bulging nets of melons on their backs and red hurricane lamps tied to their tails. There were steaks, cigarettes, beer and whisky, and a delicious buffet at the Gezira Sporting Club. On Gezira Island in the Nile, the cricket and polo matches continued in the obliterating heat. Mostly the friends swam at the club and played pool at the Turf Club, where rattan ceiling fans stirred cool air musky with wood polish and cigarette smoke.

Moorehead filed his first story on Monday, 4 June, describing the exodus of Italians from Egypt and the ongoing round-up of Germans, including 'engineers and girls from cabarets'. 'A typical incident in the country-wide arms clean-up is that of an Italian fisherman found with an undeclared revolver. Picturesquely he declared it was for "shooting savage fish." He was fined £30.' It ran in the *Express* the next day, as the last remaining units of the British Army in France were being hauled off the beach at Dunkirk.

---

* 'Nothing will quite convey the astonishment and abhorrence with which the elderly colonel and the polo-playing messes received the newspapermen,' Moorehead wrote. '"The only time I want to see anything about my men in print is when the honours lists come out," a brigade-major told me sourly.'

British Cairo heard the surreal news from France on the radio; by the time the newsreels reached its open-air cinemas, the North African situation had become more urgent. Hoping to snaffle a share of Britain's beleaguered Empire before it was gobbled entire by Germany, Mussolini declared war on 10 June. The formidable Italian navy closed the British supply route through the Mediterranean. Lucy was in London, and three months pregnant, and there was no realistic prospect of seeing her any time soon. 'Quite seriously,' Moorehead wrote, 'we expected never to see our families again.'

Yet for all the disastrous war news from afar, neither he nor Clifford seems particularly alarmed by their predicament. This was still, Clifford wrote, 'the era of blind confidence. In view of what was happening in France it had to be blind, otherwise it couldn't have remained confidence.' The next morning Moorehead and five other correspondents filed into General Wavell's office to hear what he planned to do about General Balbo's 250,000-odd Italian troops in Libya, not to mention the 300,000 the Duke of Aosta commanded in Eritrea and Ethiopia, where they directly menaced Anglo-Egyptian Sudan and the Red Sea shipping route.

§

To grasp the context of Moorehead's war all you'll need is the most basic mental picture of the North African campaign. The Desert War rambled bloodily to and fro along the 1000-mile littoral for nearly three years. Four times the British and Empire forces – the Army of the Nile, as Churchill grandly designated it in 1940, later the Eighth Army – would drive its caravan of guns, tanks, its dust and supplies westward through a string of coastal settlements, some of them hardly more than marks on the map (Fuqa, Mersa Matruh, Sidi Barrani, Sollum), some of them – such as Tobruk, Derna and Benghazi – old Arab settlements now shared with desperately poor Italian colonists. Thrice the British forces came scrambling back before the screeching tracks of Afrika Korps panzers, blowing fuel dumps, abandoning airfields, dragging damaged equipment, hurrying ambulances along the edge of the narrow road past jammed transports. The campaign began in June 1940 and began to end in October 1942, when victory at El Alamein launched the final Allied push across Libya and up into Tunisia, which finally fell to the Allies in May 1943.

For three years, North Africa and the Mediterranean theatre was the only place where Britain, with its dominions, faced its enemies on the ground. Though it began with what Clifford called a 'puny little baby of an army', and at its height never involved more than a dozen divisions at any one time,* the Desert War has taken on a legendary grandeur in the annals of British arms. When it began, though, it really did feel like a sideshow. Only a handful of newspapermen were there to hear Wavell announce that his little force had raided some Italian outposts on the Libyan border. Many of the fighting troops themselves, once Moorehead got among them, seemed bemused to find themselves fighting for their British way of life in a godforsaken African desert. 'I heard this a thousand times: "Why aren't we at home defending England?"'†

The obvious answer was Suez, the carotid artery of the Empire. Protecting Suez meant protecting Britain, as well as the Iraqi oil fields beyond it. But there was an even simpler explanation. The British government needed a fighting front somewhere. It needed to show the world it was still standing. And through its Public Relations Unit, the army would do everything it could to help the correspondents provide the glorious story of victorious battle in the African sands.

The first glimpse of those sands was not promising. Driving out past Alexandria for the first time, Moorehead's convoy was caught in a choking *khamseen*. This is, he told readers, 'in my experience the most hellish wind on earth'. They struggled through the gale of sand beyond the Red Cross tent hospital at Daba; through the airfield at Fuqa. By the time he got to the war correspondents' camp at Bagush, visibility was down to just a few yards.

---

* In 1942, the year of the El Alamein battles, some 300 divisions were fighting on the Eastern Front.
† This view would change. After months of digging and fighting and burying friends, the defenders of Tobruk during its long siege of 1941 came to believe, Moorehead wrote, 'that they were defending London and their own homes across its [Tobruk's] scarred sulphur-coloured plains and the perimeter was as real to them as the cliffs of Dover.'

In front of the car little crazy lines of yellow dust snaked across the road. The dust came up through the engine, through the chinks of the car-body and round the corners of the closed windows. Soon everything in the car was powdered with grit and sand. It crept up your nose and down your throat, itching unbearably and making it difficult to breathe. It got in your ears, matted your hair, and from behind sand goggles your eyes kept weeping and smarting. An unreal yellow light suffused everything.

Any movie-goer of the 1930s might have been led to expect golden rolling dunes and romantic green oases in the desert. Instead, the press-men found themselves surrounded by an 'unvarying disc of flat brown gravel'. Driving through the bleak little resort town of Mersa Matruh, Clifford remarked that this was where, 'centuries earlier, Cleopatra had dallied and bathed with Antony' – a shred of glamour in the general mono-tony that no correspondent failed to mention in his dispatch. Moorehead slept on the sand that first night, in a sleeping bag zipped over his head to keep the dust out. In the following days he observed from a safe distance a diversionary tank attack on one of the Italian forts – the confusion sur-prised him; the noise of the artillery was appalling – and gradually accustomed himself to life under canvas at what passed for the front.

There was an improvisatory quality to the early fighting that flared up in isolated skirmishes fought around forts and fuel dumps, and the cor-respondents had to improvise ways of describing it, the halting tempo, the longueurs and sudden eruptions of action. Groping for analogies that might help their readers understand what it was like, they compared the atmosphere of the country to the novels of H Rider Haggard and PC Wren; they likened the experience of watching the battles to being in a cinema, watching a drama 'as rounded and directional as a motion picture'.

In fact, they never really saw a battle, 'only a great deal of dust, noise and confusion'. Patterns in the fighting emerged hours or days afterwards. Moorehead saw how the Italians were clinging to forts designed for impos-ing imperial order on pesky Bedouin raiders but helplessly vulnerable to modern artillery; how the Italians patrolled the useless barbed-wire fence at the border, 'with the persistence of a goldfish edging along the confines of his glass jar'. He realised that modern desert war most resembled war at sea, an observation that became a truism, but only after Moorehead observed it.

Each evening the pressmen settled down with their tea and typewriters to bash out what they'd seen. Absorbed in the 'onward rush of the present', Moorehead had no time to worry about posterity, and no time to polish the reports he sent back to the *Daily Express*. Contrast was the key, he thought: it was 'the spectacle of ordinary people (in this case the soldiers) reacting to a strange place'.

'Reporting,' he wrote after the war, 'requires a quick and concentrated enthusiasm ... and, above all, a sense of wonder and curiosity in life as it goes by at the moment.' Through the static of the intervening decades something of the astonishing moment is still transmitted by these reports, which place the reader if not right at the front, then on the road to battle, senses on full alert:

> Lying on open ground in this bitter wind I wake at night to see flashes against the brilliant moon and wake again at dawn to feel the desert floor trembling with the impact of high explosives ... We are all dirty, cold, unshaven and enthusiastic.
>
> Men pressing up that filthy road from Sidi Barrani in thousands have faces caked white with dust and two staring eyes peering out under each tin hat. Sometimes, as we did an hour ago at dusk, we pressed down among icy rocks for safety. Twelve Italian bombers, playing the old game of coming straight at us out of the sunset, suddenly shot across the skyline with twelve fighters ... But ... you can't destroy an army scattered almost invisibly over hundreds of miles of desert.

'What a time and what a place – congratulations,' someone cabled in December. There's no doubt that Moorehead felt the same way. It all seemed to write itself, he remembered. 'Within an hour of arriving in the desert ideas came crowding into one's mind, and if there was no action for days together it made no difference. Life there was so completely abnormal.' Abnormal, but soon so familiar to the pressmen they became blasé about their bizarre environment and its hazards. During a lull in a tank battle one day, Clifford recalled, they cracked out the cards to pass the time, while just on the other side of a nearby crest, unspent rounds in a burning tank burst intermittently until none were left.

Often the reporters were left behind by events, and had to hitchhike to the next hopelessly confused battle when their vehicles broke down, or cadge seats on RAF transports. They lost their supplies and searched for improvised meals in captured stores. They went off into 'the blue' in search of different headquarters, where they foraged for scraps of fresh news from other parts of the front. When the day was done, they set up camp near any HQ they could find. That meant digging slit trenches so that they had somewhere to dive if a stray Savoia bomber should appear. Sometimes half a dozen correspondents would sit around belting out stories with a workshop clatter that was, one reporter wrote, 'powerfully evocative of the final half-hour of any public examination'. They wrote on beaches, in truck cabs, in abandoned houses where broken glass crunched under foot, on the running boards of trucks; they perched on warm rocks with their typewriters on their knees while the sun went down. After dinner they resumed in flickering candlelight or with an electric torch trained on the keys. They'd bash their messages out – 1000 words or more, sometimes – then try to work out how to get them back to the nearest press tent for the censor's stamp, and thence to Cairo, preferably on the next supply plane or, failing that, by road or rail with anyone willing to take them.

Colleagues recalled that Moorehead had a way of sitting at his typewriter, eyes narrowed, head cocked at a calculating angle, cigarette dangling from the side of his mouth. 'It was a new kind of reporting,' Moorehead wrote: 'exasperating, exciting, fast-moving, vivid, immense and slightly dangerous.' And it suited him perfectly.

His stories were constantly front-paged through that first campaign. In December Sutton cabled from the foreign desk: 'YOUR EXCELLENT MESSAGES HAVE SENT EDITOR NUTS HE TALKS ABOUT QUOTE LOVELY FLOW YOUR WAR DESCRIPTIVE STORIES BRINGING DESERT SANDS INTO HIS THROAT UNQUOTE.'

Why? Partly, he thought, because his mind was so clear. This was life stripped back to its essentials. In the Desert War the issues were as simple as the landscape was monotonously, elementally flat; no civilians to worry about here, no money, none of Cairo's fifth column types muttering in Arabic or French, no politics at all. 'The desert had an antiseptic effect upon nearly everyone who went there in the war,' he wrote later: 'it destroyed most of the small indulgences and even the vices that eat like parasites into our lives in normal times.'

In the desert, nightfall was a deliverance. When work was done, someone conjured dinner from a cut-down petrol tin, some pilfered onions and a few cans of rations. Someone else cleaned up. Then there was nothing to do but crawl into your bedroll and sleep until the 'mad glaring eye' of the sun returned, bringing with it the day's first flies. But for a few quiet hours they could enjoy the wonderful cold, and the primeval brilliance of the cloudless night sky. Darkness brought a release.

In the early days, it was often just Moorehead and Clifford, 'Mutt and Jeff', as some others had taken to calling them. Isolated from their past lives, Moorehead wrote later, they were like 'two strangers who cling together in a shipwreck'. Moorehead discovered that Clifford was hopelessly shy and always insisted that Moorehead enter an office first; he wasn't especially driven: there were too many other things besides journalism he was interested in. He had a deep and informed love of music, but otherwise wasn't a sensualist. While the belly dancers at Madame Badia's held Moorehead spellbound, Clifford was unmoved. Gardening was more his line. And golf. He didn't smoke. Unlike Moorehead, he gave money to beggars, but was otherwise slow to reach for his wallet, and could be peevish about shared bills. Now, laid out side by side on the moon-silvered sand, they talked whatever nonsense came into their heads. It was the start of an 'effortless, absorbing conversation', Moorehead wrote:

> We talked at first of the things we had had done that day, and of how we thought the front would develop and of where we should go on the morrow. We talked of our writing and of how to improve it, and finally we talked about ourselves ... Our two camp beds sailed out into space and time and we were exactly poised and at peace. There we sat like birds in the wilderness, we were free, and there seemed at last in this murmured

exchange of ideas to be an explanation for the mystery of simply being alive. To speak the dream – that was the thing: the backward dream of all that had already happened and the forward dream of what we hoped would be; and this was not difficult because we were, in fact, perched on a kind of mental frontier; our old lives had come to an abrupt stop with the war and with our arrival here in the desert, and no one could say what was going to happen to us after the war was over.

This passage is so affecting partly because we know now what happened after the war. But also because it conveys a depth of friendship few of us will ever experience – at a time in life, and a time in history, when the future seemed full of possibility, an endless vista perfectly scaled to this heaven of silently blazing stars.

§

One of the odd things about Moorehead's desert landscape is that there are so few women in it, apart from sightings of the occasional Bedouin tending her flock in full tribal regalia. It's only when a woman appears that the monotonous maleness of everything is revealed. A few women reporters made their way into the battle zone in 1940, including Eve Curie, daughter of Marie and a correspondent for the *New York Herald Tribune*, Clare Hollingworth, and later Clare Boothe Luce, wife of *Time* proprietor Henry Luce, each one provoking a tremendous flap among conducting officers and much conspicuous unconcern from their male colleagues.

This story's most important woman was about to arrive in Cairo. Moorehead had become so close to Clifford after only a few months in the desert that he began to dread what would happen next. What if Alex and Lucy didn't get on? How could he make her understand how important a part of his life Alex had become?

Moorehead was there in Cairo to see his heavily pregnant wife rowed in from the flying boat to the launching stage, the last tiny leg of an onerous journey that had taken several days and cost £300. His memory of this moment wins him no points for chivalry, but sounds honest: the 'slim active woman' he remembered from Rome had become, in a shapeless maternity dress, a sweaty and exhausted blue-and-white bundle. Moorehead took her to the Carlton, where the flowers Alex had reminded him to buy drooped in the sultry air. Lucy took in her husband's cramped quarters; they went for lunch in the gloomy salon downstairs and watched flies circling interminably above the warm pressed meat. Later they went to an open-air restaurant in the city with Alex. It was an enjoyable evening, but there was no indication that Alex and Lucy were particularly taken with one another.

Moorehead headed out for a week at the front, resigned to the end of 'haphazard communal life' with Alex, and 'the establishment of a rigid home' with set times for meals. But he returned to find that Alex and Lucy had not only found a flat on Gezira Island for the Mooreheads, but that a room in it had been set aside for Alex. As they so often would, others had taken care of things, and Moorehead was delighted.

§

In early December 1940, after some months of feints and raids designed to discourage the massive Italian Tenth Army from rolling further into Egypt, Wavell struck at the enemy's fortified positions. Not an *offensive*, as such – 'You might call it an important raid,' the C-in-C told the small group of pressmen summoned to his Cairo office. It took Moorehead a day and a half of rugged driving to get to Nibeiwa, a fortified Italian camp twenty miles south of Sidi Barrani, and when he arrived the fighting was already over. With the help of some new Matilda II tanks, the 4th Indian Infantry Division had visited terrible violence on the defenders, and moved on. Moorehead's prose wanders in amazement around the battlefield. There are the silent horrors of aftermath: 'Here and there before the breaches in the walls a dead man lay spread-eagled on the ground, or collapsed grotesquely at the entrance of his dugout under a gathering cloud of flies.' The corpses included that of the Italian general Maletti, who had died at his machine gun: 'body covered with a beribboned tunic [he] still lay sprawled on the threshold of his tent, his beard stained with sand and sweat.' But it was the 'luxury and elaboration', as Clifford put it – he was there, too – of the Italian outpost that added an extra layer of the surreal

to the already bizarre experience of watching European armies trying to
annihilate one another in an African desert.

> Extraordinary things met us wherever we turned ... Officers' beds laid
> out with clean sheets, chests of drawers filled with linen and abundance
> of fine clothing of every kind ... dressing-tables in the officers' tents were
> strewn with scents and silver-mounted brushes and small arms made
> delicately in the romantic northern arsenals of Italy.

Underground tunnels linked superbly provisioned hospital tents and lavishly furnished dugouts. For five miles around, Moorehead wrote, there
were handwritten letters 'in a thin spidery schoolboy scrawl full of homely
Latin flourishes' strewn in the sand. He wandered among corpses, battle-
stunned donkeys and pack mules braying for water, discarded hand-grenades
and ceremonial swords, and sappers stripping abandoned enemy machin-
ery. He picked through astonishing stores of food and drink: wines, tinned
tongue and tomato paste, vegetables and packets of freeze-dried mine-
strone, stacks of 'Parmesan cheeses as big as small cart-wheels and nearly
a foot thick'. And all of it, Moorehead wrote in *Mediterranean Front*, 'all
this richness and its wreckage, all the scars of the battle and all the effort
of ten thousand men, it seemed, would not prevail longer than a week or
two'. The bodies, the loot, the burst-apart cases of food and bullets, were
all sinking beneath a wind-borne film of sand. Soon, Nibeiwa would be
'restored to the featurelessness and monotony of the surrounding waste'.

The first of the Desert War's five great pendulum swings was underway;
this one would end six weeks later and 800 miles to the west at the Battle of
Beda Fomm with the capture, or obliteration, of the entire Italian Tenth Army.
For six weeks Moorehead raced along the coast in the wake of the rumbling
spearheads. Today it's easy to read every single word Moorehead wrote for
the *Express*: thanks to digitisation, the old fish'n'chip wrappings enjoy a ghostly,
fully searchable immortality in online archives. We can read his dispatch from
Sidi Barrani, say, on the terrific naval bombardments laid down to soften up
the approach to Sollum. 'In one camp alone a thousand men were wiped out,'
he reported. 'From the sea the enemy was pounded with 15in shells

containing shrapnel as big as cricket balls. "Pretty fast bowling," as the intel-ligence officer just said as he got the report here over the field telephone.'

That tally-ho note sounds ridiculous now, even as reported speech. But perhaps it played well among Londoners waking from another freezing night of bombing and grinding anxiety. Moorehead was finding a way to convey to readers what was mostly impossible to see ('From first to last we never "saw" a battle in the desert') but could be *sensed*, the experience of being surrounded by fighting without knowing what's happened until after-wards. His best reports vividly convey the scale and shambles and confusion of the battles fought in and out of towering screens of dust, where tank units wheeled around blindly trying to find an enemy to lash at, all under 'the terrible, blasting, stultifying heat of the sun'. During the battle in which the Afrika Korps broke into Tobruk after its famous siege, chaos *was* the story.

> There is no front line. British and German tanks have met and wiped each other out. That is all. On both sides there are thousands of prisoners, thousands of casualties … Just this is definite … The hard armoured cas-ing around both armies has been pierced and broken and the soft inner core of the infantry, light gunners and supply columns stand opposed and at places hopelessly intermingled. Occasionally, tanks from both sides are cutting loose in this soft stuff … It is like a shark among the mackerel.

This was the kind of opportunity of a lifetime that could also very eas-ily get you killed. One day in early 1941 Moorehead and Clifford were following a headlong advance through the wooded foothills of the Green Mountains towards Barce. It was early evening. Everywhere on the road was the wreckage of retreating Italian forces: abandoned vehicles, groups of surrendering troops waving white hankies, trucks upended or torn apart by the Hurricanes that were operating up ahead. Moorehead and Clifford were in their Morris truck with their conducting officer and War Office photographer Geoffrey Keating when they rounded a bend and saw a group of Italians laying mines a few hundred yards up the road. Nothing to be alarmed about. They were travelling with some British armoured cars and Australian troops and all day they had been overrunning lost or terrified Italian soldiers who had gratefully surrendered when presented with the opportunity. While everyone waited for this lot to surrender also, British sappers leapt from their cars and began ripping up the freshly laid mines. But the Italians didn't surrender. They just stood there, in the middle distance, watching. Time for a bit of that fast bowling, perhaps. "'Give them a burst," someone began to say, and then from the hill ahead, a long whining scream of bullets came at us down the roadway.' It was an ambush.

Breda guns, two-pounders and mortars crashed their shell dead among us. Clifford and I made for the wooded bank on the left, but it was hopeless – the enemy were firing almost at point-blank range, two or three hundred yards away. The rest of the British patrol also tried to make for cover, some of them shooting as they ran. One Breda-gun burst set the armoured car next to ours ablaze, killing the men inside. I heard the muffled scream of another man, hit half a dozen times in the legs, being gallantly dragged back along the gutter by his comrades. The enemy's tracer-bullets made long criss-cross sheaths of light down the road.

Then I saw Keating, full in the face of the fire, running down the line of empty armoured cars trying to get a first-aid kit. Our driver had been cruelly hit on the arm by an explosive bullet as he had leaped from the truck. I ran over to him, tearing off a bandage from a sore on my knee, but he was huddled crookedly in the shallow drainage gutter, quickly drenching in his blood. Clifford joined me, and together we tore off his greatcoat and cut away his sweater and shirt. But then the Italians creeping closer saw us – the last of the British left around the cars. They blew our truck to bits while we lay four yards away trying to stem the wounded man's flow of blood. Then Keating, who had somehow got up the roadway, joined us with a first aid pad which we fixed in the wounded man's arm. The fire was very close and very heavy and our cover not more than eighteen inches, so we had to stop and lie still from time to time. Then a piece of shrapnel struck Keating in the forearm, while a bullet tore a ragged hole in his leg. He fell forward softly upon the driver in the shallow trench. Clifford was nicked neatly in the behind. Another bullet passed through the folds of the sleeve of my greatcoat, and, certain I was hit, I remember waiting frigidly for the pain to come.

By now the line of cars was blazing, and although the enemy could see Clifford and me alone, trying to bind up the wounded men, they concentrated all their fire upon us. It was madness then to stay. We dragged the driver into a bush – I pulling him by the heels, Clifford pushing his shoulders. Keating, who continued directing us, urged us to go ahead while he looked after himself. He, too, succeeded in following slowly. Forcing the driver to his feet – he was in great pain, but trying very hard to help us – we crouched and dodged from bush to bush. All this was at dusk, and as we crossed each open space the Italians unloosed their fire again.

Three hundred yards further on they stopped to dress the driver's wounds again. The shelling eased slightly. After a 'long, bad walk' flinching at the sound of each rattling salvo from the road, they were safely among their own armoured cars.

This is the account in *Mediterranean Front*, the book Moorehead began writing a few months later. The story is quite different when Moorehead returns to this 'first acquaintance with death' a decade on, writing during long, dull days aboard a passenger liner taking him to Australia in 1952. Back he goes to that dirt road outside Barce. Now he can add that when he and Clifford tried to dress the driver's wound three hundred yards from the cars, his hands were 'shaking so much the whole contraption fell into the blood, the broken glass as well as the iodine. When I picked up another phial Alex took it away from me and broke it in the proper way.' And he can remember how it felt, pinned to the ground in terror.

> I never thought of surrendering. I thought only: this is too cruel, they cannot realise what they are doing to us. If they were here with us they would see it and they would stop ... There could be no hatred or anger in the world which would want to hurt us so much. I thought again and again: 'I am not hit yet ... I am not hit yet.' I did not pray or think of my past life or of my family; I simply wanted to get away. If I had had a gun I doubt that I would have fired it. I did not swear, except softly under my breath, until the driver cried out pitifully that he was in agony and could go no further, and then I shouted, 'Get on you little bastard'. If I helped my companions

at all it was done mechanically and without any real volition; with all my
senses I longed for the darkness so that I could get away and hide ...

I do not think that I ever recovered from this incident.

The next day they went back to collect their gear from the truck, but
their typewriters were wrecked, smashed into a heap of twisted typebars. A
wheel of parmesan cheese Clifford had looted from Nibeiwa was so riddled
with bullet holes it now resembled Swiss cheese. A beloved pair of Italian
naval trousers he had stored behind the cheese, however, was unharmed.

§

In Cairo, seventy years later, in the jet-lagged euphoria of arrival, I sat on
my bed at the Carlton that first night and tried to tune in to Moorehead
frequency across time. But I was distracted by the view. My room was
quite high up, and from my window I could see the roofs of several other
buildings, all of which seemed to be piled with heaps of rubble and plastic bags of rubbish. Directly across from me was a tangle of garbage and
building debris on a roof six floors above the street, as if the top half of
the building had collapsed on the bottom half. I thought of Moorehead
in Sousse, Tunisia, 1943, and the landscape bombing had produced there.
'It was not so much the general devastation, it was the violence with which
everything had been done. A grand piano had been picked up from a
basement and flung on to a house-top. The roof of one apartment building had been flung bodily on to the next building.'

Over the next few days I found it easy enough to find links to
Moorehead's experience. 'Nearly all night long,' he wrote of those early
days, 'in the Egyptian café below, the clients banged down their dominoes
and backgammon pieces with a noise that had the same power to destroy
sleep as a creaking door.' In 1940 there was an open-air cinema across the
street and 'until midnight the Arabic dialogue, the incidental music and
the pistol shots of the westerns came up to us in a loud, meaningless explosion of sound'. The cinema had gone, but there were still crowds looking
for entertainment. The hotel now fronted onto a street of stalls and shops
specialising in auto and boating accessories. Every horn, wailer and siren

invented by humans was for sale in this little strip; for those passing by it was an irresistible temptation to try every last one of them, just for fun. All hours of the day until well past midnight, I could hear Keystone Cops–style sirens and electric honks, each one usually followed by delighted clapping and cheers.

Some nights at the Carlton, as I lay awake listening to the festival of car horns, I pondered Moorehead's success in reporting the Desert War. I'd always liked this part of the story, and now I felt invested in it – how sudden the success was, and remarkable. Christiansen always maintained that before the war Moorehead had given useful service, but 'it was not then apparent that his literary skill even existed'. But 'something happened to him. His sense of observation, his gift of words, brought the battle of the desert clearly before the eyes of everyone in Britain.' The Cairo cable office ran hot with notes from friends like Monks, who was still loyally cheerleading from afar – 'VERY PROUD YOUR MAGNIFICENT EFFORTS FELLA' – and regular sobriquets from the foreign desk: 'WE SMELT POWDER TOO' or 'YOU'RE ONCE MORE MILES AHEAD OF YOUR COMPETITORS'. Several of Moorehead's competitors agreed. Moorehead's dispatches 'had undoubtedly been the best war-reporting from the Middle East', wrote Clifford, whose professional rivalry with his friend had a civilised veneer, but a subliminal bitterness to it as well – or so Moorehead thought.* Clare Hollingworth admitted that Moorehead was regarded among his rivals as 'the best reporter/correspondent'. The *Evening Standard* declared him 'one of the really great reporters of war'†; another time Christiansen cabled to tell his star: 'London editor of *Life* says if you American would win Pulitzer Prize'.

Later Christiansen declined to take any credit for this success. Moorehead's miraculous sprouting was all his own work. But he did do everything he could for his star's name-recognition, which, after all, was in everyone's interest. In June 1942, in one of his daily editor's bulletins,

---

* Moorehead: 'We were constantly trying to outdo one another in the dispatches we sent to our newspapers, and later on, in the books we wrote. It was a cross-current beneath our friendship, a kind of private, professional bitterness. We never rejoiced in one another's successes, we enjoyed hurting one another.'
† The *Standard* was, it should be noted, a Beaverbrook paper.

Chris deplored the fact that Moorehead's by-line had been combined with someone else's: 'Moorehead is a big shot, an expert on Libya. He is entitled to be regarded as a distinguished correspondent.' And that's how Moorehead had been treated almost since the fighting began: no one was misspelling his name anymore. On 13 December 1940, Moorehead's front-page report was by-lined 'Daily Express War Reporter Alan Moorehead' and accompanied by a rare headshot of 'Front-Line Moorehead' himself. In February 1941, as the heady British advance gained momentum through Sidi Barrani and Sollum, the front page announced: 'Moorehead bathes in Graziani's Bath'. Your correspondent, home-front Britons were assured, had entered the abandoned villa that had served as Italian headquarters in Derna and now had unchallenged command of the enemy general's hot and cold faucets. By late 1941 *Time* magazine was referring to Moorehead as 'Beaverbrook's ace correspondent'; *Life* magazine printed a long piece about the battle of Sidi Rezegh in late 1941, introducing him to a whole new continent of potential readers. When Moorehead and Clifford got back to Cairo after that battle they went through the mail that had piled up while they were away. Moorehead had notice of yet another handsome raise in salary, his fifth in eighteen months. Clifford got a demand for so much income tax that he wrote, 'I still can't believe it's true.'

Success was a tonic, Moorehead thought. ('I believe success does improve people,' he admitted later.) Whatever else success did in 1941, it certainly changed the way people saw him. And not everyone was sold on the idea of Moorehead's genius. Plenty of reporters, especially the news service correspondents, spent more time at the front among the troops, anonymously gathering the plain news. They were often months away from Cairo. As a 'special correspondent', Moorehead's job was to turn the news into long stories with the colour and shape that could grab readers and explain the overall situation. Chester Wilmot, then a correspondent for the ABC and later the author of the classic *The Struggle for Europe*, seems to have thought Moorehead was a little too comfortable at HQ. In a letter home to Australia he wrote, 'The test which I apply is this... "Could I face it, if I had to sit beside a man who took [part] in that action and listen to my broadcast"?' He doubted if Moorehead could pass such a test:

With Montgomery in the desert. Clifford is second from the left.

I know that most correspondents think military knowledge is an embarrassment – they prefer to write in blissful ignorance ... Alan [Moorehead]
writes a very readable story – but his stories have only a casual acquaintance with the truth. I believe that truth is more dramatic than
fiction – especially if you get the whole truth.

Moorehead didn't let fact-checking slow him down, it's true; as Clifford
put it later, his friend's 'approach to detail is artistic rather than historical'.
Moorehead was certainly capable of improvising an atmosphere of eyewitness from second-hand accounts. Having missed the evacuation of
Crete in 1941, for instance, he was obliged to file a few 'magic carpet' stories patched together from communiqués and second-hand reports.
During the thirty-hour battle for Chania, he told readers, the hand-to-
hand fighting was 'indescribable' – which was hardly surprising since he
was trying to describe it from an office in Cairo.

I picture him at daily military briefings in Cairo's Immobilia Building
as the Desert War rolled on, spilling crumpled cables of congratulation
each time he pulls his cigarettes out of his tunic pocket. What did the
newcomers make of their acknowledged leader as he lolled there in the
best chair, nodding familiarly at the general, murmuring something to
him about lunch when the conference was over. Perhaps there *was* a new

swagger in his step; perhaps his frank interest in success could have been dialled down a little.

It is also striking how smoothly 'Front-Line Moorehead' seems to have won the confidence of so many high-ups. By mid-1941, for instance, he and Lucy were in the habit of lunching with Eighth Army Corps commanders 'Strafer' Gott and Willoughby Norrie. In early November Lucy began working as private secretary to General Auchinleck, who had replaced Wavell that summer; her appointment gave rise to much muttering among rival pressmen about unfair access to inside information. Clive James's observation that Moorehead's 'renowned social mobility was employed mainly among the upper classes' sounds about right. Moorehead found it easy to talk 'with men of unusual talent' and didn't mind telling you about it. If he's not getting along tremendously with Admiral Cunningham in Malta, he's dining with the Governor of Cyprus in his splendid residence, or talking tactics with Auchinleck during a post-prandial stroll in the general's rose garden. He returned from one such lunch, Clifford wrote in his diary, 'very pleased with himself'.

This air of determination – ruthlessness, for those who didn't take to him – especially chafed with Australians, who were often struck by the accent, all the proof you needed that Moorehead was bent on becoming more English than the English. Moorehead was pointed out to Patrick White in Barce. 'Here I only brushed up against the professional reputation; it was years before I met the man and found him the waxwork so many successful Australians become.' (White, admittedly, could find an unkind word for anyone.) Moorehead's near-death experience in Libya may have had got him mentioned in dispatches, but it irked an old friend from Melbourne University, Lieutenant Allan Fleming, who happened to be in command of some armoured cars which found themselves fighting off the ambush. 'I could read in Alan's eyes the opening of his dispatch, "I was first into Benghazi,"' Fleming wrote later. 'For Alan to get himself into this "I was first" situation, one of our men was killed. I had a rather sour outlook on him after that.'

Moorehead had tried not to think about Australia since he left six years earlier, but his native land had, disconcertingly, come to find *him*, in the form of the Australian 9th and 6th divisions and the correspondents sent out to report on their feats. There was Fleming in Barce; later Chester Wilmot at Beda Fomm. A large-spirited man, Wilmot shamed his late-arriving competitors by freely sharing his scoop on the collapse of the Italian Tenth Army, complete with helpful map references. There were other old friends from home working as correspondents, including John Hetherington from the Melbourne *Herald* – who remembered years after that they used to call Moorehead 'the little tick'. I could find no evidence that Moorehead sought out their company in Cairo.

Perhaps there were advantages to his split loyalty. 'As an Australian living abroad,' he wrote in *A Year of Battle*,

> I had had many arguments about [the Australian troops]. I had tried (quite unsuccessfully) to explain to Englishmen that the Australians' manner was the sign of their independence and the freedom of their way of life and that some of their physical vigour might not come amiss in England. To the Australians I tried (even more unsuccessfully) to point out that the Englishman's voice and reserve did not indicate animosity or contempt or weakness, and that some of the Englishman's quiet mental tenacity might not come amiss in Australia.

Yet when you audit the *African Trilogy* for patriotic sentiment it's surprising to see how little Moorehead writes about his countrymen, especially considering the substantial part they played in the campaigns.

§

As the days went on in Cairo, I felt less and less desire to go out at all. Every morning as I headed off with a bustling itinerary in mind I was stunned afresh – as though it hadn't been exactly the same yesterday – by the brilliant heat, the choking exhaust and noise of the traffic, the pedestrians milling in impenetrable thickets. I longed for the dim quiet of indoors, any indoors: a museum, a mosque or a hotel lobby. When I did get out, my Moorehead goggles sensitised me to some aspects of the terrain, but blurred much of what was right in front of me. I was so caught up trying to channel the spirit of my quarry in the Carlton, for instance, that it took me several days to see that the rubble heap on the roof just across from my window, at which I gazed every morning wondering how I might include it in my book, was not an exotic detail of squalor but someone's *house*. A large family was living in that rubble, behind the belts and cranes of the elevator works. Once you saw it, you couldn't not see it. It was a makeshift home of old bricks and tin sheeting, with rooms subdivided by sheets pegged to string, a giant plastic tub of washing (how did they fill it, I wondered?), an aerial, and at night I could dimly make out from deep inside the structure the blue flicker of a TV screen, evidently powered by electricity tapped from the elevator head and run in on loops of black wire.

Still, Cairo had been daunting for visitors in the early 1940s too. It was then probably the second most important city in the British world. Soldiers, attachés and diplomats and their families were blowing in from everywhere, from places like Scandinavia, Chungking or Delhi. Officers, wrote the already renowned adventurer and Arabist Freya Stark, would 'salute you unexpectedly on the terrace of Shepheard's or the Continental'. Flats were offered for rent in the *Egyptian Mail* at scandalously inflated rates. The febrile glamour is what everyone remembered.

White women were almost as scarce in Cairo as in the desert – they 'were outnumbered a hundred to one', Moorehead wrote, 'and even that remaining one was on the point of being evacuated' – but if an officer could find one to ask, there was always a show on the rooftop terrace of the Continental or an open-air cabaret down by the river with low lighting, a band with the trumpeter streaming sweat, and a waiter in black tie and fez serving good champagne. A strange air of nostalgia for this world was in the air already, even before it was threatened by Rommel. Perhaps because he was a newcomer, Moorehead could see right away that on a broader scale, nostalgia was virtually a war aim in 1940. North Africa would be, among other things, a battle to preserve a geopolitics and a view of the world that was unlikely to survive no matter what happened in the desert.

Moorehead felt unwell a lot of the time. He was smoking endless cigarettes. Like everyone else, he suffered from exhausting stomach complaints. The crowded city could be wearying, too, though rich in human comedy. Simply boarding a train at the chaotic Ramses Station, for instance, was a feat achieved only in spite of all the people determined to help you. 'As your taxi pulled up,' Moorehead wrote:

> three or four Egyptian porters flung themselves inside, tore your luggage out and disappeared with it into the crowd ... On your way to the ticket office you were offered in turn by the vendors a fly-whisk, an officer's stick, a pornographic magazine, a glass of yellow syrup, a lottery ticket, a bar of partly unused chocolate and a booklet on how to avoid paying income tax.

(That 'partly unused chocolate' is an especially nice touch, concealed in the palm of the sentence until almost the last moment.) But the extreme poverty was a culture shock. Mutual incomprehension and distrust made interactions with ordinary Egyptians difficult. 'Alan and I drove out along the road south-west of the Nile to photograph some Egyptiania,' Clifford wrote in his diary in July '41. 'We managed to line up various picturesque girls, goatherds, old women, floundering water buffaloes, date palms, et cetera. But even in the country the revolting Egyptians flocked around yelling for baksheesh, trying to sell us their women and generally behaving in a thoroughly abject way.'*

Moorehead didn't disown these attitudes later. Egypt, he thought, was no advertisement for British rule. But everywhere he and his British generation went in Africa and the Middle East, he wrote in *A Late Education*, 'we remained on what we liked to think of as "British soil". Like the children of very wealthy parents it seemed quite natural to us that we should occupy the best houses and hotels, that we should have at our command cars, motor launches, servants and the best food, best hotels, etc.' It was how things were. Jan Morris – then Lieutenant James Morris, another wartime traveller – has referred to it as 'a spirit of imperial arrogance'. 'I felt,' he wrote, 'like most British people my age, that I was born to a birthright of supremacy; out I went to exert that supremacy.'

In 2011 the Continental wasn't open, and you couldn't visit Shepherd's

---

* This awful line is entirely out of character. Among the very few who made an effort to learn some Arabic, Clifford was, Moorehead attests, 'much kinder and gentler than I was in his dealings with the Egyptians.'

Hotel anymore. That essential item in the memory inventory of wartime Cairo, with its storied Long Bar, its garden planted with exotic flowers, its little zoo, burned to the ground in 1956 during the Suez Crisis, along with all the other British fantasies of postwar suzerainty in the Middle East. But those days weren't that hard to imagine. From the roof of the Nile Hilton you could look down at barges strung with ropes of electric lights jitterbugging in sync with distantly throbbing music. And there were relics that had been preserved in one way or another, like the Windsor bar, and perhaps certain rituals, too. Breakfast at the Carlton, for instance, which comprised a boiled egg and a toothsome croissant the size of a hat, and was served by a very old and formal gentleman in fez and waistcoat. He moved with an exquisite lack of haste, and managed to radiate such a long-suffering contempt for both me and his tasks that his carriage of the tea tray from kitchen to table was a kind of performed critique of the colonial legacy. And on Gezira Island the Club still stood, sprinklers shimmering spray onto its luminous green lawns.

§

Once baby John was born in the American hospital in Cairo, the Mooreheads kept a modest profile in the social whirl that was British Cairo. Sometimes they entertained at home. People seem to have played an extraordinary amount of bridge in those days – leave a few people alone for a moment in 1941 and they'll have whipped out the cards and dealt a fresh rubber. The Mooreheads resumed cordial relations with Geoffrey Cox, who was in Cairo; both Alan and Lucy became friendly with Freya Stark. Their social circle included Geoffrey Keating, Eddie Ward and many other names that would fill the visitors' book in Porto Ercole twenty years hence. Christopher Buckley enters Moorehead's world about now, too. The *Daily Telegraph*'s correspondent was a classicist – he once referred to Moorehead and Clifford as 'the Orestes and Pylades of the desert war' – who wrote gloriously recondite prose, and was impatient with those he considered stupid. But the war thrilled him. He was apparently fearless, and he played bridge. With the addition of Buckley, 'Mutt and Jeff' now became 'The Trio' – though Buckley naturally preferred 'triumvirate' – a contemporary legend revered and resented, often simultaneously, by other less senior, less favoured correspondents.*

§

Towards the end of July 1941, Moorehead started writing *Mediterranean Front* in the living room of the first-floor flat on Gezira Island.

He had just turned thirty. Till now, 'I had been a non-entity among the average,' he wrote in the 1960s. 'I had no reputation, no money, no connections and no particular prospects. Then all at once it seemed that everything had conspired to help me.'

In the desert he'd gotten into the habit of typing his dispatches at night; a book seemed to call for a more considered technique. He got up very early in the morning and in the dark cool of the living room, while their Egyptian cook Sulieman fumbled pots in the kitchen, produced, mostly in longhand, between 2000 and 2500 words a day, sometimes working for ten or twelve hours at a stretch. On the very first morning of work, Clifford was summoned from his room by the racket of Moorehead's pre-dawn typing, and was startled to learn that his friend – and professional nemesis – was now, damn it all, writing a book.

Moorehead could be high-strung and demanding when a book was in the works, but these were probably the best writing conditions of his life. He had a publisher – from several suitors, including Victor Gollancz, Moorehead had chosen Hamish Hamilton, whose offer of a £150 advance was the largest. Moorehead also had a lot to say, and he had a ready-made audience eager to hear it. Essentially a 'pouring out of personal experiences', *Mediterranean Front* proved a relatively easy book to write. 'As war correspondents we were constantly beset by feelings of inadequacy. It seemed to us impossible to describe the things we were observing within the narrow limits of our daily messages,' he wrote later. Now he had a chance to tell the full story, 'to make a pattern, to draw deductions, to indicate a beginning, a middle and an end'. The work continued so well and so fast

---

* This 'Trio' label has always sounded faintly silly to me – a bit *Dad's Army*, a bit music-hall. I can't imagine anyone actually using it in conversation, especially with panzers in the vicinity. But it seems that they did.

Moorehead had managed to get most of it done before seeking Christiansen's blessing, which he duly gave: 'As you've been a good boy will give you permission to publish book.' Seventy years later the exhilaration is still palpable in its pages. It was a book that was written on a power surge of revealed talent, and its effortless confidence and style set the tone for the two others that would follow: *A Year of Battle* (1943) and *The End in Africa* (1943).

§

Much of the time in Cairo I spent in Groppi's Garden Café, a survivor from the war years that is, for that reason, name-checked in all the guidebooks. The garden is sunken and tiled; there are cane chairs with tables with glass tabletops and several beautiful big trees busy with dusty little birds and tiny leaves that gently fall from the air into your water glass. It's all over-looked now by a half-derelict ten-storey slab building with broken windows through which men can occasionally be glimpsed moving about with plastic sacks of stuff and planks balanced on their shoulders, but the garden has blessed breezes, especially in the late afternoon, and so I spent a few late afternoons there with my copy of *African Trilogy*. I'd brought it with me with the notion of seasoning its pages in the dry-spiced African air in which it had been conceived. There were 692 of those densely printed pages in my copy. They were chased with rubbed-out pencil pressings, marginal exclamations, dog-ear wrinkles, scribbled cross-references and underlinings: the private cipher of the obsessive. I'd now been annotating this book for at least as long as the campaigns it describes had taken to fight.

I'd read the trilogy maybe three times before. When Moorehead finally got his hands on a copy of *Mediterranean Front* in February 1942 – two earlier consignments had been sunk en route – the new author spent most of the day, Clifford noted drily in a letter, absorbed in reading it. But what sort of story was it today, in Groppi's, now that the onrush of the present had faded out of its pages? Reading it again, I hardly noticed the battles. What I saw was the adventure story it contains, a story of travels through a world summoned to life in sweeps of lightly amassed detail. And – strangely – freedom. The ordinary soldier in North Africa, wrote one ordinary soldier, moved through Cairo and the desert with 'the appetite of a tourist but the opportunity of a prisoner'. Not Moorehead. In this time of total war, of blockades, conscription, movement orders, border crossings festooned with barbed wire, he had a golden ticket. One gets the 'eerie feeling', wrote the *New York Times*' reviewer of *Eclipse* (1945) 'that he wandered untrammeled from one end of the war to the other': so long as he kept filing reports, the *Express* was happy to let him have his head. In the twelve months after his arrival in Egypt, he covered by his own estimate 30,000 miles across Africa and the Middle East. By 1943 he had visited Kenya, Somalia and Abyssinia; he had flown in bombing raids over Eritrea and the Red Sea; he had toured the Eastern Mediterranean in Admiral Cunningham's flagship; and made his way to Cyprus, Iraq, Syria and Palestine. He made a special trip to Ceylon and India – where he and his colleague, Richard Busvine, secured personal interviews with Gandhi, Nehru, Jinnah and Lord Linlithgow – and flew the length of Africa in a flying boat, before making a brisk tour of America and its military factories.

Some of this remarkable *laissez-passer* came with the job. But the energy for it, the focused wanderlust, seems to come from his nature, the same restlessness that had him climbing the walls in Gibraltar. And getting around a world at war required energy, endurance, the ability to just shut your eyes. Once Moorehead was obliged to tranship between navy destroyers in a whale boat in heavy seas; he ended up desperately clinging to the rope netting while waves repeatedly smacked the whaler into the destroyer's side. (At the ship's railing, the crew watched his landlubber's strife with lively interest: 'I don't see you taking any notes,' the captain cheerily boomed through a loud-hailer.)

But flying was the worst. Moorehead hated it, and in rough weather he hated it even more – 'I just give up and lie back, pea-green in the face.' One cross-Atlantic trip involved lying prostrate on the floor of a Liberator for twelve hours, 'buttoned up to the eyebrows' in a flying suit, heavy boots, parachute, oxygen mask and life-jacket, and tightly wedged among fifteen others similarly encumbered. But flying was essential to his work, and he did a huge amount of it during the war, especially in North Africa, scrambling for the last seat on an oversubscribed Dakota, Liberator, Glen Martin or flying boat. In baking tin passenger sheds in the remotest parts of East

Africa and the Middle East, he cobbled together routes to get to where he needed to be. His willingness to push his way to the front of a queue served him well, but he still spent days at a time languishing in all kinds of strange places 'kicking his heels' waiting for a seat out, surviving on whatever rations he could pick up – perhaps a tin of bully beef whose contents, Buckley once observed, 'are apt to wear a peculiarly corpse-like aspect', especially on a hot day. At Khartoum Zoo, for instance, he sat out a long wait reading among deer and pelicans, and was startled one afternoon to look up and see General de Gaulle anonymously feeding the ducks. Marooned without transport at Jijiga aerodrome in Ethiopia, Moorehead helped a squadron of South African pilots in their mess drink a case of newly arrived whisky and 'slept blissfully that night on the camp bed of a pilot who had crashed the day before'. Quite often no one knew exactly where he was. He hardly knew himself. On the Sudan–Eritrea border, near the Italian redoubt at Kassala, he dined one night at a camp where all the talk was of a giant crocodile someone had just shot. The evening was spent listening to the BBC on a wireless set perched in a thorn bush.

Sometimes the war felt like a leisurely retracing of old Imperial routes. In late 1940 Moorehead was with a group of correspondents heading up the Nile from Khartoum towards the fighting in Ethiopia by paddle steamer. There was an authentically Victorian tempo to this trip; time puddled as they progressed with 'deadly excruciating slowness' up the river. Moorehead passed the days on deck, stripped to the waist in the wet heat, slumped in a wicker chaise, reading Churchill's *The River War*, the writer-soldier's account of the expedition that culminated in the Battle of Omdurman in 1898. Everywhere he went in Africa Moorehead found tableaux of semi-comic Imperial senescence he couldn't resist describing. Nairobi in 1940 was 'so improbable a place, such a survival from some lost world', so faithful to stereotype, he could hardly contain his writer's glee. 'The lovers *are* frequently tall, good-looking counts and earls; the ladies more often than not move glamorously about in Paris evening gowns and furs. They *do* drink champagne, they *do* dance through the night occasionally on soft-lit terraces ... The men *do* go out on safari with beaters and servants and emerge later from the forest bearing the skins of savage animals.'

India, 1942

More often, though, the picture of colonial life is a picture of entropy: of enervation, decay. The great story Moorehead's *African Trilogy* tells is that of an empire's last desperate fight for survival – *his* Empire, the one he'd grown up in, hearing stories of Gallipoli, reading Rider Haggard and Kipling, singing 'God Save the Queen' in the crackling heat of a Melbourne schoolyard in late summer. His mixed feelings about that inheritance haunt the whole triumphant tale.

A photograph from the chronological centre of the war: Delhi, March 1942, a month after the fall of Singapore. Moorehead is perched on a bench of decorative marble, fresh from lunch with the Viceroy, perhaps. He is in tropical kit: shorts, socks pulled up to the knee. His feet don't reach the floor and his sun helmet seems too big for him. The most famous war correspondent in Britain looks like a boy trying out his father's chair, wearing his father's hat.

§

'We saw the most astonishing things,' Moorehead wrote in one of his last *Express* columns after the war: 'giraffe stampeding in the Abyssinian valleys, destroyers chasing U-boats off Gibraltar, the monstrous jet-black night of the mid-Atlantic (ourselves a tiny lighted steel box in endless space), Germans and Italians fleeing in panic in the Libyan Desert, and great fires along the Rhine.'

As a traveller, Moorehead's responsiveness to place is not existential, like DH Lawrence's; it doesn't have that mystical intensity. It's not like Patrick Leigh Fermor's, either, with its lyrical raconteurship, its 'truffled style and dense plumage', in Lawrence Durrell's phrase. Moorehead's prose is plainer. The author seems a plainer chap, too. Some thought Moorehead arrogant, or conceited, but he wasn't arrogant on the page. The narrator of the *African Trilogy* is wry and alive to the absurdity of things, including himself. Like many bookish people on the home front, JB Priestley was contemptuous of the emerging 'cult' of the war correspondent, but in his review of *Eclipse* it was precisely Moorehead's modesty that he singled out for praise. Another reviewer called him 'a very modest man'. In *A Late Education*, too, Moorehead seems to find just the right weight of authorial presence: he's an everyman who happens to be on the spot, offering the reader a stream of sense impressions of a world undergoing violent transformation.

Every wartime journey Moorehead made was one from which there might be no return. Is that why, paradoxically, his writing is so responsive, and sounds so free? Who knew when it was going to end? Roberto Bolaño says somewhere that 'genuine travel requires travellers who have nothing to lose'. Moorehead had plenty to lose, but an infinity of sensations to gain; his writing would never be as flushed with the communicated joy of seeing as it was when each new place might be the last he ever saw.

Sometimes, Clifford noted, the warcos' travels felt 'more like *tourisme* than war'. The fact that the fighting took place on the same battlegrounds three years running probably contributed to this air of unreality. The scale of the fighting had grown enormously since the first sweep west to Al Aghcila in late 1940. By early 1942 Wavell's 'little piratical army' of 36,000 troops was 500,000 strong. The forlorn little desert outposts now thronged with people and equipment. They had seen enough since the war started to feel pangs of regret for the early days. 'It's like doing a Cook's tour of the battlefields,' Moorehead remarked as he contemplated the very spot where he had nearly been killed in the ambush a year before.

But it only felt like tourism sometimes. Mostly it felt like a journey into a world beyond reason, where, Clifford wrote, the 'mind jibbed at trying to assess the significance and horror of it all', and language simply couldn't follow. A 'suave phrase' like *heavy casualties*, Clifford wrote in his book *Three Against Rommel*, contains 'an unthinkable amount of agony and tragedy'. The words *heavy shell-fire* 'cannot even faintly hint at the tight, taut feeling you get while you are waiting for the shell to come, and the whining, whimpering scream of it, and the nerve-jarring crack of the explosion, and the whirring and the tinkling of the fragments flying round you, and the quick pang of the relief that that one did not hit you, and the immediate realisation that the next one may'. Bouncing forward one day in November 1941 during the battle of Sidi Rezegh, they crossed the smouldering battlefield, passing corpses and other broken, wasted things, and argued all the while 'rather acrimoniously' about Jane Austen. They paused to examine an intact-looking Afrika Korps truck. Its driver, a blond boy, was still gripping the wheel, though his brains were spilt out on the seat beside him. On the ground they found a postcard from the German's mother, which promised, in Clifford's translation, that 'she would bake him another cake when she could, but there was nothing in the house for the moment'.

It could have been either of them, after all. Correspondents did not often face the mortal danger of front-line troops; but the front was never far away, and for years at a time. 'I don't think Alex and I ever approached it with any other feeling than that of dread ... nearly always it was dread and nothing else, and the joy we had in coming away was so great it was like a sudden release from physical pain.' Days after they saw the truck and its poor dead occupant, Moorehead and Clifford escaped capture during a German counterattack at Sidi Rezegh. A number of colleagues, including Eddie Ward of the BBC, a lifelong friend of Moorehead's, were captured where they lay in their slit trenches huddled in terror while a tank battle raged around them. At a base camp once, a colleague who had heard that Moorehead had been killed expressed nothing more than mild surprise at finding him alive. 'Was I really as hard-boiled as all this?' Moorehead wondered. Maybe he was just too honest about how exciting it all was: just as he'd savoured the 'ghoulish release' provided by the bomb-shattered *Deutschland* in Gibraltar. 'It was difficult not to enjoy it,' Clifford remarked of a shattering night-time bombardment of Tobruk, 'just as one cannot help enjoying the sight of a house burning even if one knows the owners.' The extravagance of the destruction could be mesmerising. Watching the plague of violence return, year after year, to Barce and Bardia and all the hardscrabble colonist towns with their lonely sugar-cube houses and starveling crops, sometimes tipped the correspondents into a kind of end-times lyricism. A German workshop overrun on the road into Tobruk in late 1941 seemed to Moorehead 'like some Doré etching of a forgotten and spellbound village'. A bombardment of Bardia takes place in a scene of Turneresque eventide, as Moorehead paints it, a day 'full of warm, yellow, winter sunlight. Now in the evening, like flights of migrating birds, British bombers kept sliding across a sunset magnificently red. And far into the night, the red fires in Bardia expanded and continued the sunset.'

§

In March 1943 there was another unhappy flight, this one out of a muddy airfield in Algiers. It was a mystery flight for the planeload of pressmen: they hadn't been told where they were going. Gibraltar and Ceuta passed under the wing. The destination was actually Lyautey, in Free French Morocco, but the pilot muddled his bearings and descended with mistaken confidence into Larache, a Moroccan harbour town under the control of neutral Spain. The error was only discovered a few hundred feet off the ground, when anti-aircraft fire began splattering into the plane. Bullets flashed through the cabin. While the pilots jigged away from the *ack-ack*, everyone flung themselves down, 'sprawled in a confused mass of arms, bodies and legs on the floor near the tail, some of them clutching parachute packs to their chests, some wedging themselves under the benches'. But the Canadian correspondent seated next to Moorehead was already hit in the temple, and 'blood and grey brains were pumping out of the wound and spilling down his cheeks'. With others, Moorehead did what he could to staunch the bleeding and wash away the gore, but the young man who'd been chatting and munching bully beef sandwiches half an hour earlier was beyond help.

When they landed, the surviving correspondents were bussed to Casablanca, and the war's biggest presser so far. I found Moorehead in agency photographs of the conference. Clear as day, there he is: one of thirty reporters perched on the damp grass in the garden of the Anfa Hotel – 'irresistibly like a Sunday school treat with the children gathered at the feet of their two school-mistresses,' he wrote – within spit-ball distance of FDR and Churchill, Giraud and de Gaulle. He's smiling politely down at his notes in one shot, as though at a presidential *bon mot*; in another, cigarette in mouth and giving the president a considering look.

This was the 'unconditional surrender conference', as Churchill urged the reporters to describe it, but that was all the censors would pass. The journalists weren't allowed to tell their readers anything about the limp handshake of mutual distaste performed for the cameras by de Gaulle, leader of the Free French, and Giraud, the rehabilitated collaborator. When it was over, all the journos were herded into another room at the hotel to pound away at their typewriters. In the photos, I looked for signs of weariness, or traces of damage. But in Moorehead's face, still so startlingly young, there's no hint of the postwar *cafard* or a descent into the materialist void. He looks relaxed and focused, like a man who has found his rightful place and knows exactly what he's doing.

Yet this was the low-point of Moorehead's long war. Having missed the climactic battle of El Alamein – granted a leave-pass by Christiansen, he was on a working holiday in the US at the time, marvelling at the suprahuman scale of its iron smelters and munitions factories – he had rejoined the war in Tunisia, soon after Operation Torch landed US troops in Morocco and Algeria in November 1942. Nothing was the same. With the arrival of the Americans, the war's scale had been transformed. Unfamiliar new equipment was arriving in Algiers Harbour in gargantuan quantities, and new and unwelcome bureaucracies were set up to manage it all. Control of the news flow was being centralised. Pooling, an arrangement under which a few randomly selected reporters would witness an operation and then share their copy with other papers, became commonplace. One has to 'condition oneself to a war that is run politically', he wrote to Lucy after a run-in with those bureaucrats, but until he did, and he never really did, red tape left him with a feeling of 'distress and irritation'.

Perhaps, too, Moorehead saw his great days in the desert, his *annus mirabilis*, fading into history's margins. The old days of the knights' tournament in empty space were a quaint memory. Tunisia would be a vicious, sodden slog through mountains. Civilians were caught up in the maelstrom, along with their pretty, proud old towns. No longer a distant pillar of dust rising on the horizon, or a red line on the map, the enemy was right there, across the valley from you, with his carefully ranged artillery and his binoculars trained on your jeep.

In the third volume of the trilogy, *The End in Africa*, Moorehead describes his visit to a brigade headquarters in a cowshed on the plain below Longstop Hill – officers red-eyed with fatigue and shock, silent staring casualties laid out on a wrecked tennis court behind – then a few paragraphs later, he's moved up the hill and, looking back, sees the cowshed disintegrate in a shell burst. 'There had been so much killing all around here that the only emotion I felt was: "I'm glad I'm not still in the cowshed."' In another scene, he shares a dugout with some exhausted soldiers near the summit of Longstop. One asked him: 'Are you the bastard that wrote in the paper that we're getting poached eggs for breakfast every morning?'* The summit was finally taken by the Argyles in late April 1943 after a famous and especially bloody sequence of attacks. Major Anderson, a 25-year-old who had assumed command when the battalion CO was killed, led bayonet charges into a series of enemy machine-gun pits. He was later awarded the VC. 'Anderson, to look at, was not very different from the other officers in this battalion,' Moorehead noted mordantly when it was over, 'except he was still alive and most of the others were dead or wounded.'

Longstop Hill was a famous fight at the time, another terrible battle: bloody, costly. And Moorehead's account is another little gem of its genre. In a few lines he has you there on the hill with him, breathing the drifting

---

* Not *exactly* what the man said: 'Every second word was an adjective I have not quoted here.' And no, Moorehead wasn't that particular bastard.

cordite, stepping around the strange flash burns mortar rounds left in the hillside wheat fields. Moorehead had developed a tremendous facility for work like this. But he seems to be only half-focused on the daily firefights. His pocketbook is full of unrealised ideas for features on strategic questions and the misunderstandings between the Americans and the British, the difficulty of conveying to the home front and its armchair strategists the grisly truth. 'It is useless to picture these men who were winning the war for you as immaculate and shining young heroes agog with enthusiasm for the Cause,' he wrote. 'They had seen too much dirt and filth for that. They hated the war ... the real degrading nature of war was not understood by the public at home, and it never can be understood by anyone who has not spent months in the trenches or in the air or at sea.'

§

A month later, the war in Africa was over. For those who had been there at the start, there was an understandable note of nostalgia mixed in with the triumph. On 10 May Moorehead wrote: 'Here was the positive and absolute end of the Tunisian war, of Montgomery's 2000-mile march, of [Lieutenant-General] Anderson's six months' battle in the mountains, of the whole African war. And you will understand that after three years' campaigning it was an overflowing pleasure to see a handful of Montgomery's and Anderson's tanks and armoured cars going down the hill together before us to take Tunis and with it all Africa.'

Some of the old swing was back in his messages now. When it was time to leave, Moorehead and Clifford expertly looted supplies from a captured German store on Cape Bon. Into a Volkswagen, also pilfered, they piled their booty of cameras, clothes, binoculars, tinned food and fine wines. Military police in Algiers would confiscate whatever they couldn't consume, they knew, but who cared? It was the joy of looting that mattered. In the meantime, they set off for the three-day coastal drive to Algiers. It was beautiful weather. They put the car's windscreen down, paused to swim in the sea when it got too hot, and ate huge dinners in farmhouses in the evenings.

Now for Europe.

5

HANGING ON BY EYELIDS

clipse opens in August 1943, with the Trio following the leading platoons of the British 50th Division into Giardini, a mile-long strip of white-washed houses hugging the east coast of Sicily. After the success of the July landings, and the 'deep draught of triumph', as Buckley sonorously put it, of the first weeks of the campaign, progress had been slow. Moorehead missed the landings – he had been in London, taking a break from front-line reporting – and had only just arrived for the march north from Catania. The Germans were conducting a staged withdrawal up the coast, and like most of the places they left behind, Giardini was on fire. There was a sickly stink of burning chemicals, but no one much about. In the last few villages, they had found no sign of the enemy, just the usual skinny children crying out for *biscotti* and climbing like monkeys on any Sherman tank unwise enough to stop. While the riflemen edged carefully forward, Moorehead munched on sunwarmed grapes and watched smoke curling into the 'blaring cobalt blue' of the midday sky. There seemed to be no Germans in Giardini either, just a handful of stunned old people, and a few groups of Italian soldiers waving white flags and vainly trying to semaphore their surrender to a British gunboat circling just offshore. The Germans had gone, they said. No ambush. 'There was the usual hush over this gap between the advancing army and the retreating enemy,' Moorehead wrote. 'Everything goes to earth ... You smell the enemy. Here and there, for no explained reason, a house burns quietly and there is no one to quench it; it burns in a vacuum with not anyone to watch.' Carefully stepping around mines laid with clumsy haste in the macadam, the three correspondents followed the road to the far end of the village. From here, their objective lay in clear view: Taormina, 'one of the fairest sights in the Mediterranean ... A 1000-foot cliff laced with vines rises sheer from the sea and along the lip of its dizzy heights stand the great luxury hotels in their flowering gardens.'

The correspondents decided to go on ahead. Clifford led the way up the zigzag goat track. Some Italian machine gunners were dug in along the track, but they just wanted to surrender. Sobbing for breath, the correspondents advised them to throw their rifles down the cliff, then dragged themselves upwards into the brilliant heat. Above, they could see that people were gathering along the stone parapet of the piazza, 'making a queer staccato ululation that might have been a warning or a welcome'.

It was a welcome. The Trio collapsed at café tables on the main piazza; overjoyed proprietors rushed to fetch them 'English tea' and warm beer. Had they just captured one of the most romantic pleasure resorts of Europe? Well, not quite. To no one's surprise, it turned out that Geoffrey Keating had got there first. Now a major, and heading up the 160-strong Army Film and Photographic Unit, the Trio's old pal and fixer from the Western Desert had cycled into town a few hours earlier as if to a particularly promising picnic. Having ascertained that there were no Germans left, Keating negotiated a formal surrender over a bottle of champagne at the police station, and then enjoyed a personal tour of the Greek and Roman ruins before he cycled off again.

On the next day the Trio chose a villa from a range of baroque piles on offer. And then, as if by unspoken consensus, everyone in Moorehead's circle seemed to decide that it was time for a rest, a 'holiday out from the war'. The villa had several floors that stepped down the steep slope of the hill. Moorehead and Clifford installed themselves with Keating and the war artist Edward Ardizzone. Buckley found a room in the home of an urbane architect who lived across the street. It was a spectacular billet. Moorehead slept on a camp bed on the tiled terrace. When the sun woke him, rising 'through a green light over the Straits ... everything – the

Moorehead and Alexander Clifford, c.1941

ravines that tumbled down to the sea, the houses perching on the crests, the pine trees outside, and even the wine bottles left on the terrace from the previous night – was cast either into full light or full shadow'. The wife of the architect chaperoned her two delightful daughters on regular visits to lunch or soirees with dancing; a cook produced rabbit stews from the provisions the men brought back from afternoon foraging trips in the car. Lunches could last all afternoon and spontaneous dinner parties filled with a changing cast of blow-ins from past and future campaigns. The wine flowed, the conversation was learned and generous, then drunkenly argumentative. 'Topics began with violent generalizations and ran quickly into abstracts,' Moorehead wrote in *Eclipse*. 'Manners became everything and behaviour nothing. We made a hundred extravagant sublimations on any theme – food and chess, painting and gambling, books and wine, music and clothes.' Luxuriating in 'an infinity of days here in the sun', everyone could forget where they'd been and take a break from where they were going.

This little bacchanal of talk and drink and dances on the terrace marks a climacteric in the story of Moorehead's war: it's the start of a new struggle to make sense of it all, a slow but unmistakeable turn from the question of how battles were fought to why. And that meant a new book, and a new *kind* of book. 'I have an idea for the next book so fragile and reeking that

I scarcely dare to write about it,' Moorehead wrote to Lucy six months after this.

> It's a book about our summer school in Taormina and our winter school in Naples. Alex and Geoffrey and I have really succeeded in setting up two extraordinary salons in these two places in these six months ... It is a compression and a cross-section of the war ... The book must begin quietly with us walking ahead of the Army into Taormina and then I have all my characters and situations ready made. I want to write it.

The End in Africa had been published by then, and the reviews had again been very good. But they didn't assuage the doubts Moorehead felt about the value of his work. A letter about the book from Evelyn Montague, who had been Africa correspondent for the *Manchester Guardian* before he was invalided home to Scotland with tuberculosis, gave those doubts a concrete shape. 'You're too good a man to be slipshod and invent atmosphere which you have some reason to think might once have existed, and talk cock about not caring about minor details,' he wrote. Montague thought Moorehead's first book had been 'plain but good', and his second 'sophisticated, amusing and not so good'; despite patches of brilliance, however, this third one was 'fretful, worried ... and bad'. 'I've watched your work going off nearly all this year; do come home and not write a book – get the tangles out of yourself, give yourself time to relax and take stock and get your ideas sorted and your nerves in some sort of shape.' Moorehead greatly admired Montague and perhaps his opinion carried the gravitas that attaches to the mortally ill. Hearing it straight like this left him winded, he told Lucy. But Montague's critique was also somehow a release from grinding worry, permission to start again with something different, and better.

That beautiful, trembling idea for a book, the dream-perfect book every writer has dreamed, became *Eclipse*, Moorehead's fourth and final narrative memoir of the war. It was to be a work of atmosphere as much as fact, he wrote in its foreword, 'of hopes and fears and miseries: the truths underneath the more obvious noises and movement of the war'. By the time he wrote that, the dream had long since been abandoned. The events

Eclipse narrated – the final collapse of the Third Reich – were just too sprawling and disordered for such a delicate scheme. On publication, *Eclipse* was acclaimed, though – and largely for those parts dealing with Normandy and after. But it was the first twenty pages I'd always loved: the part in Sicily, in Taormina, where the war recedes, and for a moment we can see its recorders relaxing behind the scenes of history, pausing to try to comprehend how far they'd come.

§

It had been two years since my trip to Egypt when I got to Taormina. I was making my way to Moorehead's house at Porto Ercole again. But the chance to see the place that loomed so large in Moorehead's memory of the war years was too good to pass up.

The village was quite different to the diorama I'd constructed in my mind – in that weirdly emphatic way of real places. There was no hope of finding the right villa, but there was no need, either: my hotel was in roughly the right spot, set on a steep hillside about ten minutes' hike from the Corso, Taormina's narrow and gently winding main street. Like Moorehead's villa, and like most of the grand old buildings in the village, my hotel overlooked Mount Etna – it could hardly help it. The goat track they had scrambled up – which I intended to walk – was still there, too. And the cliff-top piazza was exactly where it should be. Only now it was prosperous and peaceful. No 'frightful smell of shit' that Ardizzone noted when he and Keating were mobbed by overjoyed residents that first afternoon.

I spent a couple of days idling receptively in shaded spots, waiting for the landscape to reveal something extra, to add another dimension to my favourite twenty pages of *Eclipse*. Taormina felt like a museum devoted to the living history of the European holidaymaker. While gazing out at sumptuous views of sea and mountain and ruins, you can browse racks of postcards showing sumptuous views of sea and mountain and classical ruins. All 'disgustingly pretty', Ardizzone called it. Other postcards were black-and-white snaps of *la dolce vita* 1960s-style, in all its aspirational nostalgia: images of other peoples' holidays, of those long-gone or famous folk who have also ridden the funicular down to the rocky islets and grottos, who have swum and lunched in years past. The heat was stupendous. In the piazza, people flopped with half-folded maps in corners of shade, staring dazedly at the baking cobblestones.

I felt conspicuously unrelaxed, anhedonic even, as I tramped around trying to map Moorehead's time here to the terrain. I hiked upwards, mostly, up the rocky peak. Each day brought the kind of dazing sunlight that makes you duck your head, and I ended up in a kind of trudging trance, squirting glossy orange pulp from fallen prickly pears and scattering countless sunbaking lizards, little ones with lime-green speckles on their backs.

At the top of each knotty staircase the view became magnificent and vertiginous in a slightly different way. But there was always Etna, vast and distant, and yet somehow right there in front of you; and the sea, pearl grey in the milky light of the afternoons, the surface creased here and there by the breezes or the trailing wake of a yacht.

Above Taormina itself is Castelmona, a tiny village built on a second, even steeper crag of rock. No wonder grand conversation took flight so easily. Each view was so vast that you could, if you wanted to, and if you had a clear day, trace a mental map of the entire British campaign in Sicily. It wasn't hard to see how you might, given a rest from fear and constant work, feel your spirit expanding into all that space.

On the way back down I dawdled past the shops. The souvenir hustling – 'the business done in charms against the evil eye, hand-made lace and tiles of glazed pottery,' as Moorehead put it years later – was intense. Handmade lace was everywhere, and tiles, but no charms. Unless you counted the tremendous array of cocks on display in the shop windows: hundreds of penises, carved with careful realism, in beautiful polished wood.

As if this story wasn't male enough already.

§

On the second day at the villa Moorehead sent off two reports to the *Express*. Then he spent some sober hours composing a long, self-denunciatory letter to Lucy. There had been some bitter rows in London a week before. They had been apart for six months; in his letters during that time,

Moorehead had promised that they would settle down as a family for a while. But when they were reunited it was immediately apparent that her husband intended to get back to the front as soon as decently possible. He'd been 'callous' and 'indifferent' in London, he admitted; he'd acted like a bastard. 'What can I say? I can't forever ask you to go on and on waiting.' Moorehead then goes on to implore Lucy to forgive him. She is his great love and he can't imagine living without her. With all that off his chest, he spends a cheerful evening playing bridge under the palm-leaf pergola, with atmospherics provided by the off-stage rumble of British guns calibrating their range up north in Messina.

That terrace is the principal setting for Moorehead's 'summer school' in Taormina. My own hotel had a terrace that fit the part, and I sat out there some nights with my notes while the hotel cat gnawed placidly on a lizard as thick as my thumb. It wasn't at all hard to conjure up the 'infinity of days in the sun', and the rowdy evenings of the furlough. Much was drunk. Sometimes a little 'mariachi' band set up on a corner and sang some Sicilian folk songs with tremulous emotion. Moorehead sometimes recited from memory the love poems of John Donne. One night someone accidentally dropped a lit cigarette on Moorehead's bedroll, incinerating it. Everyone was in a mood to talk. For Moorehead conversation was a serious pleasure, and never more than now, with all the main characters of his war gathered together – Clifford, Buckley, Philip Jordan, Keating and Ardizzone. They solved all the problems of the world, or thought they did, which was close enough.

What they didn't talk about, it seems, were the terrible things they'd seen. Take Buckley, for instance, who found a discarded copy of *Barchester Towers* and spent his Taormina nights re-reading it 'with delight'. Barely a week had passed since he had crossed Primasole Bridge in a jeep and seen a lorry a few hundred yards ahead hit by a shell. The explosion flung the incinerated bodies of the lorry's occupants 'hither and thither all over the road and into the ditches on either side'. Buckley was renowned for his apparent imperviousness to fear. The only weapons that unnerved him were landmines. He was enjoying the war enormously. 'It is I know, not easy to justify ethically an exhilaration which comes from being in close proximity to a place where numbers of one's fellow creatures are being violently torn in pieces by lumps of flying metal,' he wrote in his memoir of the campaign. 'But the instinct is there; it is as old as Homer and the book of Genesis.' Back on the road to Catania, Buckley had gingerly descended from his own truck and proceeded on foot. 'We passed the burning lorry (I hadn't realised before that men can still go on burning for quite a time after they are dead), and plodded on through the glaring afternoon heat.'

That's as close as anyone in Moorehead's milieu gets to sounding disturbed by battle. To the modern reader raised on the truism that war is hell – and psychologically scarring for survivors – this apparent absence of psychological stress takes some adjusting to. It feels like an error in translation, perhaps related to the strangely jolly style of Moorehead's wartime in general. Those boy-scout shorts hitched high on the waist, for instance, which always looked insufficiently serious for a modern industrial war; or the Biggles-y lingo of baby-faced fighter-pilots chirping 'Toodle-pip!' as they taxied away towards the likelihood of horrific burns, wounds or death. Like Buckley, Moorehead was realistic about the business they were in. During a trip on a Royal Navy corvette earlier that year, for instance, he had been impressed to learn that one never claims a submarine kill without 'something very definite to show for it. A piece of human body preserved in the ship's refrigerator – that is the sort of evidence the Admiralty requires.' But none of them writes as though any of this might be too much to bear. When he reviewed *The Naked and the Dead* in 1949, Moorehead remarked that during the war 'a pattern of euphemisms' had usually been found for the experiences explicitly described in Mailer's novel. Euphemism was an aspect of self-censorship, of course, for the sake of soldiers' families and home-front morale. Perhaps it also became a kind of auto-suggestion that protected them from the unendurable.

§

Even during this hiatus in lovely Taormina, the war overshadowed everything. When they went down to the beach to swim and pick through baskets of red mullet for dinner, an endless convoy of lorries rumbled by on the coast road to Messina, where the Eighth Army was gathering to launch itself across the Messina Strait to the mainland. When Moorehead and Keating spent the blazing afternoon haggling for souvenirs in the bombed-out antiques shop in town, or drove out to make a sight-seeing tour of the villages around Etna, they found Sicilians still stunned by the turn events had taken in the past few weeks, but totally uninterested in the war. Finding Italians in this state – hungry, sullen, often friendly, indifferent to the fate of Europe – raised questions about the postwar world, a world that was gradually becoming easier to imagine.

On my last afternoon I went down to the Corso, sat at a café table right in the main piazza, and ordered a coffee. The prices listed on the tariff card suggested this was a reckless thing to do, but I needed to be right here. Moorehead had returned to Taormina in 1961 to write a travel piece for *Holiday* magazine. It's mostly a fairly undemanding tour of Sicily's attractions, but it contains one of the very few 'return to the battlefield' passages in his entire career. Moorehead describes how he leant against the wrought-iron parapet of the Piazza IX Aprile – about twenty metres from where I was sitting – and looked out at the ancient sea, and down the scrubby slope he'd scrambled up in August 1943. He felt like 'just another conquering hero cut down to the size of a normal, rather uninspiring tourist with a camera slung around his neck'. What was down there, now, for this middle-aged writer in peacetime?

> My friends and I – just three or four of us in our army uniforms – must have thought ourselves to be great men that day. But of how it felt to be there, the emotions one experienced, the things one said, the exact place, as it were, of this scene in one's personal history – all this had disappeared. It was as though one was remembering not oneself but some stranger, some character one had read about in a book.

It's only in the Greek theatre that it all comes back to him. 'The eternal stillness of the stones, the glimpses of gleaming sea through the open arches of the stage suddenly collapse time and the pleasure of reverie floods in: 'the feeling of delight I was experiencing now was precisely the same as that which I had experienced in 1943 ... If I were to return here another seventeen years hence precisely the same pleasure would be evoked, the same sense of the continuity rather than the loss of time.'

Tucked away in a travel piece full of pleasant sights and charming *osteria*, a few paragraphs of private pilgrimage: a return to a place impregnated with private meaning and feelings more intense than anything he will experience again.

The idea that, for good or bad, places retain traces of the things that have happened in them is implicit in so much of Moorehead's work, especially in his books about explorers and old wars. It's not a novel idea: it's what impels so many travellers and pilgrims. It was the reason I was here in the first place. I'd been down to Giardini earlier in the day. The town was cheerful enough on the beach side, with its café tables and sunbathers settling on the rocks to bake themselves. But on the long street behind, the endless road Moorehead and the others had walked in 1943 – seeing no one but one crazy old woman who 'yammered at us unmeaningly from her toothless gums' – time seemed to hang a bit heavier. The buildings pressed against the narrow street so that it was sunk in clammy shadow. It felt forlorn below the shuttered apartments, oddly quiet, a bit shabby.

There isn't much logic to the in-the-footsteps method. My idea was that if I followed the thread linking Moorehead's words to the places where he wrote them, I might, with some intuitive effort, some narrowing of the eyes, get a fuller imaginative sense of what his world felt like. Sometimes I got nothing – like in Paris. But the path back up to Taormina felt different. There are no vines now, no goats, but the track is still there, clearly rubbed into the weeds and baked brown grass. On the scrubby escarpment, I felt closer to the ground of the unfolding past. Those machine gunners Moorehead had stumbled by: one jittery trigger finger would have cut the story short right here: no books, no glorious 1960s, no stroke, no Moorehead Papers at the NLA. They were uniformed soldiers, but they were also just some Italian men and boys with aching haunches, maybe too excited to eat. The climb itself took longer to do than read about; it would have been even longer if you were worried about snipers and mines. And if you didn't know what was waiting for you at the end.

When I got to the top, things were abruptly normal again, and it was difficult to see the battlefield for all the Versace. I re-entered the world of gelati and sunglasses, people shouting into their phones and gesturing indignantly at no one, looking out at, but not seeing, the savage sparkle of the sea; and over there a salesman dreamily smacking his little gel orbs onto the pavement, picking them all up again after they'd recovered their globular shape, glancing around each time for potential customers.

It's easy to feel a traveller's nostalgia – or envy – for the distant past, and a time less homogenised and tour-packaged than ours. But I was delighted with Taormina. This felt as close as I'd got to the ordinary reality of Moorehead's wartime – the boredom, the uncertainty, but also his feeling of being thrillingly alive at a moment when history was out of its cage. Perhaps it was an illusion; but if so it was an illusion in the spirit of Moorehead's own growing preoccupation, from *Eclipse* onwards, with the bewildering fluidity of human time, and his sense that in places of intense experience, the past is never completely past.

I was sitting at the café looking at the implausible figure on the bottom of my bill when it started to rain. *Rain?* I jumped up. I'd turned off the Corso for the climb up to my hotel when the rain suddenly became more intense. I ducked into a doorway. The noise of it was incredible, a swarming roar on the roofs and in the trees. Up and down the street people were pinned in huddles under awnings and café brollies. There was a momentary let-up; then it came down in apocalyptic earnest. Rain boomed onto canvas awnings and gouts of water jumped knee-high from swarming puddles. People stood in doorways laughing and shrieking at the water ricocheting off walls and gutters. The length of the street was lost in a bright, seething haze. Figures ran by slap-footed, frantic for cover; a young couple swirled past, sopping and exultant. There was one grimacing elderly woman I noticed plodding along, whose small umbrella imploded around her head. When it was possible to pick a path up through the waterfalling staircases, I made my way upwards. The rain had given the place a good flushing out. The cataracts flowing past carried cigarette butts and wrappers, bobbing nuggets of cat shit, a straw hat and the ragged remains of at least two rats.

One afternoon in Taormina Moorehead and Clifford polished their shoes and went off to tea with Montgomery. It was Geoffrey Keating who set it up, but the General was shrewd enough to know a public relations opportunity when it strode into his parlour. He immediately requested copies of Moorehead's books. 'I must say I found him very charming indeed,' Moorehead wrote to Lucy: 'a curiously direct missionary, hard-headed and shrewd and with this gaiety and good humour.' Reviewing the biography this relationship eventually produced, one critic was moved to observe that 'in these days of the mob-mind, the self-effacing go to the wall, while the man who builds for himself his own legend not only catches the headlines, but creates the conditions for his further employment in great enterprises.' Neither author nor subject would have quibbled with that. When Monty crossed the Strait on 3 September, sailing into the smoke from the massive artillery barrage that preceded the Allied landings, Moorehead was right there on board beside him.

Securing the southern tip of the peninsula proved to be a fairly straightforward task, since the Germans had abandoned the Italian boot from the ankle down, leaving Calabria, Brindisi and Taranto undefended. It also made for uneventful copy. The Eighth Army's next target was the vast complex of airfields at Foggia on the Adriatic coast (the airfields Joseph Heller's Yossarian flew from in *Catch-22*); at a methodical pace not calculated to thrill readers of breakfast newspapers, Monty led his army thither.

Meanwhile, General Clark's Fifth Army had come ashore at Salerno and was in desperate trouble. That's where the excitement was. Moorehead and Clifford took a truck and set out with another party of correspondents to cross the coastal no-man's land separating the Allied armies. While the German retreat continued somewhere in the mountains on their right flank, the pressmen felt their way forward into an information vacuum. They backtracked around blown bridges and skirted roads where local people had seen German armoured cars. There's a fantastically knockabout feel to this little adventure. Sometimes they simply asked village postmasters to telephone ahead to the next town to see if the enemy was there. At Vallo they heard that German patrols were heading in their direction, and so retreated into an oak forest to wait out the night. Then one of their conducting officers remembered a chateau nearby whose owners he knew well, so everyone decamped there and enjoyed such 'an awfully good meal' Buckley wrote, that 'we all completely forgot that we were slap in the middle of no man's land'. The next day they proceeded cautiously through the villages along the Campagnan coast until eventually they made contact with some American sappers at the edge of the Salerno beachhead.

Technically, this unauthorised sortie by three vehicles full of war correspondents had linked the Allied forces. Everyone posed for photos, then wrote up their 'I story' exploits as fast as they could. Moorehead's, alas, got lost at the telegraph office. By the time it was found again, the *Express* had been obliged to run someone else's account. That was mortifying. Worse was the news that the American authorities at the Salerno beachhead wouldn't allow the British correspondents to stay with the Fifth Army. So, while the ferocious battle at Salerno continued, these British correspondents would have to return to the Eighth Army's slow procession through Calabria. Now Moorehead faced the prospect of missing the fall of Naples, possibly even Rome. 'I feel baulked and restless and very much like throwing the whole thing in,' he wrote to Lucy. To Christiansen, he described it as a 'humiliating and ludicrous' situation. 'There are of course advantages in holding a steady job writing nature notes on Calabria but I feel that even with your patience you will tire of that subject.'

Back with the Eighth Army, Moorehead and his dispatches now enter a period of thumb-twiddling, with only irritations to report. The Trio requisitioned rooms in a nearby villa from an indignant old contessa. They rose at 5.30 a.m. to type their dispatches about nothing much. For inspiration, one could lean back in one's chair in the grand salon and contemplate the lolling goddesses and fat cherubs sporting on the painted ceilings high above. By 10 a.m. they were thumbing the cork out of the day's first bottle of Asti Spumante. 'But for the fact that we know we are wasting a good deal of our time as war correspondents,' Moorehead wrote to Lucy, 'it would be most agreeable.'

Allied dithering gave time for the Germans to reorganise their defences, and reinforcements rushed south held up the Eighth Army advance on the mountainous river valleys on the eastern side of the peninsula: the Trigno, the Moro, the Sangro. (Young Major Anderson, the hero of Longstop, was one of hundreds who lost their lives in the grinding battles along the Adriatic.) The campaign was being fought along a continuous front now and the correspondents roamed between coasts, searching for the crucial story. Much to the frustration of their editors in London, the professional rivals made most of their trips together. Driving up to the Campobasso front in late October the three of them decided that people at home wouldn't want to read 'little tactical pieces' about the daily fighting. Surely the thing to do, Moorehead wrote to Lucy, 'was to write of such things as the psychological feelings of the troops'.

'The strange thing about Alan,' a colleague said of him during the Italian campaign, 'was that he doesn't *like* war.' And he certainly never felt, as Churchill famously did, that there's nothing so exhilarating as being shot at without result. Yet hereabouts an almost mystical belief in the transformative effect of combat creeps into his dispatches. Moorehead wasn't often in the front-lines in these last weeks in Italy, but when he is, he seems to be watching the soldiers more intently than ever, as if seeking in their faces some essential truth that eluded him. To Lucy, from Naples: 'All war is bad for any purpose whatever except for this one thing – the wonderful, majestic fullness of the soldier walking up to the precipice to look over at the unknown and coming away again.' That *majestic fullness* sounds a bit iffy – like someone working out an idea and trying to convince himself it could be true. To a mere observer, Moorhead wrote in *Eclipse*, the risk the soldiers take seems to be 'no bad thing'. Of course the soldier going up to the line is afraid: 'It is a dread of going up to the abyss and looking over into the unknown, and of risking the chance of falling over into the unknown. As he goes up to the front the man has to say: "Now I gamble everything. I put all my life and everything I hope to do and all that part of everyone I love – I put this in the way of death. I stake it all."' For those who return there is the reward of having regained what he staked. He 'seems to be a more considerable being, and to have gathered some profit from the risks'.

Till now I'd been trying to find out how much we could still see of Moorehead's war. But now the more pressing question seemed to be: what

was the war doing to *him*? This quasi-mystical turn about the transforming power of combat seems linked to new doubts about the point of it all.
Of course the war was necessary to destroy fascism and the Nazi slave
state. But Moorehead knew that was an unimaginably remote goal for
troops camped in Italy's shell-churned mud for weeks on end. Was it too
much to ask that the experience of combat might contain something of
value in itself – that mortal wager leading to an inner expansion? 'Five
years of watching war have made me personally hate and loathe war,' he
wrote at the very end. 'But this thing – the brief ennoblement inside himself of the otherwise dreary and materialistic man – kept recurring again
and again up to the very end and it refreshed and lighted the whole heroic
and sordid story.'

§

The End in Africa came out in November. Richard Moorehead didn't
receive his copy in faraway Melbourne until February the following year,
by which time his son was back in London. 'Intensely virile lasting literature,' he glowed in his telegram. 'Are you all safe?'

Moorehead and his colleagues spent most of December 'barracks
happy', and more and more reluctant to leave their flat. They had, according to Buckley, 'the best flat in the best block on the sea front of Naples';
it had high gilt ceilings and a balcony that overlooked the bay. Naples in
1943–44, like Cairo in 1940–42, is one of those cities of legend that comes
into existence briefly and then vanishes again, like a collective hallucina-
tion. Extreme deprivation collided with bored soldiers and vast piles of
US Army food and gear in a lawless festival of profiteering, exploitation
and crazy nights. The city was full of Americans and tarts, Ardizzone
wrote; the combination produced a firestorm of syphilis that raged through
city for months to come. Women and men alike sold sex for food in the
'incredible squalor' of the slum alleyways. Swarms of *sciuscià* boys, or
street kids, slept rough in the rail yards and ruins and stole wallets and
cars, and sold to the Allied troops doctored spirits and fake cigarettes.
Moorehead managed to buy a Fiat on his expense account, and on one
occasion they motored down the coast to Sorrento and hired a ketch to

take them over to Capri. In the flat there were cocktail parties and poetry readings with American officers and Eighth Army brigadiers. Crowds of blow-ins gathered around the piano for impromptu concerts and sing-alongs. At one dinner party they threw for twenty guests, Ardizzone recorded with a sour whiff of *droit de seigneur* that clings to their relations to local women, 'a fearful little tart' inveigled herself and stayed until 3.30 a.m. She later returned with a 'pretty little girl who looked about sixteen and was almost prostrate and trembling with fright ... The idea being that she should be Alan's mistress.' They gave the girl some tins of Spam and sent her away.

Naples was Taormina all over again – 'the winter school' this time. Sometimes in their talk of the future Moorehead could be 'Tolstoyan', friends noted, and gloomy. But then, he was reading *War and Peace* at the time. He was always strongly affected by what he was reading: great writing entered his system like dye. Along with the conversation about art, war and the future, it was Tolstoy's example that inspired the dream idea of *Eclipse* – a different kind of war book, a personal, thematic story that would explain the last phase of the war 'sociologically and politically, psychologically'.

Everyone knew now that there was to be another major landing up the coast, but everyone also knew that whatever happened, the war wasn't going to be decided in Italy. Moorehead didn't want to get stuck in a side-show, much less get killed covering one. Having survived this far, he wrote later, they all became 'more cheerful and yet more selfish, more materialistic than we were before'.

Materialistic is a word that starts to appear with increasing frequency. It dismayed Moorehead to see first-hand how little Sicilians and the half-starved population of Naples cared for ideas of liberty and freedom. Food was what Neapolitans craved, he said in a 1945 radio broadcast, 'Just food. They weren't interested in anything else. They had no hatred, no pride, no notions about the rights or wrongs of the war – at that time they didn't much care who won the war.' He understood this, but he found it depressing. There was still enough of the young freedom-seeking dreamer in him to despise materialism, but he was beginning to feel its strong anaesthetic grip. Not just in the simple desire to survive the war, which grew more ardent the longer it went on. But also in the desire for the things money could bring: to be comfortable, successful, to eat well, to travel and write.

In the first week of 1944 the *Express* announced a series of articles examining the 'second front' – in France, or Belgium, or wherever the Allied assault on the Reich's western wall would come. Would Montgomery and Eisenhower get along? '*Express*man Alan Moorehead knows them both,' bragged the page-two teaser, 'and he has a fascinating and important story to tell.' Moorehead had to get back to London and tell it. He returned to Lucy in London via Gibraltar and Algiers, flying in General Eisenhower's personal Flying Fortress.

These were contented months. Lucy and John were living with Osbert and Karen Lancaster, Lucy's old friends from her days on the *Express*. Through the Lancasters, and people like Jamie Hamilton and the film producer Sidney Bernstein, Moorehead's networks flourished. Most of his time he spent following Montgomery around England from camp to camp, watching the weirdly magnetic little general build up the morale, one stump speech at a time, of the largest invasion force ever assembled. But when Moorehead wasn't filing stories about the battles to come, he continued his crabwise push into literary circles, lunching with people like Harold Nicolson, John Betjeman, Irwin Shaw and Ernest Bevin. At one lunch he was cornered by JB Priestley, 'who said, "I hate war correspondents." I–"The war's worse." P.–"There is not much to choose between them." But thought my last 3 chapters [of *A Year of Battle*] had "epic quality". Nuts.'

In late May, he farewelled Lucy, now several months pregnant, and his three-year-old son, and reported to a holding camp in the south of England to sit out the last days before the Allied invasion of occupied Europe. The days of terrorised apathy spent in the camp inspired some of *Eclipse*'s most remarkable pages. Soldiers were forbidden even to speak to members of the public passing by; everyone had been reduced to numerical inputs in vast and complex actuarial calculations, and it felt like it. 'It was not fear that oppressed you, but loneliness. A sense of implacable helplessness. You were without identity, a number projected in unrelated space among a million other numbers.' Again, there was the shocking banality of preparations for extreme violence.

War correspondents weren't magically shielded from bad luck by their typewriters, as Moorehead knew very well by now. 'I ask you not to be too bold,' Eisenhower's chief of staff said to a gathering of reporters before the invasion. 'Too many war correspondents are getting killed, and a dead war correspondent is no good to anybody.' In fact, Moorehead's D-Day came and went in a blur of almost comic mishap and anticlimactic safety. He watched the unspectacular and 'curiously toy-like' scene on the beach from the railing of his landing ship, which circled 500 yards offshore trying to disembark troops into smaller craft that drifted aimlessly away or smacked helplessly against the hull. He didn't get ashore until D-Day +1. All around, people sank in the shallows or clung to the gunwales of craft that milled around in confusion; when Moorehead's landing craft shelved on the beach a burly soldier conveyed him to the tideline on his shoulders and deposited him, perfectly dry, onto French soil, among the charred trucks and twisted metal. The battle had groped its way beyond the beach, past the burst pillboxes and gutted seaside villas. Hailing a jeep, Moorehead went in pursuit. By lunchtime he was installed at a table in a bright little provincial hotel in Bayeux, eight miles from the coast, contemplating with happy astonishment a six-course luncheon menu of omelette, cheese and steak.

On that first day he jotted down the things he saw and heard in a navy-blue linen notebook small enough for the breast pocket of his tunic. His pencil scrawl is faded, and almost illegible, just a few words per line, the lines skittering down the page. This, from a random page, gives an idea of the sheer chaos of conflicting information he would use to write his pieces:

Gaps in our landings ... speed carried us right over beaches and some distance inland. Ex 1 case.

Concrete boxes bypassed w enemy still in them.

... No good digging in on beach. So when we 3 mi inland had to go back & fight boxes ... Inside our area were [a considerable number] of loose Gers and snipers. One pocket still holding. Also women snipers & these have been killed in action ... Sector defended by non coastal division as elsewhere. [illeg.] div just moved up to thicken coastal thrust and was in proces of exercise. V heavy fighting went on all day long –

v. heavy & by enemy not more 100 yards – hanging on by eyelids ...

He was back in his element, back with the Trio, in the vanguard of
what was now an enormous multinational press contingent. 'They form
a close and formidable caravan,' a colleague drily noted. 'Brigadiers trem-
ble at their frown, they live and move *en prince*, and genuine danger and
discomfort ... may be mitigated by captured German delicacies and
mysteriously-conjured champagne.' With Clifford he went out to see the
Americans smash their way into Cherbourg. In early July he was back in
the British sector to see another assault on Caen, which was supposed to
have been captured weeks before this. Failure to progress at the British
end of the beachhead was holding up the whole plan. It was also eating
into the Commander-in-Chief's legend of invincibility. Montgomery, the
official British history of the Italian campaign would note, 'had the unusual
gift of persuasively combining very bold speech and very cautious action'.
Eisenhower and Churchill were calling for bold action, so Monty ordered
up a massive tactical bombing raid against the enemy positions. Most of
the bombs missed, but the next day the Germans began to withdraw, and
in the afternoon Moorehead was with a group of correspondents observing the situation from a ridge at the northern end of Caen when they came
under shelling. They scuttled off the ridge in search of cover, and sought
shelter in Caen's northern suburbs. But there were no suburbs left. Just a
new type of man-made landscape, the type 500 or so heavy bombers leaves
behind. Houses had become hollows in the ground. New hills had been
dragged up out of the earth.

> There were no longer streets or footpaths or any decided evidence that
> human beings had once been here and lived. There was a kind of anarchy
> in this waste, a thing against which the mind rebelled; an unreasoning
> and futile violence ... There seemed to be no point in going on. This was
> the end of the world, the end of the war, the final expression of man's
> desire to destroy. There was nothing more to see, only more dust.

The silent city of rubble was soon a familiar sight, but Moorehead
never got used to it. Contemplating what remained of Cologne in early

1945, he wrote: 'A city means movement and noise and people; not silence and emptiness and stillness ... A city is life, and when you find instead the negation of life the effect is redoubled.' In a 1940 essay about the *Iliad* Simone Weil called the destruction of a city 'the greatest calamity the human race can experience'; but such Homeric calamities had become a weekly event by 1945, all across Europe and beyond: Hamburg, Dresden, Warsaw, Tokyo, Stalingrad, Berlin. The lesson Moorehead was taking from Caen's obliterated homes and churches, from Krefeld's fetid, squalid bomb shelters, from the mass slaughter at Falaise, was that this is what ideology and noble causes led to: meaningless wreckage. No principles were vindicated by these ruins; all they told you was that humanity's capacity for destruction was steadily increasing.

I had to keep reminding myself that Moorehead's war ran almost the full gazetted span. Most people who came that close to the front experienced it for a few months at a time, coming and going again with death or incapacity, or capture or redeployment. Yet 'in the last four years of the war,' a former tank commander wrote in a review of *Eclipse*, Moorehead 'has probably been consistently nearer to the battlefield than any fighting soldier in the British army'. It would be a mistake to see those years as one coherent bloc of experience. So much changed. The kit; the new fighter-bombers, the flail tanks; the sheer scale of numbers. So much had come and gone. The battle cruiser *Hood*, that vision of pride and power glimpsed during the *Tinos* voyage in 1937, had been lying at the bottom of the North Sea for three years. Moorehead had seen the destruction of the colonists' towns in Libya, the gore and shock of the great battles in the desert and Tunisia, and the winter fighting over the rivers in Italy. But not this. Moorehead's dispatches from Europe record a sense of terrible escalation in the scale and brutality of the conflict – terrible most of all because there seemed to be no limit to it. In 1942 Gandhi had said to him that it was better to submit to violence: 'In the end the aggressor will become sated with killing and desist.' But by mid-1944 the war Moorehead was describing had become a insatiable firestorm that seemed to be feeding on its own ferocity, and would go on, no matter what anyone did, until there was nothing left to burn.

In August 1944 the Allies broke out of their bridgehead. Under Bradley and Patton, the Americans stormed west through the Cherbourg Peninsula, broke through Saint-Lô, and then at unprecedented speed turned south into undefended country, until, hooking back east towards Le Mans, they had formed a giant armoured jaw beneath the bulk of the German forces still concentrated near Caen. In a calamitous misjudgement, Hitler ordered his armies deeper into the hinge of the jaw – that is, west, towards the coast at Avranches. This meant that when obliged to retreat again very soon afterwards, almost 300,000 Germans were nearly surrounded. The only exit from the giant trap was at a little town called Falaise, just south of Caen. On the Allies' campaign maps, the Battle of the Falaise Pocket was a thing of almost flawless tactical beauty, a case study for the ages; on the ground it was three days of continuous chaos in which human life lost all value. Moorehead was in the village of Saint-Lambert, where the Germans had tried to fight their way out 'with the sort of panzer battle array that the Germans have used to terrorize Europe for four years'.

> We knew no combination to stand against it. And now, here in the apple orchards and in the village streets, one turns sick to see what has happened to them. They met the British and the Allied troops head on, and they were just obliterated. Until now I had no conception of what trained artillerymen and infantry can do, and certainly this is the most awful sight that has come my way since the war began.

The Germans had entered the village in long horse-drawn columns. Moorehead's description of what happened is all the more awful for the attention given to the horses, whose dumb suffering becomes indistinguishable from the animal helplessness of the German soldiers.

> The horses stampeded. Not half a dozen, but perhaps three hundred or more. They lashed down the fences and the hedges with their hooves, and dragged their carriages through the farmyards. Many galloped for the banks of the river Dives, and plunged headlong with all their trappings down the twelve-foot banks into the stream below, which at once turned red with blood. Those animals that did not drown under the dragging

weight of their harness, or die in falling, kept plunging about among the broken gun-carriages, and trampled to death the Germans hiding under the bank. The drivers of the lorries panicked in the same way. As more and more shells kept ripping through the apple trees, they collided their vehicles one against the other, and with such force that some of the fighter cars were telescoped with their occupants inside.

At some places for stretches of fifty yards vehicles, horses and men became jammed together in one struggling, shrieking mass.

Nothing on the battlefield would get – could get – any worse than Falaise. Moorehead wanted to see the liberation of Paris, but he wasn't sure he wanted to see anything else. 'Unless some major crisis develops I would like to return to England in early September,' he wrote to Christiansen in July. He wanted leave. A month or two – enough to be in London for the birth of his second child, and to get to work on his new book. Quite understandably, though, Christiansen blanched at the thought of his senior correspondent sitting at home tapping his teeth with a pencil while the free world smashed headlong into the Third Reich and the *Daily Mail* sold millions of copies describing it. Books could wait, surely? In another message, Moorehead tried to make Chris understand how frustrating it was to see so much and have so little room to describe it. Newspaper columns couldn't hold it all. 'We can't get it into a newspaper entirely, it's too big, it needs a fuller pattern, so much solid, right writing that can't be done from the back seat of a jeep humping round the beach-head every day ... That wonderful real stuff ... gets lost in a forest of quick clichés half the time. And so some of us say, "Can I write a book? I never had time to tell the story."'

Christiansen's patience with his champion reporter seems remarkable, given that the fall of Paris is only days away. Moorehead had already canvassed his future at the *Express* at length. It wasn't so much that the paper's politics were 'simply awful', as he matter-of-factly put it. No, the issue was sticking with journalism or taking the big leap into books. 'One fluctuates between the two: history or journalism; an intellectual satisfaction or a bank balance and a little present power.' Proposals and counter-proposals were exchanged. Christiansen tried a lateral tack. 'Do you think you could get yourself fixed up as General Montgomery's biographer – with, of course, the idea of such extracts as would be newsy for the *Daily Express*?' He outlined the terms of a very generous three-year contract that would give Moorehead more time to write his beloved books.

Just days after the fall of Paris, Moorehead wrote to Jamie Hamilton about Christiansen's offer, asking if Hamilton could match it with a contract for three books: the current one (*Eclipse*), Montgomery and another book still to be decided. Jamie's letter in reply was hugely encouraging. He begins by saying how exciting times must be for Moorehead with 'a front row seat (and by no means a safe one) at one of the greatest spectacles in the world's history. Your dispatches have been magnificent …' He wants the Montgomery book and *Eclipse*. What subject for the third book? Hamilton's idea was to put together a kind of salary deal, possibly in combination with Harper's in the US, that would come as close to possible – which wasn't all that close – to matching whatever the *Express* would offer.

The sheer speed of the breakout from Normandy forced these negotiations into the background. After Falaise, nothing stood between the Allied armies and Paris. Short of final victory, the liberation of Paris was the fragile dream that had been kept alive over four years of defeat and despair. On 24 August the Trio headed north. In a zippy new Volkswagen claimed from a dead German captain, they roared along dusty roads, ducking between trucks and tanks and jeeps, bumping along the verges alongside a caravan of military vehicles that stretched, Moorehead estimated, for 200 miles, 'gargantuan, frightening, thunderous'. At the outskirts of Paris hysteria was mounting. French troops were guarding the city approaches against Allied interlopers because the triumphal entry had been reserved for the Free French division. But Moorehead found a ratrun through the backstreets, and was soon bowling into Paris's southern suburbs. The city centre was magnificent chaos. A sea of human beings filled the square in front of the Hotel de Ville, where the indiscriminate kissing continued (though 'after so much kissing, the soldiers in selfdefence were seeking out the prettier girls'). Moorehead's party headed for the Ritz, thinking they might even be the first into the historic hotel. 'It was a little galling to find Ernest Hemingway sitting in the dining-room over a bottle of Heidsieck.' Leading a group of guerilla fighters he'd picked up somewhere, Hemingway had liberated the Ritz just hours before.

On the Champs Élysées the correspondents found de Gaulle making his victorious procession from the Arc de Triomphe. There was an impossible crush. They leapt back into the Volkswagen and, with his unerring instinct for the historic moment, Moorehead managed to edge the car into position in the centre 'directly behind' de Gaulle.

> A hundred other cars came swerving forward through the crowd and soon
> we were locked together, twenty cars abreast, the mud-guards touching,
> another row of cars behind ... One was conscious only of repeated waves of
> noise from the people. Once when I got a moment to look up from driving
> I turned and saw with astonishment that everyone in my car was crying.

Moorehead's feelings were mixed at first. 'One had been prepared and braced to plunge down to God-knew-what excesses of emotion and hysteria,' he wrote, but it was 'beyond even anti-climax' to find that everything was the same. 'Everything was here waiting to be taken up again as though those four years had never existed, and now there was nothing to get excited about, no need to shout.' This lugubrious stuff soon passed. Not even the eternal spectator could stand apart from the delirium of the crowds. One colleague recalled seeing Moorehead at one point gazing across the city, arms outflung, crying: 'My city!'

And he did feel it as a homecoming. Christiansen kept sending him cables asking him to get what he could about Gestapo atrocities, but Moorehead was too busy. There was too much to drink, too many people to talk to, too many special places to revisit and find magically unaltered. 'If it is true that the greatest joy humanity can experience is release from pain,' Moorehead wrote, 'then this was it.' Parisians kept saying the same thing, AJ Liebling recalled: '*Enfin on respire.*' At last, one breathes. Moorehead was experiencing an epiphany too. Six years older than when he last saw Paris, and so much heavier with experience, he was wrestling with something more personal than the shared joy of liberation and victory: something to do with time, and the pleasure-pain of persisting memory. On that first day, 'warm and brilliant sunshine' had succeeded the rain:

At the Porte d'Orléans the crowd was out in the streets. Nothing had changed, nothing really altered. The cobblestones. The flapping signs in red and gold over the pavement cafés. *Patisserie. Charcuterie.* Three golden horses' heads over the horse butcher. The newspaper kiosk at the corner. *Café des Sports.* The Metro maps with the broad blue lines. The flics with their flat blue kepis ... Had we ever been away?

The *Café des Sports* – where young Alan had sat so many midnights, tired, content, nursing one last beer and dreaming of the future in the fluorescent glare. *Nothing had changed.* Six long years evaporated in an instant, leaving him gazing at the blast silhouettes on the wall of time.

All these emotions were having their effect on some of Moorehead's closest acquaintances, too. Mary Welsh, Lucy's old friend, and till now the wife of Noel Monks, suddenly realised she was in love with Hemingway. Cupid's most audacious arrow, however, flew for Alex Clifford, who had always seemed immune to romance. Jenny Nicholson was a former ballet dancer, radio writer and cabaret soubrette, and now an officer in the WAAF. She was also the daughter of the author and poet Robert Graves, though it was her family's extensive painting pedigree that Alex stressed when he wrote home to announce the match. Jenny possessed, Moorehead wrote later, 'with an almost bewildering completeness those very qualities which were so much lacking in [Clifford's] own life, a natural vivacity, an unaffected assurance in her own social background, a flair for the unusual and optimistic decisions and an astonishing energy in carrying them through.' What this meant for his friendship with Alex he couldn't yet imagine.

For now, he was preoccupied with something else: the discovery that everything the correspondents had been telling themselves and their readers for five years turned out to be true. On the surreal drive into the centre of the city people had repeated the same thing over and over: '*Nous vous avons attendu si longtemps*' – we have been waiting for you so long.

What had they been waiting for exactly? Terrible things had happened in Paris, of course: the Gestapo had arrested more people here than had been killed by air raids in London. Prisoners had been tortured. Tens of thousands of Jews had been put on trains and sent to the death camps in the East. For most people, though, these infamies lay below the surface of everyday life. Life in occupied Paris had been workable. By contrast with Naples, there was enough food. The buses ran. So why this implacable hatred of the Germans? What exactly is it that was so unbearable about occupation? An entire hard-working chapter of *Eclipse* is spent 'trying to get to the bottom of this mystery', because the answer has to justify all the waste and suffering Moorehead has described for the past five years. Then it becomes clear: the one thing Parisians were unable to bear had been 'the lack of freedom to think, to trust the facts in the newspapers you read, to speak your mind, to criticise'. People will not put up with any censorship from outside. They will not put up with limits on the right to speak one's mind. The very naïvety of this argument 'blinded a good few of us to its force', he wrote. 'A man summed it up for me in one revealing trenchant phrase: "I'll tell you what liberation is. It's hearing a knock on my door at six o'clock in the morning and knowing it's the milkman."'

'It is when one grasps this point – a point round which I am trying to bind the theme of this book – that I imagine one begins to see some hope for the future.' This was the best news Moorehead could bring readers from the killing fields of Europe 1944–45, the revealed truth that gave some meaning to it all: 'the ordinary human desire for the sense of freedom always in the end triumphs over laziness and venality and ennui.'

Meanwhile, the war went on, at a much slower pace than had been hoped after the German collapse in the south. Moorehead missed the capture of Brussels, but was on the spot for Arnhem, Monty's doomed attempt to leapfrog into Holland with a massive paratrooper assault. Surveying the results of air raids on the little Dutch town of Eindhoven during this operation, Moorehead pondered 'the endless pain stretching ahead indefinitely into the future'.

> This was a microcosm of all Europe. It comprehended all Holland, all Germany, all the coming battlefields. No one here in Eindhoven was ready to confess guilt or admit that they had in any way deserved the bombings. Nor was anyone in any bombed German town going to admit that they had been guilty. That was the last thing they would admit ...

And the people of London, who had probably endured as much as any-one, thought that too. The war, in fact, in this sixth year, was ending very much as it had begun, in a welter of fear and revenge. All the acts of courage and endurance and technical efficiency were doing nothing to establish an ethic for the war or obtain the acceptance of a moral right for either side.

It sounds like a witness come to the end of his belief that witnessing does anyone any good. It sounds a bit like a resignation letter. Postdated, per-haps, but final.

§

The passages of *Eclipse* that stand out seventy years on are the ones that pull the great events of those days into vivid, momentary focus. The Germans' Christmas offensive in the Ardennes is in full murderous swing when the reader emerges from a maelstrom of clashing tanks and tree-bursts and steps into a near-silent panning shot. 'All round Brussels and Liege it was milky fog,' Moorehead wrote.

> But when you drove past the frozen canals and the tobogganing children up to the heights of the Ardennes, the sun broke through and it was like a spot-lighted stage, mile upon mile of untrodden snowfields under the clear and frosty lamp of the winter sun. If you turned your back to the ruined villages and forgot the war for a moment, then very easily you could fancy yourself to be alone in this radiant world where everything was reduced to primary whites and blues; a strident, sparkling white among the frosted trees, the deep blue shadows in the valley and then the flawless ice-blue of the sky. Flying Fortresses went by, immensely high, spinning out their vapour trails half-way across Belgium.

Not bad for a passing paragraph in a long piece probably bashed out in half an hour in the freezing cab of a lorry: simple sentences, but full of sly movement that brings us from daily life in the lowlands, past the rubble of yesterday's battles to an ageless landscape, and beyond it, in those remote and creaturely planes, a chilling glimpse of the world to come.

Lucy had given birth to a daughter, Caroline, at the end of October. By Christmas, she was herself in uniform, and accompanied her husband on several of his grim field trips in early '45. 'We tended to be more sickened by ruins than stimulated by danger,' Moorehead wrote of the final phase in Germany, where each new battle 'seemed to us repetitive and useless folly'. Gradually Moorehead drifts further back from the front-line. He didn't need to see every firefight. What you could see in the areas already recaptured was in some ways more profound: the Germans eking out a life in their obliterated cities; stockades full of captured Nazis; the roads packed with a chaotic westward migration of liberated slave-workers, sad groups of women and children clustered on church steps and in doorways.

Most of the war's impact on Moorehead's development as a writer is in place by now. All that remains is one final glimpse of the abyss. In April 1945, in gorgeous spring weather, British Second Army reached the little village of Belsen. When the British discovered the camp on its outskirts, General Dempsey had special passes issued to the pressmen so that they could see for themselves. Belsen wasn't a death camp, like Auschwitz or Treblinka; but the horrifying conditions in which its slave labour population were kept made the distinction seem almost moot. A typhoid epidemic had just raged through the camp; the emaciated bodies of its victims were piled in grisly heaps. Moorehead was given a personal tour of the cells where camp personnel were being held. The women guards: 'twenty women wearing dirty grey skirts and tunics were sitting and lying on the floor … the atmosphere of the reformatory school and the prison was inescapable.' The SS guards, many of them spattered with blood: 'Unlike the women they looked not at us but vacantly in front, staring at nothing'; and the doctor, who, Moorehead is told, had one 'trick' that involved injecting creosote and petrol into the prisoners' veins: 'The man was lying in his blood on the floor, a massive figure with a heavy head and a bedraggled beard. He laced his two arms on to the seat of a wooden chair … "Why don't you kill me?" he whispered.' Deeper in the camp, soldiers were bulldozing the dead into burial pits 500 at a time. The bodies' 'withered skin was sagging over the bones, and all the normal features by which you know a human being had practically disappeared'. This was bulldozer work he didn't want to see at all, let alone describe. 'What we were seeing was something from the dark ages, the breaking up of a medieval slave state ... It was all like a journey down into some Dantesque pit, unreal, leprous and frightening.'

The war correspondent Martha Gellhorn, who became a close friend of Lucy's in the late '40s, believed that it was the job of journalism to do something about suffering. And if you couldn't do anything, then you should just scream. Moorehead was constitutionally milder than that. But here, at Belsen, he bore witness as decently and clearly as he could. *All the living are guilty*, Vasily Grossman wrote, reflecting, after Stalin's death, on the legacy of totalitarian terror in the Soviet Union; Moorehead felt something like that in Belsen, too. In varying degrees, everyone, he believed, and not just the German people, was contaminated by the camps. They only existed because of our indifference.

> Worse camps existed in Poland and we took no notice. Dachau was described in the late nineteen-thirties and we did not want to hear. In the midst of the war three-quarters of a million Indians starved in Bengal because shipping was wanted in other parts, and we were bored.*

Many months later, Beverley Nichols, who had also been a war correspondent, and had reported from Dachau, wrote to Moorehead about the dispatch he filed from Belsen. 'I do think that it is a most important document, because of its deadly accuracy, and because you obviously wrote it with your heart's blood, and stabbed your pen deeper and deeper, to get at the truth, no matter how much it hurt.'

§

When Montgomery accepted a general surrender of the German armies at Luneberg Heath, Moorehead wrote a letter on behalf of all 21st Army correspondents congratulating the field marshal 'on the brilliant end of your long journey from the desert ... The best story probably of our lives'.

And yet in December 1946 Moorehead filled space in one of his last columns for the *Express* with a tale told to him by a salvage diver during

---

* The real number of people who died in the Bengal famine is thought to be almost 3 million.

the war – a 'trivial tale' perhaps, but to Moorehead one of 'singular beauty, a weird sort of mystery'. During a dive on a sunken German ship in a captured Belgian port, the man's torch picked out the corpses of the ship's crew lying undisturbed in the hold. Stirred by the diver's current, the corpses raised themselves off the floor and seemed to follow him. He tried to get away. He fled out of the hold, and out into the open water. 'They clustered round him, touching him … He went on. They followed; faster as he went faster, slower as he slowed … They reached out to him again.' It's hard to imagine that many *Express* readers would have wanted to read this over their ersatz coffee and powdered eggs. On this day, however, war stories were all an old correspondent had to offer. He sounds like someone laying out his proprietary wares for whoever cares to buy – take it or leave it. There is no moral to this tale, he admits – 'only a cold reflection that there is no end to the infinite horror of a war'.

6

JUICES OF GENIUS

In the summer of 1945 an 11-year-old girl answered the doorbell at her London home, opening the door to a sight she never forgot. It wasn't the small uniformed man standing there on the stoop: she knew him already, and though he was famous, he wasn't as famous as her own father, *Express* cartoonist Osbert Lancaster. It wasn't his Australian Army slouch hat, either. No, it was the astounding object balanced on his shoulder: a huge bunch of ripe bananas.

What other miracles might Moorehead now produce? Now that the battlefields lay silent, the possibilities seemed endless. 'Things had really gone very well for me,' Moorehead wrote in his 1960s notes for the autobiography:

> From a very minor reporter ... I had become the chief foreign correspondent of the paper and had achieved the sort of notoriety which attaches (especially in wartime, when news is so vital) to anyone whose name appears in a mass-circulation newspaper almost every day.

He calls it notoriety; we'd call it a kind of stardom. When his *Montgomery* came out a year later, one reviewer declared it apt that 'the first biography of Britain's most successful military leader in the war should have been written by Britain's most successful war correspondent'. *Time* magazine in America referred to him, less deferentially, as the *Express*'s 'topflight war correspondent, tiny, toothy Alan Moorehead'. A reviewer of *Eclipse* wrote that 'without achieving the glamour of Ernie Pyle' he was 'the best of the British war correspondents'. I don't want to overdo the acclaim (though here's some more: 'his battle pieces stand comparison with the famous battle descriptions of Stendhal and Tolstoy' – the *Observer*) but I do want to log the evidence of the genuine and high standing Moorehead had achieved by 1945. Because there would be no great books, not for another ten years.

Moorehead's career is a natural three-acter, plus epilogue; and we now enter the stifled, struggling middle act. His goal was clear, if the means were vague: it was time to cash in the chips he'd won with war reporting and recreate himself as a substantial literary figure. It didn't go like that. Not immediately, but implacably, like an Eisenstein pram tipped lightly down a decade's great staircase, Moorehead's career frustrations will very slowly gather pace over the late '40s, and though his fortunes bob up here and there, the downward plunge will gather an irresistible momentum until it crashes, with a succession of humblings and sorrows so tightly bunched it can seem to verge on the slapstick, into the worst imaginable thing: a nine-to-five job in PR. Actually there were other worse things. The very nadir is hard to pick, but it may be October 1952 when an anonymous review of *The Traitors*, a book about Britain's atomic spies, accused Moorehead of being, as his lawyers paraphrased it in their writ, 'a time-server without patriotism or loyalties' who in the event of an invasion by a foreign power 'would be amongst the traitors, collaborators and quislings'.

It wasn't a future he could have imagined as he stood on the Lancasters' stoop with his bananas. But the postwar plague years were a part of the story that had always intrigued me: there was something unexplained about them, something extravagantly unlucky. And now, as I made my way north from Taormina, the pleasures of crisis lay ahead in delicious prospect.

§

In July 1945 Christopher Buckley held a drinks party at his London flat to introduce his new fiancée to his friends. Tall, like Lucy, and also like Lucy, a little exhausted by Jenny Clifford, whom she found 'frightfully gushing', Cecilia Brown was a mother of three and not yet divorced from her first husband. Her recollection of that night, still clear in 1989, is a rare glimpse of what the Trio looked like to a civilian outsider. 'It seemed rather like the end of their last term at a school where they had been happy,' she told Moorehead's biographer, Tom Pocock.

Since their return from Germany the three friends had met often at the Savoy Hotel to gossip and dream up the future over drinks. But there wouldn't be many more reunions like this. Clifford was no keener on London than Moorehead was, so he and Jenny were planning to set themselves up in Paris. Buckley was off to report the end of the Pacific War. At one point in the evening, Cecelia found herself alone with Moorehead on the balcony and realised that he was flirting with her. He didn't mean anything by it, she decided; and anyway, he was so much shorter, 'and that makes a chap look a bit of an ass in that situation'. But it stuck in her mind. Cecilia enjoyed Moorehead's conversation, but she never quite warmed to that hungry quality – that old capacity to be tempted. In his approach to everything in Europe, she told Pocock, 'he was like a small boy with his face pressed up against a sweet-shop window.' I've always been struck by the pathos of that remark: even after a decade in Europe, he hadn't yet learnt how to mask his desperate need to catch up.

The other event that marks a clearing of the decks is Moorehead's trip at the end of 1945 to Australia. The flight was, as ever, a wretched experience. The final leg from Ceylon was eighteen hours in the air 'staring at an endless nothingness of sea and clouds until the mind began to reel with the mere idea of space, pure space, insubstantial, entirely uncharted and probably hostile'. And something else was bothering him. He felt embarrassed by an imbalance that had emerged in his friendship with Clifford.

> I had at that time a feeling that we were drifting apart. It was not just his
> marriage to Jenny that was separating us: I was beginning to realize that
> I had more affection for him than he had for me and this was a little
> humiliating. By going to Australia I would demonstrate that I could live
> without him.

He'd left it far too long. He hadn't seen his mother since her trip to Paris before the war; his father, he hadn't seen in a decade. In his notes for *A Late Education*, he writes of his first return home: *In effect broken off with family, friends – the idea of Aus. Had deliberately put Aus out of mind – lost accent.*

No trace remains of the words that passed between Alan and his parents, and his adored sister, Phyllis, when he appeared at Essendon Airport, but it proved to be the 'happiest of homecomings'. When Lucy and the children joined him in January, the extended family took a holiday house in Mornington on Port Phillip Bay for the summer. Moorehead could swim again, which was always good for his mood. And he caught up with many old friends and colleagues, and on terms that can only have been good for his confidence.

There's something insubstantial about this six months out of Europe, as if Moorehead was too engrossed in his *Montgomery* manuscript to be fully present. By his standards, he was writing slowly now, mostly working on the verandah of his parents' house in Croydon. Lizards darted between the legs of his writing table; at night the possums nesting in the verandah roof sometimes crept in through the window and nibbled flowers from the vase by his bed. As he sat there describing Monty's bloody experiences in Belgium in 1916, he smelt the lemon-scented gums in the garden, listened to the cackle of the kookaburras and gazed out at the Dandenong Ranges beyond his father's orchard, a plantation fondly recalled by the family and long since erased by Melbourne's urban sprawl.

This visit also marks a way-point in my search for Moorehead's world: we've entered the realm of living memory. Phyllis's two girls were in Mornington in 1946 and both recall it well. 'I remember Alan sitting out on the edge of the cliff in a deckchair in a howling gale, and I said, "What are you doing?"' Gillian told me. 'He said, "I've just bought this windcheater, and I'm seeing if it works."'

It was unsettling to meet the nieces. Years of document-sifting and note-taking hadn't prepared me for the warmth of living memory. What a presumption it was, I suddenly thought, to decide to write about another person's life. Gillian had googled me, she said, in a tone that suggested this precautionary check of my *bona fides* hadn't been entirely satisfactory. So I rushed to reassure with a fumbling explanation of how obsessed

I'd become with her uncle's work, of my hard-to-describe identification with him, of my hopes of dragging his work out of its unreasonable obscurity. (It seemed wise to keep the madder stuff to myself – that I'd anointed him my proxy escapee from Australia, made him my remote probe into the depths of the mid-twentieth century – let alone my suspicion that, at some murky, furtive daydreaming level, I wanted to *be* him.)

What Gillian and Rob made of this they were far too urbane and hospitable to say. It didn't matter anyway, because it was clear that we shared an admiration for Alan's work – we were all *fans*.

Gillian had dug out the letters Moorehead wrote to Phyllis. She turned the pages, setting aside some that were too private. With some she couldn't decide. 'I'm not sure yet whether I'm going to show these to you,' she mused aloud. 'I understand,' I said, trying to appear as principled as possible. (But also wondering, naturally, how I might go about getting hold of them.) While I photographed approved letters, Rob kept remembering favourite passages which he urged Gillian to find so she could read them out. He was right: they were funny. A new side to Moorehead was emerging: the affectionate, relaxed, bird-loving brother and uncle of the '50s and '60s. There were other things Gillian showed me too: watercolours Moorehead had painted after his stroke. These were wonderful things to see.

But the most important documents, the ones that would get inside the inward turn to novel-writing, were the letters and journals held by Moorehead's surviving children, Caroline and John. I'd studied Pocock's citations, and had calculated that behind the snippets he quoted lay a stash of intimate journals and at least 140 letters. I didn't want to sip at these from Pocock's proffered spoon – I wanted to plunge my face into the whole pot. And that's what I hoped to do in Italy. Caroline Moorehead had kindly offered to make the letters available to me in Porto Ercole, as long as she could find them. This was the material that offered the best chance to see inside the unhappy workings of Moorehead's postwar struggle.

§

In early 1946, there was as yet no sign of the difficult times ahead. As he embarked on his *Montgomery* research, Moorehead could draw on his extensive army contacts, but also on a new set of acquaintances furnished by his celebrity. Introductions smoothed the way into the inner reaches of London literary and political salons, largely thanks to London hostesses such as Lady Rothermere (later Mrs Ann Fleming) and Lady Sibyl Colefax; he was also 'taken up, inevitably, by Nancy Cunard', an *Express* colleague recalled, 'and soon knew everyone in London. A hot property, and charmingly aware of it.' The rippling circle of his acquaintance took in figures as varied as George Bernard Shaw, Cyril Connolly, John Gielgud, Harold Nicolson and Ernest Bevin.

Yet Moorehead was never entirely at home in London society. Beneath the confidence, the noted pushiness – as networking was called before it became a critical life skill – there was a streak of provincial unease. He envied the confidence of England's arts & letters caste, its storied families, such as the Betjemans and the Murrays (of the publishing dynasty), and the one Clifford had just married into. Class snobbery had been rife in the Melbourne of Moorehead's youth, but he never grew wholly accustomed to its more complex nuances in Britain.

I was coming to feel some of this bewilderment myself. When I read Artemis Cooper's biography of Patrick Leigh Fermor I felt like a horse trainer coveting the glossy coat of a rival mount. With sheer good breeding and charm Paddy seems to progress across Europe in a series of borrowed tuxes from *schloss* to monastery to hayrick and then back, to high-spirited weekends in stately English homes where everyone knows what to tip the butler, and where people with titles and triple-barrelled surnames go by nursery names like Poopsie or Bodger. Moorehead never got the hang of all that. He couldn't quite tune his ear to U and non-U English, either. As late as the 1960s Lucy was vetting her husband's work for low-class solecisms like *toilet*, 'terribly non-*u*', she scribbled on one draft, 'the word "loo", which you hate, is awful too, but *u*.'

Around this time Moorehead was involved in plans to establish a new political weekly called *Harvest*. The magazine never made it to the newsstands, but the draft manifesto Moorehead prepared for it is telling. The magazine was to serve the interests of the ordinary reader against the vested interests of the elite, he wrote. The magazine's ideal reader is the person whose formal education ended 'at around sixteen' but who has a strong desire to acquire knowledge. 'Our first objective should be to break the intelligentsia cartel who keep the real basis of policy from the electorate ... Many people feel that they are being kept on the outside of a complete conspiracy of silence by the press.'

High hopes for a bold, inclusive postwar settlement are clearly audible in this document. But so is an unmistakable note of kicking against the pricks. And maybe one prick in particular. The *Express* had been 'a splendid paper to work for during the war,' Moorehead admitted. 'So far as I can remember no report of mine was ever altered, even when I opposed Beaverbrook's opinions and policies.' But Moorehead could no longer stomach working for such a conservative paper. Christiansen proposed that he return to Paris on a salary of £4000 a year plus expenses. With the advances and royalties on the books he planned to write in his spare time, this package would amount, Moorehead privately calculated, to 'something like £30,000 a year'. But he still didn't sign.

So Beaverbrook invited his star reporter down to Leatherhead, Beaverbrook's country seat, and dialled up the charm. Over Krug they discussed Kipling and Arnold Bennett, both of whom had inscribed books in their host's library. After dinner there was a film in the private cinema. But the denouement came when Beaverbrook showed his guest up to his room (sun-lamp, butler's bell, sunken bath) and sat on the edge of Moorehead's bed, for all the world like an abandoned lover, Moorehead thought, wheedling and pleading until 2 a.m. In the library the next morning Beaverbrook mounted a sober but impassioned defence of the paper's coverage of the 1945 general election. Moorehead remained unconvinced. Baffled and angry, Beaverbrook ordered a car to run his guest to the train station. *Did not realise at time what this dismissal meant*, Moorehead jotted later – 'that I was condemned to the outer darkness as far as he was concerned. Henceforth no book of mine could be reviewed in any of his papers, nor could my name even be mentioned. He had backed me, paid me well & I had failed him. That was that: I cld go to the devil.'

Moorehead was perfectly at ease around powerful people, but he wasn't a courtier. He'd misread Beaverbrook, and he'd underestimated the price he would pay for his obstinacy. Even after he was bundled onto the train, he was naïve enough to hope for a generous bonus from the *Express* in recognition of a decade's outstanding service. Instead, he copped a mugging. As previously arranged, parts of *Montgomery* ran in the *Express* in late 1946. Then, after it was published, the paper ran a vicious review. This was such a strange turnabout that even *Time* magazine in America picked up the story.

> Last week the *Express* abruptly gave the back of its hand to Alan Moorehead, who had just quit the *Express* to write more books. The *Express* warned its readers that perhaps the biography was not so authentic after all … In an acid review in the *Express*, Brigadier A.H. Head (retired), a Conservative M.P., snorted that some passages dealing with top-level goings-on 'are filled with inaccuracies and even distortions …'
>
> An angry reader had called this radical change of tune … His name: Winston Churchill.

What Churchill objected to was the story, recounted in the book, that in early 1944, Montgomery had told Churchill that he wouldn't allow him to meddle in his preparations for D-Day, and would resign if he insisted on doing so. This was perfectly true. So was another detail Moorehead tactfully omitted: that Churchill broke down and wept during that meeting with Montgomery. But this was a time when for many, including Churchill, criticism of Churchill's war leadership was tantamount to *lèse-majesté*. Moorehead had been knouted for his temerity.

One reader unreservedly pleased with the book was its subject. Montgomery read it fondly three times. 'I never really knew what sort of chap I was before,' he wrote in a note of thanks; 'nor I suppose do you until you see yourself as others see you. I think it is first class.' Overall, reviewers agreed with him, and even after the *Montgomery* imbroglio, Christiansen hoped he could entice Moorehead to stay. But eventually he, too, gave up. 'I could not retain those fine writers, Alan Moorehead and James Cameron,' Christiansen recalled in his slightly Woosterish memoirs of 1961. There is no trace of hard feelings, but no real warmth either. 'My part in [Moorehead's] career,' Christiansen concluded, 'was to put up

his salary so fast that by the time he was reporting the German surren-
ders at Luneburg Heath he was in a higher pay bracket than Field-Marshal
Montgomery himself. But I lost him just the same.'

§

All across the world young novelists were rolling up their sleeves. The war
was the great subject of a generation, and everyone was trying to pull the
sword from the stone at the same time, including Moorehead's friend
Irwin Shaw. Some were hyperventilating with the strain. 'To the writer,
war is a gigantic, inexorable, relentlessly terrible panorama,' the young
marine William Styron wrote to his father in 1945, 'which, although at
every hand fraught with mists of beauty and pathos, swirls about him so
swiftly and chaotically that he is unable to find a tongue to utter his
thoughts.' JD Salinger, who had talked eagerly with Hemingway at the
Ritz in Paris, and then in the Ardennes offensive seen enough battle for
a lifetime, also recognised the challenge, though in gentler terms: 'The
men who have been in this war deserve some sort of trembling melody
rendered without embarrassment or regret.'

Moorehead agreed. He was determined to write his epoch-defining
novel. But the move from journalist to literary author was a bold leap in
1946. A barrier existed between newspaper journalism and literary creation; getting over it, journos felt, was a Herculean feat achieved only in
the face of disdainful bookmen. One newspaper profile from 1966 was
still marvelling at how Moorehead had, in the late '40s, 'crossed the great
divide which – so snob reviewers like to think – separates journalism from
literature'. In 1947 Clifford wrote in the *Strand Magazine* that, with the
war over, his famous friend was 'inevitably reconnoitring the idea of
switching from fact to fiction'. *Inevitably* because, as Robert Hughes wrote
decades later, in those days 'difficult as they now are to remember, successful fiction was considered the ultimate proof of a writer's prowess'.

Novels were still central to what their readers thought of as culture.
Moorehead's sense of the prestige that attached to novelists comes through
best in his account of his first real meeting with Hemingway, a few years
later. Moorehead had twice brushed by the writer he admired more than

any other: in Spain, and then at the Ritz during the liberation of Paris. But they were still barely acquaintances when Lucy's old friend Mary Welsh had married Hemingway in 1946 (chucking Noel Monks to do so). 'Don't you dare become an intellectual,' Welsh wrote to Moorehead the following year; 'Papa shoots one every day before breakfast.' Perhaps a little nervously, then, Alan and Lucy drove up from Florence to Cortina to stay with the Hemingways in 1949. 'Papa' was out when they arrived at the ski lodge, but when he trooped in with his shotgun, glowering and sour, with a dusting of snow in his wild beard and 'cartridge belts and strings of teal and mallard hung in festoons from his shoulders', he looked very much as though he wanted to shoot someone, intellectual or other. He was in a foul mood.

For a while it seemed that this had been provoked by the rumpled telegram which he now produced from a pocket. It was from Harold Ross of the *New Yorker*, declining Hemingway's offer to write something on Venice. Nothing could be better than such a piece by you, Ross wrote, 'but it so happens we have got someone called Alan Moorehead who may be doing it one day'.* This was unexpected and embarrassing. Hemingway also had a bad cold. He didn't want to ski. He didn't want Mary to ski either, because she didn't know how, and would probably break her leg. Nervously laughing this off, the Mooreheads promised to take good care of her. Out onto the slopes they went; Mary promptly crashed and broke her ankle. When Moorehead relayed this news from the medical centre, Hemingway swore so violently down the phone the Mooreheads thought they might have to flee in disgrace. But he calmed down. Over the next few days, while Lucy tended to Mary in the room upstairs, he and Moorehead sat a long wooden table in the chalet with a fiasco of red wine between them, and talked.

They talked for the best part of three days. The real thorn in Hemingway's paw, Moorehead soon realised, was writing. Hemingway was working on

---

* In a letter that accompanied his cable, Ross wrote that it 'broke [his] heart' to say no. Ross had been begging Hemingway to write for his magazine for years. Interestingly, though, both cable and letter were two months old at this point. So unless it had somehow gotten mislaid, Hemingway must have dug the telegram out in anticipation of the Mooreheads' visit, knowing that if it embarrassed Mary's guest it must also flatter him.

what would become *Across the River and into the Trees*, and was unhappy with his progress. 'He was in the midst of one of those dreadful depressions in a writer's life when nothing flows, nothing comes, the words lie dead, banal and empty in the head.'

Hemingway was soon discoursing candidly on the writing craft, on its demands, its subtleties. For Hemingway's number one fan, it was like a half-drunken one-on-one masterclass. He told Moorehead he had written thirty different endings to *A Farewell to Arms*. He had sold 300,000 copies of the book in Denmark alone *since the war*. Who cared about the money, though? Hemingway didn't. It was the struggle that drove him, the honourable labour. 'I do not know how he talked to other people,' Moorehead wrote years afterwards, 'but with me he always talked books, always of writing, and with the humility and doubt of a writer who reads for five hours or so every day, and who writes and rewrites for as long as his brain will work, knowing that it is only by a miracle that he will ever achieve a phrase, even a word, that will correspond to the vision in his mind'.

Moorehead was ready to make his own lunge at greatness. It began at the new house in Wells Rise, near Regent's Park, in late 1946. But he'd barely had time to replace the ribbons in his little Olivetti before he was packed off by the *Observer* to report from Greece and northern Italy. He returned to London in April to bank his cheques and collect the family, then headed to Italy to spend a long summer with the Cliffords in the seaside village of Portofino, south of Genoa.

Every day he rose early and sat on the terrace of the Cliffords' hilltop house with his paper-clipped sheaf of foolscap while the early morning sunlight swept up the hillside below. Till now, he'd had a constant flow of outside events to feed into his typewriter. All his books so far were essentially by-products of his war-reporting. Now they would have to be fought into being from nothing, hauled up from the inner well in little buckets. But he'd already experienced one astonishing expansion, in the desert in 1940; why not another now?

In August 1946 Moorehead took belated delivery of all the things he'd put into storage in Paris in 1939. Scattering these effects on the floor, he wrote in one of his last *Express* columns, 'seven long years suddenly rolled away and I had a most complete (and embarrassing) view of myself [then].' Compared to postwar austerities, life 'seems like one long, scandalous debauch. The eggs I consumed! The casual mountains of grilled steak.' But what struck him most was the carefree, careless way he and his friends had lived. 'Life seemed then to have a curious lightness and irresponsibility. At the drop of a hat one rushed off to foreign places, picked up acquaintances and ideas and lost them again.'

As we have seen, whole chunks of the novel that resulted, *It Is Later Than You Think*, would reappear, decades later and scarcely altered, in *A Late Education*: Spain, Gibraltar, and the glorious voyage of the *Tinos*. But it is not a carefree book. On the face of it, Spain is its tragedy. The story pits commitment against detachment in the form of a protagonist unable to commit to anything and his friend who decides to risk his life for the Spanish Republic. Moorehead's hero subsides into a bitter quietism: 'I want your side to win,' he says in a strenuous *mea culpa* towards the end:

but I'm not really prepared to do anything about it … And if you ask me what I do believe in – what thing would actually make me fight I simply can't answer … The eternal spectator … I hate it. I despise and detest it.

There's something else in the book's sadness: nostalgia. Not the sentimental kind, but the kind that's more powerful for the utter helplessness with which we experience it, suddenly understanding that everything we have done and loved is gone, and we can't go back. His protagonist has no choice but to submit to a rolling surge of memory:

> one of those fixations which we develop as children unconsciously; a memory of perhaps some corner of a garden where we played, or of someone we loved at some special place and time, and the mind cannot now go back to these things without dissolving into tears, with a sense of insupportable loss.

It Is Later Than You Think was meant to be his *For Whom the Bell Tolls*, his *A Bell for Adano*, his entrée to the elite caste of journalists who were also acclaimed novelists – such as Hemingway and John Hersey. Instead, it was a humiliation. One reader's report from the US was especially blunt. 'I am terribly sorry, the Moorehead novel just is no good. It has some brilliant spots, but they are purely journalistic and, as a novel, it just stinks. It would really do his reputation a lot of harm if this were published … This will be the Kiss of Death.'

If most of Moorehead's output has faded from view today, none of it has disappeared as completely as the novels. That alone made them irresistible to me. I read the *Later* novel in the National Library of Australia, wrestling with the yards-long scrolls of galleys held together with browning sticky tape. It was a humbling experience: it was hard to believe this was the same writer who'd produced *Eclipse* only a year or so before. As literature, the obscurity of this novel – of all three, actually – seems perfectly justified. But Moorehead's flailing foray into fiction is also remarkable for the enormous effort and misery it cost him, and for what it suggests about his struggle to deal with the psychic residue of his war.

Cautiously proceeding around the pit-traps of biographical fallacy, what do we see in the novels, apart from lots of pretty good travel reportage? A preoccupation with materialism, and the fatalism that remains when all transcendent causes have faded away. Ideas in general weren't Moorehead's strength; abstractions eluded his pen like butterflies dancing away from the net. But since Naples, and perhaps even earlier, he had been conscious of something dispiriting in the culture – the shift to the mass society of the *homme moyen sensuel*, the ordinary sensual man. He came to this idea decades after many others had identified technology and mass culture as the essence of modernity, but he clung to it with the fixity of the convert. All his novels lament the loss of a higher purpose. Without some kind of shared hopefulness, his protagonists argue, life is just a long descent from hope into conformity, a moulding into the soft upholstery of daily routine a body-shaped impression too comfy to leave. He has several goes at this theme over the years, but you can hear it most clearly in, of all places, an oddly reflective passage from *Montgomery*:

> Perhaps this despair presses most heavily in adolescence when we have so few habits and when the vision of what we might do in life is strongest and our capacity for disappointment is most acute. But then the adolescent dream is thrust down by the material necessity of making a living. It is appeased a little by a love affair or the distraction of pleasure or the illusory sense of power as we advance in our careers or even in our hopes for our children, and in the end it is forgotten: all that we really hoped and all our inmost desires in life become as strange to us as they would be to other people. And we accept what we have become as inevitable and true to ourselves. Yet might it not be that we are no more than a mass of habits and adjustments to society, that we have imprisoned our real individuality which nevertheless goes on living somewhere in the background, growing weaker and weaker until we die?

How to escape this painless defeat? Utopian politics offered no solution, not if it involved violence. Moorehead never doubted that the destruction of the Third Reich by force was right, despite the horrific cost; he didn't demur when, in India in 1942, in a personal audience with Gandhi, the great man said to him, 'What is the point of talking? You and the people you represent are committed to violence.' But he also believed that for the

individuals doing the suffering, the 'situation' can never fully justify the
pain. 'Do you really think it's worth all this?' his protagonist pleads, thinking of the heavy body bags he'd seen swung off the charred decks of the
Deutschland in 1937. 'I mean the pain and the cruelty and the awful waste.
Can any situation be so bad that it's worth undergoing all that to change it?'

This hand-wringing about violent means to necessary ends could just
be the quietism of someone doing nicely in an unfair world. But
Moorehead's deep ambivalence about violence was a bolder view in 1947
than it seems now. Many European writers and thinkers had emerged
from the war convinced that political killing is not merely necessary, but
often desirable. Many would have answered the 'Is it worth all this?' question with a Gallic shrug. Of course it is.

Moorehead wasn't alone in his humanistic impasse. He shared it with
much more celebrated thinkers, like Albert Camus and Cesare Pavese.
For Pavese war is always about death first, and causes second. 'Even beaten
our enemy is someone,' he wrote in *The House on the Hill* in 1949:

> One feels humiliated because one understands – touching it with one's
> eyes – that we might be in their place ourselves: there would be no dif-
> ference, and if we live we owe it to this dirtied corpse. That is why every
> war is a civil war; every fallen man resembles one who remains and calls
> him to account.

Moorehead had seen too many dirtied corpses, any one of which might
have taken *his* place. But his attempts to say something true and difficult
about this, about the postwar anomie and the uneasy retreat from shining causes it led to, have disappeared from the record even more completely
than the novels. People who knew him later as the celebrated master
craftsman in Porto Ercole saw little of the resister of materialist nihilism.
Not even his admirers detected much concern about political justice. The
man Robert Hughes got to know in the 1960s was 'essentially apolitical',
he thought; in the late '80s Martha Gellhorn told Pocock she thought
Moorehead had no social conscience. But Moorehead did have an ideal-
istic side, a generalised hopefulness for the world. It's there in his plans
for a new newspaper, his belief in postwar reconstruction along social

democratic lines. One of the poignant things about reading the novels, and *It Is Later Than You Think* in particular, is seeing what painful labour it was to write about losing a political optimism, a faith in the possibility of a better way of organising human affairs, that few suspected he had.

Precisely when Moorehead realised the novel was doomed is hard to say. Well into 1948 he was rewriting it and trying to sell it off in chunks to American magazines. A decade afterwards, he said that it was being set up in type 'before I had the sense to get it stopped ... It was really very bad.'

§

It Is Later Than You Think had taken a miserable year or more to write and rewrite. The next one, *The Rage of the Vulture*, he knocked off in about ten weeks.

Again, *Rage* was a thinly fictionalised version of events. In September 1947, Lucy and the children left Portofino and returned to London – leaving Moorehead feeling bereft, as he often did when granted his cherished liberty. Alone, he made his way along the Italian Riviera and caught the BOAC flying boat from Marseilles to Karachi to cover the Partition of India for the *Observer*. He went to Bombay and Delhi, where he reported on the humanitarian disaster unfolding as tens of millions of people reshuffled their lives between redrawn borders. It was in Kashmir, though, that Moorehead got his idea for a new novel. A scenic thriller, it would be based on an attack by mountain tribesmen on the Kashmiri town of Baramulla in December, which left 3000 people dead. Moorehead's hero is a war-damaged, cynical arms smuggler, Pearson, who flies into Kashmir aiming to profit from the turmoil; his love object is a blind and ravishingly lovely English girl. Her reason for rebuffing Pearson's gruff overtures is revealed in the final pages: she has a terminal brain tumor. The problems with the novel start with the plucked-out-of-a-hat title, and go on from there.* There's cynicism and love, exquisite scenery and flurries of rugged action. Robert Hughes called it 'a wooden dog'.

---

* It's a title that cries out for the substitution-game treatment. Not *The Anger of the Eagle? The Spleen of the Egret?* Or *The Froideur of the Finch?* And so on.

But there are also, among the 'compensations for the basic failure of the central story' – as the *New York Times* put it – some fine documentary flashes of what British India looked like as it passed into history, including a decomposing still life of the lounge of the besieged British Club, a scene Moorehead never tired of describing, wherever he went in the old Empire. Even during the war Moorehead had foreseen the fate of these sahibs, whose long colonial afternoon was ending. 'What a crude and tragic Hollywood thriller it has since turned out to be,' he wrote in 1942, surveying an English Club in Iraq: 'the natives creeping through the jungle, the sudden arrow embedded in the bar-room door, the settlers spilling their drinks as they run for their guns, the war whoops in the jungle, the ammunition gone and the final overwhelming rush of the enemy, and then the house going up in flames.'

It's a bizarre irony, but one consistent with the hapless state of Moorehead's career in these years, that this passage precisely describes the crude and tragic Hollywood thriller that *Rage* became. Charles Vidor's *Thunder in the East* (1952) starred Alan Ladd and Deborah Kerr, but is almost impossible to find now – the DVD I ordered took a month to arrive from the US, and turned out to be a bootleg copy. In the movie's unsmiling climax, the tribesmen descend on the remote outpost of 'Ghandahar', where the town's sclerotic Britishers have barricaded themselves in the English hotel. Back in 1942, Moorehead had suggested that it mightn't be a bad thing if the English Club in Iraq *had* been burned down – 'and some of its old ideas destroyed with it'. But there's no room for qualms in the movie. Our arms-smuggler hero, Pearson (Alan Ladd), breaks out his unsold rifles. Pearson and the pacifist maharajah (Charles Boyer) – pacifist till now, anyway – stand shoulder to shoulder in the final frames, emptying their magazines into the crowds of whooping tribesmen as they storm the Brits' redoubt. Vidor filmed this in such a way that the comrades in arms, narrow-eyed in the billowing cordite, are actually firing *into* the camera – at an audience probably grateful to be dead by this point.

So *Rage* was strike two. Long before it reached the bookstores, Moorehead was hard at work on a third novel. After an extended tour of the US in the early months of 1948, the Mooreheads returned to the Cliffords' house in Portofino for the summer. Work began right away. *A Summer Night* would be a detailed account, perfunctorily disguised, of expat life in Portofino's summer of 1948. It was a season of crises, some remote, some closer by. The Berlin Airlift, which many feared might trigger a new European war, began in June. In July, a failed assassination attempt on the communist leader Togliatti in Rome prompted a strike that reverberated even in tiny Portofino. Some young communist workers from Santa Margherita cycled into town one morning, Moorehead reported in a *New Yorker* article, and solemnly instructed all the shopkeepers to close. Shutters clattered down all around the piazza. The English hotel guests were rather put out, in their undemonstrative way.

> 'May I swim while the strike is on?' one of the English tourists asked mildly.
>
> 'You may,' one of the young men said, 'provided you do not have the appearance of enjoying yourself.'

'A political crisis every five minutes,' Moorehead wrote to Phyllis. 'We live with our bags packed and you can imagine the state of our nerves.' The two couples at the centre of *A Summer Night*, frustrated English painter Philip and wife Prudence, and their American friends, Howard and Celine, also live with their bags packed. Their long restless summer is punctuated by the strike, by debates about what makes life worth living, materialist ennui, a diving accident, a car accident, drinks and adulterous love. More literary and docile than *The Rage of the Vulture*, and full of gorgeous landscapes as well as war rubble, the novel is of a type that was in considerable demand in the late '40s. At a time when few people could afford to travel, florid tales set in exotic parts offered readers a few hours' relief from grey skies and the pinched austerity of postwar Britain; they were a way of basking in borrowed sunshine, delighting in foreigners' curious ways, and imagining it was you who was living it up in Italy.

Moorehead didn't have to imagine. Portofino was a ridiculously pretty little village in 1948, and it still is, which is why it has become a deluxe tourist ant-heap. Coach-loads of people pour into the cobbled square each day to look at the charmingly preserved piazza. Most browse the upmarket shopping arcades, bargain uncomprehendingly with the ancient ladies selling the handmade lace by the church steps, gawp at the luxury yachts and take pictures of the fishing nets drying decoratively on the Roman stones of the mole. It's cheerful, overcrowded and a bit squalid, like the buffet deck of a large ferry.

In 1948 Portofino was already a holiday spot – English milords had been wintering here for generations – but it was much quieter and much poorer. The Cliffords' house was built out of an old Saracen watchtower and 'surely one of the most beautifully placed houses in the world', one visitor marvelled. 'The Castelletto stands on the highest point of the headland, 900 feet above the sea, overlooking Portofino's miniature harbor and the hillsides behind.' It had a garden terrace with views of the sea. Branches of fragrant ilex nosed through the open windows of guestrooms. A sense of life there can be gleaned from the novel, as well as letters: warm days filled with bathing off the rocks below the promontory, long lunches of scampi, pizza and melons; naps in cool stone-floored rooms afterwards. Sometimes there were excursions to Rapallo or Genoa for shopping or sightseeing. The postwar oils craze was at its height, and everyone was painting ungainly daubs of the Ligurian coast. In the evenings, while nannies managed the children, everyone lolled in cane chairs with their cold drinks, playing bridge and canasta, or danced to the phonograph while fireflies flickered in the dim olive orchards below.

I couldn't find the Cliffords' house. But perched on a thickly treed headland above the marina I found a plausible stand-in: another turreted stone villa that had also been renovated by an English couple just after the war. It's now a local museum, with a garden terrace with dry-stone parapets and towering views of the windy sea and sky.

Trying to relate oneself to a lost civilisation is, as Moorehead said, 'an elusive operation', and the months when he was here trying to become a novelist of the world seemed impossibly distant, even *in situ*. It's easy enough to feel some sentimental envy for the carefree simplicity of those long-ago summers; the ambient fear of another war is harder to recapture, and the lingering presence of the last one hardest of all. When Eddie

Bangor dropped by in 1947 he'd just come from Milan, where he'd visited a home for children mutilated in the war. War damage and poverty crept into Moorehead's novel, too. On day trips his characters motor through the 'animated desolation' of primitive villages, past 'ragged children playing in the bomb rubble, beggars crouching on the churchyard steps, tin cans and flies and lines of washing strung across the street'.

Perhaps, I thought, things would have gone better for Moorehead in a less aggressively lovely spot. But then the popular image of the *poète maudit* – the asocial writer-genius, tubercular, garret-bound – had never appealed to him. 'Every writer I know under sixty,' wrote Cyril Connolly in 1950, 'is ruining his talent through hack-work and part-time jobs: there is always a fistula through which the juices of genius are leaking away into some disgusting receptacle.' Connolly thought serious writers should learn to be poorer. Moorehead didn't. His energies may have been depleted by a heavy schedule of *Observer* articles, but he wasn't going back to the genteel bankruptcy of his childhood. And he wasn't going back to the provincial obscurity of Australia, either.

I'd found a surly little piece published in Cyril Connolly's *Horizon* in early 1947 about Moorehead's visit there the year before. Moorehead had been looking harder at his homeland than I'd realised. Sure there was fresh food in the shops, he wrote; but overall 'the country lay in a trough of postwar weariness, of disillusion, of materialistic cynicism, of spiritual ennui'. The Australian accent, he remarked, 'grates on the European ear' – he meant *his* ear. The drabness of the cities reflected the mediocrity of their inhabitants who 'avoid at all costs any show of eccentricity or exhibit any interests beyond those of the average man'. And the creative life? The bush was there for painters, but a writer would go mad for lack of company, stimulation and *history*. 'Perhaps Proust preferred to work in a padded cell in the Faubourg St. Honoré,' he writes – you can almost hear the leathery creak of the club chair as he prepares the *coup* – 'But could he have worked in a padded cell in Wagga Wagga?'

In 1948 Moorehead doubted he could write in Wagga Wagga. He was certain he didn't want to live anywhere near it.

Nothing he produced in Portofino was lasting literature either. But I realised as I loitered up there in the villa garden, among all the Russian honeymooners taking selfies with the Bay of Rapallo in the background, inhaled the sappy air under the cypresses and tried to imagine what it looked like on one of those still nights in 1948 when hundreds of fishing boats put out from Portofino with their acetylene lamps shining down into the black water, that that didn't matter. What mattered was Moorehead's determination to make a life in the great elsewhere. He was in most ways a measured and sober personality, but there was something deeply unreasonable about his insistence on escape, this pattern of self-propulsion and continuous flight from suburban drudgery, from obscurity, from the ordinary – from Australia. It was the unreasonableness that I found so appealing, even if I didn't yet understand it. And the question remained: escape into what?

§

When they left Portofino at the end of the summer, the Mooreheads moved to a large rented house in the hills of Florence. The Villa Diana was originally built for the Medici tutor and neurotic Renaissance genius Angelo Poliziano. The earliest parts of the building dated to the fifteenth century. It had its own chapel. There was a room where Poliziano himself was said to have slept. It had sheltered troops of six different armies during the war. Guests reported ghostly visitations, albeit friendly ones. Mary Welsh (Mrs Hemingway) thought it 'rambling, drafty and lovely'. It had an enormous fireplace and ponderous furniture. There were electric lights, but no fridge, gas or telephone. In winter, they had to plug the cracks under doors with towels to keep out the freezing drafts.

Moorehead loved the business of setting up the new home, employing domestic staff, managing their picturesque crises. 'It seems madness that anyone could willingly not live like this,' he wrote in the new journal, where he would record his rebirth as a man of letters. A typical day: he worked for a few hours on the novel, then clipped some hedges in the *second* garden, and supervised some landscaping improvements to be carried out by an ancient gardener 'of terrifying aspect'. Lunch? Boned rabbit done over charcoal. There was excellent wine from the cellar. It took all his discipline 'not to take four glasses with each meal'. In the afternoon he read. The children were happy in their schools; they had an adored pet duck called Luigi, named in honour of the author Luigi Barzini, who had presented it to them during a visit. Culture would be Moorehead's country, a country he shared in Florence with a floating community of expatriate lotus-eaters. The lotus was, as advertised, delicious. 'Absence of jealousy, suspense, antagonism, ambition, ennui. How long will it last?'

Reviews of *The Rage of the Vulture* were starting to trickle in, and were surprisingly friendly. Novelist Elizabeth Bowen found it 'tautly, commandingly and totally exciting'. Gratifyingly, the novel was banned in Ireland. The *Guardian* praised the reportage: 'the exotic background is brilliantly described' – but 'there is more of the arresting war reporter in *The Rage of The Vulture* than of the imaginative artist'. Moorehead still had some work to do to fight his way out of the journalists' ghetto and into the city of literature.

And work he did. There was *A Summer Night* to be going on with. And book reviews, a new line for Moorehead. He dashed off a review of André Gide's *Journals*, which impressed him, and suggested an exemplary way of life. One has a picture, he wrote:

> of the incessant, never-ending work which feeds a really cultivated mind. Two hours' practice on the piano, an hour writing letters, two hours on translations, five hours on a novel and every other spare minute … given up to reading. This is how the days of Gide's middle age went by.

Another model of the cultivated life lay over the hillside of vineyards and stone walls at I Tatti. An even more influential figure than Hemingway for Moorehead's literary ambition in the postwar years was Bernard Berenson, the renowned art historian, connoisseur and diarist. For Moorehead, this 'brisk, disenchanted old man, crackling and sparkling' was a living link to what he considered an age of giants, to the Edwardian culture of Arnold, Strachey, Gosse and Wilde. Now nearly eighty, Berenson lived in Fiesole above Florence, in a villa that had dozens of staff and was frequently full of celebrity house guests. The rule, writes one biographer, was 'that those invited be either clever, witty, famous, and titled, or adept at making Berenson himself feel clever, witty, famous, and titled'. When, as was his habit, he led tours of his fabulous gardens, guests would fall into processional order behind, Moorehead wrote, 'as polite, as self-conscious and as gracious as the figures in a Japanese print'.

The two first met in 1947. Berenson had read and admired *Eclipse* and *Montgomery*, which had been sent to him by one of Moorehead's London patrons, Sibyl Colefax ('London's most indefatigable people-collector,' according to one historian), and extended an invitation to Moorehead to visit. The place struck Moorehead as terrifyingly grand. On the first evening, he wandered the rooms 'tense as a cat among the dishes and the Venetian fingerbowls' and awoke the next day to find a valet with a thermometer running his bath. More startling on that first visit was Berenson himself, whose *ancien régime* worldview made Beaverbrook look radical.

> When the old man says, 'So you believe that the mass of the people can be educated,' and laughs; when he says, 'Universal suffrage is rubbish. Why then not give domestic animals the vote?' ... I find I have nothing to bring against such Edwardian quaintness. It's not worth answering.

But in the late '40s a real friendship grew up between them, nourished by Moorehead's evident yearning for a mentor of some kind – 'the foster-father I so badly needed'. Berenson's watchful tutelage was vital to Moorehead's belief that he could make himself a man of literature, a real writer. He provided advice, and also solace, as it soon became clear that *A Summer Night* was going nowhere. From this distance the battle with the novels sounds like a long, luckless day in the workshop: the rough sawing of the timber, the groans, the clumsy thwack of the hammer, occasional yelps of pain. This thankless struggle seems like a simple category error: being a writer, sometimes a very fine one, didn't make him a novelist. But, alas, his determination didn't waver. Hadn't Hemingway told him he'd rewritten the last page of *A Farewell to Arms* thirty times? Moorehead was always encouraged by anecdotes from other writers about the practical mechanics of creation. He loved hearing, when he met CS Forester on an Atlantic crossing in 1956, that the creator of *Hornblower* sustained his success by writing a book a year, and relying less on the Muse than on simple maths: 1000 words a day, Forester explained, for three months each year: '1000 words × 3 months = 90,000 words = a book.' Simple.

Except it wasn't. Self-discipline wasn't helping Moorehead lift his tale out of its source material. Following the progress of the *Summer Night* drafts, Lucy had cracked the *roman à clef* at a glance: she identified herself as Prudence, the sensible, long-suffering wife of the adulterous painter Philip. And 'Philip is a portrait of yourself but a portrait without depth and one is never entirely in sympathy with him,' she wrote in some editorial notes. A couple of weeks later, more bad news. 'Darling; I have just read the two last chapters of your book and must write at once what I feel about them. I think they are excellent, far and away the best things in the book.' But ...

> Your dialogue is always beyond reproach: when your characters talk they talk as people would talk; or rather; more complicated, they read as they would sound if they talked. (You <u>must</u> write a play.) But in themselves your characters are not really true. You do not seem to me to be suffi-ciently interested in, say rather intensely fascinated with, people to re-create them in a book.

Soon, with *A Summer Night* flat-lining, Moorehead was gratefully accepting any reason to get out of the house. At the end of 1948 he was a British delegate at the 3rd UNESCO General Conference. Then he went to Berlin for the *Observer*. He was also writing a movie synopsis for Pinewood Studios about the Berlin Airlift. That came to nothing and all too soon he was back at Villa Diana, back to the old problems. 'I think I know myself as a writer now,' he wrote in his diary.

> Description of scenes, places, action: excellent. Readableness, continuity, tempo, construction: first class. Writing: often first class, sometimes bet-ter or worse. Dialogue: natural and fluent but without wit or any particular subtlety or inspiration. Characters: very bad with the exception of occa-sional flukes drawn from life. Plots: hopeless. Ability to state a meaning, a philosophy: hopeless.

In late summer 1949 Moorehead began to write a play, just as Lucy had urged.* Again, Moorehead didn't look far for inspiration: it was about a novelist who can't write, and who lives in a villa in Fiesole. Moorehead prepared a key to the cast of characters, explaining who they all were in real life, including the Italian servants, and the real name of the woman he calls 'Claire' in the play – the one with whom the bored writer (not named) wishes to have an affair. In his notes Moorehead keeps switching between characters' names and their real-life models as if he keeps forgetting that there's a difference. 'Wife having miscarriage' – the writer's wife, that is. She's called Mary in the play, and Lucy in half the notes.

In early June Lucy had, in fact, suffered a miscarriage at the villa. The pregnancy was advanced, and she was suddenly bleeding so profusely, Moorehead wrote in his diary, that 'no towels could cope with it'. It was terrifying. A thunderstorm was raging outside. Lucy 'said suddenly that she believed she might die and there were many things she wanted to say'. While they waited for the doctor, she asked him to read to her from Wordsworth's *Intimations of Immortality*. Then the storm cleared, and in a surreal detail, like something out of Tarkovsky, a religious procession passed below the bedroom balcony, with a noisy band and children in white communion outfits. Lucy was transferred to hospital, and eventually made a full recovery.

This harrowing experience makes an eye-watering reappearance just weeks later in the play Lucy had urged Alan to write. During a thunderstorm, and while his wife lies abed upstairs recovering from a miscarriage, the blocked writer, John, perhaps stirred by all that virile thunder, coolly attempts the seduction of their houseguest, Claire.

CLAIRE: We're not children. This is not something that we can just pass off casually, without caring.

---

* This business with plays remained a mystery. There's no evidence that Moorehead went to the theatre often or with much enthusiasm; I can definitively place him in a theatre only a handful of times in his entire adult life. Yet throughout the '40s and '50s, he constantly breaks off whatever he's doing to take another crack at the stage. It's possible he saw this as a roundabout route into the movies; perhaps he just used plays as a kind of purge valve for ideas he didn't know what else to do with.

JOHN: And yet we must make love.

CLAIRE: Yes, we must.

What was this – creative desperation? Or just a ruthless exercise of the artist's prerogative? These parallels to real life can't have escaped Martha Gellhorn, who read the script for him when she visited a couple of weeks later. Moorehead dolefully recorded her opinion: 'It is no good, never can be any good and ought to be abandoned.'

I'm only surprised she didn't say worse.

§

Up to this point, Moorehead's story, with its travel and love and war, seems broadly representative of his era. But in the darkest working days at Villa Diana, he seems to slip back into his own singularity, as a writer and a person. His hopes and fears seem so nakedly exposed in the solitary struggle to dredge something new out of himself. I could see him there at my elbow, at the long table in the dark room in the Villa Diana, with its two small bright windows high in the wall, smoking, sighing as he turns the pages in books loaned from Berenson's library, trying to do what writers have always done: writing in the hope of escaping death, of being loved, of making meaning from the chaos, of paying the rent.

But daydreams weren't going to cut it. I badly needed those letters and diaries.

Perhaps, like the Italian towns nearby that were still half rubble, he was recovering from the war. It's true that he 'didn't like war' as one colleague noted; but that doesn't mean he wasn't drifting in the weightlessness of peace, or that he didn't also miss the intensity of wartime, the freedom in the chaos, the constant stream of new faces and places. Moorehead was not in later life one of those people who refused to talk about the things he'd seen in the war. But he didn't dwell on it. Caroline Moorehead didn't realise her father had seen Belsen until twenty years afterwards, she told me, simply because he never discussed it. If he suffered nightmares, he didn't write about them. The nearest is a short story Moorehead wrote in late 1947 for *Collier's* magazine actually *called* 'Nightmare': it imagines a war crimes trial in which various Allied leaders are being prosecuted by the victorious Nazis in Paris. Goebbels, in a particularly horrible detail, is living in Lucullan splendour at the Crillon.

§

The *New Yorker* was the one thing that was going right for Moorehead at the time. His twenty-year association with the magazine had begun in 1948 during his American tour. With his usual pragmatism, Moorehead had collected letters of recommendation from people he knew, and from some he didn't – including the novelist Rebecca West. 'I can't think that you really need advice from me,' she replied to his note, 'but if I can give it I should be glad and proud … I have very greatly admired your stuff always, but never so much as now.' He didn't really want advice; he wanted introductions. West duly provided glowing ones, to Harold Ross and others, describing him in one note as 'the finest newspaper correspondent in Great Britain'.

The meeting with Ross concluded satisfactorily, and six months later Moorehead submitted his first article, about Portofino. 'We were delighted,' wrote Ross's deputy, William Shawn, 'though not at all surprised, that you hit the mark exactly with your first piece'. Encouraged, Moorehead submitted more pieces in the following months: on the UNESCO General Conference; a piece about villa life in Florence full of comical vexations and local characters; and one on the Palio, the ancient and anarchic horse race run around Siena's vast piazza. The *New Yorker* was a glamorous place to be published, and it paid much better than English newspapers could.

But this was a time in Moorehead's career when there was a fly at the bottom of every cup. Rebecca West privately complained to Ross about factual errors in the Portofino article; in Portofino itself, the piece went down very badly. Ann Rothermere, wife of the *Daily Mail*'s proprietor Viscount Rothermere, was staying with the Cliffords and lunching with them in Rapallo one day when she produced a clipping of the article sent to her from London by her lover, Ian Fleming. Jenny was incensed. Moorehead's article, she fumed, was a rip-off of a piece she had herself written and had been fool enough to show to the Mooreheads. Her rage only escalated as Ann's husband, also at lunch, proceeded to read Moorehead's story with evident enjoyment and admiration. 'It cast a great shadow over the day,' Ann reported to Fleming that evening, 'for whenever we passed a post office Jenny sent abusive telegrams to Alan while Alex was dumb and miserable but unable to save the Clifford–Moorehead axis from becoming an Italian vendetta.'

There was trouble with the Siena piece, too, which Moorehead barely recognised when it appeared in print in 1949. He wrote a polite but unhappy note to William Shawn, objecting to all the changes. Shawn's reply was as courteous as Harold Ross's four pages of editorial comments on the story – which Shawn delicately enclosed – were withering and exasperated.* Sensibly, Moorehead made no further protest.

By mid-1950, Moorehead himself thought his *New Yorker* pieces were becoming stylised and forced. But the magazine took everything he sent, and it's not hard to see why. His journalism still had that likeable eagerness to explore that his fiction conspicuously lacked; he still had that talent, as his American agent once put it, 'for invoking the reader's friendly feelings'. Most of these pieces were published as *The Villa Diana* in 1951, with illustrations by Osbert Lancaster. It's a sad, strangely distant book to read now: a book of ghosts that is itself haunted by the atom bomb and the aftershocks of Italy's catastrophic war. And perhaps by the author's struggle to deal with his own war experience. In one chapter, Moorehead visits the monastery town of Cassino, in central Italy. Five years had passed since the place was destroyed by an infamous Allied bombing raid. He notes, literally in parentheses: '(Land mines are still being uncovered: a boy was blown to bits a week or two back).'

There's something in the breezy diffidence of that sentence that seems unnecessarily cruel – or *hardboiled*, as Moorehead termed it. It was a hardboiled time, of course, even in sunny Italy, where the neo-realist landscape of the local towns were a constant reminder of how hard life could be. But if Moorehead's postwar retreat from action to the study had one clear effect on his work it was a deepening of his sense of history, of just how

---

* 'Undoubtedly Moorehead doesn't know what he's talking about here,' Ross wrote, inter alia, *'and we've got to do the best we can … This wording strikes me as awfully weak.'* Ross was notorious for his stringent edits, and he didn't apologise for them. 'The worse the writer is,' he once confided to another contributor, 'the more argument; that is the rule.'

long people had been fighting wars, dying of disease and still somehow struggling on. He was coming to see it all – the eruptions of domestic farce at Villa Diana, the private tragedies, the wild outbreak of ugly neon signage in Rome – as part of time's endless parade. To say that *all this will pass* mightn't sound like much more than fatalism. But in an age of dislocating shocks the continuity of village life and its ancient seasonal rhythms were a consolation.

In March 1950 he began to explore alternatives to the struggle at the Villa Diana. On a visit to London to meet his publishers, he sounded out some old friends about possible jobs. He also bumped into Christiansen, who couldn't resist twitting the man with a calling too lofty for the *Daily Express*: 'How much are you earning now, Alan?'

In spring, the Mooreheads were once again house-guests of the Cliffords at Portofino. The village was lousy with literary celebs. There was one dinner party down in the village for the Castelletto crowd and Truman Capote and Evelyn Waugh.* But Moorehead's postwar period was winding down now, like one of Gatsby's late summer parties, into the grey sober light of morning. Clifford had been diagnosed with Hodgkin disease and would be seeking treatment in London. No one yet knew what this might mean, or was prepared to think about it. The final fling was on Ischia in August 1950. The Bernsteins and Lancasters were there, too; in the evenings they all mingled at candlelit *trattorie* with Roberto Rossellini, Ingrid Bergman and the composer William Walton.

Moorehead was still on Ischia when he received the news that Christopher Buckley was dead. His jeep had run over a mine in Korea. He was forty-five. In an unpublished tribute, Moorehead remembered that shortly after the Normandy invasion, while the war raged all around, Buckley had heard of an eighteenth-century sedan chair for sale in Harrods. It was an item so splendidly out of time at that moment, and anyway so tempting to a connoisseur of the Regency period, that he

---

* It's hard to see what Moorehead and Capote might have had in common, except a great admiration for the novels of EM Forster. But Moorehead had met and befriended the 23-year-old literary sensation aboard *The Queen Elizabeth* during a trans-Atlantic crossing voyage in 1948. When they arrived in London, Moorehead introduced Capote to several friends, including Harold Nicolson, who gratefully – though unsuccessfully – tried to seduce him.

arranged to buy it immediately, for 100 guineas. The otherworldly item occupied the living room of his London flat for several years before Buckley's growing book collection forced it out, and he donated it to the local museum. The Regency period, Moorehead wrote, was one of his friend's manias. 'One was the game of cricket. Another was the art of war.'

§

They closed up Villa Diana in September 1950. Moorehead was going back to London to a job as press attaché for the Ministry of Defence, and his first taste of anything resembling an ordinary job in a dozen years.

Lucy went ahead with the children while Alan stayed on for a few days to tidy things up. Where would Luigi the duck go, the children asked as they piled into the car. What would become of him? Unfortunately, Luigi's time was up too: the cook served him up to the unsuspecting *signore* that very night. I'd always had this pencilled in as the most dismal moment in Moorehead's professional life, as he sat at Villa Diana's dining table with a last bottle from the cellar, a mouthful of Luigi on his fork. But maybe that underestimates how ruthless he was with himself. He really did need to get away from the 'sickening vacuity' of a freedom that had somehow curdled into its opposite. He needed to kick-start himself again. And he needed money, and not just for his own family. In these years he supplemented his father's pension with a regular allowance. On the way back to London, he stopped in Paris to take delivery of a Connaught-green Rover 75 saloon. It cost £785.

The letters on the numberplate were NGW: for Moorehead, they stood for *never good weather*. It looks like a harsh re-entry to reality after a long spell away from it – as though pitch-forked from a dusty pink Tiepolo cloud to the smoggy streets of London – but it was really a fairly gentle return to earth. He'd been parachuted into a good job, as chief PR flack for the Ministry of Defence, and all thanks to wartime contacts. His appointment was arranged by Philip Jordan (an old colleague from Tunisia, now press secretary to Prime Minister Attlee) and endorsed by Montgomery (now Chief of the Imperial General Staff) and on generous terms. It was all a bit irregular, actually, and some muted complaints about it made it into the papers.

If he'd been more interested in the work, 1950 would have been an exciting time to do it. This was a nervy moment in European politics. Britain was urgently re-arming for the Cold War while its diplomats tried to pull together a North Atlantic Alliance. British scientists were hard at work on their own atomic bomb program. New weapons systems were coming online; British aerospace contractors were leading the world in the race to build more powerful jet aircraft to deliver them. As spokesperson for the Minister of Defence, Moorehead's task was to get all this across to the public in a firm and soothing manner.

Too proud to return to Fleet Street, Moorehead nonetheless felt the usual journalist's misgivings about moving into PR, as well as a few uniquely his own. It seemed a backward step; 'perhaps an unexpected choice of job,' remarked one columnist, 'for a writer who shows every indication of becoming a first-rate creative author.' In the end, he only drew a salary for eight months. At the *New Yorker*, Ross urged Moorehead to get back to writing as soon as possible. 'My argument always is that writers should write, except in states of great emergency.' Moorehead agreed. Another possible subject for a *New Yorker* article had already presented itself: the German-born British nuclear scientist Klaus Fuchs, who had been convicted of treason in early 1950 for passing on nuclear secrets to the Russians.

There is a helpless inevitability about the way Moorehead plunged into the quicksand of *The Traitors*, his book about the spies. The dreaming novelist in him was drawn to the Fuchs story because it seemed so reminiscent of *Crime and Punishment*, which he was reading. 'Here, it seemed, was Raskolnikov all over again: the split personality, the desire to hide and the desire to confess, and, ultimately, his intimate trust in the policeman who has come to destroy him.' And the spies were a major story; a book might sell lots of copies. But the tale would also lead him into the realm of ideas and abstractions, always a dicey area for Moorehead.

In mid-1950 he petitioned the Home Secretary for permission to interview Fuchs in prison and was denied. Moorehead's brush with the golden age of Cold War espionage might have ended there. But in 1951, the defection of 'Cambridge spies' Donald MacLean and Guy Burgess further embarrassed a Secret Service already under pressure over the scandal of the atomic spies. The Americans blamed sloppy British security for the fact that not just Fuchs, but two other traitor-scientists, Alan Nunn May and Bruno Pontecorvo, had managed to infiltrate joint US–British war-time research programs. So arrangements were made to provide Moorehead with access to classified material so that he might produce what Churchill (now prime minister again) described in parliament as 'a truthful and substantive account of these three spy episodes'.

The Traitors appeared in July 1952. 'This is in no way an official book,' Moorehead wrote in the opening pages, 'the original idea of it, the pattern, and the opinions expressed are entirely my own.' It was a commission, though. He still couldn't interview Fuchs, but he had a brief, which he stuck to, and he had the classified material. Unfortunately, the documents he'd been given had been selectively edited – *redacted*, we would say now. So on the most politically sensitive point, Moorehead concluded, as he was expected to, that MI5's vetting procedures had been perfectly sound. Fuchs had been subjected to four rigorous checks, but always during breaks in his spying activity. This detail, writes one historian, was 'MI5's fiction, ped-dled to Moorehead as fact, on the explicit instructions of [Sir Percy] Sillitoe'. Moorehead's indulgent conclusion, that it is anyway impossible for free societies to inoculate themselves against treacherous bacilli without turn-ing into police states, MI5 got for free.

As a story, *The Traitors* is a small triumph. Moorehead's depiction of the nuclear plant at Harwell has the fluorescent vividness of an old sci-fi movie – all the bright lights and lab coats can't quite contain a horror of what's brewing in the reactor. His knack for capturing a vibrant likeness of a minor character in just a line or two is becoming a striking talent; and his traitor-scientists are richly human studies of men fumbling their way into the destiny of their own flaws. The climax of the Fuchs story, in particular, shows what a compelling novel Moorehead could write when he didn't have to make anything up.

Literary quality wasn't the problem with *The Traitors*, though; the prob-lem was with moral philosophy. For all their mistakes, Moorehead wrote, we can *understand* the spies. Yes, Fuchs's megalomania told him he should decide on behalf of humankind whether to pass on nuclear secrets to the

USSR – but 'who hasn't felt that prim egoism', that 'adolescent dream of a world that is perfectly pure and good, and oneself a shining hero in it'? Still, we cannot *forgive* them. Like the early Christians, the traitor scientists 'were so convinced of their rightness that they were prepared to destroy the State in order to have their way'. In what became an infamous phrase, he continues: 'there is no place for such men in an ordered community. They belong where Fuchs now is, sewing mailbags, in Stafford Gaol.'

This remark was met with a collective recoil of distaste; it was as though Moorehead had peed in the fountain of English humanism. 'Is this not to throw the democratic liberal-humanistic, individualistic baby out with the totalitarian bath-water?' the *Times Literary Supplement* demanded. Moorehead 'has stirred a wasps' nest', the Manchester *Guardian* said, with his 'fallacious generalisation that there is no room in society for men who consult nothing but their consciences'. Eminent critics lined up to give him a kicking. Philip Toynbee called the sentence 'a piece of straight Fascist or Communist morality'; William Empson decried the moral logic by which Moorehead damned the spies 'for having had the impudence to obey their own consciences', instead of understanding that a citizen's duty is 'to concur with any herd in which he happens to find himself'. The sharpest cut came from an anonymous review in the *Listener*. 'What [Moorehead] complains of is that [Nunn] May and Fuchs both acted as their consciences bade them, and that according to Mr Moorehead, will never do … One cannot help wondering which way Mr Moorehead will jump if, and when, we are "liberated".'*

Moorehead was bewildered by the fuss, but no one else was. 'What on earth made you write that awful sentence?' a sympathetic friend wrote. Before he knew it, Moorehead was explaining that awful sentence in a BBC radio special. Attempting a clarification, he argued that consciences are not always reliable guides to goodness: they're shaped by society, sometimes desperate and traumatised ones, like the 1920s Germany in which Fuchs grew up.

---

* The author of this piece was Rebecca West, who had so recently extolled his virtues to every American editor in her contact book. After her objections to the Portofino story, and now this, Moorehead could have been forgiven for thinking she was becoming his personal gadfly.

Perhaps what stung most was a sense of being misunderstood. In taking the measure of who and what the scientists had betrayed, *Traitors* contained some of the most affectionate passages Moorehead ever wrote about Britain, his adopted home. Despite strong sales, the hurt lingered. Several months after the *Listener* review appeared, he issued a writ in the High Court. He dropped the suit eventually, even though, as he put it in a letter to his solicitors, doing so seemed to be 'buying peace of mind at too high a price'.

That was a hard thing to come by in the early 1950s. Home life seems to have been content enough, though money was often tight – at least by later standards. (Lemonade, John recalls, was strictly a Sunday treat.) A third child, Richard, would be born in late 1951, and in many ways the household at Wells Rise was a happy place. Professionally, though, this was a period scattered with the wreckage of failed projects, and a sense of chances squandered weighed heavily. 'On the whole,' Moorehead wrote in the journal he'd all but abandoned, 'less ennui than in Florence but a much less healthy life and a pointless one.'

Even before *The Traitors* blew up in his face, he was hunting for a new book idea that would lift him out of his slump. Biography seemed the most promising direction. Within two years of his return to London he began, then abandoned, biographies of John Derry, a test pilot who died in a horrendous crash at the Farnborough Air Show in 1952; Renaissance sculptor, goldsmith and action man Benvenuto Cellini; and, most painfully, the painter Augustus John.

Moorehead would always be attracted to painters and John, once the leading portraitist of Edwardian London, brought the extra allure of veteran bohemia. Moorehead was mesmerised by his subject's 'air of wild but absolute authority'; at an early meeting 'the snowy beard fairly bristled, the piercing blue eyes bored through one like a cat's and these effects were embellished with a flowing scarlet tie and a huge, sombrero-like hat'. The book would be a kind of collaboration, Moorehead hoped. 'I believed that with persistence I could enter, in terms of writing, into that close relationship that presumably exists between a painter and his sitter ... He seemed to like me, I certainly delighted in him, and in the end it was agreed that

I should go to those of his friends who had not committed suicide and obtain from them the facts about his life.'

After *Montgomery*, Moorehead had promised himself he would never again write the biography of a living subject. Monty proved to be a pussycat compared to his new subject. John cultivated an aura of dandified eccentricity, but he was also a vain, temperamental man now in unhappy decline. After a few months of research and interviews with friends, Moorehead sent his subject 15,000 words to look over. John's response stunned him. 'I dislike the way you have thought fit to perpetuate a lot of foolish gossip besides repeating matter which I have already recorded more accurately in my book,' he wrote. 'ALL your statements of fact are wrong. I prefer the truth. Your own observations I find quite incredibly out of place.'

Moorehead was 'appalled and humiliated' by this, and then so nettled that he decided to confront John about it. An opportunity arose at a book launch. At the lunch itself they bristled past one another; afterwards, with art critic Tommy Earp tagging along as a referee, they retired to the back room of a wine shop in Soho. Over several hours they drank themselves into a soggy détente. The book was still dead, but honour was restored. Later, John sent an emollient note. 'I don't suppose you could be more distressed than I have been. By all means let us both forget it and remain good friends.' Still, it was a major blow. Many years later Moorehead described the episode as 'the worst set-back that I have ever experienced in my attempts to write.'

And all this time, Alexander Clifford was dying from Hodgkin disease. For a while he and Jenny had remained in Portofino, only moving to Rome in mid-1951 when the climb from the village became too much. They visited London often to see specialists and have X-rays. In January 1952 Alex was feeling well enough to ski, so on a whim he and Jenny met the Mooreheads in Kitzbuhel, Austria, for a week of picnics and madcap downhill runs. There was no 'atmosphere of alarm or gloom', Moorehead remembered, not until, at the end of an eight-mile downhill run into a neighbouring valley, Clifford suddenly felt terrible. Within days he was admitted to St Mary's Hospital in London. At first he seemed optimistic, taking a lively interest in his treatments and undoubted recovery. But as the weeks went on he became increasingly listless and remote.

There's something strangely unrevealed about Clifford, even in his own perceptive and thoughtful books. He was a gifted, well-connected and well-liked man, but he didn't like noise or fuss; he didn't impose himself. Describing him, Moorehead often used the word *unambitious*, and he meant it as strong praise – like many people self-conscious about their own ambition, it was a quality he wonderingly admired. Clifford's watchful intelligence had nurtured Moorehead's own ambition throughout the dozen years that had passed since the afternoon they'd sat arguing over ouzo on a sunny Athens street. His loyal, clear-eyed friendship had, more than any place, been Moorehead's home in Europe. Now his dying brought into brutal focus how much Moorehead was about to lose.

Jenny and the Mooreheads kept up a bedside vigil as Alex drifted away from them. One day Jenny and Lucy popped out for lunch, leaving Moorehead alone at the bedside. After a while Clifford's breathing became horribly laboured. Moorehead dashed for the telephone, but then realised he didn't know which restaurant the women had gone to. The nurses told him that if he had anything he wished to say he should say it now.

> What was there for me to say except that I loved him? I said this but there was no answer. I called to him again. The nurses stood around listening. When Jenny and Lucy came in his breathing was barely perceptible and presently it stopped altogether.

Moorehead sat down to write to his sister when he got home from the funeral. 'We went through the war together,' he said simply. 'He, Lucy and I were inseparable and I find it odd continuing without him.'

Clifford's loss was only the hardest in a season of deaths: Buckley, Montague, Harold Ross and Philip Jordan were all gone by mid-1952. It felt like rock bottom. So Moorehead did what he always did when he was stuck and wretched – he packed his bags and went travelling. And for the rest of his working life, he never really stopped.

7

THE OTHER SIDE OF THE HILL

I made it back to Porto Ercole in late 2013. It had been three years since I'd first walked up the drive full of vague notions of pilgrimage and laying a claim to a lost literary hero. It felt different now. I'd been invited this time – by Moorehead's daughter, Caroline, a distinguished biographer and historian in her own right. And I knew much more about what I was looking for. I'd been to Cairo, I'd hunted down Moorehead's haunts in London, Rome and Paris, and I'd spent a lot of time in libraries. My sense of Moorehead and his era was much fuller and less misted over with romanticism.

Yet as soon as I got inside the house, I was struck by the 'combination of the spiritual and the concrete' to which Muriel Spark once attributed the mystique of writers' houses. At one level, on any normal level, this was a sunny and practical holiday house. It looked lived-in and comfortable. The open sitting room was just the spot you could imagine someone reading one of Moorehead's books – perhaps in that armchair by the picture-window. But to me, it was a treasure-house of potential fetish objects. This bookshelf, for instance, which was essentially un-rearranged, Caroline said, since the '60s: I could see Moorehead first-edition hardbacks and translations, and books by friends and acquaintances like John Cheever, Harold Nicolson and John O'Hara, wedged in among Moorehead's own working copies of Burton's diaries and Darwin's *The Voyage of the Beagle*. On a table Caroline had set out some boxes of photos, a guest book, and a 'weather book' from the early days of the house in which her father had logged observations about, well, the weather, and the progress of the garden. If this story of elusive, perpetual movement had a primary location, this was unmistakeably it.

Or *nearly* it. Before I settled down to work, I stepped out onto the terrace garden with its waist-high stone wall, followed a path down past the swimming pool pump shed to the tennis court, and then circled back up through damp grass to the studio and pushed the door open. It had been full of bric-a-brac last time. Now it contained nothing but an old school desk, which certainly wasn't the Livingstone copy, and was in the wrong place – facing the window of forbidden distraction. Through it I could see the light screen of gum trees Lucy and Alan had planted, and beyond them, in the cool sunlight, a little smoky in the distance, the lower slopes of Mount Argentario, which coursed down in a grand bowl-shape, knotted with vines and olive groves, towards the town.

The Blue Nile, *Cooper's Creek* and *The Fatal Impact* had all been written here, as well as chunks of the autobiography. There were no more sacred sites after this, no more Taorminas or Carlton Hotels or Portofino castles. The trail that had begun here had finally led back here, to an empty room.

§

The chief purpose of this trip was to study the letters. But the letters still hadn't turned up. No one in the family could remember seeing them since Pocock had gone through them in 1989. This was bad news, but it didn't properly sink in then, because I was sure they'd turn up sometime. They were too important to have just disappeared. In a note to the NLA collections staff from 1990, Pocock had remarked that someone should do a volume of Moorehead's correspondence 'because he was such a wonderful letter writer'. Stuff like that can't just vanish.

In the meantime, my attention was soon diverted by the contents of the two folio-sized cardboard boxes on the sitting-room table. Each box contained hundreds of unsorted photographs. After my first sighting of the archives at the National Library, this was the most astonishing moment in my search for the life behind the books. I instantly recognised dozens of places from Moorehead's postwar travels especially; there he was reading on a beach in Ischia, 1950; standing under a flame tree with Mount Kenya rising like a snow-tipped dream in the far distance behind. That would be 1956. My dry list of dates had suddenly become chaotically illustrated. And so had the scale and tenacity of Moorehead's wanderlust.

Did anyone ever look like they were enjoying themselves so much? Even in the cheesy pics of Alan grinning atop jungle temples, fists on hips, hat tilted back, he always seems to be exactly where he wants to be. The tedium of hold-ups and missed connections and grotty hotel rooms never got close to spoiling the pleasure of contemplating a nice long itinerary, of being on the move. 'I suffer from a complaint which you might describe as "other side of the hill" disease,' he once wrote in an Australian newspaper. 'I travel constantly out of pure curiosity, merely to discover how green is the next valley.'

'Other side of the hill' disease: a harmless-sounding ailment. But it was more than pure curiosity, more even than a chance to slip the yoke of money worries and boredom. In the early 1950s, travel was the key to Moorehead's resurgence as a writer. Travel starts to look like a kind of daydreaming in space: the physical enactment of a longing to be anywhere but here, and as far from modern life as possible.

§

Two long trips of the early 1950s make a double-hinge for this swing away from modern times. The first was a working trip to Australia, just weeks after Clifford's death. The idea had come from Colin Bednall, editor of the *Courier-Mail* in Brisbane. Though Moorehead hoped to produce something about Australia for the *New Yorker*, his chief purpose was to write articles for Keith Murdoch's newspaper group, which was footing the bill. Bednall's proposal also dovetailed nicely with a standing invitation from novelist Nevil Shute* to make a trip together somewhere.

---

* Properly, Nevil Shute Norway, aircraft designer and, as a sideline, bestselling popular novelist.

Australia, of course, represented a complicated kind of escape. In the weeks before he departed he had been corresponding with Shute, whom he had met only briefly before, and who was now surprised to learn that Moorehead was himself Australian. 'I imagine you have been going through the fairly common process of thought,' Shute wrote.

> So many Australians when they are young seem to find Australia narrow and stultifying, and escape as soon as possible to the larger world. The fact that their birth place happens to be the happiest country in the world to live in doesn't appeal to adventurous young people who want to mix in great affairs, and it is only when great affairs begin to pall that one starts looking for the really happy places.

This was shrewd. Only a few years earlier Moorehead would have scoffed at that idea. But the pull of 'great affairs' *was* weakening. It just wasn't clear what would replace it. In the colonies, he wrote to Lucy, Europe seems:

> filled with the most splendid and glamorous things, richer than anything in colonial life ... Over there is the mirage, the dream-city and the escape. Here one is down to earth and does the washing-up. The time is now – there is no past ... Over there the time is past and, seen from this boarding-house, it is full of Napoleons and Tintorettos.
>
> What the colonial does not realise is that the washing-up still has to be done in Europe.

He spent most of his time on the voyage shut away in his cabin, writing about Clifford as part of a memoir he had in mind. But as he strolled the deck promenades, thoughts kept drifting back to the country he'd left. 'I did not ... feel that I really belonged to Australia at all,' he wrote.

> On board the *Himalaya*, I felt that I was outward bound. [My Australian upbringing] had been excised from my mind almost as though it had never existed. But now, as the weeks at sea went by, it began to exist again, now I started to remember, and it was not altogether the sentimental glow which the exile is supposed to feel about his birthplace.

The *Himalaya* docked at Port Melbourne on 28 April 1952. Through the chilly autumn rain he could make out the pier where his boyhood self had often stood, reading the names of the freighters and their exotic home ports. The purpose of this trip, Moorehead had written to Bednall, 'is not to hold a mirror up to the Australians: it is to enable a man who lives abroad to say how the scene strikes him by comparison with Europe and America'. That is, how it all looks to 'the eye of a foreigner'.

But Moorehead wasn't a foreigner; he was a prodigal son. The book of *New Yorker* articles written about this trip, *Rum Jungle* (1953), was spruiked on the flyleaf as 'an account of [Moorehead's] rediscovery of his own country'. His arrival was marked by a big press conference and head-lines ('Famed Author Revisits Australia'), during which he posed good-humouredly for pictures. One shows him in a three-piece suit and dark woollen overcoat, one foot resting on a chair, and a book open on his thigh; his cigarette hand is holding the book open, the other is a jaunty fist on the hip which adds to the impression that even reading is some-thing he does with a hungry zest. An old friend gave him a formal dinner at the Melbourne Club ('barrels of oysters and millionaires in spats') and there was a luncheon put on by the directors of the *Herald*. 'All the old chums sniffed about me like dogs looking over an imported champ,' Moorehead wrote to Lucy, 'and reserving the right to bite later on.'

If Australians hadn't yet developed a hang-up about successful expat-riates, Moorehead's visit – maybe that photo – seems to have made some people wonder whether it wasn't about time they did. It was the critics who eventually bit, when *Rum Jungle* appeared a year later, in 1953. 'Ideal for a tedious train journey,' wrote one, with perfect ambiguity. Another was intrigued by the 'subconscious conflict' and guilt he detected in the passages about Moorehead's childhood. The literary journal *Southerly* was lukewarm about his visit. 'It is evident that he feels an enduring fascina-tion in the bush and the aborigines, and is not without hope that the arts and civilization will develop here. Meanwhile he prefers Italy.'

Which was true enough. Still, Moorehead at least spared his compa-triots the most irritating thing a returning expatriate can say: that nothing has changed. A great deal had changed. The cities had grown beyond recognition, and their inhabitants were more worldly than they once were. But the cities were just like modern cities anywhere. The egalitarian ethos, commendable in its way, meant that everyone was wearisomely insistent about being as good as anyone else. Without servants, the women were suffocatingly bound to their homes. Pubs still closed at six o'clock. Suburban life was still dull, cream-bricked and hedge-clipped. 'Very little unexpected happens,' Moorehead wrote home, 'except a slow progression to a known end and they sweeten the process with golf, drinks and bridge.' But that small portion of it that belonged to his own family was a source of simple happiness. The verandah at his father's house in Croydon where he wrote *Montgomery* inspired an autumnal reverie in a letter to Lucy: 'An amber light on the hills. The lemon orchard is a tangle but the garden is bright and full of autumn leaves ... The light is going and the sky on Dandenong is pink. I must go inside to the fire.' That was the last time he would stay in his father's home. Richard Moorehead, whose long, heart-felt, newsy letters had been a precious link to family during all Moorehead's years away, died in 1954. His last words, Phyllis reported, were 'I won't stand this a minute longer.' And, finally, 'Damn!'

§

The first line of *Rum Jungle*: 'There are no lost cities in Australia.' No time-less ruins, he meant, no ancient roads. Moorehead experienced this lack of human history – 40,000 years of Indigenous Australian history some-how didn't count – as an almost vertiginous void; it was the cause, he thought, of the confident tedium of suburban Australia. In a chapter unpromisingly titled 'A Nameless, Hopeless Distress' he wrote that European settlers, 'because they believed that the imitation could never be as good as the original ... were afflicted always with a feeling of nos-talgia'. Even as a schoolboy, Moorehead had 'a nagging feeling that something is missing ... A vague unrest, an impression that life was pass-ing by at second best'.

That was childhood life in an Australian city; the countryside, on the other hand, had been an open-air *wunderkammer* for a white child in 1920. This return to Australia in 1952 opened a sluicegate of joyful, if painfully remote, memories. Even as a boy, he wrote, 'there was a quality of excitement and revealed truth in the bush ... You could not walk for half a mile without coming upon things that were unknown anywhere else in the world.' In a passage set on a train, as so many of Moorehead's happiest passages are, he describes coming home from a day of bush adventures at his uncle's house in Melton, outside Melbourne:

> The luggage racks above our heads were filled with the bags of apples, the specimens of beetles, rocks, and flowers, and the bunches of aromatic gum leaves we had gathered. The train jogged on through the darkness, stopping and starting; the vapor of our breath condensed on the window-panes; and I leaned against my mother's knee, thirsty, exhausted, and very dirty. But this mattered nothing for I had been ranging the hills all day, breaking into new worlds, and I had actually seen a kookaburra dive on a snake. And now I was sailing back to port with the booty – the dead lizard in the cardboard box, the jam jar full of frog spawn that would hatch into tadpoles by and by, and the chunk of rock with the yellow specks that might easily turn out to be gold.

This sounds like the onset of a chronic case of 'other side of the hill' disease. Perhaps it was meant to.

In Adelaide Moorehead stayed with an old Eighth Army friend from the desert, General Norrie (now governor of South Australia), then continued by train, riding the Ghan to Alice Springs to meet Shute. It was a strange pairing of two writers who'd changed places. Shute had immigrated to Australia in 1950, partly out of disgust at the high-taxing Attlee government, and made his home in Mount Eliza, on the Mornington Peninsula, not an hour's drive from where Moorehead had grown up. He was a decade older, politically conservative, and diffident about his own literary gifts. Designing planes was his true *métier*, he thought.

But they got along splendidly. For two months they bivouacked and drove and rode in trains. From Alice Springs they travelled north to Darwin; they visited Katherine, Mount Isa and Dajarra. They ate beetroot sandwiches; they hitched lifts in little planes across the enormous spaces between homesteads and stations. They stayed with friends, sailed on the

Arafura Sea; they spent hours watching birds and animals, and were welcomed wherever they went. A Darwin gossip columnist wrote that Moorehead's 'nice sardonic smile' reminded her of the actor James Mason. Moorehead thrived in all the space and enjoyed the old pleasure of camping and hiking he'd known in the Libyan desert. He was feeling so well, he wrote to Lucy, so 'alive physically', in a place where 'all day long one wants, and can do, so many exciting things', he was even thinking it might be possible for him to live here. 'What have we in Europe anyway now that Alex is dead and Christopher and Philip [Jordan] ...?' The next week: 'I must warn you I am constantly thinking of the possibility of our all coming to Australia ... There is so much I want to explore on this side of the world.'

Yet not much of *Rum Jungle* has this easygoing sound. Much of it today seems strangely out of focus, partly because Moorehead plays up the exotic angle – the eccentric fauna, the eccentric people – for the *New Yorker*'s faraway readers. Numerous factual errors, fastidiously itemised by local reviewers, didn't help. And then, the decades that have passed since have made it hard to visualise the country the way Moorehead did. His fatalism about Aboriginal Australia, for instance, wasn't unusual then, but some sentences still leave you rubbing your eyes. 'For one hundred years the aborigine has been trying desperately to catch up,' he wrote 'to jump from the stone age straight into the atomic age – and now, when he has almost accomplished this it seems to be too late; his race has been pretty well exterminated in the process.'

Near Darwin, our travellers found the closest thing they could to a 'lost city': a series of abandoned camps and airfields left over from General MacArthur's hurried fortification of the north in 1943. The ruins were only eight years old, but they brought out Moorehead's growing taste for the time-worn and forlorn. 'Every few miles you come on mouldering huts and the wooden skeletons of hundreds of tents; and occasionally there is an abandoned aircraft falling to bits among the trees. From year to year the jungle creeps over it all ... Even the airfields in moderately good repair have the sort of desolation that clings to a summer holiday place in the winter-time, except that the effect is redoubled here because the neglect is permanent.'

THE OTHER SIDE OF THE HILL 187

This is what Moorehead *did* find in the uneasy quiet beyond Australia's cities: an uncanny sensation of endless time. He wasn't the first European to sense something mystical and unexplained in the 'Dead Heart', as it was still sometimes called. But in a book of travel journalism the references to the 'infinite oldness', and to time's pressing weight ('so silent, so incredibly old. An infinity of unexciting time') are remarkably insistent. Moorehead felt the listless eons everywhere: in the dry rustle of hot gum leaves, in the juxtaposition of 'the infinitely primitive and the infinitely new' of the Woomera rocket range, or the Rum Jungle uranium mine in the Northern Territory, where straggle-bearded bushies stalked the outcrops and gullies with Geiger counters and humans had 'made as yet only a slight impression on the enormous silence'.

Back at his desk, the haunting silence of the outback stayed with him, and for a while work went well. 'Almost writing with the same ease I had five or ten years ago,' he jotted in his diary in late 1952. 'Particular pleasure writing about birds and animals.'

Traitors had sold well while Moorehead was away; the acrimony it had caused was easier to forget once Alexander Korda announced plans to film it. But the old lack of inspiration remained, and Moorehead now made one of his periodic blind turns into the movie business. This one, a commission to write a treatment for a film set in India, was probably urged on him by Sidney Bernstein. Co-producer of Transatlantic, the company that produced several of Hitchcock's early films, and later founder of Granada TV in the UK, Bernstein, a tall, quiet man with a senatorial bearing, was a formidable force in Britain's entertainment industry. They had first met through their wives – Lucy had been good friends with Bernstein's first wife, Zoe –and had both been at Belsen in 1945, where Bernstein had implored Moorehead to look inside the camp and describe what he saw to the world. Now, in late 1952, Moorehead was spending several soporific afternoons in an upstairs Soho office watching Hindi films with a translator at his side, in what looks like an oddly postmodern bid to learn enough about Indian life from the movies to write a movie about Indian life. Ideas didn't flow. Moorehead sought advice from Graham Greene. 'I should be delighted to see you and be of any help I can,' Greene replied in a note: he suggested Moorehead nominate a 'drinking time'. Yet whatever came of this meeting, it didn't solve the problem.

Still, as the hours passed in the private screening room, a memory resurfaced – of the Ajanta Caves, not far from Hyderabad, which he'd tried and failed to visit during his 1947 tour for the *Observer*. The idea of an Asia trip was hatched one weekend at Coppings, Bernstein's country house in Kent. One night everyone was talking, Moorehead recalled, 'of those journeys one dreams of as a child, the fantasy journeys that one will never make'.

> Sidney said that as a boy he longed to see Mount Everest, my wife had always had a romantic image of Angkor Wat in Indo-China, while for me India was the place … Having once begun to think of the east, we also spoke of Burma and the temples of Bangkok, the teak forests of Siam where the elephants worked, Hong Kong, China itself, Singapore and the Dyak villages of central Borneo: the wide, wide world.

There was nothing to stop the Mooreheads going. Bernstein cleared his diary and publicly announced that he was making a 'fact-finding' trip to the Far East: he was scouting for a film that would capture 'the vast panorama of the East in a modern sort of John Buchan story'. Moorehead pitched some Far East pieces to William Shawn; they all had their jabs; on Regent Street, Sidney and Alan bought the Box Brownie that took all the photographs I found sixty years later jammed into old paper wallets at Porto Ercole. At the last moment Lucy had to stay behind to care for baby Richard, who had fallen ill. She would follow later, but it was just Sidney and Alan who left from Heathrow in late January 1953, in a brand-new Comet jet.

Only six years before, Europe to India had been a three-day journey by train and flying boat. By BOAC Comet it was a whining blur. 'To fly at 500 miles an hour was a fantastic break with the past.' On the plane, Moorehead chatted to Vivien Leigh, who was flying out to Ceylon to shoot *Elephant Walk*. Lady Mountbatten came aboard at Rome and plopped into the seat next to Moorehead's. They talked all the way to Beirut, where refreshments were taken and Miss Leigh posed on the tarmac in the middle of the night for local photographers.

'the wide, wide world', early 1950s

This was his first taste of the jet age, and that quintessentially modern experience of leaping through the night into the strange morning of another hemisphere. It was a futuristic beginning to a journey that was entirely preoccupied with the past, or a dreamed version of it. The paintings at the Ajanta Caves were a revelation, a fabulous vision of 'all the things I had naively hoped to find in India: the maharajahs, the jewelled courts, the elephants and the peacocks – in fact the myth of India.' Many hours passed in a 'gentle coma' of absorption with the old paintings and their 'phantasmagoria of maharajahs and tiger hunts'. But at the end of each day 'the spell was broken off like a receding dream at the moment of awakening'. It was an experience, Moorehead wrote, that 'makes one realise how deeply one is enmeshed in the present'.

This was the theme of the entire five-month journey, through Darjeeling, Rangoon, Cambodia and Borneo. Tracking the elusive scent of past worlds in one promising spot after another, they avoided present realities as much as possible. In several places they skirted political trouble: in Indochina, where the French were mired in a bitter war for empire; and in Malaysia, where the British were busy protecting tin and rubber production from communist insurgents. But even as new eras were rising around him, what seems to have stirred Moorehead most were glimpses of an old one ending. In the teak plantations around Chiang Mai in northern Thailand, Alan and Sidney chatted with old timber men on verandahs where women were still *mems*, dinner still tiffin – straight out of Somerset Maugham, Moorehead noted.

> They still take the English papers; they rise at six and dine at seven (almost but not quite changing into a black tie and a dinner jacket) … Scattered around their bungalows are the tiger skins, the pieces of jade, the Chinese scrolls, and the carved wooden figures they have picked up during the last fifty years, and perhaps a silver polo cup stands on a desk in the corner.

It was all just as Maugham had described it. But Moorehead got closest to the atmosphere of a different age in Kuching, the port capital of Sarawak, where he was a guest of the adventurer and amateur anthropologist Tom Harrisson. In the late 1930s Harrisson had co-pioneered the Mass-Observation movement, a program which used anthropological field techniques to study the habits and habitat of modern British city-dwellers. In 1944, he parachuted into Sarawak to incite a guerrilla uprising against the Japanese occupation. And he had stayed on. Now he was making regular, months-long forays into the remotest reaches of the country and returning with specimens for his museum of arts and crafts in Kuching. In the mornings, Harrisson would startle his guests awake with a bellowed cry of 'Room Service!', at which signal several Kelabit tribesmen collected on Harrisson's last field trip and temporarily installed in the house's annex, would troop in 'wearing feathers in their hats and leopard's teeth in their ears, to serve the morning tea'.

It could be a scene out of Ionesco: three white chaps, sitting on the bamboo mat, drinking tea in the woolly heat, playing their parts in an absurdist recreation of the colonial adventure. With Sidney, Moorehead set off on a three-day jungle trek to the remote Land Dayak village of Tapuh. They were feted as a tremendous novelty with ceremonial dancing and singing. The deeply unmusical Moorehead was enjoined, at one point, to improvise a song of his own, which he found surprisingly easy in such a cheerful place. 'One gets the uneasy feeling that our own civilization has taken a wrong turning somewhere – that it has left behind many of the things that contribute to genuine happiness in life.'

No other literary genre has suffered such an embarrassing downgrade in esteem as travel writing of this kind: the search for a distant, undiscovered Eden, complete with naked tribespeople and all the comic ordeals required to reach it. By the middle of the twentieth century, literary adventurers were running short of places that *National Geographic* photographers hadn't already found. They had nowhere to go but into a more or less ironic mode of *re*-discovery. Anthropologist–philosopher Claude Lévi-Strauss described the loss this entailed in his 1955 classic, *Tristes Tropiques*. Journeys of genuine discovery, 'those magic caskets full of dreamlike promises', he wrote, 'will never again yield up their treasures untarnished'. It was too late: the longing for places untouched by humans had exhausted all the hidden corners of the globe and was fast filling them with rubbish.

Moorehead was too much of a realist to get carried away with the noble savage theme or whimsical re-enactments of discovery. While he enjoyed the 'somewhat bogus sentimental glow' of the traveller far from home among strange new friends, he could see that life in Tapuh was 'far from idyllic – Rousseau's conception of the noble savage simply isn't true in Sarawak'. It was unsanitary; life could be brutal and, for lack of medicines available in any London pharmacy, tragically short. But his travel writing and histories belong to that era of geographical disappointment. His *Nile* books, *Cooper's Creek* and *The Fatal Impact* would be so successful precisely because they recaptured the curiosity and romantic *idea* of discovery, even as they remained unillusioned about its bitter consequences.

As I sat at the table at Porto Ercole inhaling the scent of musky old cardboard, and the faint perfume of old developer chemicals, looking at those pictures of the Asia trip, I wondered how much of the appeal of Moorehead's work now lay in nostalgia. These sixty-year-old photographs of a journey in search of the past have now acquired their own kind of vintage glamour, with all the dressing for dinner, the passenger steamers, the dinners at governors' residences. Moorehead certainly had reservations about modernity. 'Ever since I arrived in the East I have felt like a man walking down a street where everyone is hurrying the other way,' he wrote in his diary at the end of this Asian trip – hurrying towards 'speedboats, air-conditioning, big city buildings, and aeroplanes, anything modern'.

All my objects seem to lie the other way. I want to get away from noise
and cities ... I don't want to be modern at all. I want to rediscover the
simple non-political life from which the coloured peoples are busily
hurrying away. They want a duplex apartment in a skyscraper: I think
I would be happy in a grass hut beside the sea.

Somewhere in the early 1950s Moorehead's imagination seems to cross
a private line of meridian; his 'other side of the hill' disease had been complicated by a growing fascination with the past: his own, and the world's.
But I don't think his turn to history was driven by a romantic dissatisfaction with the world-as-it-is. It was less an escape than a discovery of new
terrain, a new kind of elsewhere in which time seems suspended, pregnant
with its own meaning. Passing through Libya in 1954, he went out to look
at the old battlefields, the old tanks subsiding into the sand and the old
dugouts, and the thousands of crosses pegged out in the scrubby desert.
All he could see was time. 'It is almost impossible to believe,' he wrote.
'The armies vanish and the desert is empty again.' It was this baffling human
experience of time that intrigued him. 'Lying back on deck one idly
observes the flight of birds,' he wrote of another Nile cruise in 1959.

> One dreams, one lets the hours go by, and nothing can be more satisfying
> than the sight of the brown pillars of a ruined temple that has been stand-
> ing alone on the edge of the desert for the last two thousand years. This
> is the past joining the present in a comfortable deceptive glow, and the
> traveller, like a spectator in the theatre, remains detached from both.

That 'comfortable deceptive glow' sounds mild enough. But that sense that
time is itself an illusion – that events in the past do not exist at a fixed, safe
distance from us – often has a disquieting force in Moorehead's work: it's
like a daydreamer's peyote that brings you momentarily into contact with
the giant tide of the past behind us, invisible, but vast, and insistent.

§

Since the end of the war, Moorehead had been visiting the States regularly, usually at the end of other trips, drumming up commissions and

dealing with agents and magazine editors. In 1952, just after the Australia trip, he visited the Philadelphia offices of *Holiday*, a luxury travel magazine, and talked himself into a new and financially rewarding line of work.

Holiday was not 'an organ of the intellectuals', its editors explained in its ten-year anniversary issue. '*Holiday* is a magazine of civilized entertainment. It aims at satisfying and spurring the leisure-time interests of a sizable number of moderately well-heeled Americans. It is wedded to no doctrine except that of making propaganda for the politer pleasures of our time.' In the early '50s, with the postwar boom well underway, its moment had arrived. Travel was becoming a major industry. The magazine's pages are full of ads for luxury items, cruise wear and new airlines. And those ad-buys funded an impressive roster of 1950s (male) talent: Cheever, Steinbeck, Thurber, O'Hara and Hemingway all wrote for *Holiday*; people like Ansel Adams, Inge Morath, Robert Capa and Henri Cartier-Bresson shot its dazzling photo spreads.

Moorehead wrote about a dozen pieces for the magazine across the '50s and '60s, mostly on Mediterranean destinations. It took me months to track them all down, and cost me a small fortune in shipping freight from America, where copies have become collectors' items for fans of retro design.

When I set out to track the elusive war reporter through the postwar decades, I never expected to find him somewhere like this. The *Holiday* spreads lack the brooding mystery of the pre-war pics from Gibraltar and Istanbul and Spain; colour has arrived, and *Holiday* is saturated with it, quaint streetscapes and harbourside vistas blazing with the lobstery scarlets and solar blues. It's a vision of the globe as a luxury consumable, complete with servants, and foreigners living in charming and photogenic simplicity; an old dream of Abroad laid out in gorgeous four-colour process. Turning its heavy pages, you can almost smell the sun-warmed skin slathered in Coconut Super Oil™, almost hear the chinkling of the drinks cart as it traverses the concourse of a Bermuda beach hotel one afternoon in 1953. I knew there was something wrong with this world that existed solely for the pleasure of taking a vacation somewhere in it, but I found it very hard to resist.

So did Moorehead. *Holiday* suited him. This isn't his best stuff, but it's some of his most personable and easy-going. It paid extremely well. And the long-format pieces gave him time and space to noodle around in mostly comfortable places, taking his time, pointing out all the pleasant things the armchair curious traveller might expect to find, gently introducing his reader to exotic customs (Genoese cooking, for instance, involves such curiosities as *pesto*, 'a sharp herbal sauce', and 'various savory pies known as pizzas'). 'Mine is not the telescopic view' is how he characterised his travel-writing technique. 'It is the microscopic one. Not Cyclorama and the Wide Screen, but the snapshot for the family album.' And it's all very pleasant. If *scene* is the most overused word in Moorehead's mature prose, *pleasant* (sometimes, for variation, *not unpleasant*) runs a close second. A strangely complacent word, with its sense of modest needs well satisfied. But it gets a good run in *Holiday*, where Moorehead sometimes seems so relaxed you wonder if he shouldn't be trying a bit harder. Of the pyramids he finds he has 'nothing whatever to say. There they are: Big ones. Little ones. Medium ones.'

The full-colour escapism of *Holiday* was accommodating to the soft brush-strokes of reminiscence that were coming into Moorehead's journalism. He'd been in Europe nearly twenty years now; many trips were return visits to places where memories act like a wistful seasoning agent. Having set his scene, he is soon hunched over a local detail, peering through the loupe of memory, searching for alterations. Without damning progress per se, he sometimes registers change as a loss. 'One regrets all this a little, of course,' he writes, dreading the conversion of the old Saracen castles of the Balearics into gas stations. Revisiting Rome in 1950 he finds that in the dozen years since he lived there, American money has transformed 'a leisurely Mediterranean place into a boom town, a sort of Coney Island of free enterprise'.

> Airline booking office art is probably an international cult these days, and
> there is no getting away from it anywhere. But it looks strange here among
> the baroque Churches; those tubular steel chairs, the strip lighting in
> relentless shades of mauve and bluish-white, the glass placards suspended

like bird-cages from the ceiling, and all those cute advertising signs, the streamlined sea-horses and sea-gulls, the flying pegasuses and the comic hotel porters with wings. Somehow that fearfully bright laboratory-like atmosphere, half functional and half fey, just does not go with Rome.

§

Moorehead was still based in London, but you wouldn't know it. 'Operating at the end of a piece of elastic' as he put it, the pattern of his life was shaped more and more by long trips abroad. The longest of these he spent on the Greek island of Spetses. He lived there for six months in 1955, in a house set among some olive groves, overlooking the sea. He worked long hours, savouring his solitude. The solitude couldn't last. The family joined him for summer; in September half a generation of English letters turned up on a yacht chartered by Paddy Leigh Fermor, who was spending the year on nearby Hydra. There was Cyril Connolly, 'glooming about his runaway wife and asking what's for dinner', and Nancy Mitford*; the publishers Jock and Diana Murray, critic Maurice Bowra, and Paddy's partner, Joan Rayner. And the uncontainable Geoffrey Keating, now working as a PR man for BP; Geoffrey arrived on an enormous yacht belonging to renowned hostess Elsa Maxwell. (Oh, the Mooreheads said to one another fondly, watching Geoffrey lumber up through the olives towards them, 'he's gotten even fatter'.) Most visitors brought their oils and brushes. 'The house grows dizzy with being painted', Moorehead wrote. He added: 'I watch birds.'

There were lines in Moorehead's diary from the months before this as despondent as anything from Villa Diana: only by writing what he wanted to write and 'feeling again' would he escape his old aimlessness, 'the awful hysterical emptiness and ennui'. Now, though, as he picked goat hairs out of his pungent cheese, swam and watched birds, and worked, the misery of indecision was behind him.

When the longed for inspiration had finally come, it didn't so much strike as quietly reveal itself, like something that had been waiting to be

---

* Or Nancy Rodd, as Moorehead calls her in a letter from the time: Mitford and Peter Rodd divorced in 1957.

found. In 1954 Moorehead had spent a few weeks rewriting his novel *A Summer Night* at the Tuscan villa of an old friend, Gallipoli veteran and former boss of BBC India Lionel Fielden. One evening Lionel brought out his old war diary and showed it to his guest. Something fell into place as Moorehead turned the pages. For several years Moorehead had been conscious of parallels between his career and Keith Murdoch's, who had made his name as a newspaperman during the Gallipoli campaign. There was a family link too. Moorehead's uncle was killed on the first day at Gallipoli; another uncle lost his arm there. As he read Lionel's diary, the dim, banked coals of an idea began to glow red.*

To write about Gallipoli, however, Moorehead would have to overcome a lifetime's distaste for the very word. A boy when the Great War ended, Moorehead had grown up surrounded by its maudlin remembrance, bitterness and human wreckage. Anzac Day was a torment in the 1920s. He hated it all: Kipling's poetry and the turgid speeches; the 'bitter, hopeless grief', the boozy sentimentality and the 'endless stories about what old Joe did on Hill 60'. It all 'bored me and bored me and bored me'. Not that you would ever dare say so. Children were expected to remain 'reverent' through the crushing tedium; 'and even now I have the feeling that I am dragging a shameful secret out into the open'.

At the end of 1954, Moorehead visited the Gallipoli peninsula. He knew right away he'd found what he was looking for: a story packed with the action and crisis he was so good at, but which also seemed to resound through time. Everything he could see from the heights above the beaches evoked the past, he thought: the ruins of Crusaders fortresses, the snow-capped peak of Mt Ada, the Homeric islands looming out of morning mists, 'even the local shepherds who have herded their black-nosed sheep among these rocks time out of mind'. In the cemeteries the millennia dividing the Trojan wars and 'the generation in khaki that arrived only forty years ago' seemed to disappear on the breeze. In the *New Yorker* article he wrote about this visit he describes lying on the grass between some

---

* Fielden may well have hoped his diary would have this effect. 'It seems to me that you just are not a novelist and never can be,' he once wrote to his friend. 'You have such supreme gifts in other directions ... It makes me a bit mad that you will write novels!!'

graves as his Turkish guide recounted the story of some attack or another. 'While I was waiting for the interpreter to translate', he wrote,

> I would look at the lizards scuttling along the stone wall with an odd clockwork motion, and, beyond them, at the silver cloud of the olive trees, the heather on the cliffs, and the sea. There seemed to be some stereoscopic lucidity in the air that brought all these things into one plane, so that the fisherman's caique with red sails drifting by in the bay appeared no farther away than the lizard on the wall; one felt one could reach out and touch either of them. In 1915 ... the visual effect must have been extraordinary. Even apart from that, there was a closeness about all the events of the Gallipoli campaign that makes it now seem almost as intimate and archaic as the siege of Troy itself.

The project obsessed him. Geoffrey Cox, who had become a good friend in the years since their fractious Paris days, thought it was a mad idea. 'I asked myself is anyone going to read about World War I?' But they did, 'and this was the first of a fashion ... He had a bloody good eye for news.' Research absorbed nearly two years. Moorehead studied maps, generals' diaries, and archives. He wrote to everyone he could think of who might be able to help with original documents or interviews. Beaverbrook ignored an appeal for assistance (*the ban still on*, Moorehead noted) and Churchill, again prime minister, couldn't see him either. But Turkish archivists threw open their records, and even translated Ataturk's diary for him (it proved to be disappointingly dull). On Spetses he was working from a trunk full of books loaned from the London Library and countless letters and notebooks entrusted to him by veterans of the campaign.

The year passed in a blur of concentrated work. When he looked up from the manuscript at the end of the October, he realised he hadn't made a penny from writing in twelve months. But it was time well spent. *Gallipoli* would be the book that ended the decade of frittered energy and relaunched his worldwide reputation.

The most striking thing about *Gallipoli*, apart from its stunning critical success, is its seeming artlessness. The writing, said the *TLS*, 'is superb'. But isolating 'the secret of his skill is not easy'.

He seems to have no tricks of style, even in the best sense. Though he graduated in popular military journalism, he never seems to raise his voice. His prose is deceptively plain. And yet the power of evocation in his pages is altogether remarkable.

Of course there's plenty of art in that power of evocation; if there weren't the artlessness would just be naïvety. It's hard to resist the pull of the story long enough to notice how skilfully it's been arranged. The inspired ruthlessness, for instance, with which Moorehead shapes a three-act tragedy from such an inchoate mass of human experience; or the way different parts of the story unfold simultaneously – or seem to – so that the action on various fronts is kept running in the reader's peripheral vision while we pause to consider a new development elsewhere. Like a Shakespeare tragedy, it all seems to be unfolding now in an everlasting present, where what *must* happen next, and what *could* happen next, still seem equally possible. 'No matter how often the story is retold there is still an actuality about it, a feeling of suspense and incompleteness,' Moorehead wrote. 'Although nearly half a century has gone by, nothing yet seems fated about the day's events, a hundred questions remain unanswered, and in a curious way one feels that the battle might still lie before us in the future; that there is still time to make other plans and bring it to a different ending.'

This feeling of suspended inevitability pervades the book; it contributes to what the *Times* called a 'new strain of haunting lyrical beauty' in Moorehead's work. That strain is hard to convey, since it's a cumulative effect. But if there is one exemplary strophe in *Gallipoli* that readers recalled even years later, it was the quiet falling note with which the book ends. The peninsula's cemeteries are beautifully maintained, Moorehead wrote: 'Yet hardly anyone ever visits them. Except for the occasional organized tours not more than half a dozen visitors arrive from one year's end to the other. Often for months at a time nothing of any consequence happens, lizards scuttle about the tombstones in the sunshine and time goes by in an endless dream.'

Those empty cemeteries are hard to credit today. So is the novelty of Moorehead's subject matter. *Gallipoli* has all but disappeared beneath the great cairn of Anzac books that have piled up since, but this was the first account of the campaign written for the general reader. For many of those readers, it was a living memory, not the beatified martyrdom it has become. 'I find it difficult to express, in the hackneyed superlatives of literary criticism, my admiration for [Moorehead's] accomplishment,' wrote Gallipoli veteran and novelist Compton Mackenzie. It was all so lucid, 'one can hardly believe it was written by somebody who, when it happened, was a five-year-old child in Australia'. Veterans lined up to acclaim the book's success in recapturing 'so much of the atmosphere and spirit of those adventurous months', as General Freyberg put it. Among them were the former prime minister, Lord Attlee, who praised the book's success in 'evoking the spirit of the time' – and Australian war historian CEW Bean: 'a brilliant and sympathetic reconstruction of the Dardanelles campaign.'

'People,' Moorehead hummed in his notes, 'come out of their holes to praise a good book.' The praise that meant most was from Berenson, who had *Gallipoli* read aloud to him, and wrote from Settignano: 'You have achieved a masterpiece of historical writing, and I certainly have read nothing as good among histories of my time.'

The only dissenter in this din of praise was Norman Podhoretz, whose review appeared (of all places) in the *New Yorker*. Like many others, he thought the character sketches were 'done with the touch of a professional novelist'. But he accused Moorehead of pandering to a wrong-headed British sentimentality about the glory of sacrifice. To link the industrial butchery of trench warfare to the Trojan Wars, he wrote, is to misunderstand the gulf between the 'obsolete spirit' of old battlefields and their codes of honour, and a new terrible one in which 'rifle and artillery fire raging anonymously in no man's land is the voice of another universe'.

That's the review that Moorehead would always remember of course. That was the one he brooded over even as he was welcomed into the Royal Society of Literature, even as the book gobbled up the *Sunday Times* book prize, and then the inaugural Duff Cooper Memorial Prize, which came with a cheque for £1000 and the right to have it presented by a person nominated by the winner.

Winston Churchill volunteered to present the prize in its first year – either out of regard for the Cooper family, or as a favour to his son

Randolph, who'd been tasked with organising it, perhaps both. But it's hard to imagine Moorehead would have chosen anyone else. There's a photo of the intimate ceremony at Porto Ercole: among a handful of seated dignitaries, including Lucy, in a fur stole, Alan stands in a dapper three-piece suit and gleaming shoes, hands clasped before him like a prefect about to have rowing oars pinned to his blazer. It was a 'moving occasion', wrote Harold Nicolson. How satisfying it was to see Moorehead there in his triumph of perseverance, after so many years of floundering. I kept coming back to this photo, to the look of delight on his face. Sometimes I thought I could see something else in that grin ... a flicker of vindication. Moorehead admired Churchill, but he had complicated feelings about the man who had, albeit at a distance, so profoundly shaped his life. *I never liked him*, Moorehead wrote in his notes for the autobiography. Churchill had run a bitter and divisive campaign against Attlee in 1945, just when Moorehead's social-democratic ideals were at their most fumbling and ardent; his supporters had had Moorehead roughed up over *Montgomery*. Churchill had defended Moorehead's integrity in parliament during the *Traitors* mess of 1952, it's true, but he had declined to speak to Moorehead about Gallipoli, the campaign of which, as First Lord of the Admiralty, he had been chief proponent. Moorehead had even just published a brief, admiring biography of the ageing premier, but without any encouragement or acknowledgement from its subject. 'We have grown used to living with Churchill through many years,' Moorehead wrote in the book. 'He is as familiar to us as the headmaster at school or the captain of a ship on a long voyage.' Now, at least, for one delicious moment, the 82-year-old giant of the age, was obliged, if only out of decorum, to peer over his spectacles and see Moorehead standing there.

§

The photo of Moorehead with Churchill posed a question, one that is implicit in any book about a writer, but which I had managed to ignore till now. Was the life more interesting than the work? Or, more specifically: had the life aged better than the books had?

No one had ever queried whether Moorehead's life, with its war, its colonial-made-good arc, its famous friends, its striding appetite, was interesting enough to write about. If anything, time has made all that *more* enticing. But what has time done to the books? In the 1950s, it was the general consensus that *Gallipoli* was a modest masterpiece of popular history; a few years later Moorehead bettered it, many thought, with *The White Nile*. But was this just the inflated estimate of an outdated sensibility? (One that esteemed 'detachment' to a puzzling degree?) For years I had been urging *A Late Education* and *Eclipse* on anyone who'd listen. But what I really treasured in Moorehead was the intimate access his restlessness gave to so many shadowy corners of the middle twentieth century, to so many sunlit afternoons lost to time. His work was milled from that restlessness. If nothing else, I was certain, his books stood for the solace, the sober joy, of curiosity about the world.

But my faith in the objective value of Moorehead's books was wavering by the time I got to Porto Ercole. I'd just been rereading the novels, and all that jobbing *Holiday* work. And a few weeks before, a friend who had read a couple of draft chapters suggested I cool it a little on my praise for Moorehead's prose. Important the reader knows you don't think he's in the top deck. Let's face it: he's not *Nabokov*. Not *Saul Bellow*.

It was a good time to meet another fan of the work.

At the end of that first day working through the photographs, Caroline offered to introduce me to someone called Betty, who had been a good friend of her parents' in the Porto Ercole years, and was still living nearby. In the late afternoon the three of us drove down the hill to Betty's house. Several people were wandering about as we settled into a tiled sunroom, including a young woman and a couple of cheerful Americans in cycling gear. At the centre of all this activity, regarding it with an air of contented exasperation, was Betty herself. She had lived in Italy for many years, but her Southern accent was still strong, and she filled the room like my idea of a grand hostess out of Charleston or Savannah: charismatic, warm, welcoming. 'I'm not going to say a thing,' she said to Caroline, passing around glasses of wine while more people wandered by. 'Even if I could remember, I don't think I'd tell him!'

A little crestfallen, I joined in the general laughter. It was getting dark outside. In the square window panes our reflections were ghosted over a dim view of shrubs and a gravel path. The cyclists clomped off in their cleats to shower, and talk turned to the neighborhood's wild boar problem. Then conversation trailed off, and it was clearly time to plunge in and charm some details from Betty. I pulled my notebook out of my backpack. Betty eyed it. 'I don't think I'd like him to quote me,' she said.

'That's fine,' I said.

'Because it's *so* long ago …'

We all murmured our universal acknowledgement of time's cruel passing. Maybe it didn't matter. Moorehead rarely took notes as a reporter. He thought the notebook made people clam up. I thought this probably meant he'd had to half-invent a lot of quotes.

Betty gave an appealing laugh. 'And anything I do remember I'm quite sure I don't want in print!'

At some point Caroline and Anne left for a dinner appointment down in the village, and at Betty's invitation I stuck around – her son was coming, and he would want to talk about Moorehead. I'd settled in, now. The American cyclists (whom I'll call Ted and Sandra) had reappeared, freshly showered and terrifically friendly, and even they had heard of Moorehead. They lived in Washington, where Ted wrote a blog on politics. It was strictly a hobby, he modestly added, but it had deepened his appreciation for what real writers did. Sandra asked how I'd gotten interested in Moorehead, and was giving a convincing impression of being engrossed in my answer when Betty's son arrived.

Betty's son turned out to be the Italian author and journalist Andrea di Robilant. He had known Moorehead when he was a boy, he said; he had grown up reading Moorehead's books. They had been an important inspiration for his own books about the past, *The Venetian Navigators* and *A Venetian Affair*. What a subject, he said seriously, shaking my hand as if it were an entirely unexpected privilege. An absolutely wonderful writer.

I felt a surreal calm come over me.

Andrea asked how Moorehead's reputation was holding up in Australia these days. I said it hardly was. I mentioned that a major anthology of

Australian literature published a few years earlier had omitted him
entirely.* Andrea looked dismayed, I was pleased to note. On a surge of
shared indignation, I ploughed on: He's considered very much a figure of
the past ... Dead White Male ... middlebrow ...

Andrea actually flinched. *Middlebrow?*

I was glad Caroline had left.

Ted looked at my notepad, which I'd put back in my bag, and then
taken out again. 'Are you going to interview Andrea?'

No, no, Andrea assured him, he's just looking for background. I was
grateful for the collegial air with which he said this.

Sandra said to Ted that they should leave us to it.

This is terrific, Ted beamed, crossing his legs comfortably. As an amateur I find all this fascinating. I want to see how the professionals do it.

I wasn't sure how the professionals did it, but was so happy to meet
such a credentialled admirer, I didn't worry. We talked for a while about
Andrea's work, and about the '50s and '60s in Porto Ercole, how it had
been such an exciting time here. Finally I got down to it: What exactly
did Andrea think was so good about Moorehead's books? He exhaled
through his nose, and frowned handsomely at the tabletop. For several
moments he didn't speak. Was he disappointed by the banality of the
question? Seconds passed. Ted jiggled his sandalled foot. Then Andrea
began to talk. In a long fluent paragraph of thought that impressed me
almost as much for the concentration and care with which he spoke –
as though nothing could be more important than a question like this – as
for precisely what he said (and I can't pretend this was *precisely* what he
said, since I wasn't recording) he talked about how, as a young writer
setting out, he had always deeply admired Moorehead's uncluttered sto-
rylines, the clarity of his thought, his economy, his ability to bring the
past to life with such easy authority. If it is not too extravagant, he said,
one could say he had a Ciceronian quality of never saying too much, but
expressing everything necessary with a vital detail. His great ability to

* *The Macquarie PEN Anthology of Australian Literature* (2009). It omitted lots of people, of course, and Moorehead's
non-appearance may have had more to do with the fact that he lived so long outside Australia than anything
else. The old cultural visa trouble.

see through the eyes of the past is still an example for other writers to aspire to ...

Yes, I thought: *yes*. I wrote down the word *Ciceronian*. Of course! I thought, though I'd never read a word of Cicero in my life. I didn't know whether I wanted to hug Andrea or just listen to him talk for a few more hours. But then he was called away to the phone.

Ted and Sandra dropped me back to the village that night. In my hotel room I scribbled down everything I could remember from Betty's. I can't read most of those pages now, but whenever I look at them I'm reminded of the kindness of strangers. It was late, now, but the pontoon café anchored a few metres offshore was still open. The castle on the western headland, La Rocca, where John Cheever had spent the summer of 1957, was brightly lit, and the lights were reflected, faintly shattered by the chop on the black water. I thought of Eddie Ward, an old friend of Moorehead's from the Desert War, who had bought a flat here in the late '50s, just as *la dolce vita* was about to arrive in Porto Ercole. 'Dining one evening at a restaurant high above the harbour,' Ward wrote, 'we had watched the fishing fleet setting out, all the boats lit up. Away in the distance stretched the purple hills ... It was indescribably beautiful.'

Time, I thought, it's all about time. We're only sentimental about time because it's such a bewildering element – 'that most abstract of all human- ity's homes', WG Sebald called it. My Moorehead was constructed from the printed word, mostly, and my own preoccupations. But the actual man existed most truly in what people could remember of him; in what remained in fragile containers of memory. Walking back to the hotel I passed the spot where, in 2010, my kids had had so much fun chucking pebbles into the water and I felt a sudden sharp pang for them, those lit- tle children who had been so altered by the years since that I could no longer picture their faces then.

8

BARAKA

In May 1956, Moorehead travelled alone to America on the Cunard Line *Mauretania*. *Gallipoli* hadn't yet won any prizes, or even begun to sell very well, but already he was beginning to feel a sea change in his fortunes. The novelist CS Forester, who was also making the crossing, invited him to dinner. The old pro was happy to talk shop – this is when Moorehead learnt that Forester got by on a scandalous minimum of work (only three months of writing a year, only *two hours* a day) – and that he considered Moorehead 'a distinguished operator'. A young American debutante he'd never met before developed an ardent admiration of her own, and one night – 'to my stupefaction', he reported to Lucy – she burst into tears mid-conversation. 'She was struggling quite helplessly with an intense emotion of love: not love for me physically but at [sic] some skein of feelings I happened to release, a storm of hero-worship. I suppose this sounds awful.'

It doesn't sound too good. But his blushing confusion is understandable. Even in London, Moorehead hadn't been a public figure since the end of the war, and despite a steady critical following, American readers had been largely indifferent to his books – it had taken his American agent, Ann Watkins, nearly a year to find a publisher for *Eclipse*; in fact, in May 1956 *Gallipoli* still didn't have one.

But the panhandling days were nearly over. Moorehead strode off the *Mauretania* into the 'equatorial heat' of early June and, it seems now, into the twentieth century's cocktail hour. For the next decade he would return like a honeyeater to New York almost every year, replenishing himself in its literary scene, visiting his many friends there and savouring the rewards of a steadily reinflating reputation.

Summer was Moorehead's favourite time in Manhattan: the galleries half-deserted, salary men in their 'absurd pork-pie hats' making their way to a favourite uptown bar after work to survey the universe. Life on the street outside his Washington Square hotel was like a *New Yorker* cartoon, he thought: 'surrounded by apartment blocks with their marquees, their uniformed porters at the door, a glimpse of cool mirrors and gladioli inside, men taking poodles for a walk.'

Manhattan in the late '50s is such a rich fossil assemblage of pop imagery Moorehead's biographical traces are hard to make out for all the glitter. Still, it's easy to imagine him stepping lightly from the kerb in his high-waisted trousers, coat over the arm, in the background of a scene from *The Apartment*, or *The Seven Year Itch*, off to meet Alistair Cooke or John O'Hara in an Upper East Side bar. After a dinner where he rubbed shoulders with Steinbeck, Charles Addams and PG Wodehouse, he retired, perhaps a little unsteadily, to his suite at the Stanhope. There is, he wrote to Lucy, 'a whiff of the Scott Fitzgerald world about all this'.

Yet he wasn't a complete outsider here. The *New Yorker* made him welcome; and in the '50s he also resumed an important friendship with Alwyn Lee, a friend from Melbourne University, now literary editor of *Time* magazine. Alwyn and Essie Lee had a house in Croton, New York, where Moorehead stayed frequently over the next decade. Another of the era's fantastic drinkers, Alwyn Lee was extremely clever, well-read and well-connected; through him, Moorehead would become good friends with John Cheever, *Time* writers Charles and Lael Wertenbaker, and Charles Gleaves, whose wife, Susie, became a regular correspondent. Doors swung open to the lightest touch, at the *Atlantic*, *Holiday* and *Harper's*. Suddenly lots of editors were pressing projects on *him*: the *New York Times* wanted a story commemorating the twentieth anniversary of Munich. And *Holiday* had reserved for him the lead article for its annual 'Travel America' issue, to appear in summer the following year.

With Moorehead, the magazine promised its readers, they were in the hands of 'a fine novelist whose many articles in *Holiday* place him in the great tradition of Englishmen who have written of foreign lands'. Moorehead shared the *New Yorker*'s famously foreshortened perspective of America – Manhattan in the foreground, everything else over there somewhere – and within days of setting out on his clockwise tour of the mainland states for *Holiday*, in June 1956, he felt he'd entered a new world. After listening to a distinguished southern gentleman discoursing through a lunch served by 'Negro servants' on the 'negra' problem, he retired to his Charleston hotel, where 'the television was competing with an electric organ in the bar, the ladies' bridge club was replaced now by an eager group of men listening to the results of an election for a local sheriff. I turned up the air conditioning in my room and I read the hotel's pamphlet on what I was to do in case a hydrogen bomb fell on us in the night. I found the whole of this day slightly surreal.'

In the gentle bewilderment of the prose you can hear the dislocation among the plastics, freeze-dried meals and tourist attractions. In Reno, he blinked at the dude ranches charging $150 a week; everywhere he noticed neon-lit motor courts. He took the bus out to Folly Beach in South Carolina to take in the 'immemorial American seaside scene' of hamburger and ice-cream stands, the beach umbrellas, the dismal trill of the fairground carousel in the distance. 'People nice,' he wrote privately, 'but oh my god the horror of it. Teenagers nearly naked.' He seems to be trying to grasp the contrasts of American life, and never managing it, perhaps because he seems to be dripping with sweat half the time. In the shattering heat of summertime Dallas, Moorehead noticed 'a burlesque show of an incomparable sordidness' doing lively business with sad young men just a block or two from the upmarket Neiman Marcus store.* Americans 'are more exposed to pleasure', he mused in his diary. 'American passion for bright packaging – food, presents, cars – is an attempt to bring excitement to life,

---

* It's striking just how many cabarets and burlesque shows Moorehead seems to have sampled in his journey through the middle decades of the twentieth century. From the seamy boîtes of pre-war Paris, to Madame Badia's in Cairo, and the grim nightclubs of Calcutta, he seldom missed a chance to take a look and – in the spirit of diligent product-testing – tell us about the deplorable stuff he saw.

to live in the present.' As a traveller always keen on 'a pleasant whiff of for-
lornness and despair', he found the headlong pursuit of maximal comfort
and efficiency created a strange 'bloodlessness, a lack of flavour', detected
in the traveller's zone of hotels and train compartments as he swung through
Nevada, Los Angeles and back up to Philadelphia. 'The traveller takes
another pill in another antiseptic paper cup of water and dreams of home.'

The social democrat in him unreservedly welcomed the impact of the
postwar boom on poverty and the Jeffersonian ideal of equality between
free individuals; the writer in him worried about all this aimless pelf, and
what he called, in a lecture in London the following year, the 'appalling
uniformity – the respectability – which seems to have overtaken all but
the best minds'.

But even this sentiment – a ripened, less fierce form of the existential
dismay we saw in his postwar novels – didn't mark Moorehead as an out-
lier. When he finished his lap of the States in New York he returned to
intellectual circles fully briefed in the ennui of rat-race materialism, where
books like Whyte's *The Organization Man* (1956) and, soon, Galbraith's
The Affluent Society (1958) were doing a brisk trade warning about the
spiritual dangers of mass culture and advertising.

§

There was one American friend Moorehead was particularly anxious to
see in 1956. One of the first stops on his American tour was a side-trip
down to Cuba to visit Mary Hemingway and her husband at Finca Vigía,
their hillside estate outside Havana. That June he and Hem drifted up and
down the pool 'as lazy as crocodiles'; in the evenings they relaxed on the
verandah: 'sitting there in the tropical heat one looked out over little broken hills … [The] swimming pool, surrounded by tropical trees, was like
a pool in a river in Africa. In the little guest house where I lived there
were piles of wild animal skins which had not yet been unpacked after
the last safari.'

They fished, of course. They went out on Hemingway's fabled 38-foot
wooden cruiser, *Pilar* – the one he'd hunted U-boats in – which gave
Moorehead a chance to see a legend in his element. Reeling in a marlin,

Hemingway balanced himself 'with the sort of springiness a boxer has, but with his big forearms very steady, and every time the marlin jumped, a shining blue splinter in the sky, he peered at it with great gravity and concentration'. No fisherman himself, Moorehead nonetheless got into an epic battle during which he staggered across the deck, getting tangled up in the Stars and Stripes flying from the stern – 'Careful with Old Glory, son,' murmured Hem – before he finally landed an undistinguished and inedible fish called a horse-eye jack. Back ashore, they drove past a bar in their red Cadillac convertible and collected daiquiris wrapped in paper napkins to absorb the moisture on the glass. They sipped their drinks through the half-hour drive home, where the butler was waiting for them with more drinks.

In private, Moorehead sounds more impressed than chastened by the Finca Vigía lifestyle: the exotic house ('exotic beyond belief', he wrote to Lucy), its nine servants, its constant flow of Cuban characters, and trespassing American tourists. In the little Moorehead wrote publicly about Hemingway, he was unvaryingly loyal.

> [If] the world came to think of him as a bully-boy with a flair for publicity and a secret fear of lapsing in his virility, it did not know him. He was a violent, quick-tempered man and an egotist, he could behave meanly and outrageously in his private life, but he was not frightened, and he was certainly not a bore, and publicity sought him out, not he it; for thirty years or more he buried himself away in the country, refusing ever to lecture or to appear on television … No one ever got him to deviate from his work. And with his work he was a lonely man.

In the few extant photographs from that trip to Finca Vigía, Moorehead just looks thrilled to find himself at the dinner table. The photos remind me a little of the prize ceremony for *Gallipoli*, in fact – he looks like a man a little dazed by an unexpected promotion.

§

Earlier that year, while Lucy was going through the *Gallipoli* proofs in London, Moorehead had taken a brief trip through the Middle East and then down to Kenya and Tanganyika. He was thinking of writing something about the African explorers, he told Hemingway at Finca Vigía; Hemingway was keen to help, eagerly dragging books off the shelf, quizzing his guest about who he'd read, recommending this or that – 'You've read Baker on the Murchison Falls?' But Africa would have to wait. One idea suggested to him in New York was to write a new history of the Russian Revolution, drawing on newly released German Foreign Office archives; publication would coincide with the fortieth anniversary in 1957. His US agent Armitage ('Mike') Watkins, who had just taken over the business from his mother, hammered out lucrative serialisation offers in both *Time–Life* and the *Sunday Times*. Berenson was adamantly against the project. ('You mustn't do it. You know nothing of the country, you know nothing of the language. You can't do it.') Perhaps dizzied by the sharp upturn in his fortunes, Moorehead accepted anyway, and began work immediately. He did his reading in airport lounges, on liners and around campfires in Africa, where he made more trips in early 1957. Then he wrote it up in a villa outside Rome in about six months flat.

The Russian Revolution is a badly dated book now, and curiously dull. Moorehead wasn't able to visit the USSR before he wrote it, which only confirms the idea that he needed to pace out the terrain of a story before he could bring it to life. This, he said later, was the only time he'd gone against Berenson's advice, as well as his own better judgement: 'How much I regretted it later on.' But fate is an ironist, and it was this book, his weakest ('a great flop after *Gallipoli*,' the *Spectator* remarked), that established him as a popular author in America. It was serialised in *Time–Life* and, thanks to lobbying by Cass Canfield at Harper & Brothers (who had also picked up *Gallipoli*), it became a Book of the Month club selection in 1957. This was a transforming accolade for a relative unknown, a stamp of mainstream excellence that guaranteed the attention of booksellers and half a million subscribers across the country.

It's hard not to conclude that the times suited Moorehead – or that he was getting better at suiting himself to the times. It's true that professional historians weren't impressed. The scholarly disdain in one academic review of *The Russian Revolution* set the tone for the rest of his career: after politely demolishing various of Moorehead's claims and suggestions, and fluently rubbishing his conclusions, the author finished: 'All the same, the book is superbly written and a pleasure to read.'

The general public seemed to notice only the last part. (Raymond Mortimer: 'Does any writer about the past now possess a greater gift for gripping the general reader?') There was a substantial trans-Atlantic audience for the general-interest non-fiction Moorehead could hammer out and make 'a pleasure to read' even when the facts were iffy and his heart wasn't quite in it. Geoffrey Cox always thought that Moorehead had been fortunate in his timing, that his career grew out of the success of the *African Trilogy* and the 'wartime appetite for books – so he had his big readership before TV corrupted writing'. Perhaps that's so; but Moorehead's most successful books, full of school-reader facts and great events, also appeared at a time when serious reading was an ingrained habit in the educated middle class. It was a habit that was, for many people, rooted in an ethic of unembarrassed self-improvement. Published in 1957, *The Russian Revolution* sold 40,000 copies in the US in the first year. 'I keep getting letters,' he wrote to Susie Gleaves after it was published, '"Dear sir, may I point out that you have made out a serious error, etc." No. They may not. Let 'em tell the editors of *Life*.'* Let 'em tell the accountant ... Moorehead's income that year amounted to almost £32,000, something like half a million pounds today.

When an American writer strikes it big, Martin Amis wrote once, life can change entirely. 'You become a millionaire. You are mobbed in the street.' For a British writer, sudden literary success effects a more modest transformation: 'do radio interview; have lunch with publisher; get boiler mended.' Moorehead's case was somewhere in the middle. Aside from the odd debutante, he wasn't going to be mobbed, though when the *Sunday Times* ran a billboard campaign for a series of wildlife articles in July 1957, Moorehead felt obliged to warn his son John, at Eton, about the coming fuss. Finally there was freedom from the 'long harassed battle over money'

---

* Factual accuracy had never been his forte: 'During the war,' Clifford wrote once, colleagues accused Moorehead of 'refusing to collect any more information, in case he should come across a fact which might spoil the story already formed in his mind.'

that had soured London life in the early '50s. Literary success in America meant rewards on a scale he could barely believe. 'Did you hear what *Harper's* paid *on account* to LIFE for the Bolshie book?' he wrote to Susie Gleaves in January 1958. '33,000 dollars. Are they mad?'

Moorehead had been itching to set up home in France or Italy again, and after an exceptionally wet and grey summer spent in Sussex, Lucy gave in. In late 1956 they moved to Rome, renting a flat near Piazza del Popolo. While Moorehead was off travelling in Africa, Lucy began looking around for a bigger place. 'Get a glamour house for him,' Martha Gellhorn advised. Lucy did. Soon the family relocated to a villa in the Alban Hills that had been rented by Audrey Hepburn, with a view of the coast at Anzio, a dog called Rimsky-Korsakov, and a steady stream of guests who liked to be driven into Rome to look at ruins.

But Moorehead was seldom in any one place for long. Success was its own goad. 'Jesus, how we all go rushing off after things, trying not to be too beastly on the way,' Moorehead wrote to a friend in early 1958. 'And then what happens? Usually we get what we want and then, wham, we go haring off again. It beats me.' He was now working at a tremendous tempo. He made trips to Africa in early 1956, 1957 and (twice) in 1958; he was in New York at least once a year, and often twice. 'I keep traveling – about six months every year … And I get worse and worse about traveling: I worry about missing the train and losing my passport and I hate all air trips. But I can't stop. It's a disease and I see no help for it.'

Of course he didn't want any help for it. He sounds as happy as he has ever been. The old hatred of flying remained, but even the planes weren't so bad now. On a Stratocruiser flight from Rome to Entebbe or New York, he could retire immediately to the cocktail lounge, light a nerve-steadying Chesterfield and consider his fellow jet-setters over the rim of a whisky glass. Success paid for top-end dentistry ('My teeth gleam like a lighthouse'), the splendid villa, gifts for Lucy, the bills from Eton, where Richard would soon join his older brother. More importantly, it gave him *carte blanche* to get on a plane and go and see somewhere new.

Lucy accompanied him on some of these trips, but more often she stayed at home in Rome, answering letters, revising galleys, handling the requests to give talks, provide blurbs, introductions, discuss translation rights, consider book club deals, and banking all the proceeds. There were more proceeds to bank when *The Rage of the Vulture*, that unloved title from a decade earlier, was caught up in the paperback revolution sweeping American publishing, and reissued by Ace Books with a tagline (*Moorehead's famous best-seller – a story of passion, ecstasy and dark tragedy*) that was as misleading in every detail as the salubrious cover art. Caroline remembers glimpsing a Christmas bonus cheque from the *New Yorker* around this time, and being startled by how much it was for. Moorehead's regular visits to New York now included meetings with his American stockbroker, who took a relaxed view of wealth management: 'Oh you writing chaps, you know nothing about money. Good thing, too, or you wouldn't write so well.' And with his literary patrons: there was another meeting with William Shawn, which Moorehead sketched in a letter:

> The *New Yorker* office.
>
> MR SHAWN: Why not go to China?
>
> ME: I'm tired.
>
> MR S: Or Russia?
>
> ME: I want to go home.
>
> MR S: The Moon?
>
> ME: No.
>
> MR S: Oh, there's no holding you chaps, you're always on the go.

Preparing for a trip to Africa in 1957 he wrote: 'Got to go there and gobble the place down first-hand myself.' *Gobble it down . . .* This appetite, this primitive gladness in lighting out for new places, is one of Moorehead's most appealing traits. But there were costs associated with all this hardworking freedom, many of them borne by others – Lucy especially. He admitted as much himself. If a volume of Moorehead's letters *were* ever published, one of the busiest index entries would be for *travelling, self-reproach regarding*, from Portofino, 1947: 'Dear puss, I abandon you to so much alone . . .' From New York in 1956: 'I go away only to come home, for how long now, 17 years? I have a brief illusion of escape when I am travelling . . . and that is the only reason I travel.'

The wanderlust had developed complications by now. That trembling debutante on the ship to New York wasn't the first woman to find Moorehead powerfully attractive. Many women did; Moorehead often warmly reciprocated their attentions. He had been passingly unfaithful during the war, and intermittently, but regularly, ever since.

His unfaithfulness probably wasn't untypical for his time and milieu. But no half-sober account of his life can miss it. Robert Hughes blithely referred to various affairs*; judging from Pocock's notes, every woman Pocock spoke to seems to have volunteered an opinion on it. 'Let's just say,' Cara Lancaster told me when I visited her in London, 'my mother wasn't absolutely certain that she cared for Alan's lifestyle that much.' You could say that the womanising was an aspect of the freedom he had demanded as of right since he arrived in Europe – and had warned Lucy about from the start. But that would be to elevate to principle what looks more like habit, or business-trip opportunism. Moorehead was an outrageous flirt, Betty told me; he *loved women*, in that curious, all-forgiving phrase; quite a few women adored him too. Knowing that he was sexually attractive always mattered to him.

Sometime on that American trip of 1956, Moorehead met and fell for Jane White Cooke, a talented painter who was married to the expat English broadcaster Alistair Cooke. A few of Moorehead's flings became long-lasting attachments – he had a lover in South Africa whom he saw on and off for more than a decade – but Jane was different. What may have begun as a fling was soon a serious love affair, and it continued long after Lucy innocently discovered it (an opened letter left lying about), long after it brought lasting misery to both marriages. For the next ten years Moorehead's frequent trips to New York would include a few days at Long Island, where Jane often had the Cookes' weekend bungalow to herself. Sometimes they met in Europe during Jane's increasingly frequent trips abroad.

---

* Though with uncharacteristic delicacy, at least in public. In his memoirs, for instance, Hughes refers to 'the wife of a Melbourne financier whom Alan was visiting in a Rome hotel'. Hughes' own letters to Moorehead suggest that Alan's womanising was no secret between them, either. In 1965 Hughes mentioned in a letter to Moorehead that when he'd brought up his name to a newly arrived Australian diplomat, the man turned 'a shade of purple' and started 'spluttering about people who parked their cars in other peoples' garages'.

Unlike most marriages, in which many others have an interest, affairs tend to have few friends, and leave few traces. We'll never know what Moorehead's part-time shadow-life with Jane meant to him. The novels give some of the flavour of his attitudes to infidelity, but of course none of the facts. (*A Summer Night*, in particular, is full of impatience with pieties about marital fidelity, something the novel seems to consider an unreasonable suppression of the animal spirits.) All I found of this relationship was a pair of photographs, circa 1965. In one, Moorehead is standing by a painting in a sharp suit, a fudge of smoke escaping the corner of his mouth. He's looking at the camera, not smiling. The painting, choppy dabs of acrylic drying in low sun against a brick wall, is a freshly painted portrait of Moorehead himself. In the other photo is Jane: smiling, her hair falling across her eyes; straight-backed. She's also posing with a painting, in this case a self-portrait of the artist at her easel.

Jane painted him; he didn't write about her – except, it seems, in some difficult letters to Lucy. 'As soon as I get back I am going to throw myself into the business of making life more bearable,' he promised in a letter home from the Manhattan whirlwind in December '57. And a week later: 'Poor Puss. At the bottom of a well. Who threw her in? I did.'

§

In 1963, Ethiopian Airways ran full-page magazine ads that showed a relief map of the African continent in lunar monochrome crisscrossed by the new carrier's routes. The tagline, *Jets over the Lands of Hemingway and Moorehead*, referred the eye to the lower left-hand corner where hardback copies of *The Snows of Kilimanjaro* and *The Blue Nile* were propped up like distinguished guests. This is one of the few places I ever saw Moorehead and Hemingway in the same sentence; proof of how famous he had become, at least among readers. And it shows how strongly identified his name was with Africa. In 1957 he began publishing articles about his trips to South Africa, Rhodesia and Kenya; for the next five years, he hardly wrote about anything else. By the time this ad was running, the pearl-gray continent had furnished the crowning triumphs of Moorehead's Indian summer, and the most commercially successful books of his career: *No Room in the Ark* (1959), *The White Nile* (1960) and *The Blue Nile* (1962).

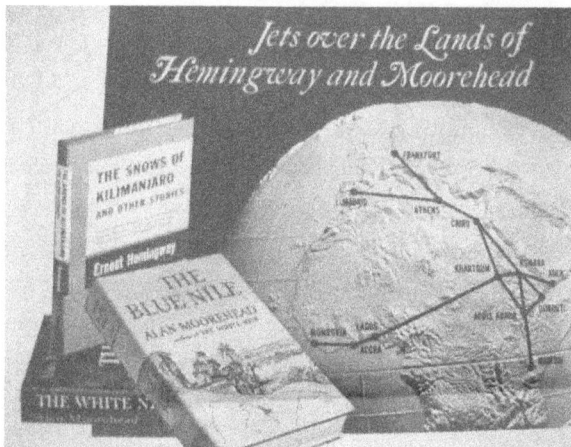

In 1942 Moorehead had travelled the length of Africa in a Sunderland flying boat, following the 'green ribbon of the Nile' south from Cairo in a series of hops, through Wadi Halfa, Khartoum, Malakal in southern Sudan, Kisumu on Lake Victoria, and thence via the Zambesi and Victoria Falls, before finally reaching Durban. During a break in Khartoum, Moorehead drank ice-cold beer on the Grand Hotel terrace for breakfast, and read all about the riverine tribes of the Sudd, where the 'naked girls were reputed to be of unusual beauty'; he browsed photographs for sale in bookstalls that showed 'extraordinarily sexual native dances'. They flew low on the next leg; images of life on the river flashed passed beneath the bulky gunwales of the Sunderland like an enchanted slide-show. At a stop on the Zambesi, BOAC staff had to shoo hippos out of the way before the plane could make its final approach. 'I conceived that the river had a compelling and mysterious charm,' he recalled in the late 1950s; 'the inhabitants of its banks were an extravagantly beautiful race living the true idyllic life … all unspoiled and uncontaminated.' It was an illusion, of course, but a thrilling one: it 'filled me with an intense desire to come back one day … It was, I suppose, nothing more than the usual tourist thirst for the Africa of the tribal drums and the jungle in the raw, but it was none the less genuine for that.'

He came back first in early 1956, to write some articles on wildlife for the *New Yorker*; and then he kept coming back, until he had enough material for a book, *No Room in the Ark*. On that first return trip, he and Lucy began in Johannesburg, where hopes of seeing 'the primitive African communities' Moorehead dreamed of were swiftly quashed by informants on the dinner-party circuit. 'I very much doubt,' one white resident told him, 'if you will find many Africans going *naked* any more.' His best chance, she thought, was in Uganda. He might try there.

Passages like these gently satirise the outsider's African fantasy, but Moorehead's disappointment at African suburbia, at its deflating familiarity, was authentic. A dinner party in the hills out of town was 'the usual thing': all white, evening dress, and a round of entertainments after the meal – liar dice, poker, canasta, bridge. More Portofino than darkest Africa.

The primary object of the trip was to see animals in the wild. This passion is the one thing in Moorehead's postwar life that seems completely new. Apart from the pocketed birds' eggs of childhood bush trips there's little sign of it before the 1952 trip to Australia. But animal-watching had developed into a genuine joy of his middle age – it was his one mad enthusiasm. Even in the histories of the 1960s, animals scuttle onto the page where they're not strictly required, as if the author can't bear to keep them out. 'I have become more of a bore about animals than ever,' he confessed in a 1958 letter, describing the green Brazilian parrot he had just acquired and named Loretta ('It eats with me, sleeps with me, and walks in the rain with me').

Apart from Loretta, this wasn't a sentimental attachment. He found animals hypnotically absorbing; watching them allowed him to forget himself. Sometimes in his encounters there is, in the rapt stillness of his attention, a hint of the metaphysical: as if the unillusioned rationalist in him was approaching a form of spiritual communion he couldn't get anywhere else. 'I had not been prepared for the blackness of him,' he wrote of his first glimpse of a gorilla on Mount Muhavura, Uganda, after an eight-hour slog uphill through hypericum and giant bamboo.

> He was a great craggy pillar of gleaming blackness, black crew-cut hair on his head, black deep-sunken eyes towards us, huge rubbery black nostrils, and a black beard. He shifted his posture a little, still glaring fixedly upon us, and he had the dignity and majesty of prophets. He was the most

distinguished and splendid animal I ever saw and I had only one desire at that moment: to go forward towards him, to meet him and to know him: to communicate.

No Room in the Ark begins in a spirit of leisurely safari. But it soon becomes a wider story about the peril facing Africa's wild animals amid the turmoil of decolonisation, and about the West's apparent indifference to their fate. The tragedy of Africa, Moorehead wrote, is 'the glee for killing'. It had been since white men first arrived. Now the new governments in Kenya and Uganda were struggling to fund the gamekeepers required to keep poachers out of their fragile national parks. If nothing is done about it, Moorehead wrote in a script for an unproduced Granada TV program, 'pretty soon there won't be a wild animal alive larger than a rabbit outside the game parks in the whole of Africa.'

No Room in the Ark was a conservationist *cri de cœur* but it works not by belabouring the destruction of the wildlife, but by making the author's amateur enthusiasm the reader's own. It's really a book about the tremendous enjoyment Moorehead took in looking at animals, then conveyed in his inconspicuously absorbing way. 'One year,' Moorehead wrote,

> when I was travelling through Tanganyika I was doing a good deal of reading about the Russian Revolution ... And it was an odd thing to look up from Trotsky or the collected letters of Lenin and see, only a few yards away, a group of lions watching me from the long grass; or perhaps meet the eye of some great gaunt bird like the marabou, which in its own way could be as grave and relentless as Lenin himself.

He was daunted, at first, by the task of doing something new with such an iconic cast of creatures. But advice from William Shawn 'at once resolved my greatest difficulty. Take no notice, he said, "of the fact that the hippopotamus, the elephant and the other animals have been described so often before. Say what you think, say what you felt."'

Although his descriptions of animals tend to the anthropomorphic, his delight is contagious. Storks massing for their annual migration leave behind a few older birds, he writes, 'who don't feel equal to this journey, and often … you will see them loitering about in the swamps and the marshes in South Africa through the winter, like elderly holiday-makers who linger on in half-deserted seaside hotels long after the season is over.'

All this deeply impressed one credentialled naturalist. 'Alan Moorehead has put me in a quandary,' wrote Gerald Durrell in the *New York Times*. 'He has written a book so good that any praise of mine seems inadequate. He writes with such strange brilliance that he evokes the color and scents of the African scene with tremendous power; more than any other book I have read on Africa this one made me feel I was sharing the experiences with the author.'

§

The book was published in early 1959. In the first three months it sold 30,000 hardback copies in Britain alone. Even the *Daily Express* begrudgingly reviewed it, setting aside its ban on all things Moorehead. It was translated into four languages, serialised in several of the world's leading newspapers and magazines, recommended by the Reprint Society, and various book societies, including, again, the Book-of-the-Month Club in the US, and eventually sold nearly half a million copies worldwide. In faraway Melbourne, copies were piled up into stupas in bookstore windows.

In the 1950s *No Room in the Ark* seemed to belong to a boom in popular naturalist and conservationist books – fitting in between Durrell's own *The Overloaded Ark* (1953), for instance, and Rachel Carson's *The Silent Spring* (1962). But hardly anyone knows it now. It's been out of print since the mid-1970s. It had always been one of my favourites, partly because it seems like an undisturbed relic of its time. But mostly because it is full of that odd Moorehead quality of being both bound to its historical moment and also strangely outside it.

The trips that furnished his three Africa books, and much journalism, took place during the high tide of decolonisation; most of the countries he visited to write *No Room in the Ark* – Uganda, Tanganyika, Kenya, Rwanda and Sudan – achieved independence between 1956 and 1963.

The flags of the European empires were being jerked down flagpoles across the continent. But the politics of decolonisation and self-government, and the impact of urbanisation, is a barely perceptible hum in the background of Moorehead's Africa. In Nigeria in 1963 he noted the appalling poverty in remote inland villages, but was pleased nonetheless to report that the political tension observed in the lead-up to independence two years before had apparently evaporated. The Nigerians he met impressed him with their solicitousness, amicability and spontaneous dancing. 'If you are riding by in a car and the Nigerian cannot reach forward to shake you by the hand,' he reported, 'he will wave instead, apparently very much refreshed by just this one quick glimpse of you.'

An equally upbeat take appears in a 1960 article for *Horizon* magazine about depictions by colonised peoples of white invaders:

> It is pleasant to glance at these souvenirs of the first contact between the two groups of races and to know that the colored man so often looked upon the whites not too unkindly, not as a threatening monster, but as an enlightened and benevolent extension of himself.

It's unlikely the Mau Mau insurgents Moorehead saw rounded up behind barbed wire at Lodwar felt this way. Others who witnessed the eclipse of white rule weren't nearly so indulgent towards its legacy. Ryszard Kapuściński, for instance, spearheading the next generation of European writing about Africa, arrived in Dar es Salaam in 1962. He saw the same structural racism there he'd seen all across Africa: 'the whites possessed the best plots of land and the cities' richest neighborhoods, and they controlled industry, while the blacks were consigned to crowded, wretched scraps of semi-arid land.'

That sort of systemic analysis was alien to Moorehead's essentially eye-level view of the world-as-it-is. And to his fatalism: many times, he wrote in *No Room in the Ark*, he saw animals tearing one another up for food and never thought to wish that things were other than they were.

> One develops a curious indifference, and it is always possible to dismiss the most brutal things with the phrase, 'Oh well, it's the law of nature. It's

bound to happen anyway.' ... It is the inevitability of these things, the idea that since they do happen it is right they should happen, that excuses you from feeling pity; and in Africa it is quite easy to let this same indifference insulate you from human tragedies as well.

Moorehead's real interest in Africa lay in what lay beyond the cities, in the remotest reaches where some imaginary essence of Africa – the one he'd seen from the flying boat in 1942 – was most likely to be found. And this is what you can still feel in the pages of *Ark*, especially: a kind of tipping point in Western longing for the wilderness beyond the monotony of modern urban life. As one review put it, 'wildlife casts over the nerve-worn men and women of the modern world an increasingly fascinating spell.' Perhaps readers were also responding to the note of shrinking-world elegy struck in the book's blurb, which described journeys like these ones as 'probably the last adventure left today that has nothing to do with the atomic age and the conquest of space ... Nowadays it is getting increasingly harder to escape from the city, from civilization, from other people.' It wasn't just the charismatic fauna that was on the cusp of being lost forever, but also a gilded twilight before remnants of pre-modern Africa disappeared forever under a tide of irrigation schemes and Coca-Cola.

Ark is partly a report on this vanishing idea of Africa. Moorehead did find his 'naked tribespeople': the Dinka of the southern Sudan were still there, 'a proud and truculent people'; the Turkana people of Lake Rudolf, observing their 'ancient tribal customs', and the cattle-herding Karamojong of north-east Uganda whom Moorehead admired for their independence and undiluted exoticism (a diet of fresh milk and cow's blood). Many of these people are there in his travel pics – smiling group shots with a shirt-sleeved Moorehead squeezed in the middle. And he also found places where his own tribe continued to observe its hallowed rites. At Lodwar, near Lake Rudolf in Kenya, Moorehead came across a British fort of the type he'd seen during the early days of the war in Africa, functioning in 1957 exactly as it had then, exactly as such forts did in movies like *Beau Geste* and *King of the Khyber Rifles*. It stood on high ground; a Union Jack still flew; camels squatted under the waterhole palms while soldiers drilled inside and sentries watched over the 'appalling waste of sand and stark rock' all around. All the details, including a bugler to sound the recall, were preserved with 'almost painful thoroughness'.

There's an air of Sunday evening ethnography about these pictures of tribal life – and maybe about that fort, too – that is powerfully redolent of a historical moment when *National Geographic* was in its heyday, and when the joy with which its photos celebrated the diversity of humankind was inseparable from anxiety about its future. In Africa, English was imposing itself as a *lingua franca*, as travelling salesmen and officials flocked into new airport hotels in remote townships. New cropland daily encroached on wildlife habitats. The old circular African huts on the lake shore at Jinja were now made of prefab aluminium rather than grass, 'and they are dry, practical, and hideous.'

For African romantics, the truly sinister rumble of change was the one emanating from the giant hangars and welding bays at Boeing and McDonnell Douglas: the jets were coming, and they were about to open up intercontinental travel to millions of middle-class Westerners. The safaris and pan-African road trips that had till now been the exclusive preserve of adventurers and rich game-shooters were now a possibility for 'the born tourist type' that travel writer Peter Fleming was already deploring back in 1936, 'the happily goggling ruminant' he found spoiling his view of exotic sights, and which was about to descend on the game parks in thousands of coach-loads. And in a feedback loop familiar to every tourist who has ever found herself, at Macchu Picchu, or the Alhambra, inwardly raging at all these fucking tourists, the scramble to see the last of authentic Africa would only accelerate its corruption. 'The tourists of our time are an implacable, a ferocious phenomenon who recognise no authority but their light-metres,' groused Cyril Connolly (way back in 1953), 'who require local colour for their colour film and folk-lore in action for their cine-camera.' This is exactly what was happening in 1957 at Lake Kivu, in the Congo, where Moorehead found a native population bewildered by its new role as a tourist spectacle. Where the Belgians 'have encouraged them to cling to their ancient habits a weird kind of surrealism sets in', Moorehead wrote. For a few pounds, the celebrated hunters of the Watusi 'can be induced to perform their war dance', a production which proved both impressive, and ineffably pitiful. The warriors seemed 'a little self-conscious in the way that children sometimes are when, against their instincts, they have been persuaded to dress up and make a performance at a party'.

Moorehead didn't blame the tourists for this. As ace far-flung correspondent of the *New Yorker* and slide-night raconteur of *Holiday* magazine, he was clipping his ticket on the booming travel industry, and he had the good grace not to complain. He was, anyway, a conviction democrat about travel. The war – which, among many other things, was a vast exercise in state-funded mass travel – only strengthened his belief that everyone should have a chance to see the world. But of course mass tourism was a threat to another endangered species: the travel writer. It didn't just ruin the view; it threatened a cherished monopoly on adventure. In the late '50s, remote destinations were easy enough to get to if you had contacts, and money and time, but were still prohibitively expensive for most. This period between the steamships and the rockets, travel writer Jan Morris has said, was a blessed time to go out into the world and write about it. 'If I'd been born a generation earlier,' she wrote in the 1970s, 'I couldn't have seen so many places; a generation later, I might not have bothered to try.' For some writers who had thrived in that gilded interregnum, all the new souvenir stands and sound'n'light shows dulled the appetite. Shirley Hazzard noted her friend Graham Greene's declining taste for the world as the twentieth century rolled on. In the '30s and '40s Greene's travels had been partly impelled by 'his wish to test the dangerous margins of his world', but twenty years on,

> that addiction and intoxication had, with age, been diluted by indifference. The round-trip ticket of the jet era, in making the travel trajectory dramatically brisker, had eroded those elements of risk and rigour that once sent Graham on lonely journeys to enigmatic places.

Moorehead permitted himself the odd elderly grumble – even the best of the temples, he admitted during a 1962 trip up the Nile, seem mundane 'when beset by crowds in straw hats and coloured shirts'. But he was largely immune to this generational disappointment. Perhaps because what he found most enigmatic about places was time, and the unsettling transformations it produced.

§

By the time *Ark* appeared in bookshops, Moorehead had long since begun work on the project first conceived in 1956: a history of African exploration. In 1958 he embarked on a fury of reading for a book about the Nile, and in September he made another research trip to Africa, travelling with an old family friend, Dick Waller, with a plan to retrace the steps of the Victorian explorers. In September they sailed from Venice for Dar es Salaam, where they stayed at Government House as guests of the governor, Sir Richard Turnbull (the last British governor of Tanganyika), before moving to Zanzibar, where they were put up by the British Resident, Sir Henry Potter. In a Land Rover they tracked inland following a map specially prepared for them by the chief draughtsman of the Royal Geographic Society, pegging their way along the Burton–Speke path of 1857 in daily leaps, across wadis and waterholes, sometimes finding a friendly verandah at a district commissioner's station, sometimes laying out the bedroll under the stars.

When Pocock spoke to him thirty years later, Waller remembered how much Moorehead relished tracking his quarry on this storied ground. *We must try to get into the minds of the old explorers*, he would say. Or *This is exactly what Burton and Speke would have seen*. Waller remembered, too, Moorehead's eagerness for the physical challenge; he was 'unsparing' with himself, and unsympathetic to those daunted by the pace. And keen *always to move on*: that quality of reckless, almost violent resentment of wasted time, the need to get to the next thing – a character still recognisable from the one James Cameron knew in the war, 'erratic, aggressive, full of terrier enthusiasms, eaten by the curiosities of the naif Australian'. That bounding energy is unmistakable in the book he finished the following year, *The White Nile* (1960). The successor to romantic old novels of Empire, one American critic said, is the true adventure story, and 'Alan Moorehead tells such stories ... better than anyone else. He is really our contemporary John Buchan ... right on target when it comes to the reconstruction of a good adventure.' But the special quality of *The White Nile*, and *The Blue Nile* that followed in 1962, is not just the reconstruction of adventure, but reconstruction of our *need* for it. What really shocked him about the fort at Lodwar was the realisation that places like this 'have become as out of date as the illustrations in old Victorian adventure books'.

> It seems incredible that the camel-driver and the native soldier in his kepi ... should have become anachronisms so completely and so quickly ... and I remembered with a curious sense of embarrassment, how important all these things once were to me, how I gobbled them up in the movies and the adventure books. And now I had arrived at the reality of them at Lodwar, it was the reality, and not the fiction, that was unreal.

For all their sobriety and good sense – and the 'Ciceronian restraint' Andrea had alerted me to – Moorehead's late histories are suffused with a wide-eyed wonder that he seems to have rediscovered in memories of his childhood. Passing through Istanbul in 1957 for a *Holiday* story, Moorehead mentions a book he'd owned as a boy with stirring lithographs of life in old Constantinople.

> A bright vision of the East grew up in my mind: I saw a horizon of gleaming mosques, of caiques and feluccas sailing across the Golden Horn, of trains of caravans coming in from Samarkand, of fierce caliphs ... of beautiful women looking down through barred windows on to the waters of the Bosporus. Neither age nor experience has succeeded in dimming this vision ... I still secretly see the city in this way.

Seeing a city that way, with your head full of Arabian Nights, you're going to miss plenty of historical reality. But maybe you gain access to the delight, as Orhan Pamuk writes of his own earliest memories of Istanbul, that comes when you discard 'historical grievances and enjoy it fully as a child, to long to know more'.

The man who had grown up reading Buchan, Ballantyne and Kipling by the light of a gas bracket 'that sprouted from the wall with a naked flame' had found a way to transpose the childhood appetite for ripping

yarns into his stories for grown-ups.* His best work revives in the reader
the wide-world wonder we felt as children, spinning the classroom globe
with a fingertip. The urge to dive into lost worlds might be called escapist, but it is also enlarging: a state of mind, Pamuk called it, 'ultimately as
life affirming as it is negating'.

In the mid-nineteenth century, the source of the Nile was the last great
mystery on the geographers' books. *The White Nile* tells of the great
European expeditions that set out to solve it, only 100 years before
Moorehead's return to Africa: there's Burton and Speke in 1856; Speke and
Grant in 1860; Samuel and Florence Baker's upstream trekkings of 1863;
Livingstone's seven years of gently mistaken wanderings around the Upper
Congo and Lake Victoria from 1866.

The blurb promised 'half a century of British achievement which makes
us proud of our Victorian ancestors', which is a strangely jingoistic take on
a book that describes how those very ancestors opened the Nile valley to
ruthless exploitation. Still – there *is* a kind of admiration for the explorers.
In 1856, Speke and Burton were heading into regions almost as alien as
the moon, and not much easier to reach. Expeditions were massive under-
takings; funded by scientific societies and private subscription, they
comprised in some cases hundreds of people, including native porters, and
countless wagons, camels and horses. The obstacles were daunting. The
explorers were constantly losing porters to desertion and death. The worst
that befell Moorehead and Waller as they retraced the tale in 1958 was an
attack by a broody hippo that sent them scurrying into the bush so fast
they needed help to find their way back to the river. A hundred years before,
the explorers were constantly lost. If they weren't lost they were involun-
tarily detained: Speke and Grant were 'guests' of King Mutesa's court at
Buganda for six months. They were constantly ill from disease.

The world they wandered into still seems hallucinatory. Mutesa would
prove to be a cunning and subtle politician; but when Speke and Grant
first encountered him they saw a man who 'affected an extraordinary

---

* It's not surprising that Moorehead's African books translated so readily to junior editions with lots of illustrations –
and excellent captions. '*Gordon's head shown to Slatin while still a prisoner of the Mahdi*', for instance; '*Theodore's
prisoners pitched over the precipice*'.

stiff-legged strut which was meant to imitate the gait of a lion' and ruled his court like a sulky godlet; he was fond of ordering whimsical summary executions. Nearby in the court of the King of Karagwe, the Bakers saw the king's 300 or so enormously fat wives, who were force-fed goat milk 'sucked from a gourd through a straw, and if the young girls resisted this treatment they were force-fed like the *pâté de foie gras* ducks of Strasbourg'.

Strangest of all, in many ways, were the explorers themselves: Victorian megalomania, mysticism, idealism and appetites for hardship that often run ahead of their own understanding, let alone common sense. Inhuman endurance is a constant theme. Florence Baker, for instance, went everywhere her husband did during their three-year trip up the river, faced all the same dangers – sunstroke, malaria, slurping swamps, ambush by warriors armed with poison-tipped arrows – but did it all cinched into Victorian corsets and weighed down with heavy skirts and much tedious 'weaker sex' treatment.

It is the fate of the past, and everyone in it, to be condescended to by later generations, if only for their childlike ignorance of all that we now know. But Moorehead isn't interested in the distant strangeness of this world for its own sake. He wants to see the past as it saw itself; for all their extraordinary feats, his characters – doodled into life with just a few words – are remarkably like people we might know. Livingstone, he wrote, 'had that quality which the Arabs describe as *baraka*. In the most improbable circumstances he had the power of enhancing life and making it appear better than before.' Contrasting Emin Pasha, governor of Equatoria, with the monotone Stanley, who rescues him in 1874, Moorehead writes: 'Emin, one feels, was the sort of character who would have been given the worst table in a restaurant … Stanley's world was compacted into a straight line, an arrow in the blue. Emin describes a series of faint spirals in the dust.'

To a modern reader, the most alien aspect of the explorers' Africa is all the time in it: the delays, the longueurs, the hiatuses, the onerous *lento* of nineteenth-century exploration. The explorers, and the armies who came after them, proceeded at a pace that, I couldn't help but notice (and couldn't help wondering whether Moorehead noticed), closely resembles the slog of book-writing. Typically, two or three years of daily trudging are interrupted by months-long hold-ups while people sweat out a fever, or wait for reinforcements. Sometimes they wait for the season to change. Mail from Europe can take a year to arrive.

But time is also part of the mood of these books, the melancholy that attends the 'crushing and yet captivating weight of loneliness in Africa'. Moorehead's figures will themselves on through a kind of myth-field where geological time is part of the terrain, along with the ever-flowing rivers, the birds and animals, the seasons, the cycles of rise and fall. There's a fatalism in this vision of the indifferent everlastingness of the natural world, but also consolation. 'Sometimes,' Rebecca West wrote, 'it is necessary to know where we are in eternity as well as time.' And so it is for the explorers, and for us watching them, as they trudge forever on, further and further from home, as if through a darkening landscape by Caspar David Friedrich, towards slanting rays of *weltschmerz*.

'It's a dream book,' wrote Martha Gellhorn in a letter of congratulation Moorehead treasured, 'a humdinger … And what a wonderful way of life you've found, it combines derring-do (which we all pine for, or anyhow I do, sicken for want of it), with the pleasures of the mind, your mind at work.' Released in late 1960, *The White Nile* was the critical and commercial pinnacle of Moorehead's career. In Britain alone it sold 60,000 copies in hardback, just in the first year. Across the Atlantic, it ended up doing even better ('a fascinating and extremely well-written work,' declared the *New York Times*, 'absolutely absorbing'). It was the Americans' turn to grapple with what his publishers were now advertising as 'the Moorehead Magic'. 'His formula not much different from that employed by legions of diligent hacks,' mused another *Times* reviewer; none of it was new, as such; his themes and ideas were unremarkable. So how did he hold readers in his subtle spell? 'Mainly by exercising a rare ability for becoming involved while remaining detached. He is a wonderfully gifted reporter who has applied the full force of his talent to history.'

The story-telling brio had something to do with the dimension added by Moorehead's boots-on-the-ground method. 'He seems to have visited every inch of it,' wrote JB Priestley, with curmudgeonly approval; the result, suggested American travel author William Zinsser in 1990, is an interactive style of storytelling, a style Moorehead 'raised to perfection . . . his feat is not only to make us feel that we are with Burton, Speke, Baker and the other doughty Victorians who sought the source of the Nile, but that we are with him as he follows the steps of those explorers'.

The most remarkable rave for *The White Nile* came from the travel writer Jan (then James) Morris. Something in Morris deeply approved of Moorehead's work; from now on Morris's reviews for each new book turn up in the *Times* like a personal *oompapa* band ready to lead a parade of praise. Moorehead's 'books are, as every reviewer knows, a pleasure just to sniff', Morris declared, placing Moorehead among a select group of writers bringing to English letters 'a late flame of virility and derring-do'.

> They are the survivors of that old English companionship, the scholar-adventurers, a blend of the artistic and the practical . . . All are the very antithesis of the Common Man . . . and all four, each a patrician in his different kind . . . are remarkable men in an era of unremarkable celebrities. They feel fit, lucky, successful people, in an age dominated by the sick, the unfortunate and the petulant. They are, to be short, rather a relief.

One senses Morris finding a convenient outlet here for some post-Suez, anti-suburban frustrations. But that didn't stop Lucy pasting this review into the scrapbook in which such items were archived. Nor did it stop me, when I found it, adding it to the file in the back of my mind where I kept proof that I wasn't mad.

Today the obvious explanation for the success of both *Nile* books is still the best one: Moorehead had found the perfect story. His own desire to get to Africa and *gobble it down* is also the book's subject. Livingstone, he wrote, 'was one of those people who cannot bear not to look over the other side of the next hill'. Both *Nile* books are full of people with the same problem. Of course, some of them only wanted to look over the other side of the hill in order to shoot whatever was there. But Moorehead's fondest attention is reserved for scholar-wanderers, like Livingstone, Burton and Burckhardt, the mysteriously impelled types who seem to be escaping into bliss as much as exploring or campaigning, and at times he writes about them with a recognition so strong it verges on self-portraiture.

Vivant Denon, for instance, was one of the savants Napoleon brought along on his invasion of Egypt in 1798 to catalogue all the marvels discovered on the way. A gifted polymath, Denon followed General Desaix's army into Upper Egypt and spent many months in a state of barely expressible excitement – 'terrier-like in its intensity', Moorehead wrote – exploring the great pyramids, the temples at Dendera, Karnak, Edfu and Aswan. Denon would become so engrossed in his sketches of temples and statues, he often worked right through battles; his comrades were constantly doubling back to drag him out of a tomb or prise him away from the frieze before he was shot or speared.

> No sooner would he begin a sketch or start to trace an inscription than the trumpet would sound the advance, and he would have to scramble on to his horse and hurry after the others. It was intensely frustrating. He was like the enthusiast who, having come miles to see a painting, is turned out of the museum by the closing bell – except that here he never knew whether he, or any other trained observer, would ever be able to come back again.

Moorehead knew what it was like to find himself in some extraordinary place, trying to take it in, to describe it, just as the artillery got busy blasting it to bits. And he understood traveller's rapture. He could imagine how, after roaming the Sudan and the Ethiopian Highlands for several years, the Swiss adventurer and Arabist Johann Burckhardt might have felt catching his first glimpse of the ruins at Philae:

> It is an exhilarating experience to come up in the evening, or better still in the moonlight, to some such place as Wady es Sebure, and see, close to the shore, the great propylon of Rameses' temple with its avenue of sphinxes half buried in the sand. But to have been there in 1813, as Burckhardt was, and to have known that nothing but an utter barbarity lay around, that there was no easy way back to civilization, and that this sight, unrecorded, unexplored and unknown, was standing there for your eyes alone: this must have provided sensations which were the justification for all the dangers and miseries of the journey.

❦

Much of *The White Nile* Moorehead wrote at Freya Stark's house in Asolo, near Venice, in the early 1959. Lucy remained in Rome with Caroline, typing up her husband's drafts, and occasionally driving up to Porto Ercole to supervise progress on the house. When he wasn't taking walks in the spring rain with his obnoxious parrot hooked to his shoulder, Moorehead was 'hull-down' working in one room, beating out his brains, as he put it, while Stark worked in another. He sometimes felt lethargic, too: 'ill-mannered and IMMATURE,' he wrote to a friend. 'If you have any odd literary jobs you want done just send them along to us.'

A year later he was writing *The Blue Nile* in his brand-new studio at Porto Ercole, with maps and illustrations pinned to the walls, his little Olivetti to one side. Back in Cairo in 1941, Moorehead had devised a method for writing books he'd stuck with ever since. He would sketch out by hand a blueprint of the entire book on sheets of foolscap, indicating roughly the contents of each chapter, including inspired phrases or lines of dialogue, and refine it until all his ideas were in the right place. Once this 'cartoon for a tapestry' was complete, it was time for the actual writing. It was a methodical, painfully costive process that demanded a steady, unrelenting input of working time. When a book was on the go, he worked six days a week; he rose before 7 a.m., made himself a huge pot of coffee, and trudged out to the studio. There he sat, back to the tumbling vineyards and shining sea, not leaving his seat until lunchtime. In the afternoons, he corrected the morning's work, read, or redrafted. The greatest lesson Robert Hughes absorbed at the feet of the master, he said afterwards, was business-like hours. 'Whether he was writing anything or not, he'd be sitting in front of the typewriter, and generally just by the sheer process of shaming himself into sitting there, 1000 words a day would come out.' Moorehead remarked in the late '50s, 'people sometimes tell me they enjoy writing. I just look at them and wonder how long they've been at it.'

Hughes recalled reading to his mentor a line from Leonardo's notebooks: *The world is full of infinite causes that have never yet been set forth*

in experience. "'That's it!" [Moorehead] exclaimed. "That's what keeps a writer going! You don't need to make things up!'" But the celerity with which *The Blue Nile* followed its bestselling predecessor looked to some more like good business sense than a passion for *infinite causes*, particularly since, as several critics observed, the river this time wasn't a mighty stream thundering through his tale, but a tenuous thread that allowed him to string together several unrelated episodes of Europeans in Africa.

There *was* something mechanical about Moorehead's productivity, even to supporters. In his panegyric to *The White Nile*, Morris suggested that Moorehead had 'some of the attributes of a computer . . . Feed him with facts, one feels – any facts you like – and with a rumble and a regurgitation, a clicking and a whirring, an inflow of maps, excellent pictures and well-compiled indexes he will produce for you an admirable book.' Moorehead always operated on a fuel-mix with a higher ratio of perspiration to inspiration than the romantic ideal prefers, and never more than now. I sometimes wondered if his regularity, his pragmatism and steadiness counted against him.

But people could say what they liked. Isn't there triumph here, even in this 'straining shit through a sock' phase? Not so much because this was also the period in which Moorehead owned a beautiful new house on an Italian hillside, kept a *pied-à-terre* in London, was putting two sons through Eton, and would soon acquire half a yacht. But because he'd made it – again. And this time he'd found a way to channel his defining flaw – the outsiderism, the deficit of commitment he deplored in himself – into his work. The old restlessness for elsewhere is not just part of the tramping exhilarating energy of the African books. It's the fountainhead of Moorehead's ineffable talent, his ability to let us relive the past through long-ago lives in long-gone places.

9

HOME

When they moved into the house at Porto Ercole in 1960, Moorehead began keeping a weather book: a kind of captain's log for the house's voyage through the years to come. In it he recorded memorable storms and delightful stretches of weather, notable events in the village calendar, seasonal changes and improvements to the property and animal sightings. Paging through it, I realised he'd also recorded a new and unexpected Moorehead: the contented homebody. Moorehead's lifelong itch to get out and go somewhere seems salved, at least temporarily, by the pleasure of constructing a home from scratch. Apart from the townhouse in Wells Rise, this was the first house he'd owned. On the churned-up clay pan left by the builders he planted vines, fruit trees and a kitchen garden; there was a rose garden on the terrace, acacias, and mimosas and 'witches' fingers' with brilliant rose-purple flowers. In the second year they added plane trees outside the studio, a row of cypresses to line the lower drive. Nowhere does he sound as satisfied as he does reporting on the welfare of his vines and acacias.

It's not clear why Alan and Lucy chose this spot on the Tuscan coast. Perhaps they were tipped off by John Cheever, who'd spent the summer of 1957 in La Rocca, the sixteenth-century fortress overlooking the port. Outside the season, Porto Ercole was still a rustic fishing village. When the Cheevers were at La Rocca, there was one toilet that had to be flushed by bucket, and a goat and some raddled chickens in the courtyard, and a plague of beetles inside. But simplicity was part of the attraction. There was no electricity in the Mooreheads' house when they moved in. On winter evenings they'd light the fire after dinner, and Moorehead would read Saki and Chekhov aloud to the children. An access road had to be built to reach their ten acres. A water supply had to be set up, springs dug, terraces laid out for the vineyard and the olive trees. 'I am now an expert on sewerage, bricklaying, hydraulics, floor space (in square metres), horticulture, and Italian lawyers,' Moorehead boasted in 1961. In return for cooperation on several matters, the Mooreheads were advised to make a 'contribution', in the Italian custom, to a certain local identity, but how was such a thing done? With an envelope stuffed with lira, he went down to the village to see the man in his office. In his awkward Italian, Moorehead chatted for a long time without successfully raising the subject until, in desperation, he mutely proffered the payola. Without even glancing at it, *il padrone* took the envelope, placed it on his desk and went on with what he was saying.

Summers could be rowdy, but out of season this was a remote and sometimes wild coast. On boat trips to the deserted beaches of Giglio, Moorehead would turn to the beach wall and tear off his clothes. 'Who cares?' he'd say to bemused visitors, striding into the Ligurian Sea. 'No one can see you here.' Sometimes there were storms that made the return trip perilous. But Moorehead loved a gothic storm. Lots of them are recorded in the weather book. He was less enamoured with the nagging winds that plagued the area – the *siroccos*, the *tramontanas*. But by April the fireflies had arrived and the nightingales were in full voice. 'Nowhere, surely, can the spring burst out at you at quite such a speed … By May … the countryside is a paint pot of fresh green wheat and blazing wildflowers.'

This was his second springtime, too. Money wasn't a problem anymore, though Moorehead emphasised that they weren't rich.* He hadn't 'lived in the rosy glow of journalistic ready cash' since his *Express* days. But he was living well. With the help of a gardener from the village, they grafted vines

---

* A 1963 gossip column in the *Daily Express* – which seems to have lost the energy to keep up the ban – got in a dig at its eminent alumnus, the 'book-wealthy Moorehead … After fifteen books – five of them in six years – he has decided to take a long overdue rest on his farm in Tuscany.'

in March 1961; when the plants yielded a first vintage the next year, Moorehead was elated. Finally, after so many country lunches in Italy 'where the host crows "this is our own wine you're drinking", and of course, you have to down the filthy stuff ... Well now it's my turn.' When it was uncorked, that first vintage proved to be more a triumph of will than wine-making: Lucy emptied her glass into a pot plant; Caroline gave hers to the parrot.

A pool was added, then a badminton court; a new car. And there was live-in help, Bruno and Adele, who feature in every memory of the house: Bruno stick-thin, Adele enormous, a memorable sight when they both piled onto the motorbike to go down to the market. 'At night,' Moorehead's niece Jocelyn recalled, 'Adele would be cooking the pasta and picking fresh marrow flowers and things like that, and sitting on that garden table with the candles going, Bruno in the white starch serving everything.' After dinner, there were the obligatory games. Among their friends, the Mooreheads had a reputation as ferociously competitive card-players, Lucy especially. Bridge was her favourite, but racing demon or canasta would do. She also crushed all comers on the Scrabble board.

It was Lucy who set the tone at Villa Moorehead. She managed the household 'with great calm and efficiency', Jocelyn thought. 'She kept a tight rein on things in the house.' Another young woman who visited in the '60s told me that 'Lucy was someone whose good opinion you badly wanted. She was also very funny. But she had firm ideas about how life ought to be lived and you felt that those ideas were probably the right ones.' It wasn't that one was forbidden from reading novels in the mornings, for instance; it was simply that with Lucy there, no one would dream of doing such a feckless thing. Mornings were for work.

And though most visitors experienced Porto Ercole as a holiday house in exotic surrounds, it was, even in summer, a house of working writers. 'The feeling in our family was that it was perfectly okay if you wanted to be a nuclear physicist,' Caroline told me, 'but that nothing was really as good as writing.' While Alan ground out the words in the studio, Lucy was preoccupied with the cottage industry growing up around her husband, an enterprise in which she seems to have regarded herself as a joint stockholder, rather than unpaid help. With 'magnanimity, cunning and unbounded devotion', wrote Robert Hughes, Lucy 'managed everything except his actual writing for 40 years'. She was his archivist, compiler of indices, letter-writer, manager of relationships with a dozen different literary agents in Europe alone, and typist. Caroline told me that her father would finish a book and then, 'like many writers, his one idea was to get the hell out, and he would get out leaving my mother typing his book. That happened a certain amount.'

On one such occasion, when he'd left Lucy with a manuscript, he joked to friends that he'd just sent off a nice word for her in the book's acknowledgements page: 'That bastard, I can hear Lucy saying, does he think I am going to work myself to death here & him take it all for granted?'

§

Work was still all-consuming, the travel associated with it more or less constant. In 1962 Moorehead went to West Africa and Russia, both trips for the *New Yorker*, and both a chance to escape the busywork required of the well-known writer. At this time he was fielding continual offers to contribute to new magazines and anthologies*; he provided blurb quotes,

---

* Including some unlikely ones: in 1963, he was invited by Kingsley Amis to contribute to a book of science-fiction stories. Moorehead politely passed.

wrote introductions to books on explorers, and articles about conservation, an area in which he was becoming prominent. He travelled regularly to London, staying at the family's flat in Pimlico. On these trips he would see Jamie Hamilton and pop into the club to see his writer friends, John Betjeman, the Pipers, Jock Murray. There were events at the Society of Australian Authors in Britain, which he'd helped set up in the mid-1950s. Later that year Moorehead accepted an invitation to appear at a symposium in Washington DC, where he mingled with other big-name writers, including Dwight Macdonald, and fielded offers for his papers from two American universities. In a letter home he said his lectures had gone over all right, 'but the social stuff is a battle. Dear Bill Walton has spent the last hour laughing at me for even getting involved.'

As his public profile grew, Moorehead strove dutifully to meet its demands. He'd made a brief first TV appearance in 1956, to discuss *Gallipoli*, but Sidney Bernstein had been trying to talk his friend into doing something for Granada for years; Moorehead finally gave in and in 1963 appeared on a chat show to discuss the World Wildlife Fund. That year he also accepted an offer to join a Mediterranean cruise as guest lecturer; in return for free tickets and a handsome emolument, he would give shipboard talks and lead walks around the Gallipoli battlefields. Alas, public speaking badly unnerved him, and he wasn't good at it ('Terrible,' Caroline told me. '*Terrible.*')* The cruise turned out to be a harrowing experience. Moorehead briefly escaped the doting passengers when they called at Cyprus, and Steve Foley, an old friend from the *Express*, took them on a consoling picnic. He was suffering 'the penalty of fame in the attentions of the passengers', Foley wrote later. "'Poor Alan,' said Lucy. "I should never have let him take this on.'"

Exactly how famous Moorehead was at the peak of his career is difficult to gauge. In London he was considered a major author; and he was certainly the best-known Australian writer in America. But it seems

---

* Once, during the war, Lucy sat by the wireless waiting to hear her husband give a scheduled talk on the BBC. *And now, Mr Alan Moorehead*, said the announcer; then – a long agonised silence, only broken by the announcer's hasty return. *Er, unfortunately it seems we can't bring you Mr Moorehead ...* Lucy was appalled. It turned out that Alan had been seized by 'mic fright', and was unable to utter a word.

to have been limited to a kind of book-spine renown; the man himself seldom appeared.

Yet to one writer-fan who met him in the early 1960s, Moorehead was nothing less than a giant, a 'literary lion, [who] roamed all over the world hobnobbing with eminent men and women,' enjoying 'superstar status on both sides of the Atlantic'. This fulsome estimate came from the Indian novelist Manohar Malgonkar, another of Jamie Hamilton's authors. Malgonkar had specially asked if he could meet Moorehead during a visit to London. His admiration was as unreserved as his prose – Moorehead was 'a man at the peak of his career, still going on overdrive, seeking new worlds to conquer, setting off on new adventures, assured of success'. And while it's true that no one is more likely to overstate the cultural importance of writers than a writer, Malgonkar's account of a lunch meeting at Jamie's house gives an oblique glimpse of Moorehead in his heyday. Conversation flowed easily at first. Moorehead amused his companions with the story of his hellish Mediterranean cruise; they discussed the Profumo scandal, and the movie business. Moorehead reported with satisfaction that Hollywood had just bought the rights to *The Blue Nile* and was, Malgonkar recalled, 'determined to lure Elizabeth Taylor for the part of Lady Burton'.

But then the two writers got snared on the question of whether there had been any princes in India before the British came. Moorehead thought not; Malgonkar, who had just published a novel called *The Princes*, rather thought yes. Mutual ardour seems to have cooled with the coffee. Afterwards, Moorehead leapt into a taxi for Piccadilly, leaving his admirer, who was heading that way himself, to try his luck with the bus.

This slightly hard-faced character is hardly new; he goes with the old accusations of ruthlessness. In work matters, John told me, he was 'an ambitious, tough and determined man'.

Privately, though, he agonised about the value of his work and his ability to maintain his sales. During one of his sister's visits to Porto Ercole, Moorehead said to her: 'everything I can do to earn our living must come out of my mind – it's frightening.' He was bewildered, and enormously frustrated, when critics suggested, as they sometimes did, that his writing lacked wit – even Jan Morris had named a 'lack of humour' as

Moorehead's only fault as a stylist. Remarks like that fed a nagging fear that there was something fraudulent about all this success. 'It's like he'd been doing it,' Caroline told me, 'and finding it miraculous that he'd been doing it.' Sometimes a good review eased the anxiety, replenished his confidence. After a wonderful one in the *Times Literary Supplement*, he wrote to Lucy: 'I see once more a glimmering ... of the old hope that one just might still write well and if I can get a firm hold on the idea everything will fall into place.'

§

By mid-1962, *The Blue Nile* was selling almost as extravagantly as its predecessor had. So what next? There was no shortage of suggestions. By now Moorehead was fielding up to twenty book and journalism ideas a year from publishers and editors* – and sometimes reviewers. One reviewer who had greatly admired what Moorehead had done within the confines of the Nile, thought it was time for him to spread his wings, tackle something even bigger. 'One of these days the Gibbon of our declining Empire must emerge, and who could scribble, scribble, scribble better on such an immense and majestic subject than this able, scholarly and always dedicated craftsman?' Over a lunch in London, General Ismay tried to persuade him to tackle another colonial project that could do with a new coat of professional varnish: the Indian Mutiny of 1857. What he had decided to do instead was, to some in literary London, completely unexpected. He was going to write about another, less exotic part of the old empire: Australia.

The change in direction was not as abrupt as it looks. A gradual reconciliation with Australia and the idea of writing about it had been underway since the mid '50s. *Still not at home in Australia*, he wrote in his notes about the 1952 trip; *but Gallipoli changed all that*. And so it did, albeit via a roundabout set of connections.

---

* The sheer number of these suggests Moorehead was seen by some as a storyteller for hire, albeit an expensive one. Despite the scars left by *The Traitors* and *The Russian Revolution*, Moorehead flirted seriously with several projects suggested to him at this time, including a proposed book on Sarawak, one on generalship in the Second World War and also – bizarrely – a biography of the Soviet leader, Nikita Khrushchev. Arrangements for a series of official interviews were well in train when Khrushchev was deposed, and Moorehead's travel plans were abruptly cancelled.

With Sidney Nolan in Antarctica, 1964

While Moorehead was drafting *Gallipoli* on Spetses in 1955, the Australian novelists George Johnston and Charmian Clift were trying to write on nearby Hydra. When Sidney and Cynthia Nolan visited them there, Johnston showed the painter a copy of Moorehead's *New Yorker* article about growing up with the Anzac legend. Nolan was profoundly stirred by the story, Johnston recalled. From then on, 'when the retzina [sic] circled and wild winter buffeted at the shutters of the waterfront taverns, we would talk far into the small hours of this other myth of our own, so uniquely Australian and yet so close to that much more ancient myth of Homer's'. As soon as he could, Nolan got himself to Turkey and began work on his first series of Gallipoli paintings.

This was the beginning of a fertile exchange of inspiration between Moorehead and Nolan, who had much in common. Both had grown up in and around Melbourne before the war, both had been restless for overseas experience, though Moorehead's departure was earlier and more permanent. By the late '50s they were, in their own fields, Australia's best-known cultural figures. And they were drawn to landscape, and to the past, as a source of myth and abiding mystery. Moorehead greatly admired the way Nolan's first Ned Kelly series evoked 'a classical hero translated to the modern age'. Here was an artist who seemed miraculously immune to white Australia's creative predicament: the absence of a past. 'It does not distress or embarrass him,' Moorehead wrote, a little wonderingly, in an American magazine. 'Instead he makes a virtue of it ... he realizes that no one is really isolated and that the Australian scene is merely a re-creation of the ancient past. A myth, a continuous dream, explains and animates the human race.' It was Nolan who suggested Moorehead write about the ill-fated Burke and Wills expedition of 1862 from Melbourne to the Gulf of Carpentaria.

Moorehead flew to Melbourne to begin work in September 1962. Somehow ten years had gone by since his last visit. Both parents were dead*, but Phyllis lived in Hawthorn with her husband, Jack. Moorehead stayed for two months, commuting each day to the State Library of Victoria, where a room was set aside for his use. He pored over documents, savour-ing 'the copperplate writing of 19th century letters', the thrill of holding in his hands the very letters Burke buried beneath the 'Dig Tree'. In November, with a hired 4WD and guide, he set out to retrace the doomed expedition all the way from Royal Park in Melbourne, through Swan Hill and Menindie to Cooper's Creek, and on to the Gulf of Carpentaria. Then, with research in the bag, he went back to Italy and wrote *Cooper's Creek* over a bitterly cold northern winter. One day while he was pushing the explorers through the appalling heat of the Stony Desert with his fountain pen, it snowed so heavily Bruno had to shovel a path through the snow so Moorehead could get to his studio. But the work went well, and it wasn't a long book. The draft was finished in March. By May, Lucy was satisfied with the rewrites and the manuscript was sent to the publishers.

§

A typescript copy of *Cooper's Creek* is held at the State Library of Victoria; Moorehead donated it in thanks for all the help he received. A few hun-dred pages bound in oxblood covers and fastened by brass rivets. Flipping through it I thought of a line from a review: '[Moorehead] is in the very first flight of writers of prose in which every word tells and none is put in

---

* His mother in 1948; his father in 1954. In each case, the news was relayed by Phyllis to her brother from what must have seemed a painful distance, in time as well as space.

for effect.' It's true: you can see how assiduously he planed down the sentences in his quest for transparent simplicity, for that *polish and detachment*. On almost every page you can see where he has altered the typescript, a redundant adjective or sub-clause abstemiously wicked away.

It was oddly disconcerting to find Moorehead so close to home after all this time. It only now occurred to me that I could have *started* here. At any time in the past five years I could have walked down to the *Herald* building in Flinders Street, where he served his apprenticeship in journalism, and tried to imagine the world of 1934.

I *could* have. But it was Moorehead's original flight from Melbourne that I'd always understood best and guiltily envied. Now that he was back, however, I wished he'd written more about the city we had in common. But I searched in vain for anything from the postwar period that even touched on the special bottom-of-the-world melancholy of Melbourne's windy days and slanting-sun evenings, the migrant *heimweh* that suffuses its elderly inner suburbs.

He was too preoccupied with the far country, with the bush that 'imitated nothing ... was *sui generis*, the best that could be'. I'd always known this bush-bashing phase was coming, but Moorehead's research trip of 1962 seemed to lead into country I'd never much enjoyed, into the florid outbackery of writers like Ion L Idriess or Frank Cluny, who'd written his own Burke and Wills romp, *Dig*, in 1936. Just sitting there with the *Cooper's* typescript was enough to summon sharp memories of the 4WD bush treks I'd seen in countless educational films during my country primary-school days in the 1970s: the documentaries by the Leyland brothers or Alby Mangels projected through fragrantly overheating reels onto a sheet hoisted over the blackboard. Depthless hours seem to have been devoted to outback films. Black plastic would be gaffered across the windows to block out the dull afternoon light, and as the smell of sandalled feet and Vegemite sandwich rinds filled the classroom, we watched as people winched jeeps over cracked creek beds, laconic characters stuffed around with rifles and fishing reels, and pointed with inexplicable eagerness to some rocky outcrop in the distance. Someone in tight shorts would prod a snake with a stick or maybe change a tyre. On school excursions, too, we were steeped in Australiana: visits to 'historic' homesteads that were maybe eighty or ninety years old, with stables out the back where there'd be a skeletal tractor with cleated iron wheels half sunk into the dirt floor and a display of primitive shears; in the drawing room a few headless mannequins standing in a roped-off area wearing tea-stained Victorian undergarments. We were probably some of the luckiest children on earth, but that didn't occur to me then. All I knew was that Stonehenge and Portuguese forts were elsewhere; in this country it was just dry creeks and bush-band lagerphones.

But I needn't have worried. There's not a skerrick of Australiana in *Cooper's Creek*. There's no sentimentality, either. There *is* an awful lot of wandering around in the country, but the country is described with a watchful attention that restores radical strangeness to the familiar and cliché. North of Menindie the expedition moved in an 'extraordinary place', Moorehead wrote, where the 'weight of oldness in these rocks' can still be felt, where strange trees like the beefwood and the leopard tree were full of screeching cockatoos, and 'the snow-white bole of the ghost gum is still warm to touch long after sundown'. This old, mostly silent world was, to the expeditioners, unreadable; not hostile or sinister, but indifferent, unrevealing: 'nothing was communicated'. It was full of alien birds, and snakes, including the python that Burke cooked up and which left him with terrible dysentery; horrible ants with scaly wings; the mosquitoes and flies were so dense in places the men rode with veils and goggles. One of the book's 'many merits', Manning Clark wrote in the *New York Times,* is that 'although the setting was provincial, and indeed at times parochial, the story is seen in its universal significance'. I'm not sure about the *significance* of the story itself: Moorehead tells it as a colonial vanity project mismanaged from the start and only raised to the tragic by blunders, and the poignant bad timing of its fatal denouement. After he read a draft of the book, Alwyn Lee suggested to Moorehead that, without realising it, he had told a story of colonial Australians' defeat by their own country: the explorers 'discovered nothing, and died in nothing', discovering only the 'bleak and final truth that Australia would never be a great nation'.

This is partly true: Moorehead wants us to see the expedition as part of the global story of colonisation; and, more fundamentally, as an episode from the ancient struggle of humanity with nature. This is an Australia that Moorehead was only able to discover by leaving it, lapping the globe and returning again: the Australian landscape as a blank canvas for the Western imagination, one primed by tales of nineteenth-century Africa and the mythopoetic visions of Sidney Nolan. (Nolan provided a painting for the book's dust jacket.) Moorehead's ill-equipped explorers seem to ride under the eyes of the old gods in *Cooper's Creek*; the slow diurnal pulse of the expedition evokes the experience, as old as the human heart, of the encounter with the revealed world, people trudging slowly, in wonder and terror, into unknown space.

Still, the Cooper is clearly not a watercourse to compare with the Nile. Even Moorehead's staunchest fans noticed a meagre quality in the human drama. It's a dour incurious troop, this expedition of clerks and surveyors, roustabouts and incompetents; none of his characters had the soul-hunger of a Denon or a Burton to leaven the sad story, to rejoice in all the astonishing creatures or the revelatory clarity of the light, no one to wonder at the richness of the Aboriginal mythscape through which they moved, unseeing. This was the reason *Cooper's* was the only one of Moorehead's histories Shawn chose not to excerpt in the *New Yorker*: the personalities were not 'rich or strong enough' for magazine purposes. 'Much the most interesting person in *Cooper's Creek*,' the *TLS* suggested, 'is Alan Moorehead.'

This was the review that revived in Moorehead the hope that his work was worthwhile. And despite its metropolitan condescension, this review is probably the most serious and insightful appraisal of Moorehead's writing published in his lifetime. Moorehead is a cosmopolitan, the unnamed reviewer writes; he belongs to 'the nation of artists ... Now that he is writing about Australia, all the same, it is curious how Australian he turns out to be.'

His clarity and straightforwardness are perhaps specifically Australian, and so is his lack of humour; but most of all it is a certain stillness of style, poised somewhere between dreamtime and disillusion that marks him, now one comes to think of it, as a man touched by the wide melancholy of Australia. Mr Moorehead can often, almost in spite of himself, move the susceptible reader to tears; and so can Australia too, so strange and lonely is her quality, and so tinged with disappointment.

There's no doubt Moorehead's writing *was* touched by the 'wide melancholy' – or something like it – of the landscape. Like so many other white writers before him, he was attracted to and repelled by the passive grandeur of the bush, 'biding its time', as DH Lawrence had written in *Kangaroo*, 'with a terrible ageless watchfulness, waiting for a far-off end, watching the myriad intruding white men'. Perhaps he saw in the 'ageless silence' a landscape ideally suited to the elegiac mood of eternal return he'd been working into his histories since *Gallipoli*.

§

Something seemed to have shifted in his sense of the place during that 1962 trip. 'If I were younger I would not hesitate two minutes,' he said in an oral history interview recorded for the National Library in 1964, 'I would return to this country and I would write here of Australian themes.' Suddenly he was full of ideas for books he wanted to write: a biography of the explorer Edward John Eyre, perhaps; or a book, like *No Room in the Ark*, about the richness of Australia's unique fauna and the danger of losing it to development or indifference.

As a traveller, he revelled in the open spaces and animals the way he always had. All this fed a hunger for the outdoors, its simplicity, healthfulness and the vigorous, unpretentious life he thought people lived in it. Even before he came back himself, he had always intended to send his children on long gap-year trips to Australia for a character-building taste of fresh air and sunshine.

It was on just such a trip that John Moorehead met up with his father in 1962, and found him having a lovely time. The two of them joined a three-day group camping trip in the Snowy Mountains. One night John got into a strenuous argument about something with another camper. Moorehead didn't intervene. 'He sat back listening to the argument,' John told me, 'and I thought: how odd for him, to have invented this English child.' Yet it was probably an Australian child who was preoccupying Moorehead's thoughts: the child he'd once been, the one whose life he'd elected not to live.

His return in 1964 was the full-face reconciliation with the birthright of his first twenty-five years. 'It is a Rip van Winklish experience to return to the native heath,' he wrote in the *New Yorker*. 'I hardly recognize the place.' Usually, he wrote, one returns to childhood places to find everything smaller and less dramatic. Not here: the cities have sprouted towers, a babel of languages – European ones, at least – can be heard in streets seething with traffic. He depicts a young country emerging into confident adolescence: 'one can hardly see a psychologist's making a living in this fresh wind.'

But a half-decent psychologist would have had her hands full with Moorehead, you'd think. Reviewers were certainly happy to venture their own analysis. Ten years before, *Rum Jungle* had moved one to observe that it is not easy to 'bury' or 'discard' one's country: 'I do not think Mr Moorehead has escaped.' The problem with *Cooper's Creek, Meanjin* now concluded, is 'that Mr Moorehead, who prefers to live in Italy, is not really at home in Australia'. Thanks to the local success of *Cooper's Creek* he was feted wherever he went on this trip. But he seems to be reaching out for something that eluded him, and not just material for another book. He tried to explain the expatriate bind in an interview:

> For [expatriates] of the older generation, we've reached a curious forking, a dichotomy in our experience … Returning to Australia, we have a tremendous tug back to the beginnings of our lives … You must in the end, I think, if you are a writer … return at last to your roots.

That wasn't as simple as it sounds. As he refamiliarises himself with the country he'd only really seen through a long-ago haze of needing to escape it, he seems doubly dislocated. A 'block forms in my mind when I think about my youth', he wrote in *A Late Education*. 'Somehow it was wrong, it ought to have been different.' In these pages, Moorehead grapples with the cost of a life of continuous self-invention and the 'deliberate shutting off of memory', as he called it in his notes, a 'kind of self-induced amnesia', that it demanded. Might he have been happier if he hadn't been so determined to escape the colonial backwater, the shame of his second-rate origins and his penny-pinching childhood, by getting out and making his mark? And *what* had he escaped anyway? Martha Gellhorn told Pocock that Moorehead felt his Australianness as an inferiority – but perhaps she just thought he should.

He certainly seems prepared now to trade in the triumph of his escape, if only Australia would let him. When John Hetherington sent him a draft of a 1961 profile of Moorehead he had written for *The Age*, he protested that it made him sound 'anti-Australian'.* He never expressed regret about leaving as a young man, but there is a clear note of guilt in his writing about Australia: for not having tried to know the country better when young, about not having paid enough attention. In *A Late Education*, Moorehead relates an incident at a book signing in Melbourne in the 1960s where he fails, at first, to recognise an old university friend who, having shuffled to the front of the queue, has shyly introduced himself: *Remember me?* He did, though he had to ransack his memory for the name. 'I wish he had not felt he had to say that,' Moorehead wrote. After all, which of them had followed the truer path?

> My conviction that I was in charge of my own destiny and had to make things happen or nothing would happen at all, was nothing more than arrogance and a short cut to unhappiness. By moving about so much and attempting so many different things I had rejected life instead of discovering it, and like Baudelaire's Traveller had ended nowhere. Well, perhaps not nowhere, but at all events at no safer or better haven than he had reached.

To this point I'd never been able to take that *mea culpa* very seriously. Did he *really* wish he hadn't gone so far and seen so much? And had so much fun? Yet now it didn't seem so unlikely. Couldn't it be true that his 'other side of the hill' disease *was* a kind of affliction? That in his *annus mirabilis* in the Libyan desert he'd gotten exactly what he wanted, and hadn't been able to stop wanting more and more of it?

---

* The corrected version ran: 'His countrymen shake sorrowful heads over Moorehead's preference for living and working abroad; they feel he is guilty of aesthetic disloyalty by not using his uncommon talents to write about his own country.'

Certainly there's no evidence that he much enjoyed the perquisites of celebrity, even when a dusty red carpet was rolled out for him – dinners at the Melbourne Club, the reporters who swarmed aboard to interview him when his ship docked at Fremantle in 1966; the small town Caroline remembers from that visit where someone had stretched a banner across the main street: *Welcome to Moorehead!* Much more sustaining was the access his reputation gave him to leading conservationists such as Jock Marshall, and Dom and Vincent Serventy; and to new faces in the arts crowd, including Johnston and Clift, the critic Max Harris, the documentary film pioneer Bob Raymond*, and literary renaissance man Geoffrey Dutton, whose tough reviews of *Rum Jungle* and *Cooper's Creek* didn't stop him becoming a warm friend. And then there were the painters. A sometime Sunday dauber himself, Moorehead had a special admiration for the artists he'd come to know in Australia, people like Fred Williams, as well as Nolan, and especially Russell ('Tass') Drysdale and his wife, Maisie.

In early 1962, Moorehead called up Robert Hughes, then a young free-lance architecture writer. For Hughes this remarkable call came out of the blue; Moorehead had been impressed by some of Hughes' newspaper articles and wanted to say so. With an eye for the main chance reminiscent of the young Moorehead, Hughes invited 'this august stranger' to dinner at his humble Sydney flat. Astonishingly, Moorehead accepted. The evening was a bibulous success, one that reached almost hallucinogenic heights when, to top it all, Sidney Nolan turned up looking for Alan. More wine was drunk. Nolan somehow ended up in the fountain; Hughes ended up with a headache, a promise of introductions to London publishers, and a prized invitation to visit Moorehead in Italy – if he should ever get that far. 'He was the only writer I knew,' Hughes recalled in 1987, 'the guy I most admired and the person I wanted to be. I was filled with semi-filial envy at the way he could find his subjects from the real world.'

§

* Raymond had been a Second World War correspondent in Europe. An author, journalist as well as filmmaker, he co-founded ABC's *Four Corners* program with Michael Charlton in 1961.

This wasn't a universal sentiment in Australia's cultural circles. At the Adelaide Festival in March Moorehead opened an exhibition of Sidney Nolan's paintings, and then gave the opening address of Writers' Week to an all-star crowd. He stuck to familiar themes. 'Writing was a lonely job,' one reporter summarised his contribution. 'If he had been less charming and sensible,' the *Bulletin* remarked, his selection as opening turn 'might have come close to embarrassing'. The Marxist and nationalist factions of the local literary scene were not much charmed. As noted, Xavier Herbert, author of *Capricornia* (1939), decided Moorehead was a 'pompous bore'.*

I never had to look far for rumbles of hostility to Moorehead and the aura of global triumph that seemed to follow him around. Max Harris wrote to Moorehead once that he was 'spearheading a campaign to develop a sophisticated appreciation of your considerable literary virtues'. Clearly, such an appreciation was not yet widespread. The tooth-grinding with which some Australian writers greeted Moorehead's overseas success echoed in Hetherington's review of his memoir, a decade later: 'Members of that sect of Australians, all of them either university or journalistic contemporaries of Moorehead in Melbourne and some of them writers in a small way, whose envy shows out in their systematic disparagement of him, should read *A Late Education*. It might make some of them repent.'

Systematic disparagement. Now there's a phrase to conjure with: a vision of literary life circa 1963 in Melbourne: everyone bitching around a flagon of fruity lexia at a backyard barbecue in Carlton, and the footy on the kitchen radio. Or Sydney, where Patrick White disparaged Moorehead's type – without apparently bothering to consult any of his works. 'Journalism is what people seem to want to read. I'm told Moorehead is not even very good.' Privately, Hetherington wasn't above a bit of disparagement himself. A decade earlier, in a letter to Norman Lindsay, he wrote:

> He is a small man, and therefore known to some of his contemporaries as Little Tick ... many women find him extraordinarily attractive, and

---

* Herbert also took Robert Hughes aside during the festival to berate him for his insufficient Marxist zeal.

Moorehead likes women thus confirming the old saying, 'Big man, big cock: little man, all cock.' He is happily married … They are both ambitious, and his wife, whom I like, with certain reservations about her calculating attitude to life, has done everything to further Moorehead's success as a writer.

Part of the problem, Hetherington felt, was Moorehead's effort, 'in so far as such a thing is possible, to cast a veil of oblivion over his Australian beginnings'.

The odour of unpatriotic disavowal never quite dissipated. Still, people could have overlooked the accent and the bulging Rolodex, if not for his books' propensity to sell in such profligate quantities all over the world. Whispers of Moorehead's generous advances were, as they generally are, intolerable to other writers – even to Patrick White. 'Perhaps if I lived in Europe or London like the financially successful Australian writers and painters, and made an occasional graceful progress through these parts, I might feel sentimental-patriotic,' he wrote to Dutton in 1965. 'But one would have to earn quite a lot to manage it.'

And perhaps there was a feeling that Moorehead's interest in Australia was primarily extractive: that he was only here to dig up some stories and sell them at a giant profit in overseas markets. Peter Coleman, who, as editor of the *Bulletin* in the early 1960s was right in the thick of cultural debate, wrote in 2012 that 'Moorehead was one of those Australian journalist/writers of that period … who believed that the point of writing books was to publish an international bestseller, and you could not do that from Melbourne or Sydney, however grand your theme.'

But Moorehead's reborn interest in Australia was more meaningful to him than that, and more sincere. For such an ambitious writer, it's telling that he would gamble his hard-won fame on subjects so remote to an international readership. And his actions suggest that he genuinely wanted to be involved in Australian life. To Geoffrey Dutton's delight, he offered Sun Books the paperback rights to *Cooper's Creek* – 'exactly what our young firm needed: a ready-made bestseller', Dutton wrote. He contributed to the *Australian Dictionary of Biography*; he wrote introductions to several Australian books. His 1964 oral history interview with Hazel De Berg was a conscious contribution to the nation's cultural memory vault. It was when he received the typescript of this interview that Moorehead decided to donate his papers to the National Library.

But even so, he seems a marginal presence, surplus to local requirements. Many intellectuals were looking ahead to *postcolonial* Australia, a country turning to Asia and the Pacific, one that would be more worldly, urban and middle-class. This was a future turning away from bush nationalism and the 'continuing obsession with landscape' that puzzled and exasperated Donald Horne in *The Lucky Country*; an obsession that produced 'many haunted images of melancholy or despair ... Paradise has been lost and artists are disappointed.' Not much of a believer in paradise, Moorehead wasn't disappointed. But he *was* fascinated by the country, the strange intensity of the inland emptiness that seemed to absorb the millennia with barely a trace. As early as 1957 he had argued that Australian writers and artists needed to become more rather than less Australian: 'the moment has come for Australians to return to their own origins', he declared in a lecture in London, to that 'so odd combination of the very old and the very new'. He admired the artists who looked for meaning in the old bones of the continent, like Nolan and Fred Williams. But the mood of his Australian books perhaps drew on Drysdale's landscapes in particular: the uprooted trees and implacable suns and endless red horizons that would, Robert Hughes wrote, 'be a document of pessimism but for the profound compassion with which Drysdale paints the figures in it.'

Festival over, Moorehead retired with Lucy to the Duttons' station outside Adelaide. There, he wrote cheerfully to Phyllis, 'we had a snake in our bedroom and Lucy saw some galahs just before they were shot.' He set up a chair and table at one end of the verandah, where he could look up and see the wide bay, and crack on with his new book, *The Fatal Impact*. This was another adventure story propelled by exploration – Captain Cook's voyages in the Pacific – but now the tragic theme glanced at in the *Nile* books and *Cooper's Creek* was front and centre. It was about how the thrill of exploration was inevitably followed by colonisation and economic exploitation. It would be, by instinct more than intellectual analysis, a work of black armband history *avant la lettre*.

On the 2000-mile train from Adelaide to Perth, where he and Lucy would board the ship for home, Moorehead saw barely any wild animals. Not a single kangaroo. That saddened him, and 'the unrelenting promotion of the human species' he saw in huge new developments at Esperance disturbed him too. This lack of 'ecological humility', in John Gascoigne's phrase, was the subject of *The Fatal Impact* – my 'angry little book' Moorehead called it. It's 'all about how the white man has ruined the South Pacific', he wrote to a friend; 'everyone is going to love it.' If the *Ark* had been conservation by stealth – a celebration of the treasure at risk in the African bush – *The Fatal Impact* would be an unambiguous philippic, a wake-up call about the damage done since Cook's voyages, still being done, in Antarctica, Tahiti and Australia.

§

They returned home, but even in Italy, Australia wasn't as far away as it had once been. The new jet airliners brought the two parts of his life much closer together, and Australian themes – and Australians – were all around. Leaving Lucy to settle back into Porto Ercole, Moorehead flew to Turkey and spent a week in Gallipoli filming a documentary on the Anzacs with Bob Raymond. The Drysdales were constantly in and out that summer. And Sidney Nolan wanted his friend to open a show for him in London.

From this far distance, an air of timeless legend hangs over those 1960s summers. Every time Moorehead returns to Porto Ercole, the pace seems to switch to a kind of glamour montage; someone puts some crackly *bossa nova* on the wind-up turntable, the hard colours soften. These were the halcyon days of friends, plentiful work for good pay, movie contracts, flourishing roses, long, gregarious lunches in the Tuscan sunshine. The steady flow of guests became a happy deluge, especially in summertime. Bob Hughes arrived to cash in his cherished invitation; he stayed for two months, 'like a cuckoo in the nest' as he put it, pitching in with the *vendemmia* and prowling the little Italian churches of the region in a hired Fiat 600. His brilliant, unselfcensored talk dominates many memories of that time; as does Geoffrey Keating, who had a place himself in the village. John Cheever was perhaps the most significant addition to the social roster. His letters mention balmy June days spent sipping gin, eating lobster and playing backgammon. But it was Alwyn Lee who Moorehead most admired. Tall, with a heavily scored face, Lee was a brilliant critic and baulked poet, but the form at which he truly excelled was the autobiographical tall story. In his youth he had been, wrote Cheever admiringly, the 'sexual and political terror of Melbourne'; in New York he maintained 'a series of ardent and eccentric attachments to barkeeps, whores, unemployed actors and an international spy called Hong Kong Harry'. And the village was also becoming a fashionable satellite of *la dolce vita* in Rome. Movie stars came by, as well as writers, including William Styron and Gore Vidal, who stayed that summer with Jackie Kennedy. Martha Gellhorn recalled that Porto Ercole was becoming much 'smarter' at this time – which Alan liked, she thought, and Lucy liked less.

At the house itself there were plenty of eminent visitors. Famous names figured in Moorehead's correspondence – Igor Stravinsky, for instance, who wrote to express his admiration and burning desire to meet – and in his future plans, largely thanks to the movies. Moorehead's luckless, but untiring pas de deux with the movie biz continued throughout the 1960s. Publicly, he maintained a sardonic attitude to the medium that had so far yielded only one terrible B-movie. 'Film people live in a world of their own, half hysterical, half make-believe and finesse,' he told a journalist in 1965. Behind the scenes, though, he was working hard to get his books on screen. Part of the appeal was money – by late 1963 a contract for a movie of the *Nile* books and an option for *Cooper's* had brought the proceeds of unmade films to something like £10,000. In London, Moorehead sought meetings with Sean Connery, apparently in the hope of convincing the new James Bond to play Burke. When that fell through, discussions resumed with Peter Finch, who was eager to secure the rights to *Cooper's Creek* himself. David Lean was lined up to direct *The Fatal Impact* but decided he'd had his fill of deserts with *Lawrence of Arabia*. Undismayed by the failure of any movies to appear, Moorehead signed on in 1966 to write an American film about Charles Darwin, and a British biopic about

Brigadier Orde Wingate, the legendary eccentric who had led a guerrilla force in Burma in 1942.

It all contributed to a way of life in a beautiful place that made a lasting impression on a younger guest, John and Caroline's friend Anne Chisholm, whom Alan and Lucy invited to stay when they heard she was having an unhappy time au pairing in Rome. They were terribly kind to her, she said; and the Mooreheads' Italian home was, to an aspiring writer, a indelible vision of the literary life. Chisholm told me she remembers thinking: *this is what the writing life is like. This is how it should be.* 'Work in the morning, and all these people crowded around the table for lunch, and it would go on and on, everyone talking noisily, drinking, laughing. I just thought: what a wonderful way to live.'

In its blessed state, the happy days at Porto Ercole only lasted seven years, which perhaps accounts for the gilded tinge to some memories of that time. And of course it wasn't a perfect idyll. Moorehead's womanising was a continuing misery. Cheever spent several days that year sitting on the beach with Lucy, listening to her discuss her husband's 'ruthless infidelity' with 'a kind of doting detachment'.

$$\S$$

Moorehead indulged in few of the trappings of fame, but there was one he couldn't resist. 'We have become rather grand,' he wrote to Tass Drysdale in the summer of 1964. 'I have just acquired a half share in a motor-yacht complete with sailor. God knows what it's costing.' Sidney Bernstein was his co-owner; the new skippers named their 32-foot sloop *Lucandra*, a mash-up of their wives' names. The Mooreheads' pale blue writing paper now bore two addresses: *Villa Moorehead, Porto Ercole* in one corner and *a bordo del 'Lucandra'* in the other, to be circled on those occasions when one was corresponding from sea.

I've always liked the boat, and not just because it would have appalled Xavier Herbert. The boat seems to fit so perfectly a period fantasy of the

---

* Douglas was, along with Berenson and Max Beerbohm, another of the grand old Mediterranean Englishmen/ anglophiles of the period. Moorehead had visited his home on Capri in 1950 to pay his respects, it seems, or perhaps just to complete the set.

successful writer in Mediterranean exile – it's like something out of de Maupassant, or Norman Douglas.* According to Robert Hughes' possibly apocryphal, perhaps retrofitted version, the writer's boat *was* a fantasy from an earlier time. One night during the war in Italy, Moorehead, the novelist Irwin Shaw and Luigi Barzini were sitting around drinking and boasting of the famous books they would write and what they would do with the royalties. The blather turned competitive and a wager was laid: twenty years hence, the three of them would meet to see who ended up with the biggest boat. And so they did. *Lucandra*, it turned out, was by some way the smallest. Barzini's could barely squeeze into the marina at 80 feet; Irwin Shaw's was a floating palazzo staffed with white-gloved stewards.

When his yacht hove to off Porto Ercole in 1965, Irwin and his old chum had much to discuss. Disappointing film adaptations, the perplexing passage of years. 'As we sat on the terrace of [Moorehead's] house,' he wrote,

> and looked out over the dark sea we talked of friends who had died, friends who had not lived up to their promise, generals who had made extraordinarily bad decisions when we were younger men, and the usual writers' problems – insomnia, divorce, drink, critics, the income tax, and how to avoid saying the same thing in book after book without being told that your powers were waning. We ... looked at the trail of the moon on the sea below, and secretly congratulated ourselves that we were together in such a place so many years after the bombs, the land mines, the invasions, the generals.

Most of the people he might have reminisced with like this were now long dead. And he generally wasn't one to look back. He certainly liked a knees-up – 'I only know how to live like a hermit or a rake,' he admitted in 1966, 'nothing in between' – but even among the yachts and glamorous parties there's a self-sufficiency to the glimpses of happiness that survive from this period. The satisfaction of a good paragraph now and again; the huge pod of dolphins that leapt around the bows of the *Lucandra* one day in June 1965; the intriguing little creature – a marten – spotted on the road to dinner at a glitzy new resort and later described in glad-hearted detail in the weather book.

Work, with its frustrations and rewards, was always foremost. His work could make him seem distant. I knew it would be a mistake to assume that Moorehead's prose of the 1960s – that bespoke blend of unillusioned fact-finding and dreamy solitariness – was a simple reflection of Moorehead's inner world. Even so, there *is* a perceptible thread of loneliness in his middle age, particularly when he is in Australia. To Manning Clark, whom Moorehead met around this time, 'he seemed to be on the move like a fugitive ... a lonely and unhappy man.' A lover he visited in 1964 was sad to find him 'so full of discontent and alone inside'. I thought I could make out a neat biographical hypothesis here: that Moorehead was experiencing the unfashionability of his obsessions – war, hard news from colonial history, the threat to nature – as a widening gap between him and his world. Maybe celebrity added distance, too. One Australian reviewer of *A Late Education* remembered how in Australia Moorehead had seemed less a man than a glamorous phantom:

> You say you have never met him and [people] say they were sure you must have; didn't you once work in Melbourne? In Melbourne it was the same. This was where he had liked to stand or sit. This was his friend from university ... But you learned nothing of him. People did not say personal things. They only reported on him like a national monument being moved around the world.

A national monument? Perhaps – like that statue of Kemal Ataturk in Istanbul, and now just as dusty and disregarded.

§

Returning to Australia in 1965, he hoped, he told journalists, to write a book about the country's animals; he was also going to make a documentary with Bob Raymond on the same subject. And there was another project that he didn't talk about in the press, though it was possibly the one that meant most to him: an opera by Peter Sculthorpe based on the story of Eliza Fraser, a Scottish shipwreck survivor captured, or adopted, by the Indigenous people of Fraser Island in 1836. Moorehead had been commissioned to co-write the libretto. Nolan, who had first painted the subject in the late '40s, would design the sets.

He began in Phillip Island, to look at the seals there and lament the slaughter of their ancestors in the early nineteenth century. Then he went down to Fisher Island in Bass Strait for the annual slaughter of the mutton birds, and from there began to work his way north along the east coast.

He was working hard on the documentary filming: dinner at 6.30 p.m. on the dot, bed at 9 p.m., an insomniac awakening at 1 a.m. to read Patrick White, whom he admired, with reservations. 'Yes, he is real good,' he wrote to Maisie Drysdale, 'but what a sad, myopic eye, what contempt – or maybe envy – for everyone.' At almost every stop local journalists plied him for news on his book, his impressions, naturalist's tips. He didn't take photographs, he told one; he had learnt during his East Africa trips that 'everybody else was walking around with tripods and exposure meters until the leopard had gone. I had to tell them what it looked like ... I like to sit very still and sketch. I don't even take notes any more. Taking notes is an excuse for not thinking.'

In private he sounds happy enough. He was outdoors the whole time and, as ever, outdoor life seemed to simplify things. At dinner one night at Manning and Dymphna Clark's Canberra home there was excellent conversation, and delightful company. The only other guest was the young historian Ann Moyal, who had worked closely with Lord Beaverbrook. (Afterwards she drove Moorehead to his hotel where, she told me, he gave her 'a warm kiss' and suggested she join him upstairs. She declined.) Back on the road with Raymond and his film unit, Moorehead visited Eric Worrell's reptile park near Gosford, took in the dolphins at Tweed Heads, and the sea birds at Michaelmas Cay near Cairns. They all stayed in motels, and ate in places where every salad was full of pineapple chunks and the red wine, if there was any, came heavily chilled. A research assistant on the film, Suzanne Baker, thought Moorehead seemed an 'open-minded and thoughtful' man. 'My memory of it is that you could sort of sense him measuring his own emotions about what he was seeing, that he was looking hard at things, trying to understand what it meant to him being back in Australia.'

In June, Moorehead proceeded to Fraser Island with Peter Sculthorpe and his co-librettist, young music critic and writer Roger Covell, to immerse himself in the landscape of the Fraser legend. They spent three happy days on the island. Covell told me he found Moorehead 'lively, interesting, energetic', and very easy to get along with; not at all the 'august stranger' whose reputation was so awe-inspiring to Robert Hughes, or whose voice had once startled me with its gravitas. One night, Moorehead wrote, they drove twenty miles along the ocean beach and camped in a fisherman's hut.

> I sat for a long time on the step of the hut, and just as the light was failing I saw the shapes of three wild horses – one white, the others bay – detaching themselves from the trees ... When they reached the edge of the sea each animal – and I swear wild horses have a special grace – lifted up a foreleg and began elegantly scraping a hole in the sand. Later on I found out why they were doing this – they wanted to drink the brackish water that seeped into the holes as they dug – but just at that moment it was nature transferred into art.

The opera, like Moorehead's planned book on Australian fauna, was doomed, though for different reasons. Sculthorpe's delays and evasions had already exhausted the patience of his first collaborator, Patrick White; within a year they had caused everyone to give up completely. But in early '65 Moorehead was flush with ideas, getting up early each morning to 'have another crack' at the libretto. This seemed strange to me, given that he was no opera buff, and was largely indifferent to music in general. But Roger Covell sensed that Moorehead saw the opera as a chance to do something new, that he craved recognition as a creative artist, and not just as 'a brilliant journalist ... He wanted the artistic blessing.' *Still?* In 1964 George Johnston had somehow found a new literary gear to produce the instant classic of suburban Australian disillusion, *My Brother Jack*. Perhaps Moorehead coveted the sort of critical recognition his friend was now basking in.

Of course, his books *were* a kind of art. His subjects weren't new, but his voice, that blend of hard clarity and romanticism he'd discovered with

Michaelmas Cay, Queensland, 1965

Gallipoli and had been refining ever since, unmistakably was. And if to some contemporaries his work remained mere journalism, it was a journalism to which he brought – as the British travel writer Alan Ross put it – 'gifts and resources that more obviously creative artists would do well to envy'.

But perhaps those gifts were easiest to appreciate from a distance – in time as well as space. TV host Graham Kennedy gave *The Fatal Impact* an impromptu plug on *In Melbourne Tonight*, but apart from Manning Clark, few Australian critics shared his enthusiasm. The book was criticised by historians, who suggested that Moorehead relied even more heavily on the work of others than his fulsome acknowledgements managed to convey, particularly Bernard Smith's *European Vision and the South Pacific*.* Max Harris, who wrote to Moorehead after reading the galleys of the book, had graver reservations. His letter was warm but tough, and serious – a

---

* In 1998, Smith recalled that Sidney Nolan had given Moorehead a copy of the book. 'Alan sensed a bestseller lying in its depths if it were filleted for its theatrical incidents. He raided it as only a skilled author can.'

remarkable letter, actually, the sort of letter that makes you wish people still wrote letters like it. After a cordial preamble, Harris admits that the book had 'grimly disappointed my expectations'. Moorehead had chosen an excellent theme, but he'd buggered it up. He'd ignored important work already done on this subject; what he had read he hadn't read closely enough. And not even the usual Moorehead virtues ('the atmospherics are, as ever, excellent') could make up for it.

> I wanted to get in early and forestall your possible psychological reactions. If the Americans and the British all call out 'Hurrah, three jolly cheers for Moorehead's latest; jolly fascinating' and its sales are comfortingly astronomical, do not develop that characteristic reaction of thinking the critics out here are a race of knockers, and bugger them. It may be that some of them really <u>care</u> about this theme, and really know this story, and that additionally some of them, a growing number, may also really care about the innate distinction of your literary capacities ... Give us a go and contemplate that our critical reactions may be honest and perhaps more properly informed than the critic in 'Time'.

Harris had a point. There's lots of drama and vividly animated characters in Moorehead's lament for the fate of the pre-European Pacific, but only a broad-brush account of how the damage was done. Still, as the *Observer* suggested, forsaking 'definitiveness' perhaps gained Moorehead 'a concentration that allows his theme to emerge with clarity and force'. *The Fatal Impact* delivered his chastening theme to a large international audience and when it was published in 1965 it was acclaimed pretty much everywhere except Australia. Norman Lewis called it the most interesting non-fiction book published in Britain 'for a very long time'. And *Time*'s verdict? 'The superbly skilled journalist-historian Alan Moorehead takes soundings of philosophic depth – savage and civilized man in confrontations unresolved to this day.'

§

The unresolved confrontations were personal, too. For all the sober sorrow and tragedy, there's also a great longing in *The Fatal Impact*. The most compelling passage in the book, which follows Eyre's near-fatal trek of

endurance across the fearsomely inhospitable country of the Great
Australian Bight, clearly doesn't belong, which makes it all the more tempting to read as an echo of the author's own entangled need for an idea of
Australia, and in particular of the bush, that he'd formed as a boy.
Moorehead's imagination wanted to return to this country, but it was
country that wasn't easily assimilated by outsiders and their myths, and
their dreams of unspoiled space.

Perhaps what Moorehead discovered in the country was not just a new
setting for the Man v. Nature theme he had been writing about for a
decade, but also a difficult, enlarging solitude, the feeling he got from the
country itself – 'antediluvian, shy, infinitely subtle' – that infuses his last
books. It's as though the outback, with its eons of footprints lost in the
dust, its childhood hauntings and its consoling loneliness, heightened
Moorehead's sense of the impermanence of human things – and with it,
his compassion for a species that increasingly lived, he thought, amid the
consequences of its own ruinous wonder.

§

In mid-2015, Moorehead arrived in the mail on two hand-labelled discs
from Channel Nine's archives department. As far as I know, the documentaries from the 1960s contain the only footage of Moorehead that exists.
I'd kept putting off inquiring about them, I think because the older
Moorehead never felt as approachable as the younger one. But it was time
to take a sober look at where the escape artist of 1936 had ended up.

The man on the screen was instantly familiar; but also very unexpected – like someone who's been away for years. There was a slight
underbite I'd never known about, and which made the ends of his sentences look more cantankerous than they were. But he had a strong set of
uppers (New York dentist?); the lower ones were a bit more dishevelled.
And something else … What had the *TLS* said? 'Now that he is writing
about Australia … it is curious how Australian he turns out to be.' That's
what I thought. It *was* curious. In his mid-fifties, he seemed to have
reverted to the physiognomy of his birthplace; this was a dad's face from
the farming district I grew up in: big bones, skin toughened by the sun,

shaggy eyebrows, swirling hanks of greying hair freed from their comb-over by the wind.

When Bob Raymond approached him with the idea of doing these documentaries, Moorehead wasn't enthusiastic. He didn't know anything about television, he objected, and didn't have time to write a script 'even if I knew how'. But when they came to shoot *Gallipoli*, Raymond recalled in his memoirs, he didn't need a script. It was all still in his head. Moorehead simply stood in front of the camera and, 'without a note or a falter spoke simply and hauntingly'.

The *Women's Weekly* TV columnist detected some early signs of nervousness, but overall found Mr Moorehead a most satisfactory and watchable host. I'm sure this was so – in 1964. Across the years, though, he seems ill at ease, as he stands there on a bridge overlooking the Nile (1964), or solemnly strokes a wallaby's ears (1965). He speaks very slowly and tries to avoid the camera; most of the time he's looking away into the middle distance, as though his ideas for what to say next were up there in the branches of that sugar gum. The pipe he's holding in one shot – he's found another way of ingesting tobacco – is visibly shaking.

But nothing dates as helplessly as old television. When my kids got home from school, five years after I'd dragged them down to Porto Ercole, I asked if they wanted to see the man himself. My daughter frowned at the screen for a few minutes, but the black-and-white footage clearly looked prehistoric to her. She gave me a supportive little pat on the head and went off to do something else.

I sympathised. For me it was touching to see him walk and talk at last – how could it not be? But I was glad I hadn't seen this earlier. I might have lost my courage. He wasn't an old man, or tired – he was still spry in his fifties, full of the old restlessness and appetites. But he never seemed more outdated, more ripe for replacement by a generation more relaxed in front of the camera.

At least now I could appreciate the irony that he looked most dated in the most up-to-date medium. This might have been the 1960s – his last books were written just as The Beatles were going global – but they weren't *those* 1960s. Of pop culture and the anarchic energy that was about to upend Western culture when these programs were made – the New Wave, pop, pop art, pop psychology – there is not a trace in his work. The most up-to-date pop song Moorehead refers to, in a 1950 article about Rome's modernisation, is 'Baby It's Cold Outside'. It's as though he is separated from all that by a thermocline in the cultural atmosphere.

He only spoke once in public about the friends he'd lost so soon after the war, at a London literary festival in the late '50s. 'On purely literary grounds I think it is a shame that they are dead,' he said. 'They died at a moment when they were most needed – when mass communications were to burst upon the world.' They were needed, he meant, to prevent mass media smothering all the things that made life worth living: objective standards, poetry, great art, nature, pools of contemplative quiet.

Finding him looking so *preserved* in the flat film stock and rigid elocution of the old documentary made me think of how quickly the past becomes strange to us, old and strange. Any sepia-tinted figure could provoke thoughts like these, of course. But the maddening pastness of the past mystified Moorehead too. What do we do with all of those redundant decades piling up behind? In Moorehead's books the past feels like an irresistibly vast, half-explored space that brings out a kind of wanderlust of feeling, more vigorous than nostalgia, more bewildered. Is there any meaning to be had back there? Can any reader escape in any meaningful way into the space and time of old books?

I've always thought so. If I didn't, I wouldn't have been sitting there in front of the telly, with my finger on the rewind button.

10

DETACHMENT

The year 1966 doubtless felt like any other, another one slipping by in a busy and productive middle age. But from here, it seems strangely thematic, like a carefully shaped coda. Not just the travels: to Africa, Australia and America, and plans for more books and films, and the steady pleasure of life in Porto Ercole, with spring plantings jotted down in the weather book, convivial evenings and a vintage in September every bit as satisfying and undrinkable as the previous ones. But underlying it all, a return of that old feeling of dissatisfaction. Moorehead's African travel companion Dick Waller told Pocock he was surprised when, in a rare moment of grandiosity, Moorehead said to him: 'What is my future? I've done it all. Where can I go?'

Packing his bags for somewhere new had always been the cure for Moorehead's *cafards*. But the trips of that year have the quiet, tired deflation of the road already travelled. In Africa he and Lucy re-visited the Kenyan wildlife parks. In Australia with Caroline and Lucy later in the year, he was mostly beset by journalists; he handed out some valedictory-sounding advice to 'the young writer' ('who should start reading as much as he can and write incessantly') and admitted he had no specific projects in mind. He'd had to drop the book about Australian fauna, because an expert he knew and admired was already doing one. When he heard that Geoffrey Dutton was writing a biography of Edward John Eyre, he tore up his plans for that too ('very generous of him,' Dutton said). An invitation to become a visiting professor at Monash University was flattering, but all he managed to write in Australia was a pastoral vignette about Anlaby, the Duttons' ancestral home.

In America he tried to contact Sculthorpe, on sabbatical at Yale, but the elusive composer wasn't answering his phone. He saw Alwyn Lee and Jane Cooke. 'I have been doing nothing much but work,' he wrote to Tass Drysdale from Jane's Long Island house in October. 'I find a kind of flatness about America, don't know what it is, too many cars, too much cosiness and prosperity and a general feeling of where do we go next and what does it matter anyway?'

That summer he wrote in his diary:

> Nearly everything I have touched in the last twelve months has gone wrong ... My libretto has been rejected. The book on Australian natural history that I planned I find I cannot do. The film I made there has not been shown. The Hollywood producer has not bothered to acknowledge the receipt of the Darwin script and will pay only a part of my expenses. I find I cannot write my autobiography. I have nothing to do.

The Darwin movie had stalled in pre-production; the Orde Wingate biopic fell apart after a bruising and embarrassing interview with his widow in Scotland. Empty-handed, humiliated, Moorehead returned by train to the London flat, where John found him that evening gulping whisky and fuming about his treatment. 'When will I ever learn to have nothing to do with films?'

§

He and Lucy planned to spend December in Porto Ercole. But before they left London, Moorehead went to see his doctor about bad headaches he'd been having, and odd episodes of numbness and slurred speech. The doctor handed him on to a neurologist, who ordered immediate tests, including an X-ray requiring an intravenous injection of dye. On 4 December 1966 he was admitted to Westminster Hospital. He was unconscious when doctors realised that he must have been suffering ischemic attacks caused by a blockage in an artery. Immediate surgery, though risky, might prevent a major stroke. Lucy, stunned by the suddenness of events, gave her consent.

As the family entered the surreal world of medical crisis and sickbed limbo ('I have been talked at so much by so many doctors, surgeons, neurologists,' Lucy wrote to a doctor friend in Melbourne, 'I break out into a heavy sweat if I see one'), Moorehead remained unconscious for the next week. Australian papers reported Moorehead's critical condition in daily updates, but there wasn't much news until he resurfaced, and it became clear that he'd sustained serious damage during the surgery. He couldn't speak or read. He couldn't move his right arm. It wasn't clear that he even understood what had happened to him. Lucy sounds dazed, too. It is 'the waiting that is hard for us', she wrote to the Drysdales. 'It all fell on us out of the blue.'

At first the doctors were confident substantial recovery was likely, given time. But how much? Moorehead spent the next month in hospital, gradually regaining strength. When, in the first week of 1967, he was allowed to come home, he negotiated the sixty-four steps to the flat 'astonishingly well', Lucy thought. But full recovery was clearly a long way off. 'Alas,' Lucy wrote to Tass and Maisie, 'no one knows how long that will be. He is much better, but still can't use his right hand much and is bothered with speaking. He knows perfectly well what he wants to say but can't always say it and this is frustrating to an enormous degree.' Lucy was flat out making arrangements – hiring help, including a dauntingly expensive cook, and responding to letters and calls of concern from friends. 'What a bloody thing it is, seems so damned unfair,' she replied to one. Their financial situation made them more fortunate than many in the same position, and she knew it; but things were hard enough. While Moorehead endured the ordeal of dependency, Lucy did everything she could to make it bearable. Jane Cooke, distraught, wrote a series of letters to Alan which Lucy had to read aloud for him, because he couldn't read them himself.

Beyond the family, the seriousness of the situation took a long time to sink in, perhaps because of the delicacy surrounding illness in those days. I kept finding an oddly myopic optimism in peoples' letters. Geoffrey

Dutton, for instance, saw Moorehead in London in February, and went down to the Bernsteins' country place with him for the weekend. Alan, he wrote in a letter home, 'was in fine form. Wasn't it wonderful that he went to the quack when he did, that the man had the brains to diagnose it.' It's hard to know what Dutton can have meant by 'fine form' here. Moorehead could barely speak a few words.

Some crucial part of his brain was obviously damaged, but it's true that the rest of him seemed almost unaffected. His determination was completely unimpaired. In Porto Ercole, where they spent the summer, Lucy arranged for 'a charming girl' to live with them and work with Alan on his reading and Moorehead threw himself into the task of relearning letters, sounds and the names of simple objects, and retraining his limbs to swim. But as the months go by, Lucy's letters trace an arc of slowly fading optimism. 'Talking a lot better,' Lucy she wrote to the Drysdales in July, but 'not yet able to read … I am afraid he must have moments of intolerable frustration and boredom and hating the whole of his life but on the whole he is amazingly determined and cheerful. I repeat to him that it is only a question of sticking out this bad time and I think he believes me.'

§

In 1968 the Mooreheads made contact through friends with Roald Dahl and his wife, Patricia Neal, who had suffered a serious stroke a few years earlier but was now, as Lucy saw during dinner one night at the Dahls' home in Buckinghamshire, almost entirely well. Their hosts agreed that Moorehead was doing even better than Neal at the same stage and so, much encouraged, the Mooreheads rented a 'horrid little cottage' (Caroline recalls) near Great Missenden, where Alan could work with Neal's therapist, Valerie Eaton Griffith.

He was a willing patient, Griffith wrote later; 'all his enormous power for hard work, and his great will and determination' were intact. The alphabet was impossible at first, but give him the name of any place on the planet, and he could stab the place on the globe without difficulty. But concentrating for long periods was exhausting. Eaton Griffith tried anything she could think of that might interest him: maps of Africa, puzzles.

She even tried a puzzle made from a *Playboy* centrefold, in the hope that an old enthusiasm might hold her patient's attention.

Ninety per cent of his mental capacity had survived the stroke, the family believed, maybe ninety-five. But there was no Neal-style miracle. Moorehead's concentration did improve over the years. He was never able to read with any fluency, much less write. His improving speech stalled at a few stock phrases. *Bloody awful. Absolutely. Marvellous.* But that was all. He was never going to write again. In a poignant scene, Robert Hughes recalled pushing his old mentor around Regent's Park in his wheelchair. They were feeding the ducks when, in a sudden spurt of willed fluency, Moorehead said to him, 'If only you knew how bored I am' – he tapped his head – 'in here.'

Seventeen years passed like that, in unimaginable isolation. When Moorehead went out for walks in the early days, Lucy used to hang a little card around her husband's neck printed with his name, address and phone number – in case one of the era's most tireless travellers became confused and needed a stranger's help to find his way home.

They continued visiting Porto Ercole for part of each year. Notes were entered in the weather book, but in a different hand, and much less frequently. Friends still came to stay. In 1968 Moorehead was awarded a CBE. He refused to front up to the palace for the ceremony to accept it at first, but relented two years later. He accepted his gong alongside Noël Coward, who was getting a knighthood, and whom Moorehead had first met a lifetime before when he interviewed the star at the Gibraltar docks one summer evening in 1937.

At Porto Ercole, bridge was one thing Moorehead could still do well – or as well as he ever had. Holding the cards was difficult, so he propped them up in a little wooden rack and made his reckless bids with signs. His frustration was sometimes hard to witness. He 'suffered greatly', Valerie Eaton Griffith wrote, having to listen to everyone else talking away on all subjects without being able to join in. At dinner parties he might last till midnight before it all got too much but then, sometimes, he would abruptly leave the table only to be found later in another room with an audiobook playing while he tried to follow the words on the page. (He read Tom Wolfe's *The Right Stuff* in this way.) One night talk turned to dictionaries.

Which was the best? Desperately trying to make his view on this understood, Alan dragged a friend from her seat to the bookshelf, and pulled out the Chambers Dictionary: *this* is the one.

It was all too hard for some people. A loss like this can be a merciless winnower of friends, and some fell away. Others did their best: Geoffrey Keating struggled with his friend's aphasia, and coped by diverting his Moorehead-related energy into John instead. Bernstein and Jamie Hamilton stuck fast, of course, and Alwyn Lee and the Drysdales. 'I don't think Alan has had such a good time for years,' Lucy wrote to Maisie after a visit in Melbourne. 'He really pined for Tass's company when we left. We were only able to comfort him by assuring him that you would come over this summer, so I hope and pray you do.'

§

Even with its engine disengaged Moorehead's literary production continued on its own momentum, as if in angel gear. In 1967 there was a trickle of pieces for the *Sunday Times*, including the Anlaby story, the last thing he ever wrote, and an upbeat report on the healthy state of East African game parks recycled from the *New Yorker*. Pieces kept appearing in compendia and essay collections, like an Australian omnibus in which Moorehead was introduced as 'the brilliant journalist-historian' with 'a captivating style that makes the dullest history read like a Rider Haggard adventure'. As late as 1972, Moorehead is listed, between Arthur Miller and Pablo Neruda, among the contributors for a new (and soon defunct) American magazine called *Audience*. By then he hadn't written a word for six years. Lucy signed off on new translations in new territories (*Cooper's Creek* had 'rather a good sale' in Czechoslovakia, she noted in 1967; 'can't think why they would go for it') and oversaw the production of junior, abridged and illustrated editions. In 1973 *The White Nile* was reissued in a lavishly illustrated paperback. 'It should remain a classic of its kind,' the *Spectator* wrote, 'and Penguins are to be congratulated on their good taste.'

Most important, Lucy got to work finishing the books lying scattered on Moorehead's studio workbench. It was a painstaking task that required all of her editorial gifts. By stitching together notes and film scripts, and reading aloud the links for Alan's approval as she went, she managed to assemble a full book, *Darwin and the Beagle* (1969). The theme was classic Moorehead: the young Charles Darwin was another scholar-traveller, like Denon, Captain Cook, Burton or Burckhardt, making a world-changing journey in that last fragile moment when such journeys were possible. The book's irrepressible tempo struck reviewers as authentic; so did its not-quite-convincing analysis: 'an instance of attractive science journalism,' one reviewer said, 'undermined by poor historical scholarship.'

But Lucy's greatest alchemical feat was *A Late Education*. When it appeared in 1970, there was, understandably, some muffled scepticism. John gave a couple of interviews to explain how Lucy had assembled the memoir from several manuscripts his father had written before the illness. Anyone still doubtful could see Lucy in court: in a note to Jamie Hamilton she said she would not hesitate to sue anyone who suggested the book wasn't entirely the work of its author.

I spent a long time comparing drafts and analysing fragments trying to detect a ghost in the text, but I still don't know how much glue Lucy needed to hold the thing together. In the end I decided just to be grateful that it was produced at all. It's the most personal of Moorehead's twenty-one books, and the fans' favourite. John Barkham, another veteran of the war in Africa, wrote in his reader's report: 'It is recorded in that modest yet immaculate style which has made Moorehead so admired a writer – a style so unobtrusive that when he stirs your emotions (as he does here several times) you go back to see how he did it.' Moorehead wasn't getting many cables nowadays, but Sidney sent him one from Granada HQ in Manchester: 'BLOODY MARVELLOUS VERY VERY VERY GOOD LITERALLY COULD NOT PUT IT DOWN.' In New York, William Shawn read the proofs too, and was moved by them. 'Mr Moorehead's writing is so good – so elegant, really.' His magazine had run extracts from *Darwin and the Beagle*, but he declined the offer to serialise the memoir. It wasn't quite 'within our scope', he wrote to Lucy. It was the last word in a partnership that had sustained Moorehead since the lowest ebb in the years after the war.

Moorehead had always wondered whether his work was good enough to last. Now he was in the strange position of living to see if it would.

It was the man behind the work who faded first, becoming a shadowy figure, strangely enmisted in hearsay and faulty memory, especially in Australia. In a way it's not surprising. Perhaps this was the price you paid for avoiding publicity; and in biographical terms, Moorehead didn't help himself either. He often muddled the dates and minor details of his own life – several times in *A Late Education*. As Clifford once noted, facts had always been subservient to truth in Moorehead's work: if Alan thought the Battle of Arnhem read better with tulips he would put them in, never mind that in September the bulbs were still snug in the ground.

But when I returned to Canberra in 2015 for a final fact-check at the National Library, I was struck afresh by the slipshod way Moorehead's biography has gone into the national record. His entry in the *Australian Dictionary of Biography* is meticulous and exemplary. But elsewhere, in reference books, compendia, friends' biographies, it's a man-shaped blur of mistakes that a quick fact-check could have avoided: trips he didn't make; parties he wasn't at. There seemed to be an indifference to the basic data that verged on something like contempt, for a man some Australians had always found a bit hard to take. But maybe this happens to everyone in time. Perhaps I was oversensitised by loyalty. What does it matter if even the estimable Geoffrey Blainey thinks that Moorehead was born in Swan Hill?

Closer to home, memories inevitably perished a little over time too, though not out of indifference. Robert Hughes' recollection of pushing his mentor around the park, for instance, is demonstrably false: Moorehead was never in a wheelchair. (Perhaps this was Hughes' tulips-in-September moment: the pathos of the scene *demanded* a wheelchair.) Young Bob wasn't around much after the stroke.* Nor was Martha Gellhorn – unapologetically so. She told the family up front she wouldn't be doing much for Alan, and no one was surprised. They'd never really seen eye to eye.

And inevitably, Moorehead began to fade from public memory of the

---

* To be fair, he was based in New York in the '70s. In the years to come, Hughes often mentioned Moorehead in reviews and interviews, and always with gratitude and admiration.

war, too. When the BBC series *World at War* was made in the early 1970s it featured several old colleagues from the campaigns in Africa, Italy and Europe. But Moorehead was missing. So were Clifford and Buckley, of course, and Wilmot and Jordan. But only Moorehead was alive to witness his own absence.

§

What was it like to watch the world rolling on without him? Did he even notice? Certainly Moorehead was still capable of meaningful communication. John told me he grew much closer to his father in the last years of his life than he'd been before. He clearly enjoyed his grandchildren, and good company. 'He had ten different ways of using "absolutely", and "you bet your life"', Rob told me. 'He still had a wonderful way of communicating with you. He'd ask about the children, and he'd go – with his hand, showing their different heights – that one, that one and that one.'

Lord Bangor (Eddie Ward) invited his old friend to parties in London, such as the one where Tom Pocock had his first brush with a man he'd revered, when a young war correspondent himself, as the master of the trade. An awkward exchange followed in which Moorehead responded to each of Pocock's eager remarks with perfect friendliness, but oddly terse replies: 'Absolutely!' or – sympathising about the traffic – 'Bloody awful!' Seeing she was needed, Lucy stepped in, as she always did, and conversation became possible again.

Apart from people, painting was the great consolation of a cruelly contracted existence. He took art classes in London. Some of the most sustaining hours were the quiet ones he spent in the company of Anthony Fry, a young painter who lived nearby, and had the knack of companionship. In the studio at Porto Ercole, he shut himself away all day long with his canvases. It was a godsend, Lucy told friends, that he had found something that interested him and that he could still do. 'It really has made a life for him,' she wrote. He enjoyed exhibitions, though his ability to self-edit had been impaired. At shows of acquaintances' new work he sometimes mortified Lucy by audibly snorting 'Bloody awful' as he strolled from canvas to canvas.

He still had his energy. A journalist who tracked him down in 1977 found 'a man still built like a little bull, still as forceful-looking as a rolling bowling ball'. He still wanted to travel. There were trips to Morocco with friends; regular returns to Australia, another trip up the Nile in 1975. They went back to East Africa in 1970; Lucy had been concerned that it would be painful returning there, 'but I think he really did enjoy it immensely; the animals as enchanting as ever and all his old friends the game wardens so nice to him'.

But what was happening in his mind? If anyone knew it was Lucy, who stands there in Moorehead's 1970s interpreting as best she can, holding an existence together. Her stoicism was remarkable, her uncomplaining co-existence with the new reality. And with the old one … In the months after the stroke, Lucy got in touch with Jane Cooke and invited her to London to see Alan, perhaps recognising that however disagreeable such a visit would be to her, it might be reviving for Alan. Jane never abandoned him either. In the years to come the two women reached a workable entente, albeit with more pragmatism than friendliness in it. On Jane's occasional visits to London Lucy would hand Alan over to her for a weekend trip to Paris or the country somewhere. Lucy would take a badly needed break.

Hard not to admire the strength of character all round.

§

In July 1979 Lucy was killed in a car accident. She was driving Alan and Phyllis from the house to a restaurant in nearby Ansedonia when their car was struck by a lorry as they turned into the trunk road south to Rome. Lucy and Phyllis were both flung through the windshield. Alan, buckled up in the passenger seat, witnessed the whole thing. Lucy died in hospital two hours later. Moorehead was physically unhurt, but a difficult existence now threatened to become intolerable. 'We are all, of course, left completely stunned by what has happened,' John said, relaying the awful news to the Drysdales. Alan 'is a bit shaky but otherwise well: he has accepted Lucy's death with remarkable bravery, which did not surprise me: in a sense I think the last 12 years has inured him to almost any further disasters.'

§

Moorehead's world contracted even further. He moved in with John and his young family in Primrose Hill, staying a year or so, and then lived with

Caroline's family until his children found a flat for him in the neighbour-hood. An Australian nurse lived in, cooking and keeping an eye on him. Moorehead lived on for four years after Lucy's death, until he died from a second stroke, in the upstairs bedroom of his flat.

He had continued with the same uncomplaining, more or less grim determination to get to the end of each day, with a lifer's daily ration of drinks and cigarettes. Once in London, he made John understand through gestures that he was going to throw himself in Regent's Canal. John knew he didn't mean it. There was still painting to do, the pleasure of watching his grandchildren growing up. 'He was very strong. Unbelievable, really.'

He made annual trips to Australia in these years, sometimes on his own. One of his children would put him on a plane at Heathrow and at the other end someone would collect him at Tullamarine airport, like a parcel posted across the world. In Melbourne he would stay in Hawthorn with Phyllis, and see his old friends. Then he eventually grew restless and would suddenly want to get back to London. One of the last trips to Australia, I was delighted to discover, he flew by Concorde – at exactly the time I was gazing at the Concorde in the Stuyvesant ad at the corner store, trying to imagine where it was going. So, here was one last futuris-tic plane ride to add to the campaign map of a lifetime's flights I kept on my wall ... I liked to think of him jetting back to London at supersonic speed, with a tray of freeze-dried food on his lap, looking down on the bright globe from the dusky edge of space.

One of Moorehead's favourite subjects in the last years was Aboriginal art. He made a number of paintings based on photographs of rock paint-ings, some from books Tass Drysdale sent him.

Sometimes he went down to the zoo at the bottom of Regent's Park, a short walk from the flat, to paint the animals. The expatriate writer who had been so desperate to escape Australia in his youth, ending at the London Zoo, painting kangaroos left-handed.

That's not a bad image, I thought: symmetry, and tragic irony. I could end with that.

Except I wasn't quite finished.

The man himself might have faded to the point where no one but war buffs and people who had to read *The Fatal Impact* in school know who he is, but the afterlife of his work, its reputation, is more complicated. All writers date, of course. Very few books last more than a few decades. But it had always seemed to me that Moorehead's reputation faded unusually fast, beyond the standard rate of decay all but the greatest writers suffer.

How good are the books today? It was hard for me to tell, and it had never been my intention to make a great revisionist claim anyway. His work could speak for itself, and still does, in regular reissues of the best-known books. But I couldn't help feeling a twinge of defensiveness sometimes – when, say, someone suggested that Moorehead's war journalism mightn't be so revered if his reputation hadn't been gilded by the commercial success of the *Nile* books; or whenever I came across a novelist's put-down. 'If only Alan Moorehead knew how to write,' chirps VS Naipaul in the pages of *Sir Vidia's Shadow*, when Paul Theroux suggests *The White Nile* as background reading on Africa.*

Moorehead's journalism has remained highly esteemed among those journalists who know it. Phillip Knightley remembers Sam White, a star of the *Express* in the '50s and '60s, telling cadets who badgered him for reading tips to 'for Christ's sake just get hold of anything by Alan Moorehead'. James Cameron called him 'the best of us all'. In 2012, he was inducted into the Melbourne Press Club's Hall of Fame, and pleasant things were said.

Even as a yardstick of literary merit, Moorehead's work has had a stubborn afterlife. Critics always found it hard to describe Moorehead's particular quality, but in the decades since his stroke they have recognised it when it appears in new books or – more often – doesn't. The author of a 1978 book about Africa suffered by comparison, in the view of one reviewer: he 'says he has set out to do for the Congo what Mr Alan Moorehead did for the Nile. He hardly succeeds in that: it takes more than research and enthusiasm to create a work of art.' A recent novel set in the

---

* According to Theroux's memory, at least. This was around 1964.

Mediterranean theatre of the Second World War can't match the authentic article, in another reviewer's opinion: 'Alan Moorehead's *The Desert War*... makes this North Africa seem like land under gauze.'

Among professional historians, not surprisingly, Moorehead's work hasn't fared any better than it did during his lifetime. Though even here there are admirers. In 1987 Manning Clark wrote that 'as long as there is a reading public for a story teller such as Alan Moorehead we can be sure the age of the human ant-heap has not arrived in Australia.' A few years ago the brilliant biographer of Shelley and Byron, Richard Holmes, described Moorehead as 'one of the greatest Australian popular biographers and historians' whose books about Australia 'achieved a significant type of collective biography'.

Perhaps his most enduring legacy lies in those driven by his example to go out into the world in search of astonishing true stories. David Attenborough, for instance, has acknowledged Moorehead as a major inspiration: he was a man ahead of his time, Attenborough said in 1964, both as a conservationist and as a writer who used gripping historical narratives to illustrate contemporary problems. It was Moorehead, too, who first suggested to Robert Hughes that he write about convict settlement in Australia. Without Moorehead's encouragement and mentorship, *The Fatal Shore*, which Hughes dedicated to Alan and Lucy when it appeared years later in 1986, may not have been written; without Moorehead's books, Hughes may not have discovered the sound of its majestic opening lines.

Yet it's because of his writing about war that Moorehead's name most often comes up now, flickering back into view as major anniversaries come round. In the decades during which Anzac has become a kind of secular cult in Australia, Moorehead's pioneering *Gallipoli* was, oddly enough, rarely mentioned, until it was reissued on the centenary of the landings. Reviewing the glut of anniversary books, Germaine Greer called Moorehead's a 'masterful account, and still the best written of them all.'

§

The real difficulty is that for all Moorehead's detachment and clarity –
perhaps *because* of his detachment, now that I think about it – his voice
can sound as though it is crackling out at us from an old wireless with
news from a distant time. When Harper Perennial reissued *The White Nile*
into the internet age, in 2000, some readers baulked at Moorehead's
descriptions of Africans. A review on Amazon deplored Moorehead's
'overt racism' which was 'of a weird flavor, seeing as how the author also
berated the explorers for their own bad attitudes towards Africans.
Dude – don't criticize yer neighbor for having a splinter in his eye when
you have a plank in yer own, all right?'

Moorehead – the *dude*. I laughed out loud when I read that.

It's true, though, that recent, radical shifts in sensibility can make it
hard to read parts of his work without flinching. To appreciate the epic,
gloomy opening stanza of *Cooper's Creek*, for instance, requires a mental
edit of the reference to Aborigines as 'the most retarded people on earth'.
Moorehead came to deplore colonialism: the damage done, by disease
and violence, to indigenous peoples is the central theme of *The Fatal
Impact*. But his failure to imagine that indigenous peoples across the globe
might not quietly vanish, but resist what he called 'the long downslide
into Western civilisation', has come to seem defeatist, as well as wrong.
His common-sense authority, for that matter, has come to seem as though
it relies on a specifically white man's idea of common sense.

But few writers treading this terrain in the '50s and '60s fare well in
hindsight. It may be true to say, as many a postcolonial critic would, that
Moorehead's thoughtful search for new horizons in time and space is not
innocent at all, but complicit in – indeed *constitutive of* – the white violence of the Western gaze. But that doesn't tell us much about the sensibility
of Moorehead's time, or what Manning Clark meant when he called him
'the historian with the eye of pity'. Or how deeply into time and space
Moorehead's inquisitiveness allowed him to see.

'It would seem that there is little enough to thank God for in these
appalling deserts,' Moorehead wrote in *The White Nile*, 'and yet the poor-
est and most wretched of the inhaitants will be seen throughout the day
to prostrate themselves upon the sand.' That remark provoked Sudan-born

British writer Leila Aboulela to write something much more revealing about the limits of compassion.

> I remember the shock, the first inkling that the West is wrong, that the West doesn't know ... day in day out I saw that sight [Moorehead] had described, I lived it all around me, lived in it, was part of it and understood that it was independent of the 'little enough to thank God for,' knew that it was of value and of dignity in itself, that it was something beautiful, something nice ... Every religion tells us that the poor are closer to God, that they are more loved by God, that they will get into Heaven faster and easier than anyone else. Why is that? Why are they privileged? Travelling in North and Central Sudan, Alan Moorehead had seen why but not understood.

That seems right to me, and a useful reminder that compassion is not the same as understanding. *Seeing* was Moorehead's unfailing inborn gift – seeing, and transmitting the experience of seeing to the reader. Understanding how people in faraway places experience their own worlds was the hard part. It always is.

§

Back in Canberra one last time, I checked into a motel room in Queanbeyan, interchangeable with any of the others I'd stayed in. And maybe not so different from Moorehead's basic hotel room in Valencia in 1937. Except that no one was bombing this one, and this one had linen in those terrible blue and ochre, Ken Done–influenced squares and swirls that seems to be obligatory in Australian motels at the three-star price-point, and was made out of some polymerised fabric blend that probably hadn't existed in Moorehead's time. It squeaked when I sat on it.

At the library the following morning, a librarian who was checking my reader's card pointed out that I'd first requested the Moorehead papers in 2007. Jesus. I hadn't really got cracking till a few years after that. But still. In all that time I hadn't opened a non-fiction book without checking the index, more often than not finding nothing between *Moore, George* or *Moorehead, Agnes* and *Morshead (Gen.)* – a name I grew to detest, simply because it so often appeared where what I was looking for didn't. I hadn't passed a building site, and there were plenty of them in Canberra, without thinking of the phrase Christiansen had loved so much in a Moorehead dispatch from 1944: *I could stand watching a bulldozer for hours.* ('Now the man who writes that homely little touch has my money every time as England's greatest reporter.') This warm, sterile room at the NLA is where I'd always felt the strongest connection to Moorehead the living person, more than in Taormina or even Porto Ercole, here in the Gibraltar cables, and the drafts of his doomed postwar novel where Moorehead's hell-bent desire to get away and into the wide world was most unreasonable, and so most attractive. But my obsession was winding down now. I could almost feel it leaving my body, like a fever that's done its work fighting off an infection. I no longer felt a Pavlovian jolt every time I saw his name in a blog or index. Though on my last afternoon in the library I did catch myself half-hoping I'd find one last woe-begotten play from the 1940s, just for old time's sake.

That night in my room I flicked through *Darwin and the Beagle*, then lay on the squeaky doona listening to trucks grinding away from the highway intersection outside. I studied a blister of damp in the ceiling plaster. How to explain all this time I'd spent with my face pressed up against the window peering back there into the gloom of the mid-twentieth century, trying to make out one solitary man in it? Moorehead counted himself fortunate that he'd known from the age of sixteen that he wanted to write, and had never thought of doing anything else. It *was* lucky, though his calling was seldom a joy. 'I dislike writing very much and do as little as I can,' said the man who did little else. He also said: 'one is never satisfied with a book' – a consoling remark for anyone stuck with theirs. 'The best one can hope to do is a good sentence once a week, a good paragraph once a month, a good chapter once a year. A good book never.' Maybe I should go to America and examine the *New Yorker* archives, I thought. But that would be another form of procrastination, like counting *pleasants* and making a defiant list of Moorehead's best jokes. Still – perhaps I could do a scene about my visit to the grave in London's Hampstead cemetery two years ago ... how I'd found the headstone there, a modest, mottled grey slab leaning out of wet grass and parsley stalks a few metres from a suburban street. How I'd admired the excellent brevity of the epitaph. *Alan Moorehead: Writer.* But I hadn't felt anything that day. 'Nothing was communicated,' in Moorehead's phrase, and it seemed weird to imagine that it would be.

All the communicated meaning was in the books, in Moorehead's long, intimate report from the heart of his fabled era. I still felt I knew him best there, where I could be alone with his voice, and savour the shared solitude of writer and reader that linked us across the decades.

On the face of it, Moorehead was a tragic realist. In his books all the excitements of history sit alongside a calm awareness of the brutal brevity of most lives. Human destructiveness is essentially an aspect of natural history. That boy blown to bits by a leftover mine at Cassino turns up in Moorehead's work again and again: in refugee trains in Kashmir, a starved calf nudging its dead mother by a dry waterhole in time of drought; the Patagonian child bashed against a rock by his or her father and left to die in the hard sunlight of another time. It's there even in *Darwin and the Beagle*: in a story of thrilling intellectual curiosity and far horizons, Moorehead pauses to describe how Darwin travelled the pampas of South America with General Rosas, then busy with his campaign of annihilation against the Indian tribes. Moorehead treats these long-forgotten horrors with perfect detachment. A reprisal raid against a tribe near Bahia Blancas goes off with stunning savagery, and in cool disinterested prose: 'one dying man had bitten his assailant's thumb and would not let go even when his eye was forced out.' Another 'was observed to be loosening the bolas round his waist so as to be ready to strike when his pursuer came close. His throat was cut.'

> [The survivors] were lined up for interrogation and when the first refused
> to divulge the whereabouts of the rest of the tribe he was shot dead. So
> was the second, and the third had no hesitation either: 'Fire,' he said, 'I
> am a man. A man can die.' Vultures, being familiar with these scenes,
> hovered overhead.

You could argue that Moorehead's immersion in lost worlds was merely the luxury of the outsider passing through. In many places that moved him, in postwar Italy, postcolonial Africa and the Pacific, the inhabitants building a future out of wreckage couldn't afford too many memories.

But there was also something compulsive and urgent in Moorehead's incessant return to the past, a feeling that grows stronger towards the end of his writing career. In the 1965 documentary Moorehead made with Bob Raymond about the Australians who fought in the Western Desert, he revisits the Libyan town of Bardia, scene of a critical victory of 1941. Straight-backed and compact in his shell windbreaker, Moorehead stands in a street of blazing white stone and crumbling walls. Bardia, Moorehead tells us, has never recovered. 'It's a dead town still.' It looks like it. The only signs of life are some parched weeds and a small girl who emerges from a doorway in the background to wring out clothes on the stoop. As Moorehead recalls the Australian 6th Division's fierce assault on the town's perimeter, the girl glances up at the camera, and then looks down to her washing. She's probably seen it before: middle-aged men who were here twenty-five years earlier, returned to the place they'd left smashed and desolate to visit graves, or take pictures of the past in which, when they're developed, none of the terror and elation of a headlong advance will appear.

While the girl trots about, crouching to whack a bit of cloth on the ground, Moorehead faces the camera. The Australians had shown they could fight, he says, decisively. But mostly he doesn't look decisive; he doesn't look detached. He looks faintly uncomprehending, like someone struggling to explain some forgotten meaning, trying to assimilate the best days of his life with all the damage they did. But if he says anything about this, we don't hear it, because the archive print has deteriorated and there's no more sound for the rest of the film. Just pictures, just silent shots of the flat stony battlefields, the pinewood hills on the road to Barce, and the cemeteries at Mersa Matruh, where Cleopatra once came to bathe in the sea.

ENDNOTES

Notes on sources

The privately held letters and journals that Tom Pocock saw in the late 1980s and referred to in his book as the 'Moorehead Family Collection' never reappeared. Where I quote from his excerpts, I give the relevant page number in his *Alan Moorehead*, The Bodley Head, London, 1990.

Moorehead's niece, Gillian Lodge, generously showed me some letters written to her mother by Alan or Lucy. These, and photographs and documents shown to me by various interviewees and other members of Moorehead's family, are cited as 'private collection'.

Many references cite the Moorehead papers at the National Library of Australia. Properly the 'Papers of Alan Moorehead', this collection comprises 327 folders distributed among forty-three boxes, and a few folio items. References give the collection number – MS 5654 – the box number, and then the number of the folder within the box (e.g. MS 5654/2/10). The 'Papers of Tom Pocock' are also held at the National Library of Australia (as MS 8377).

Interviews were carried out with Caroline Moorehead (28 September 2013), Cara Lancaster (April 2014), Gillian Lodge (September 2013), John Moorehead (April 2014), Jocelyn Moorehead (April 2014), Anne Chisholm (September 2013), Suzanne Baker (November 2015) and Penny Pocock (December 2015).

Works by Moorehead

The following editions of Alan Moorehead's books have been used in the endnote citations.

African Trilogy, Hamish Hamilton, London, 1944.
Churchill and His World, revised edition, Thames & Hudson, London, 1965 [1960].
Cooper's Creek, Hamish Hamilton, London, 1963.
Darwin and the Beagle, Crescent Books, New York, 1983 [first published by Hamish Hamilton, London, 1969].
Eclipse, Text, Melbourne, 1995 [first published by Hamish Hamilton, London, 1945].
The Blue Nile, Hamish Hamilton, London, 1962.
The Fatal Impact, Hamish Hamilton, London, 1966.
Gallipoli, Harper & Brothers Perennial Classics, New York, 2002 [first published by Hamish Hamilton, London, 1956].
A Late Education, Hamish Hamilton, London, 1970.
Mediterranean Front, Hamish Hamilton, London, November 1941.
Montgomery: A Biography, Hamish Hamilton, London and Melbourne, 1947 [1946].
No Room in the Ark, Penguin, 1962 [first published by Hamish Hamilton, London, 1959].
The Rage of the Vulture, Charles Scribner's Sons, New York, 1948.
Rum Jungle, Hamish Hamilton, London, 1953.
A Summer Night, Hamish Hamilton, London, 1954.
The Traitors: The Double Life of Fuchs, Pontecorvo, and Nunn May, White Lion, 1974 [first published by Hamish Hamilton, London, 1952].
The Villa Diana, Hamish Hamilton, London, 1951.
The White Nile, Hamish Hamilton, London, 1960.

1 NOTES ON A DISAPPEARANCE

1   one of the best writers in the English language: Edwin M Yoder, *Washington Post* (Book World), 4 April 1971.

1   'like straining shit through a sock': Robert Hughes, *Things I Didn't Know: A Memoir*, Knopf, New York, 2006, p. 306.

1   'The choice and arrangement of the words': Unpublished typescript, *Papers of Alan Moorehead*, National Library of Australia, MS 5654/25/205.

2   dog-eared sheaf of foolscap: NLA MS 5654/27/225.

2   'all to be masterpieces': NLA MS 5654/25/201.

2–3   'I've had a gun shoved into my ribs': AM to Beth Thwaites, 18 August 1936, *Papers of Tom Pocock*, National Library of Australia, MS 8377.

4   Hemingway and Ross: Francis J Bosha, 'Ernest Hemingway and the *New Yorker*: The Harold Ross files (Notes),' *The Free Library,* 22 September 2001.

6   'exasperatingly cavalier': James Cameron, *Observer*, 2 May 1971.

6   *festschrift*: reviews by veteran war correspondents and former colleagues included those by Ronald Payne, 'Out there on his own', *Sunday Telegraph* (London), 20 December 1970; Joseph G Harrison, 'No longer ago than yesterday', *Christian Monitor*, 27 May 1971; John Hetherington, 'Phases in a life', *Age*, 1971.

7	'Johnsonian pleasure', 'sauce of the epoch': *A Late Education*, pp. 150, 152.
8	'some turreted town': *Rum Jungle*, p. 19.
8–9	'I date my life from this moment': *Rum Jungle*, pp. 19–20.
9	'a beautifully defined picture': Cyril Bentham, 'Montgomery in the field', *Times Literary Supplement*, issue 2340, 7 December 1946.
10	'like a special correspondent for posterity': Philip Collins (ed.), *Dickens: The Critical Heritage*, Routledge, London, 1971, p. 392.
10	'He wrote effortlessly': Charles Foley to Tom Pocock, 6 October 1987, NLA MS 8377.
10–11	'Before it is too late': *African Trilogy*, p. 196.
11	'descry Mount Athos': *Gallipoli*, p. 42.
13	Joseph Brodsky, 'To please a shadow', *Less Than One: Selected Essays*, Penguin, London, 2011, pp. 367–9.
14fn	'Nothing is more intriguing': *The Blue Nile*, p. 142.
16	'I wandered out': *A Late Education*, 1971.
19	'His little shithouse': Geoffrey de Groen, *Some Other Dream: The Artist, the Artworld & the Expatriate*, Hale & Iremonger, Sydney, 1984, p. 135.
22	'prim at heart': AM to LM, 26 April 1952 (Pocock p. 248).
22	'Comes over one': DH Lawrence, *Sea and Sardinia*, Cambridge University Press, Cambridge, 2002, p. 7.
22–3	'You sounded just as I had hoped': NLA MS 5654/2/9.
23	'dominating purpose': John Hetherington to Norman Lindsay, 16 January 1960 and 12 February 1960, State Library of Victoria, Hetherington Papers, MS 9740 Box 5.
23	For James, see Clive James, 'Alan Moorehead', *Cultural Amnesia*, W.W. Norton, New York and London, 2007, pp. 515ff. For Knightley, see Philip Knightley, 'Introduction' to Alan Moorehead, *Eclipse*, Granta, London, 2000. For Hughes, see Hughes, *Things I Didn't Know*; Geoffrey de Groen, *Some Other Dream*; Hughes, 'A man who did not need to make things up', *Weekend Telegraph* (London), 3 March 1990; and Tim Flannery, 'The naked critic: Memories of Robert Hughes', *Monthly*, September 2012, p. 20.
23	'What a pompous bore': Frances de Groen, Laurie Hergenhan (eds), *Xavier Herbert Letters*, University of Queensland, 2002, p. 255
24	'a unique literary category': 'Mr Alan Moorehead' (obituary), *Sunday Times*, 30 September 1983, p. 14.
24	'see through the eyes of others': Max Harris, 'Moorehead miraculous', *Australian*, 1965.
24	'There is a kind of writing': CP Snow, 'Men on the spot', *Financial Times* (London), 7 January 1971.
25	'almost as naked, as primitive': *The Blue Nile*, p. 279.
26	'self-inflicted prisons': *A Late Education*, p. 160.
27	'walked the course': or, as he put it himself, 'sniffed the wind'. See Patricia Rolfe, 'Wild Life and Civilised People: The Moorehead method of research', *Bulletin*, vol. 87, no. 4456, 24 July 1965, p. 30.
27	'sudden pools': Jan Morris, 'The saddest story', *Times Literary Supplement*, issue 3219, 7 November 1963.
27–8	'The old town of Bonny': Alan Moorehead, 'The galvanized-iron roof', *New Yorker*, 1 September 1962, p. 38.

2 CUMDEAD ETWOUNDED

29   'brightly striped Moorish counterpane': Alan Moorehead, 'It Is Later Than You Think', (in some drafts titled 'A Memory'), c. Oct 1947, unpublished manuscript, NLA MS 5654/25/205.

29   'I used to go down to the docks': *Rum Jungle*, p. 18.

29   'at the centre of things': *A Late Education*, p. 30.

30   'in the isolation of neutrality': *African Trilogy*, p. 432.

30-1   'The warships in and out of the harbour': Alan Moorehead, 'These twenty thousand Britons are suffering from nerves', *Daily Express*, 21 July 1937, p. 10.

31   'quite a pleasant fellow', 'subversive': *A Late Education*, p. 65.

32   'men at the look-out stations', 'at the cost of', 'Dear Mr Sutton': AM to Charles Sutton, May 1937, NLA MS 5654/1/5.

32   'might cost 10/': AM to Charles Sutton, 21 July 1937, NLA MS 5654/1/5.

32fn   'Rock Defences': Gibraltar notebook, NLA MS5654/35.

33   'Six years of fighting': 'It Is Later Than You Think', NLA MS 5654/27/221.

33   'I read the proofs': John Hetherington, *42 Faces: Profiles of Living Australian Writers*, Angus & Robertson, London, 1963, p. 119.

34   'generous mouth': Alexander Clifford, 'The war correspondent', *Strand Magazine*, London, 1947, p. 28.

34-5   'that supreme quality': James was writing of Adam Bede, who lacked it. Henry James, 'The Novels of George Eliot', 1866.

35   'People ate shrimps': NLA MS 5654/27/221.

36   'leading eyesore', etc: 'It Is Later Than You Think', NLA MS 5654/27/222, p. f.

36   'smugness', 'assistant bank manager': 'It Is Later Than You Think', NLA MS 5654/27/228.

36-7   'blowsy trollop' etc: 'It Is Later Than You Think', NLA MS 5654/27/221.

37   'a thrill out of living', 'too near decadence': AM to Beth Thwaites, 18 August 1936, NLA MS 8377.

37   'nagged by the feeling': *A Late Education*, p. 50.

37   'matchless blue': 'It Is Later Than You Think', NLA MS5654/27/228.

38   'mysteries of the Mediterranean': John Dos Passos, *Journeys Between Wars*, Constable, London, 1938, p. 357.

38   'the *Deutschland* appeared': Alan Moorehead, *Daily Express*, 31 May 1937.

39   'there was an air', 'ghoulish release': *A Late Education*, pp. 69, 71.

40   'the new Dark Ages': 'It Is Later Than You Think', NLA MS 5654/27/228.

40   'NICE WORK FELLA' etc: cable from Monks to AM, 31 May 1937; and cables from *Daily Express* to Moorehead, 31 May and 1 July 1937, NLA MS5654/1/5.

41   'peaceful as an English fishing village': Moorehead, *Daily Express*, 7 June 1937.

41   'As it turned out': AM to Sutton, 19 June 1937, NLA MS5654/1/6.

41   'The debris': *A Late Education*, p. 73.

41   'Jean Ross': 'Surgery by Candlelight', *Daily Express*, 1 June 1937.

42   'I am sorry it is so much': AM to Sutton, 19 June 1937, NLA MS5654/1/6.

42   'For forty minutes': Alan Moorehead, 'Thirty bombs fall by Italian ship', *Daily Express*, 18 June 1937, p. 1.

42   'I am well satisfied': Sutton to AM, 14 July 1947, NLA MS 56543/1/6.

42   'such an interesting city': editor of the Melbourne *Herald* to AM, 22 June 1937, NLA MS 5654/1/5.

42   'Gibraltar was front page': 'These twenty thousand Britons . . .', Alan Moorehead, *Daily Express*, 21 July 1937, p. 10.

42   'NOW PERHAPS': Monks to AM, 23 July 1937, NLA MS 5654/1/5.
43   'the right amount of sensationalism for the *Express*': AM to Lucy, 22 August 1939 (Pocock, p. 58).
43   'fires of Almeria': 'It Is Later than You Think', NLA MS5654/25/201.
43   'ENNUMERATE FRANCOS': Sutton to AM, 16 August 1937, NLA MS 5654/1/5.
43fn   'in a white duck suit', etc: 'Noel Coward guest in cruiser at "Gib"', *Daily Express*, 20 July 1937, p. 1.
44   little black notebook: NLA MS 5654/35.
44   'The blatant nature of these attacks': 'The Royal Navy in the Spanish Civil War, Part III', *The Naval Review*, August 1974, p. 204.
44   'IF YOURE NOT BACK YET': Sutton to AM, 1 September 1937, NLA MS 5654/1/5.
44   'The scheme at first': AM to Sutton, 28 August 1937, NLA MS 5654/1/5.
45   'OK GO AHEAD': Sutton to AM, 5 September 1937, NLA MS 56543/1/5.
45   Aletti Hotel stationery: NLA MS 5654/1/'1936'.
45   'YOU MISSED': Sutton to AM, 8 September 1937, NLA MS 5654/1/4.
45   'UNWANT AIRTRIP': Sutton to AM, 9 September 1937, NLA MS 5654/1/4.
45   'YOUR TRIP UNPRODUCTIVE': Sutton to AM, 15 September 1937, NLA MS 5654/1/3.
45   'It is impossible to continue': *African Trilogy*, p. 47.
45   'Now at last': *A Late Education*, p. 74.
45fn   Ambler's impressions of Tangier in these months are strikingly similar to Moorehead's. See Eric Ambler, 'Spy-haunts of the world', *The Ability to Kill*, The Bodley Head, London, 1963, p. 165; and his autobiography, *Here Lies*, Farrar Straus Giroux, New York, 1985, p. 128.
46   'I imagine that I am recording all this': 'It Is Later Than You Think', NLA MS 5654/25/205. The word 'book' is neatly struck out in the original, with no replacement given – perhaps Moorehead himself didn't know what to call it. Novel? Memoir? Moorehead's publisher Jamie Hamilton suggested 'chronicle' (in a letter of 27 October 1947).
46   'How did one begin?': 'It Is Later Than You Think', NLA MS 5654/25/205.
46   'plump little man', etc: 'It Is Later Than You Think', NLA MS 5654/25/205; *A Late Education*, p. 42.
46   'secret and difficult business': *A Late Education*, p. 76.
46–7   'Mr Brandt' appears in *A Late Education*, pp. 76ff and various drafts of 'It Is Later Than You Think', esp. NLA MS 5654/27/225–6.
47   '"It's my job," I said': *A Late Education*, p. 77.
47   *Russian in Istanbul*: NLA MS 5654/1/2.
47–8   'lights of the city', 'All this intensive': *A Late Education*, pp. 78ff.
48   sheepish-sounding draft: NLA MS 5654/1/1.
48–9   'by some accident': *A Late Education*, p. 86.
49   'full of the noise': *A Late Education*, p. 88.
49–50   'I went directly on to the bridge', etc: *A Late Education*, p. 90.
50   'I Run Pirate Zone in Tanker': Alan Moorehead, *Daily Express*, 7 October 1937, p. 9.
50   notes on the Victoria Hotel: NLA MS 5654/27/225.

3 ARRIVAL

51   'nice Australian girl': AM to Beth Thwaites, 25 June 1936, NLA MS 8377.

51   'struck us as being very ambitious': Tom Pocock, interview notes with Douglas Brass, c. 1988, NLA MS 8377.

52   'dampest and greenest tree', 'known by no one': *A Late Education*, pp. 38, 39.

53   'Who will ever forget', 'I woke in the morning': *A Late Education*, p. 41, 42ff.

54   'great bull-like young men': *A Late Education*, p. 45.

54   'shining-eyed look of ecstasy': 'It Is Later Than You Think', galleys, NLA MS 5654/27/223.

55   'I didn't want to pause': *A Late Education*, p. 49.

55   'two great breaks': NLA MS 5654/27/225.

55   'To stay at home': *Rum Jungle*, p. 12.

56   wife painting flowers on wallpaper: This story is something of a family legend. Moorehead also mentions it in 'An arcady of a kind', *New Yorker*, 1 August 1953, p. 25.

56   'She took things how she found them', etc: Alan Moorehead, *Observer*, 13 August 1950.

56–7   'Micawberish and futile optimism': *A Late Education*, p. 18.

57   'genteel poor', etc: *A Late Education*, pp. 17–18.

57   £2.10s a week: *A Late Education*, p. 19.

57   'all for Karl Marx': *A Late Education*, p. 20.

58   'prettiest girl I had ever seen', 'unhooks her belt', 'rather grander quarters': *A Late Education*, pp. 52, 51, 54.

58   Joseph Lyons and the whiskies: Mary Wood's notes from her interview with Moorehead, 15 March 1955, NLA MS 8377.

59   Gray and Sullivan: notes from Pocock's interviews, NLA MS 8377.

59   The disc, a 'voice-o-graph', is in the Moorehead papers: NLA MS 5654/1/6.

59–60   Arthur Christiansen's career at the *Daily Express*: see Anne Chisholm and Michael Davie, *Lord Beaverbrook: A Life*, Knopf, 1992; and Christiansen, *Headlines All My Life*, Heinemann, 1961. In 1938, the paper's circulation reached 2,329,000. The boast about how Christiansen had boosted circulation (with innovations such as removing full stops from headlines) was reported in *Time*, 22 November 1943; Christiansen always insisted it wasn't he who'd made it.

60   salacious divorce stories: Chisholm and Davie, *Lord Beaverbrook: A Life*, p. 320.

60   'outshone its competitors': Sir Geoffrey Cox, *Eyewitness: A Memoir of Europe in the 1930s*, University of Otago Press, Dunedin, 1999, p. 238.

60   in-house newsletter: 'Alan Moorehead catches glimpses of the Spanish War', undated clipping, NLA MS 5654/1/2.

61   'demands for each of us social equality': AJP Taylor, *Beaverbrook*, Penguin, London, 1972. p. 376.

61   'one last hectic spending bender', 'every week a new night club opened': 'It Is Later Than You Think', NLA MS 5654/26/219, p. 235a.

62   'required to report the parties', 'Every day': Cox, *Eyewitness*, pp. 261, 165.

62   'we tried to limit ourselves': *A Late Education*, p. 102.

63   'Didn't I tell you': Richard Moorehead to AM, 27 March 1939, NLA MS 5654/1/4.

63   'Taxi to office of *Daily Express*': Chester Wilmot's diary, 13 March 1938, Papers of Chester & Edith Wilmot, NLA MS 8436, Series 7.

63   'an air of taut', etc: *A Late Education*, pp. 103–4.

63   'Result was': AM to Lucy Milner, 7 November 1938 (Pocock, p. 34).

64 'the Seine made a wide sweep': *A Late Education*, pp. 99–100.
65 'up and up through glades', 'could see his great dog-eyes': *A Late Education*, pp. 108–9.
65 victim, or executioner: The phrase is Jean-Paul Sartre's, writing about France's war in Algeria. See 'Growing pressure for Algeria settlement', *Times*, 7 March 1958.
65 'I believed': 'It Is Later Than You Think', NLA MS 5654/26/219, p. 255c
65 'quality of impending disaster': Alan Moorehead, 'Munich in the light of today', *New York Times Magazine*, 28 September 1958.
65 'If this is cowardice': Henry Miller, *Hamlet Letters*, cited in Robert Ferguson, *Henry Miller: A Life*, Hutchinson, 1991, p. 261.
66 'knew that we were condemned': 'Munich in the light of today'.
66–7 'In all Spain': Alan Moorehead, '"Date-line town" is full of spies', *Daily Express*, 12 January 1939, p. 10.
67 'Bus Runs Babies': Alan Moorehead, *Daily Express*, 9 April 1938, p. 2.
67 'vast and frightening chasm', etc: Alan Moorehead, *Daily Express*, 2 April 1938, p. 1.
67 'humiliation seemed more complete': *A Late Education*, p. 117.
68 'I could not understand' etc: *A Late Education*, p. 116–17.
68 'wildly and irrationally generous': *A Late Education*, p. 96.
68 'love and fraternal spirit': Simone Weil, 'Letter to Georges Bernanos' in Murray Sperber (ed.), *And I Remember Spain*, Hart-Davis, MacGibbon, London, 1974, p. 260.
68 'suburban hedge cutters': Erl Gray to AM, 27 March 1939, NLA MS 5654/1/2.
69 'dead hand of suburbia': unpublished draft of *A Late Education*, NLA MS 5654/25/206.
69 'I know if I went back': AM to Lucy, 24 April 1939 (Pocock, p. 53).
69 'Hemingway came running down the stairs': unpublished draft of *A Late Education*, NLA MS 5654/25/204.
70 'I kept perversely': *African Trilogy*, p. 218.
70 'disgusting things', etc: AM to Lucy, 17 June 1939 (Pocock, p. 56).
71 Italian waiters on the train: 'Prelude in Italy', an introduction of a dozen or so pages to Moorehead's *Mediterranean Front* (1941) that was omitted from the *African Trilogy* omnibus in 1944 and from all subsequent reprintings. See *Mediterranean Front*, pp. 11–12.
71–2 'What a collection': AM to Lucy, 23 August 1939 (Pocock, p. 59).
72 'Even in the Ambassadors': 'Prelude in Italy', p. 15.
72–3 'a tall, witty, statuesque girl': Clifford, 'The war correspondent', p. 28.
73 'God knows we'll be trapped soon enough': galleys of 'It Is Later Than You Think', NLA MS 5654/27/223.
73 'I had a fine barrage up': AM to Lucy, 7 January 1939 (Pocock, p. 45).
73 'It is only the world': AM to Lucy, March 1939 (Pocock, p. 50).
73–4 'What I dread so much', etc: AM to Lucy, 18 March 1939 (Pocock, pp. 50–1).
74 'a stout gentleman': Alan Moorehead, 'Eternal Rome', *Holiday* magazine, April 1952, p. 34.
74 'And we wondered': 'Eternal Rome', p. 36.
75 'Everything is grey': 'Prelude in Italy', p. 13.
76 'Within two hours', 'Hating it all': 'Prelude in Italy', pp. 16, 19.
76 'a tiger': AM to Lucy, 20 May 1940 (Pocock, p. 71).

76 'I have watched many demonstrations': Alan Moorehead, *Daily Express*, 10 May 1940, p. 2.

77 'I have not talked so well': AM to Lucy, 26 May 1940 (Pocock, p. 73).

4 A DESERT WAR

80 'What in the name of God is that?': *African Trilogy*, p. 16.

80 'thick drowsy slabs': Alexander Clifford, *Three Against Rommel*, G.G. Harrap, London, 1943, p. 287.

80 'engineers and girls', etc.: Alan Moorehead, *Daily Express*, 4 June 1940, p. 8.

81 'Quite seriously': *A Late Education*, p. 57.

81 'the era of blind confidence': Clifford, *Three Against Rommel*, p. 9.

82 'puny little baby of an army': Clifford, *Three Against Rommel*, p. 294.

82 'I heard this a thousand times': *African Trilogy*, p. 176.

82–3 'in my experience', etc: *African Trilogy*, p. 19.

83 'centuries earlier, Cleopatra': Clifford, *Three Against Rommel*, p. 14.

83 'as rounded and directional': *African Trilogy*, p. 77.

83 'only a great deal of dust': *A Late Education*, p. 60.

83–4 'with the persistence of a goldfish': *African Trilogy*, p. 24.

84 'desert war': Moorehead uses this analogy in: Alan Moorehead, *Daily Express*, 4 July 1940, and *African Trilogy*, p. 20.

84 'onward rush of the present', etc: *A Late Education*, p. 132.

84 'Reporting': Alan Moorehead, 'Foreword' to 'A Memory' (a version of 'It Is Later Than You Think'), NLA MS 5654/26/219, p. 1.

84 'Lying on open ground': Alan Moorehead, *Daily Express*, 21 December 1940, p. 4.

84 'What a time and what a place': unsigned cable, NLA MS 5654/1/3.

84 'Within an hour': *A Late Education*, p. 61.

85 'powerfully evocative': Christopher Buckley, *Road to Rome*, Hodder and Stoughton, London, 1945. p. 82. Eve Curie made the same observation in her *Journey Among Warriors*, William Heinemann, London, 1944, p. 34.

85 'a new kind of reporting': *African Trilogy*, p. 66.

85 'YOUR EXCELLENT MESSAGES': Sutton to AM, NLA MS 5654/1/8.

86 'antiseptic effect', 'mad glaring eye', 'two strangers who cling together': *A Late Education*, pp. 61, 63, 35.

86–7 'effortless, absorbing conversation': *A Late Education*, p. 33.

87 women in the desert: Eve Curie, *Journey Among Warriors*; Clifford, *Three Against Rommel*, p. 151; Caroline Moorehead (ed.), *Over the Rim of the World: Selected Letters of Freya Stark*, John Murray, London, 1988, p. 207. Stark was warned off making the trip to the front: 'all the sanitary arrangements are so public everything just *stops* when a woman is in the camp'.

87 'slim active woman': *A Late Education*, p. 123.

88 'haphazard communal life', 'the establishment': *A Late Education*, p. 125.

88 'You might call it an important raid': *African Trilogy*, p. 65.

88–9 Scene at Nibeiwa: *African Trilogy*, pp. 66–72.

89 'In one camp alone': *Daily Express*, 16 December 1940, p. 6.

90 'From first to last', 'terrible, blasting, stultifying': *A Late Education*, p. 60, 62.

90 'There is no front line': Alan Moorehead, *Daily Express*, 27 November 1941, p. 1.

91–2 Barce ambush: *African Trilogy*, pp. 104–5.

92–3 'shaking so much', etc: *A Late Education*, pp. 127–8.

93 parmesan cheese anecdote: Clifford, *Three Against Rommel*, p. 66.
93 'not so much the general devastation': *African Trilogy*, p. 529.
93 'Nearly all night long': *A Late Education*, p. 7.
94 'not then apparent': Arthur Christiansen, *Headlines All My Life*, p. 246.
94 'VERY PROUD' and other cables: NLA MS 5654/1/5.
94 'the best war-reporting': Clifford, *Three Against Rommel*, p. 297.
94 'the best reporter/correspondent': Clare Hollingworth, Pocock's interview notes, c. 1989, NLA MS 8377.
94 'one of the really great': Christiansen to AM, 13 January 1942, NLA MS 5654/1/6.
94 'London editor of *Life*': Christiansen to AM, 3 December 1941, NLA MS 5654/1/6.
94fn 'constantly trying to outdo': *A Late Education*, p. 122.
95 'Moorehead is a big shot': Christiansen, 'Editor's bulletin', 3 June 1942, NLA MS5654.
95 'Moorehead bathes in Graziani's Bath': *Daily Express*, 3 February 1941, p. 1.
95 'I still can't believe it's true': Clifford, *Three Against Rommel*, p. 148.
95 'I believe success': Moorehead, interviewed by Mary Wood, 15 March 1955, NLA MS 8377.
95–6 'The test which I apply': undated letter, cited by Neil McDonald in 'Damien Parer and Chester Wilmot at Tobruk', *Quadrant*, July 2000, p. 86.
96 'approach to detail is artistic': Clifford, 'The war correspondent', p. 30.
96 'renowned social mobility', etc: Clive James, *Cultural Amnesia*, p. 519.
97 'very pleased with himself': Clifford's diary, 18 January 1942 (Pocock, p. 115).
97 'brushed up against': Patrick White, *Flaws in the Glass: A Self-Portrait*, Jonathan Cape, London, 1981, p. 97.
97 'I could read in Alan's eyes': Allan Fleming, interview with Tom Pocock, NLA MS 8377; Pocock, p. 98.
98 'the little tick': Hetherington to Lindsay, 12 February 1960, SLV MS 9740 Box 5.
98 'As an Australian living abroad', *African Trilogy*, p. 363.
99 'salute you unexpectedly': Freya Stark, *Dust in the Lion's Paw: Autobiography 1939–1946*, John Murray, London, 1961, p. 56.
99 'outnumbered a hundred to one': *African Trilogy*, p. 121.
100 'As your taxi pulled up': *African Trilogy*, pp. 254–5.
100 'Alan and I drove out': Clifford's diary, 13 July 1941 (Pocock, p. 105).
100 'we remained': *A Late Education*, p. 131.
100 'a spirit of imperial arrogance': Jan Morris, *Paris Review*, Summer 1997, no. 143.
100fn 'much kinder and gentler than I': *A Late Education*, p. 132.
101 'the Orestes and Pylades': Buckley, *Road to Rome*, p. 131.
102 'I had been a non-entity': unpublished draft fragments for *A Late Education*, c. 1964?, NLA MS 5654/25/204.
102 £150 advance: Richard Knott, *The Trio: Three War Correspondents of World War Two*, The History Press, Stroud, 2015, p. 106.
102 'pouring out', 'As war correspondents': unpublished draft fragments for *A Late Education*, NLA MS 5654/25/204, pp. 13, 12.
103 'been a good boy': Christiansen to AM, 25 August 1941, NLA MS 5654/1/6.
103 copies of *Mediterranean Front*: Knott, *The Trio*, p. 106.
103–4 'the appetite of a tourist': Neil McCallum, *Journey With a Pistol: A Diary of War*, Gollancz, 1959, p. 55.

104   'eerie feeling': *New York Times*, 5 May 1946, p. 39.
104   'I don't see you taking any notes', 'I just give up', 'buttoned up to the eyebrows', 'kicking his heels': *African Trilogy*, pp. 430, 115, 411–12, 117.
105   'peculiarly corpse-like aspect': Buckley, *Road to Rome*, p. 84.
105   'slept blissfully': *African Trilogy*, p. 132.
105   'deadly excruciating slowness': *African Trilogy*, p. 31.
105   'so improbable a place', etc: *African Trilogy*, p. 121.
106–7 'the most astonishing things': *Daily Express*, 4 December 1946, p. 4.
107   'truffled style and dense plumage': Durrell's undated letter of congratulation on PLF's *Mani*. See Artemis Cooper, *Patrick Leigh Fermor: An Adventure*, John Murray, London, 2012, p. 307.
107   'cult' of the war correspondent: Priestley's review of *Eclipse*, undated, 1946, NLA MS 5654/10/78.
107   'genuine travel requires travellers': Roberto Bolaño, *The Insufferable Gaucho*, trans. Chris Andrews, Picador, 2010, p. 136.
107   'more like *tourisme*': Clifford, *Three Against Rommel*, p. 68. See also p. 185.
107–8 'like doing a Cook's tour': *African Trilogy*, p. 242.
107   'mind jibbed': Clifford, *Three Against Rommel*, p. 173.
107   'unthinkable amount', etc.: Clifford, *Three Against Rommel*, p. 303.
108   'she would bake him another cake': Clifford, *Three Against Rommel*, p. 173.
108   'I don't think Alex and I', 'Was I really as': *A Late Education*, pp. 58, 133.
109   'difficult not to': Clifford, *Three Against Rommel*, p. 176.
109   'like some Doré etching': *African Trilogy*, pp. 235.
109   'warm, yellow, winter sunlight': *African Trilogy*, p. 82.
109   'sprawled in a confused', etc: *African Trilogy*, p. 493.
110   'irresistibly like a Sunday school treat': *African Trilogy*, p. 495.
111   'condition oneself to a war': AM to Lucy, 20 September 1943 (Pocock, p. 163).
111   'There had been so much killing', 'Are you the bastard', 'Anderson, to look at': *African Trilogy*, pp. 541, 540, 542.
112   'It is useless to picture these men': *African Trilogy*, p. 540.
112   'Here was the positive': Alan Moorehead, *Daily Express*, 10 May 1943, p. 1.

5 HANGING ON BY EYELIDS

113   'deep draught of triumph': Christopher Buckley, *Road to Rome*, Hodder and Stoughton, 1945, p. 78.
113   'blaring cobalt blue': *Eclipse*, p. 11.
113–14 'usual hush': *Eclipse*, p. 13.
114   'one of the fairest sights': Moorehead, *Daily Express*, 17 August 1943, p. 4.
114   'queer staccato': *Eclipse*, p. 14.
114–15 'holiday out from the war', etc; relaxing in Taormina: *Eclipse*, pp. 15–21.
115–16 'I have an idea': AM to Lucy, 1 January 1944 (Pocock, p. 173).
116   'too good a man', etc.: E.A. Montague to AM, 25 December 1943, NLA MS 5654/2/10.
116   left him winded: AM to Lucy, 9 January 1944 (Pocock, p. 175).
116   'of hopes and fears': *Eclipse*, p. 8.
117   'frightful smell of shit': Edward Ardizzone, *Diary of a War Artist*, The Bodley Head, London, 1974, p. 44.
117   'disgustingly pretty': *Diary of a War Artist*, p. 46.

118 'business done in charms': Alan Moorehead, 'The sad and beautiful island of Sicily', *Holiday*, September 1961, vol. 30, p. 85.

119 'What can I say?': AM to Lucy, 18 August 1943 (Pocock, p. 151).

119 'infinity of days': *Eclipse*, p. 15.

119 'with delight', 'hither and thither': Buckley, *Road to Rome*, pp. 151, 119.

120 'It is I know, not easy to justify', 'We passed the burning lorry': Buckley, *Road to Rome*, pp. 66, 119.

120 'something very definite': *African Trilogy*, p. 426.

119–20 'pattern of euphemisms': Alan Moorehead, 'The horrors of war', *Observer*, 8 May 1949, p. 9.

121–2 'My friends and I', etc: 'The sad and beautiful island of Sicily' p. 85.

122 'yammered at us': Buckley, *Road to Rome*, p. 135.

124 'I must say I found': AM to Lucy, 5 September 1943 (Pocock, p. 157).

124 'in these days of the mob-mind': review of *Montgomery*, *Truth* (London), 29 November 1946.

125 'awfully good meal': Buckley, *Road to Rome*, pp. 181–2.

125 'I feel baulked': AM to Lucy, 20 September 1943 (Pocock, p. 163).

125 'humiliating': AM to Christiansen, 22 September 1943, NLA MS 8377.

125 'wasting a good deal': AM to Lucy, 2 October 1943 (Pocock, p. 164).

126 'to write of such things': AM to Lucy, 28 October 1943 (Pocock, p. 169)

126 'The strange thing about Alan': 'The craft of writing', *Sunday Times*, 24 October 1954.

126 'All war is bad': AM to Lucy, 9 December 1943 (Pocock, p. 170.)

126 'dread of going up to the abyss': *Eclipse*, p. 74.

127 'Five years of watching war': *Eclipse*, p. 299.

127 'Intensely virile': Richard Moorehead to AM, by telegram, 27 February 1944, NLA MS 5654/1/8.

127 'the best flat in the best block': Buckley, *Road to Rome*, p. 253.

127–8 Ardizzone's description of Naples: *Diary of a War Artist*, pp. 77ff. Re. 'firestorm' of syphilis, see Norman Lewis's superb *Naples '44*, Eland, London, 1983.

128 'fearful little tart': Ardizzone, *Diary of a War Artist*, p. 85.

128 'sociologically and politically': 'Foreword', *Eclipse*, p. 8.

128 'more cheerful and yet more selfish': *A Late Education*, p. 141.

128 'Just food': 1944 radio broadcast, BBC Postscript program, reported in the *Observer*, 3 April 1944.

129 '*Express*man Alan Moorehead': *Daily Express*, 4 January 1944, p. 2.

129 'who said, "I hate"': Moorehead's journal, 10 February 1944 (Pocock, p. 171).

129 'not fear that oppressed', 'curiously toy-like': *Eclipse*, pp. 105, 112.

130–1 'Gaps in our landings': 'Eclipse diary', NLA MS 5654/34.

131 'close and formidable caravan': Tom Driberg, *Leader Magazine*, 11 November 1944.

131 'unusual gift': quoted in Rick Atkinson, *The Day of Battle: The War in Sicily and Italy 1943–1944*, Little, Brown, 2013, p. 300.

132 'no longer streets or footpaths', 'A city means movement': *Eclipse*, pp. 143, 236.

132 'greatest calamity': Simone Weil and Rachel Bespaloff, 'The *Iliad*, or the poem of force: War and the Iliad', *New York Review of Books*, 2005, p. 31.

132 'the last four years': H d'Avignor Goldsmid, review of *Eclipse*, *Horizon*, April 1946, p. 286.

133 'In the end the aggressor': Alan Moorehead, 'Gandhi: A last look', *Observer*, 1 February 1948, p. 4.

133–4   'sort of panzer battle array', etc: *Eclipse*, p. 155.
134   'Unless some major crisis develops': AM to Christiansen, 30 July 1944, NLA
         MS 5654/2/13.
134   'We can't get it into a newspaper entirely': AM to Christiansen, 31 July 1944.
134   'simply awful': draft letter, AM to Christiansen, undated, probably June 1944.
         MS 5654/2/12.
134   'One fluctuates between the two': AM to Christiansen, 31 July 1944, NLA
         MS 5654/2/12.
134–5   'fixed up as General Montgomery's': Christiansen to AM, 11 August 1944,
         NLA MS 5654/2/13.
135   'a front row seat': Jamie Hamilton to AM, 6 September, 1944, NLA
         MS 5654/2/13.
135   'gargantuan, frightening', 'after so much kissing': *Eclipse*, pp. 158, 162.
135–6   'a little galling': *Eclipse*, p. 169.
136   'A hundred other cars': *Eclipse*, p. 171.
136   'prepared and braced', etc: *Eclipse*, p. 161.
136   'My city!': Douglass Brass, interviewed by Pocock in 1987 (Pocock, p. 192).
137   '*Enfin on respire*': AJ Liebling '*Enfin on respire*': *Just Enough Liebling*, North
         Point Press, New York, 2004, p. xxii.
136–7   'At the Porte d'Orléans': *Eclipse*, p. 161.
137   'an almost bewildering completeness': *A Late Education*, p. 142.
138   an entire hard-working chapter: Chapter 11: 'The Four Years in Paris', *Eclipse*,
         pp. 174–88.
138–9   'endless pain stretching ahead': *Eclipse*, p. 208.
140   'All round Brussels and Liege': *Eclipse*. p. 227.
140   'We tended to be more sickened by ruins': *Eclipse*, p. 169.
140–1   'twenty women wearing dirty grey skirts' etc: *Eclipse*, pp. 261–5.
141   '*All the living are guilty*': Vasily Grossman, *Everything Flows*, Random House, 2010.
141   'Worse camps existed': *Eclipse*, p. 269.
141   'most important document': Beverley Nichols, NLA MS 5654/3/26.
141   'on the brilliant end': AM to Montgomery, 4 May 1945, NLA MS 5654/2/13.
142   'trivial tale' of the diver and the corpses: *Daily Express* 5 December 1946, p. 2.

6 JUICES OF GENIUS

143   'From a very minor reporter': NLA MS 5654/27/225.
143   'the first biography': Review of *Montgomery, The Truth* (London),
         29 November 1946.
143   'topflight war correspondent': *Time*, 9 December 1946 (vol. 48, no. 24), p. 49.
144   'without achieving the glamour of Ernie Pyle': d'Avigdor Goldsmid, p. 287.
144   'his battle pieces': 'Battle Lines', *Observer*, 21 November 1943, p. 8.
144   'a time-server': NLA MS 5654/12/98.
144–5   'frightfully gushing', etc: Pocock, pp. 203–4.
145   'staring at an endless': Alan Moorehead, 'Where Shall John Go?', *Horizon*,
         February 1947, p. 135.
145   'a feeling that we were drifting apart': drafts of *A Late Education*, NLA
         MS 5654/25/206.
146   *In effect broken off with family*: 'L.E. Scheme', NLA MS 5654/27/225.
146   'happiest of homecomings': drafts of *A Late Education*, NLA MS 5654/25/205, p. 5.

ENDNOTES

299

148	'taken up, inevitably, by Nancy Cunard': Charles Foley, notes on Moorehead, NLA MS 8377.
148	'solecisms like *toilet*': NLA MS 5654/25/205.
149	'Our first objective': NLA MS 5654/2/9.
149	'a splendid paper': drafts of *A Late Education*, NLA MS 5654/25/206.
149	'something like £30,000': NLA MS 5654/25/206. This figure seems inordinately high, considering that Moorehead's proposed wage at the *Express* was to be £4000. Perhaps a miscalculation – or a wishful typo.
149	*Did not realise*: notes for *A Late Education*, NLA MS 5654/25/205.
150	parts of *Montgomery*: Brigadier Head's review, 'Is Moorehead right about Montgomery and Churchill?', *Sunday Express*, 24 November 1946
150	'Last week': *Time*, vol. 48, no. 24, 9 December 1946, p. 49.
150	'I never really knew': Montgomery to AM, 20 December 1946, NLA MS 5654/3.
150–1	'I could not retain': Christiansen, *Headlines All My Life*, p. 246.
151	'war is a gigantic': William Styron in Rose Styron and R Blakeslee Gilpin (ed.) *Selected Letters of William Styron*, Random House, New York, 2012, p. 17.
151	'men who have been in this war': JD Salinger, in Ian Hamilton, *In Search of JD Salinger*, Faber & Faber, 2010, p. 95.
151	'crossed the great divide': Alexander Clifford, 'The one that got away', *Sunday Times*, 2 January 1966.
151	'inevitably reconnoitring': Clifford, 'The war correspondent', p. 30.
151	'difficult as they now are to remember': Hughes, *Things I Didn't Know*, p. 275.
152	'Don't you dare become an intellectual': Welsh to AM, undated letter, 1947, NLA MS 5654/3.
152	'cartridge belts', 'but it so happens': *A Late Education*, p. 156.
152fn	'broke [his] heart': Bosha, 'Ernest Hemingway and the *New Yorker*'.
153	'dreadful depressions', 'I do not know': *A Late Education*, pp. 157, 158.
154	'seven long years', etc: *Daily Express*, 2 December 1946. The theme is taken up in almost identical terms in drafts of the novel, which is separated from the time it describes by 'the black gulf of the war' and by a 'bewildered feeling that one has been whirled away from that time and dumped down again ten or twelve years later', 'It Is Later Than You Think' typescript, NLA MS 5654/26/219, p. 2.
154–5	'I want your side to win': 'It Is Later Than You Think' typescript, NLA MS 5654/26/219.
155	'one of those fixations': Moorehead, 'Foreword' to 'A Memory', NLA MS 5654/26/219, p. 3.
156	'I am terribly sorry': NLA MS 5654/3.
156	'Perhaps this despair presses'. *Montgomery*, p. 156.
156	Gandhi: *African Trilogy*, pp. 278–9.
156	'Do you really think it's worth all this?': NLA MS 5654/27/221.
156	'What is the point': 'Gandhi: A last look', p. 4.
157	'Even beaten': Cesare Pavese, *The Selected Works of Cesare Pavese*, trans. RW Flint, *New York Review of Books*, New York, 2001, p. 176.
157	'essentially apolitical': Hughes, *Things I Didn't Know*, p. 307.
157	no social conscience: Martha Gellhorn, interview notes, NLA MS 8377.
158	'before I had the sense to get it stopped': Alan Moorehead, 'The good life in Italy', *Holiday*, August 1959, p. 54.
159	'a wooden dog': Robert Hughes, 'A man who did not need to make things up', London *Telegraph*, 3 March 1990.

159   'compensations for the basic failure': *New York Times*, 10 November 1948.
159   'crude and tragic Hollywood thriller': *African Trilogy*, p. 197.
160   "'May I swim while the strike is on?'": Alan Moorehead, 'Letter from
       Portofino', *New Yorker*, 25 September 1948, p. 97.
160   'political crisis every five minutes': AM to Phyllis Whitehead, 25 July 1948.
161   'surely one of the most beautifully placed': TS Matthews (a friend of Clifford's
       father-in-law, Robert Graves) in Frank L. Kersnowski (ed.), *Conversations
       with Robert Graves*, University Press of Mississippi, 1989, p. 21.
161   'an elusive operation': Alan Moorehead, 'The Temples of the Nile', *New Yorker*,
       23 September 1961, p. 106.
162   'ragged children': *A Summer Night*, p. 65.
162   Every writer I know under sixty': Cyril Connolly, *Horizon*, February 1950.
162   'the country lay in a trough', etc: Cyril Connolly, 'Where shall John go?',
       Horizon, February, 1947, p. 138. Back in Australia, the editors of the literary
       journal *Southerly* noticed Moorehead's article all right, and fumingly
       republished several paragraphs of the visiting Englishman's gibes. When a
       reader subsequently pointed out that Moorehead was actually Australian, the
       editors conceded their error, albeit with poor grace. 'That Moorehead could
       have been taken for an Englishman shows how completely, in his article on
       Australia, he denied the country of his origin' (*Southerly*, Autumn 1948, vol. 9,
       no. 3, p. 194).
163   acetylene lamps: Alan Moorehead, 'The Italian Riviera', *Holiday*, June 1953, p. 126.
163   'rambling, drafty and lovely': Mary Welsh Hemingway, *An Overpraised
       Season*, Knopf, 1976, p. 229.
163   'madness that anyone', etc: AM's journal, 18 September 1948 (Pocock, p. 224).
163   'tautly, commandingly': Elizabeth Bowen, *Tatler*, 20 October, 1948, pp. 86–7.
164   'exotic background': Hugh A Fausset, *Guardian*, 8 October 1948, p. 3.
164   'incessant, never-ending work': Alan Moorehead, 'Intimacies', *Observer*,
       24 October 1948, p. 3.
164   'brisk, disenchanted old man': AM's journal, 13 January 1949 (Pocock, p. 226).
165   'those invited': Meryle Secrest, *Being Bernard Berenson: A Biography*,
       Weidenfeld & Nicholson, London, 1980, p. 375.
165   'as polite': *A Late Education*, p. 151.
165   'London's most indefatigable people-collector': Denys Blakeway, *The Last
       Dance: 1936, the Year of Change*, John Murray, 2010, p. 219.
165   'tense as a cat', 'When the old man says': *A Late Education*, pp. 150–1.
165   'the foster-father': *A Late Education*, p. 149.
166   '1000 words': AM to Lucy, 27 May 1956 (Pocock, p. 258).
166   'Philip is a portrait of yourself': Lucy's notes, 18 November 1948, NLA
       MS 5654/2/15.
166   'Darling; I have just read', etc: Lucy's notes, undated, NLA MS 5654/2/15.
166–7 'I think I know myself': AM's journal, 11 November 1948, (Pocock, p. 225).
167   'said suddenly', etc: AM's journal, 12 June 1949 (Pocock, p. 232).
167–8 Play script: NLA MS 5654/31.
168   'It is no good': AM's journal, 1 August 1949 (Pocock, p. 233).
168   'Nightmare' galleys: NLA MS 5654.
169   'I can't think': undated, c. December 1947, NLA MS 5654/1/6.
169   'finest newspaper correspondent': West to Morgenstern, 30 January 1948,
       MS 5654/2/12.

169   'We were delighted': Shawn to AM, 14 October 1948, MS 5654/2/16.

170   'cast a great shadow': Mark Amory (ed.), *The Letters of Ann Fleming*, Collins Harvill, London, 1985, pp. 72–3.

170   polite but unhappy note: AM to Shawn, 5 December 1949, Shawn's letter of 13 January 1950, and Ross's notes of 9 August 1949: NLA MS 5654/2/16.

170   'for invoking': Anne Watkins to Jamie Hamilton, 12 December 1947, NLA MS 5654/26/219.

170   '(Land mines . . .': *The Villa Diana*, p. 76.

171   'How much are you earning': AM to Lucy, undated (Pocock, p. 234).

171   unpublished tribute to Buckley: AM's journal, August 1950 (Pocock, p. 240).

171fn Nicolson: his diary, 27 May 1948: Nigel Nicolson (ed.), *Diaries and Letters 1945–1962*, Collins, London, 1968, p. 140.

172   'sickening vacuity': *A Late Education*, p. 162.

173   'perhaps an unexpected choice of job': newspaper clipping, c. April 1951, NLA MS 8377.

173   'writers should write': Ross to AM, 20 March 1951, NLA MS 5654/2/15.

173   'Here, it seemed': Alan Moorehead, 'Preface to new edition', *The Traitors*, Harper & Row, 1963, p. xiii.

174   'a truthful and substantive account': *Christian Science Monitor*, 30 August 1952.

174   'This is in no way an official book': *The Traitors*, p. 17.

174   'MI5's fiction, peddled to Moorehead': Nigel West, 'Fiction, faction and intelligence', in Peter Jackson, L.V. Scott (eds), *Understanding Intelligence in the Twenty-First Century: Journeys in Shadows*, Routledge, 2004. Sillitoe was Director General of the Security Service (MI5) from 1946 to 1953.

175   'who hasn't felt that prim egoism', etc: *The Traitors*, p. 121.

175   'Is this not to throw': 'Breaches of security', *Times Literary Supplement*, 22 August 1952.

175   'has stirred a wasps' nest': *Manchester Guardian*, 2 August 1952, p. 4.

175   'a piece of straight Fascist or Communist morality': 'Through the net', *Observer*, 20 July 1952, p. 7.

175   'for having the impudence': quoted in 'V.G. Kiernan on treason', *London Review of Books*, 25 June 1987, vol. 9 no. 12.

175   'What [Moorehead] complains of': Rebecca West, *The Listener*, 7 August 1952. See also West's (signed) review in *Time and Tide*, vol. 33, 26 July 1952.

175   'What on earth': letter to AM, 20 August 1952, NLA MS 5654/3/25.

176   'buying peace of mind': letter to his solicitor, NLA MS 5654/3/20.

176   'less ennui': AM's journal, 21 December 1951 (Pocock, p. 242).

176   'air of wild but absolute authority', etc: from an unpublished account of how he failed to write the biography, NLA MS 5654/26/213.

177   'a lot of foolish gossip': Augustus John to AM, 31 March 1952, NLA MS 5654/26/213.

177   'appalled and humiliated': NLA MS 5654/26/213.

177   'I don't suppose': Augustus John to AM, 3 April 1952, NLA MS 5654/26/213.

177   'the worst set-back': AM's unpublished account, NLA MS 5654/26/213.

177   'atmosphere of alarm or gloom': *A Late Education*, p. 169.

178   'What was there for me to say': *A Late Education*, p. 174.

178   'We went through the war together': AM to Phyllis Whitehead, 18 March 1952, Private collection.

7 THE OTHER SIDE OF THE HILL

179   'combination of the spiritual': Muriel Spark, *The Informed Air: Essays*, New
        Directions, 2014, p. 26.
180   'such a wonderful letter writer': NLA MS 8377.
181   'I suffer from a complaint': Alan Moorehead, *Herald* (Melbourne), 30 July 1952.
182   'fairly common process of thought': Shute to AM, 28 February 1952, NLA
        MS 5654/2/13.
182   'splendid and glamorous things': AM to Lucy, 10 April 1952 (Pocock p. 247).
182   'I did not': drafts for *A Late Education*, NLA MS 5654/25/204.
183   'not to hold a mirror up': AM to Bednall, undated, NLA MS 5654/2/13.
183   'Famed Author Revisits Australia': *Herald* (Melbourne), 28 April 1952.
183   'barrels of oysters', etc: AM to Lucy, 3 May 1952 (Pocock, p. 251).
183   'subconscious conflict': Hal Richardson, 'Australian returns to scene of guilt',
        Australian, 14 November 1953, p. 14.
183   'enduring fascination in the bush': *Southerly*, September 1955, vol. 16, no. 3.
184   'Very little unexpected happens': AM to Lucy, 30 April 1952 (Pocock p. 250).
184   'An amber light on the hills': AM to Lucy, 3 May 1952.
184   'I won't stand this': AM's journal, August 1954 (Pocock, p. 256).
184   'no lost cities', 'because they believed that the imitation': *Rum Jungle*, pp. 9, 10.
185   'there was a quality', 'The luggage racks': 'An arcady of a kind', pp. 25, 26.
186   'nice sardonic smile': 'Diana's Diary', *Northern Standard*, 13 June 1952
186   'alive physically': AM to Lucy, 22 June 1952, private collection.
186   'What have we in Europe': AM to Lucy, 22 June 1952 (Pocock p. 252).
186   'I must warn you': AM to Lucy, 27 June 1952 (Pocock p. 252).
186   'For one hundred years', 'Every few miles': *Rum Jungle*, pp. 57, 75.
187   'infinite oldness', etc: 'An arcady of a kind', p. 25.
187   'Almost writing': AM's journal, 8 December 1952 (Pocock p. 254).
187–8   'I should be delighted': Greene to AM, 9 September 1952, NLA MS 5654/2/12.
188   'those journeys': unpublished 'Ajanta Diary', 1953, NLA MS5654/26/211.
188   'vast panorama of the East': Caroline Moorehead, *Sidney Bernstein: A
        Biography*, Jonathan Cape, 1984, p. 206.
188   'To fly at 500 miles an hour': unpublished 'Ajanta Diary'.
189   'all the things I had naively hoped', etc: unpublished 'Ajanta Diary'.
190   'They still take the English papers': Alan Moorehead, 'Letter from Bangkok',
        New Yorker, 6 March 1954, p. 81.
190   'Room Service!': Alan Moorehead, 'The house on stilts', *New Yorker*,
        28 November 1953, p. 52.
190   'One gets the uneasy feeling': 'The house on stilts', p. 51.
190   'those magic caskets': Claude Lévi-Strauss, *Tristes Tropiques*, trans. Doreen
        and John Weightman, Penguin, 1974, p. 37.
191   'somewhat bogus sentimental glow', etc: 'The house on stilts', p. 51.
191–2   'Ever since I arrived in the East': unpublished 'Ajanta Diary'.
192   'almost impossible to believe': Alan Moorehead, 'The Mediterranean', *Holiday*,
        November 1954, p. 108.
192   'One dreams': *The Blue Nile*, p. 111.
193   'organ of the intellectuals': *Ten Years of Holiday*, Simon and Schuster, 1956, p. viii.
194   'Mine is not the telescopic view': Alan Moorehead, 'Travel U.S.A.', *Holiday*,
        July 1957.
194   'nothing whatever to say', 'One regrets': 'The Mediterranean', pp. 108, 121.

194–5 'Airline booking office art': *The Villa Diana*, p. 69.

195 'glooming about his runaway wife', 'house grows dizzy': AM to Walter Goetz, 6 September 1955, NLA MS 5654/5/3.

195 'awful hysterical emptiness': AM's journal, 30 October 1954 (Pocock, p. 257).

195fn 'It seems to me': Fielden to AM, undated, NLA MS 5654/2/12.

196–7 'bitter, hopeless grief', 'even the local shepherds', etc: Alan Moorehead, 'Return to a legend', *New Yorker*, 2 April 1955, pp. 106, 109, 110.

197 'I asked myself': Sir Geoffrey Cox, interview notes, NLA MS 8377.

197 *the ban still on*: Alan Moorehead, 'L.E. Scheme', NLA MS 5654/27/225.

197–8 'the secret of his skill': Cyril Falls, 'Gallipoli in retrospect', *Times Literary Supplement*, 4 May 1956.

198 'No matter how often', 'hardly anyone ever visits them': *Gallipoli*, p. 118, 362.

198 'new strain of haunting lyrical beauty': Obituary, *Times*, 1983.

199 'I find it difficult to express': Compton Mackenzie, 'The Dardanelles', *Observer*, 29 April 1956, p. 14.

199 'so much of the atmosphere': Lieut-Gen Freyberg, 'Why we failed at Gallipoli', *Sunday Times*, 29 April 1956, p. 4.

199 'evoking the spirit': Lord Attlee, *Spectator*, 26 April 1956, p. 9.

198 'come out of their holes': notes for an autobiography, NLA MS 5654/225.

199 'You have achieved a masterpiece': Berenson to AM, 4 July 1956; and ALE drafts, NLA MS 5654/25/206.

199 'done with the touch', etc: Norman Podhoretz, 'Romance and reality', *New Yorker*, 20 October 1956, p. 194.

200 'moving occasion': Nicolson, *Diaries and Letters 1945–1962*, p. 321.

200 *I never liked him*: 'L.E. Scheme'.

200 'We have grown used': Alan Moorehead, *Churchill and his World*, Thames and Hudson, London, revised edition, 1965, p. 8.

204 'Dining one evening': Edward Ward, *I've Lived Like A Lord*, Joseph, 1970, p. 258.

204 'that most abstract of all humanity's homes': WG Sebald, *On the Natural History of Destruction*, trans. Anthea Bell, Penguin, 2003, p. 154.

8 BARAKA

205 'a distinguished operator': AM to Lucy, 27 June 1956 (Pocock, p. 259).

205 'to my stupefaction': AM to Lucy, 2 June 1956 (Pocock, p. 259).

205–6 'equatorial heat', etc: Moorehead, 'Travel U.S.A.', pp. 36–7.

206 'a whiff of the Scott Fitzgerald': AM to Lucy, 7 July 1956, private collection.

207 'a fine novelist whose', etc: editors' intro, 'Travel USA', p. 35.

207 'I found the whole of this day': 'Travel USA', p. 40.

207–8 'People nice . . . but oh my god', etc: USA trip diary, NLA MS 5654/34.

208 'The traveller takes another pill': 'Travel U.S.A.', p. 52.

208 'appalling uniformity': Moorehead's Sir Thomas White lecture, given at Australia House, London, 13 April 1957.

208 'as lazy as crocodiles': unpublished draft of *A Late Education*, NLA MS 5654/25/204, pp. 220ff.

209 'exotic beyond belief': AM to Lucy, 17 June 1956 (Pocock p. 260).

209 'the world came to think': *A Late Education*, p. 158.

210 'You mustn't do it': unpublished draft of *A Late Education*, NLA MS 5654/25/206 p. 272.

210   'How much I regretted it': drafts of *A Late Education*, MS 5654/25/204, p. 239.
211   'All the same, the book is superbly written': *Annals of the American Academy* vol. 321, January 1959.
211   'Does any writer': Raymond Mortimer, 'Brave travellers across the bush', *Sunday Times*, 3 November 1963 p. 35.
211   'wartime appetite for books': Sir Geoffrey Cox, interview notes, NLA MS 8377.
211   'I keep getting letters': AM to Suzie Gleaves, 9 February 1958, British Library Add MS 63520 ff. 31–7. Subsequent correspondence to Gleaves from the same collection.
211   'You become a millionaire': Martin Amis, *The Moronic Inferno and Other Visits to America*, Viking, 1987, p. 46.
211   'long harassed battle over money': AM to Lucy, 22 June 1952 (Pocock, p. 252).
212   'Did you hear what *Harper's* paid': AM to Gleaves, 17 January 1958.
212   'Get a glamour house for him': Gellhorn, in Pocock, p. 265.
212   'Jesus, how we all go rushing off': AM to Gleaves, 17 January 1958.
212   'I keep traveling': 'Who and where', *Holiday*, November 1954, p. 33.
212   'My teeth gleam': AM to Gleaves, 17 January 1958.
213   'Oh you writing chaps', 'The *New Yorker* office': AM to Gleaves, undated, c. December 1957.
213   'Got to go there': AM to Gleaves, 17 January 1958.
213   'Dear puss': AM to Lucy, 25 September 1947 (Pocock, p. 213).
213   'I go away': AM to Lucy, 2 June 1956 (Pocock, p. 261).
214fn Hughes, *Things I Didn't Know*, p. 382; 'spluttering about people': Hughes to Moorehead, undated c. 1965, NLA MS 5654/8/63.
215   'As soon as I get back': AM to Lucy, 19 December 1957 (Pocock, p. 265).
215   'Poor Puss': AM to Lucy, 19 December 1957 (Pocock, p. 265).
216   'green ribbon of the Nile', 'naked girls', 'extraordinarily sexual native dances': *African Trilogy*, pp. 115, 119, 119.
216   'I conceived', 'an intense desire': *No Room in the Ark*, pp. 184, 12.
217   'primitive African communities', 'I very much doubt': *No Room in the Ark*, p. 13.
217   'I have become more of a bore': AM to Gleaves, 11 April 1959.
217–18 'I had not been prepared': *No Room in the Ark*, p. 133.
218   'the glee for killing', etc: outline for unproduced Granada TV documentary, 1956, NLA MS 5654.
218   'when I was travelling through Tanganyika': *No Room in the Ark*, p. 201.
218   'at once resolved by greatest difficulty': article for Reprint Society newssheet, March 1960, NLA MS 565/15/125.
219–20 'who don't feel equal to this journey': *No Room in the Ark*, p. 36.
220   'Alan Moorehead has put me in a quandary': Gerald Durrell, 'Gazelles on the skyline', *New York Times*, 31 January 1960.
220   'If you are riding by in a car': Alan Moorehead, 'The galvanized-iron roof', *New Yorker*, 1 September, 1962, p. 44.
220   'It is pleasant to glance at': Alan Moorehead, 'Image of the white man', *Horizon*, September 1960 (vol. 3, no. 1), NLA MS 5654/26/216.
220   Mau Mau insurgents: *No Room in the Ark*, p. 174
220   'the whites possessed the best plots': Ryszard Kapuściński, *The Shadow of the Sun: My African Life*, trans. Klara Glowczewska, Penguin, 2002, p. 39.
221   'One develops a curious indifference': *No Room in the Ark*, p. 61.
221   'wildlife casts': Richard Fitter, 'Wanted, more Noahs', *Observer*, 28 June 1959, p. 21.

221   'naked tribespeople', 'a proud and truculent people', 'ancient tribal customs':
      No Room in the Ark, pp. 164, 203, 168.
222   'appalling waste', 'almost painful thoroughness': *No Room in the Ark*, p. 164.
222   'dry, practical, and hideous': *No Room in the Ark*, p. 138.
222   'the happily goggling ruminant': Peter Fleming, *News From Tartary*,
      Charles Scribner's Sons, 1936, p. xii.
222   'The tourists of our time': Cyril Connolly, *Sunday Times*, 6 October 1953.
222–3 'have encouraged them', etc: *No Room in the Ark*, p. 71.
223   'born a generation earlier': Jan Morris, 'Preface', *Among the Cities*, 1985.
223   'his wish to test the dangerous margins': Shirley Hazzard, *Greene on Capri: A
      Memoir*, Virago, 2000, p. 59.
223   'when beset by crowds': 'The Temples of the Nile'.
224   *We must try to get into the minds*: Waller, in Pocock, p. 267.
224   'erratic, aggressive': James Cameron, reviewing *A Late Education*, 2 May 1971.
224–5 'Alan Moorehead tells such stories': Basil Davidson, 'Heroes and knaves in
      search of Africa', *New York Times*, 12 August 1962.
225   'It seems incredible that the camel-driver': *No Room in the Ark*, p. 164.
225   'A bright vision of the East': 'The Mediterranean', p. 114.
225–6 'historical grievances': Orhan Pamuk, *Istanbul, Memories and the City*, Faber
      & Faber, 2005, p. 50.
225   'that sprouted from the wall': NLA MS 5654/201/25.
226   'ultimately as life-affirming': Pamuk, *Istanbul, Memories and the City*, p. 50.
227   'sucked from a gourd': *The White Nile*, p. 47.
227   'which the Arabs describe as *baraka*': *The White Nile*, p. 99.
227   'Emin, one feels': *The White Nile*, p. 310.
228   'crushing and yet captivating': *The White Nile*, p. 329.
228   'Sometimes . . . it is necessary': Rebecca West, *Black Lamb and Grey Falcon*
      Canongate, Edinburgh, 2006 (1942), p. 825.
228   'It's a dream book': Gellhorn to Moorehead, 16 January 1961, NLA MS5654/6.
228   'fascinating and extremely well-written work': *New York Times*, 11 January 1961.
229   'His formula not much different': Harry Gordon, 'Civilization can be cancerous',
      New York Times, 27 March 1966.
229   'seems to have visited': JB Priestley in Ann Moyal, *Alan Moorehead: A
      Rediscovery*, National Library of Australia, Canberra, 2005, p. 76.
229   'raised to perfection': William Zinsser, 'A travel nut's library', *New York Times*,
      26 August 1990.
229   'books are, as every reviewer knows', etc: Jan Morris, 'The professional touch',
      Times Literary Supplement, 30 December 1960.
229   'one of those people who': *The White Nile*, p. 100.
230   'terrier-like in its intensity', 'No sooner would he begin a sketch', 'It is an
      exhilarating experience': *The Blue Nile*, pp. 109, 113, 148.
231   'hull-down': AM to Gleaves, 11 April 1959.
231   'ill-mannered': AM to Suzie Gleaves, 11 April 1959.
231   'cartoon for a tapestry': unpublished drafts for *A Late Education*, NLA MS 5654/25/204.
231   'Whether he was writing anything or not': Geoffrey de Groen, p. 135; and
      similar passage in Hughes, *Things I Didn't Know*, p. 306.
231   'people sometimes tell me they enjoy writing': Alan Lewis, 'Talk with Alan
      Moorehead', *New York Times*, 16 September 1956.
231–2 *The world is full of infinite causes*: Hughes, 1990.

232 'some of the attributes of a computer': Jan Morris, 'A river muddy with history', *Times Literary Supplement*, 13 July 1962.

9 HOME

236 'now an expert, 'lived in the rosy glow': Hetherington, *42 Faces*, pp. 116, 119.
236 'Nowhere, surely, can the spring burst out': AM's weather book, private collection.
236fn 'book-wealthy Moorehead': Rex North's column, *Daily Express*, 17 May 1963.
237 'where the host crows': AM to Suzie Gleaves, 23 July 1960.
238 'magnanimity, cunning and unbounded devotion': Hughes, 1990.
238 'That bastard, I can hear Lucy saying': AM to Maisie Drysdale, undated (c. May 1965), State Library of NSW, MLMSS 4191/2-4, Item 5.
238 Offers to acquire Moorehead's papers: Martin H Bush to AM, 8 June 1964, NLA MS 5654/9/68.
239 'social stuff is still a battle': AM to Lucy, 15 November 1963, private collection.
239 brief first TV appearance in 1956: This was on 4 May. The *Guardian* described it as 'completely successful': 5 May 1956, p. 12.
239 'penalty of fame': Charles Foley to Pocock, 6 October 1987, NLA MS 8377.
240 'literary lion, [who] roamed all over the world': Mahonar Malgonkar, *Dropping Names*, Roli Books, 1996, p. 35.
240 'everything I can do': Phyllis Whitehead, in Pocock, p. 279.
240 'lack of humour": Morris, 'The professional touch'.
241 'I see once more a glimmering': AM to Lucy, 15 November 1963.
241 'the Gibbon of our declining Empire': Jan Morris, 'A river muddy with history'.
241fn Khrushchev project: NLA MS5654/9/70.
242 'when the retzina': Jenny Macleod, *Reconsidering Gallipoli*, Manchester University Press, 2004, p. 216. For more on how AM influenced Nolan's *Gallipoli*, see Nancy Underhill, *Sidney Nolan: A Life*, NewSouth, University of New South Wales, 2015, pp. 261ff.
242-3 'It does not distress or embarrass him': Alan Moorehead, 'Artist from the Outback', *Horizon*, September 1962, p. 99.
243 'the copperplate writing of 19th century letters': *Cooper's Creek*, p. 211.
243-4 'in the very first flight of writers of prose': 'Heroism, muddle and death in darkest Australia', *Times*, October 1963.
244 'imitated nothing': *A Late Education*, pp. 16–17.
244 'extraordinary place', 'veils and goggles' and Burke's dysentery: *Cooper's Creek*, pp. 60, 63, 91.
245 'although the setting was provincial': Charles Manning Clark, 'To the dead heart of Australia', *New York Times*, 16 February 1964.
245 'discovered nothing, and died in nothing': Lee's reader's notes, 15 August 1962, NLA MS5654/7/61.
246 'rich or strong enough': Shawn to AM, undated, NLA MS 5654/8/68.
246 'Much the most interesting person', etc: Jan Morris, 'The saddest story', *Times Literary Supplement*, 1963.
247 'a terrible ageless watchfulness': DH Lawrence, Bruce Steele (ed.), *Kangaroo*, Cambridge University Press, 2002, p. 15.
247 oral history interview: with Hazel de Berg, for the National Library of Australia, March 1964, NLA ORAL TRC 1/54.
248 'It is a Rip van Winklish experience': Alan Moorehead, 'Letter from Australia', *New Yorker*, 10 October 1964, p. 216.

248 'I do not think Mr Moorehead has escaped': Hal Richardson, 'Australian returns to scene of guilt', *Australian*, 14 November 1953.

248 'Mr Moorehead . . . is not really at home in Australia': Marcel Aurousseau, 'The Burke and Wills Expedition,' *Meanjin Quarterly*, March 1964, p. 100.

248 'For [expatriates] of the older generation': oral history interview, 1964.

248 'block forms in my mind': *A Late Education*, p. 26.

248-9 'deliberate shutting off of memory' etc: MS 5654/26/201..

249 draft of a 1961 profile: John Hetherington to AM, 26 September, 1961.

249 'I wish he had not': *A Late Education*, p. 22.

250 The dinner at Robert Hughes' flat: there are conflicting accounts of the date: Hughes variously makes it lunch on his verandah in 1964 (Hughes, *Telegraph*, 1990); and in *Things I Didn't Know* (p. 267), a dinner in 1962. Probably 1962.

250 'the guy I most admired': Robert Hughes, interviewed by Nicholas Shakespeare, *Times*, 12 January 1987.

251 'Writing was a lonely job': Patricia Rolfe, *Bulletin*, 21 March 1964.

251 'spearheading a campaign': Max Harris to AM, undated, c. Oct-Nov 1965. NLA MS 5654 folio 4.

251 'Members of that sect of Australians': Hetherington, 'Phases in a life'.

250fn Hughes's Marxism: Ruth Starke, *Writers, Readers and Rebels: Upfront and backstage at Australia's top literary festival*, Wakefield Press, 1998.

251 'Journalism is what people': White to Juliet O'Hea, c. January 1966. See David Marr, *Patrick White: A Life*, Random House, 1991, p. 526.

251-2 'a small man': Hetherington to Lindsay, 12 February 1960, SLV MS 9740 Box 5.

252 'if I lived in Europe or London': White to Geoffrey Dutton, 18 November 1965, David Marr (ed.), *Patrick White Letters*, Random House, 1994, p. 288.

252 'one of those Australian journalist/writers': Coleman, 'Australian Notes', *Spectator*, 8 January 2010.

252 'ready-made bestseller': Dutton to AM, 9 November 1965, NLA MS 5654/8/68.

253 'continuing obsession': See, for instance, 'The Legend and the Loneliness: A discussion of the Australian myth', *Overland*, no. 23, Autumn 1962, pp. 33-8.

253 'many haunted images': Donald Horne, *The Lucky Country*, Angus and Robertson, 1966, p. 63.

253 'document of pessimism': Robert Hughes, "Painting', in Peter Coleman (ed.) *Australian Civilization: A Symposium*, Canberra, Sydney, 1962, p. 141.

253 'a snake in our bedroom': AM to Phyllis Whitehead, 19 March 1964, private collection.

254 'unrelenting promotion of the human species': 'Letter from Australia', p. 228.

254 'angry little book': AM to Tass Drysdale, 19 June 1964, State Library of New South Wales, MLMSS 4191/2-4, Item 5.

254 'like a cuckoo in the nest': Robert Hughes, 1987 interview.

254 'sexual and political terror': Blake Bailey, *Cheever: A Life*, Picador, 2009, p. 329.

255 Sean Connery: Saul Cooper to AM, 13 August 1964, NLA MS 5654/8/68; Peter Finch to AM, 1 January 1964, NLA MS 5654/8/69.

256 'ruthless infidelity': Bailey, *Cheever: A Life*.

256 'We have become rather grand': AM to Tass Drysdale, 19 June 1964.

257 'According to Robert Hughes': *Things I Didn't Know*, pp. 311ff.

256 'As we sat on the terrace': Irwin Shaw, *In the Company of Dolphins*, Random House, 1964, p. 55.

257 'I only know how to live like a hermit': Dutton, *Out in the Open*, p. 300.

258   'he seemed to be on the move': Pocock, p. 274.

258   'so full of discontent': NLA MS5654/8/61.

258   'you say': Owen Thomson, 'Monument come to life', *Australian*, 1971.

259   'Yes, he is real good': AM to Maisie Drysdale, c. May 1965. As far as I know,
        Moorehead and White met only once after the war, in February 1964, during
        a dinner at a Chinese restaurant in Sydney also attended by Nolan and
        Sculthorpe. They didn't hit it off. See Graeme Skinner, Peter Sculthorpe, *The
        Making of an Australian Composer*, NewSouth, 2007, p. 331.

259   'walking around with tripods': *Canberra Times*, 1 April 1965.

260   'I sat for a long time': Alan Moorehead, 'Foreword', in Allen Keast, *Australia
        and the Pacific Islands: a natural history*, Random House, 1966, p. iii.

260   'gifts and resources': Alan Ross, *London Magazine*, January 1971, p. 104.

261   TV host Graham Kennedy: References to the program in Jack Whitehead to
        AM, 27 April 1966, NLA MS 5654/9/70.

261fn   'Alan sensed a bestseller': Bernard Smith, *Australian Book Review*, no. 199
        (April 1998), p. 7.

262   'the atmospherics': Harris to AM, c. Oct–Nov 1965, NLA MS 5654 folio 4.

262   'a concentration that allows': Charles Osborne, 'Paradise Lost', *Observer*,
        23 January 1966, p. 26.

262   'the superbly skilled': *Time*, 8 April 1966, vol. 87, no. 14, p. 132.

262   Norman Lewis, most interesting non-fiction book: NLA MS 5654/9/70.

264   'even if I knew how', 'without a note or a falter': Robert Raymond, *Out of the
        Box*, Seaview Press, South Australia, 1999, pp. 88, 90.

264   'Baby It's Cold Outside', which Moorehead mentions as the sort of American
        nonsense you might hear a Roman milk boy singing nowadays – in 1950 –
        rather than a 'Neapolitan lament': Alan Moorehead, 'Go West, Signorina!',
        Observer, 14 May 1950.

10 DETACHMENT

267   'What is my future?': Pocock, p. 277.

267   'should start reading': Frank Harvey, 'Author speaks', *Age*, 11 November 1966.

267   'very generous of him': Geoffrey Dutton, *Out in the Open*, University of
        Queensland Press, 1984. p. 315.

268   'I have been doing nothing much': Lucy to Dr Rod Andrew, a long-time
        Melbourne friend of the Mooreheads, 6 January 1967 (Pocock, p. 280).

268   'Nearly everything I have touched': AM's journal, 26 June 1966 (Pocock, p. 275).

268   'When will I ever learn': AM to Tass Drysdale, 5 November 1966.

269   'the waiting that is hard for us': Lucy to Drysdales, 11 December 1966.

269   'I have been talked at so much': Lucy to Dr Rod Andrew (Pocock, p. 280).

269   'no one knows how long': Lucy to Drysdales, 7 January 1967.

269   'What a bloody thing it is': Lucy to Dr Rod Andrew (Pocock, p. 280).

270   'was in fine form': Dutton to Drysdale, 3 February 1967.

270   'a charming girl', 'Talking a lot better': Lucy to Drysdales, 10 July 1967.

270   'horrid little cottage': Caroline Moorehead, interview with the author.

270   'all his enormous power': Valerie Eaton Griffith, *A Stroke in the Family: A
        manual of home therapy*, Delacorte Press, 1970, p. 69.

271   poignant scene: Hughes, *Things I Didn't Know*, p. 382; Flannery, 'The naked
        critic', September 2012.

272   'I don't think Alan': Lucy to Drysdales, 28 February 1978.

272   'the brilliant journalist-historian': *Australians Abroad: An anthology*, FW Cheshire, 1967.

272   'should remain a classic': 'Bill Platypus's', *Spectator*, 14 September 1973, p. 18.

273   'an instance of attractive science journalism': Introduction, p. 62. Charles Darwin, *On the Origin of Species*, Broadview Press, 2003.

273   Lucy would not hesitate to sue: Lucy to Jamie Hamilton, 23 October 1970, NLA MS 5654/25/207.

273   John gave a couple of interviews: see 'New book by Moorehead', *Herald* (Melbourne), 7 August 1970.

273   'BLOODY MARVELLOUS': Bernstein to AM, 26 August 1970, NLA MS 5654/25/207.

273   'Mr Moorehead's writing is so good': William Shawn to Lucy, 24 February 1970, NLA MS 5654/2/16.

274   'if Alan thought the Battle of Arnhem': Clifford, 'The war correspondent'.

274   Blainey on Moorehead's birth place: Geoffrey Blainey, *A History of Victoria*, second edition, Cambridge University Press, 2013.

275   Lord Bangor invited him to parties in London: Pocock, p. 283.

275   'It really has made a life for him': Lucy to Drysdales, 26 April 1971.

275–6 'a man still': Edward Hoagland, 'In the land of sorrow: Congo', *New York Times*, 11 December 1977, p. 285.

276   'We are all, of course': John Moorehead to Drysdales, 30 July 1979.

278   'If only Alan Moorehead': Paul Theroux, *Sir Vidia's Shadow: A friendship across five continents*, Penguin, 1988, p. 27.

278   'for Christ's sake': Philip Knightley, 'Introduction' to *Eclipse*, Granta, 2000.

278   'says he has set out': Review of Peter Forbath's *River Congo* in London *Times*, 17 August 1978.

279   'makes this North Africa seem like land under gauze': Review of Adam Foulds' *In the Wolf's Mouth*, *Spectator*, 25 January 2014.

279   'reading public': Manning Clark, 'Preface', *The Fatal Impact*.

279   'one of the greatest Australian': Richard Holmes, 'Biography: The past has a great future', *Australian Book Review*, November 2008, p. 26.

279   David Attenborough: BBC radio talk on 16 August 1964, NLA MS 5654/8/63.

279   Moorehead's a 'masterful' account': *New Statesman*, April 2015.

280   'the most retarded people on earth': *Cooper's Creek*, p. 1.

280   'the long downslide': *The Fatal Impact*, p. 61.

281   'the historian with': Manning Clark, 'Preface', *The Fatal Impact*.

281   'it would seem': *The White Nile*, p. 205.

281   'I remember the shock': Leila Aboulela, 'Moving away from accuracy', *Alif: Journal of Comparative Poetics*, vol. 22, 2002, pp. 198–207.

282   *watching a bulldozer for hours*: Christiansen to AM, 3 March 1945, NLA MS 5654/1/6.

282   'I dislike writing very much': AM's entry in *Who's Who* (UK), c. 1954.

282   'one is never satisfied with a book': oral history interview, 1964.

FURTHER READING

Tom Pocock's fine *Alan Moorehead* (1990) is largely focused on the war-time life and career, and it remains the most comprehensive account of that phase of Moorehead's life. Richard Knott's *The Trio: Three Correspondents of World War Two* (2015) offers an eye-level portrait of Moorehead as he appeared to his peers, including Buckley and Clifford, and a richly detailed account of the early years of the war in particular.

Pat Burgess's *Warco: Australian Reporters at War* (Heinemann, Melbourne, 1986), Richard Collier's *The Warcos: The War Correspondents of World War Two* (Weidenfeld & Nicolson, London, 1989) and *Witnesses to War: The History of Australian Conflict Reporting* by Fay Anderson and Richard Trembath (Melbourne University Publishing, 2011) all provide valuable overviews of the role of war correspondents, especially in the Second World War. Artemis Cooper's *Cairo in the War: 1939–19* (Hamish Hamilton, London, 1989) is an evocative guide to its subject. But any reader interested in the environment Moorehead lived and worked in during the war should read *African Trilogy* and *Eclipse* – and then track down copies of the near-contemporaneous campaign memoirs produced by his colleagues. Buckley's *Road to Rome* (1944) is a particular delight, but a number of other books covering similar territory are remarkably good, especially considering the speed with which they were produced. *Three Against Rommel* by Alex Clifford, *Gullible's Travels* by Richard Busvine, *Diary of a War Artist* by Edward Ardizzone and *I've Lived Like a Lord* by Edward (Lord Bangor) Ward all give an immersive taste of daily life behind the headlines. Norman Lewis's superb *Naples '44* is a remarkable insight into that city's humanitarian nightmare in the last years of the war, and also the vast disorder of military logistics and bureaucracy in which reporters like Moorehead operated.

Moorehead's life before and after the war has attracted less attention. *A Late Education* is the best place to begin, though it ends in the early 1950s. Happily, that's where Ann Moyal's compact, elegant *Alan Moorehead: A Rediscovery* (National Library of Australia, 2005) really gets going, with its deeply knowledgeable account of Moorehead's development as a popular historian. Three brief overviews of the career have been particularly useful in the writing of this book: Michael Heyward's introduction to a reissue of *A Late Education* (brought out by Text in 1995), Clive James's profile of Moorehead in the collection *Cultural Amnesia* and David Callaghan's essay, '"There are no lost cities in Australia": Losing and Finding Australia in the Work of Alan Moorehead' (*Australian Literary Studies*, May 1999, vol. 19, no. 1). The chapters on Moorehead and Chester Wilmot in Peter Sekuless's *A Handful of Hacks* are especially shrewd on the Australian context, though again the emphasis is on the war years.

Apart from these, the most telling glimpses of Moorehead in the '50s and '60s are often in the background of other peoples' stories – such as Robert Hughes' *Things I Didn't Know* (2006), Nancy Underhill's *Sidney Nolan: A Life* (2015) and Graeme Skinner's *Peter Sculthorpe: The Making of an Australian Composer* (NewSouth, 2007) – and in newspaper interviews and articles. The most noteworthy of these are referenced, where relevant, in the endnotes.

ACKNOWLEDGEMENTS

My greatest debt is to Caroline and John Moorehead for accepting in such good faith a total stranger's determination to write a 'sort-of biography' about their father and his work. Both shared memories of their father and his milieu with me, and helped in so many ways over several years. I thank them for their generosity and support.

Thank you to Penny Pocock for permission to quote from her late husband's interview notes, and from the postwar letters and journals, since lost, cited in his *Alan Moorehead*. Penny Pocock was also one of a number of people who talked or wrote to me about Alan. Suzanne Baker, Anne Chisholm, Roger Covell, Andrea di Robilant, Michael Holroyd, Cara Lancaster, the Moorehead family, Gillian and Rob Lodge, Jocelyn Harkin, Elizabeth Stokes and Ann Moyal were others; their memories hugely enriched my picture of the man elsewhere. I am deeply grateful to them all.

Thank you to the librarians and archivists of the British Library Manuscripts Reading Room, the State Library of NSW, the State Library of Victoria, the New York Public Library and the Archives Division at Nine Network Australia. I particularly want to acknowledge the brilliant staff of the Special Collections Reading Room at the NLA in Canberra for so much friendly help finding my way around the Moorehead papers over the years.

Much of the research and travel undertaken for this book was made possible by the generosity of the Sidney Myer Foundation. I thank the foundation's trustees for that support and hope they find in these pages some of the curiosity and passion for Australian stories they hoped to stimulate with the Merlyn Myer Biography Stipend.

So many people have helped me get this story into a readable shape. A vague and murky idea for a book probably would have remained just that without a timely push from Helen Garner and James Button. I am indebted to both for that push, and for so much else, including sympathetic readings of draft chapters. I also want to thank Robert Manne, Sarah Carlisle, Sean O'Beirne and Marcus Dempsey for their rigorous and thoughtful readings of the manuscript. Their suggestions greatly improved the final version, and helped eliminate errors and dead-ends. Any that remain are, of course, entirely my own work.

I want to thank, at Black Inc., Sophy Williams and Morry Schwartz, whose enthusiasm for what must have seemed a fairly obscure subject was very encouraging early on. Later it was my tremendous good fortune to be able to commit my battered manuscript to the expert care of project manager and copyeditor Kirstie Innes-Will. Thank you to my publicist Imogen Kandel, to Peter Long for the superb jacket, and to Kerry Biram, who compiled the index. And especially thanks to my editor, Chris Feik. Calmly ignoring regular crises, Chris retained his confidence in the project throughout, and for that, as well as his artistry with the blue pencil, I am eternally grateful.

Thanks to Carl and Ali for a loan of the best writing room in Sydney, and to Jum and Sasha and family for their hospitality in the heart of Moorehead's old London neighbourhood. Closer to home, I have been sustained by the good counsel – and forbearance – of Gregor Kennedy, Anne Carlisle, Amanda Dunn, Dan Fitts, Chris McNeill, Misha Ketchell, Simon Castles, Georgia Richter, Matt O'Meara, Carolyn Fraser and my parents, Anne and Peter. Thanks to Alastair Ritchie for map-reading in Cairo, to Marcus for all the suggested alternative endings, and to Costa Coustas for the Writer's Tears. A special thank you to Sean, for keeping faith with the book and working so hard to help make it better.

Heartfelt thanks, finally, to the four people who have lived with this as long as I have: to Sarah, still and always my first reader; and to Gracie, Jonah and Hughie, for your pep talks and your patience. The next one will have a shrunken head in it, I promise.

INDEX

www.ingramcontent.com/pod-product-compliance
Lightning Source LLC
Chambersburg PA
CBHW022004080426
42733CB00007B/465